Human Resource Management

Sound HRM practices matter—they are a *sine qua non* of effective governance in democratic government—equally so at the local, regional, state, and national levels of government. The NASPAA (Network of Schools of Public Policy, Affairs, and Administration) accreditation standards demand critical competencies for public managers that are vital to human resource managers and supervisors at all levels. These competencies include skills: to lead and manage in public governance; to participate in and contribute to the policy process; to analyze, synthesize, think critically, solve problems, and make decisions; to articulate and apply a public service perspective; and to communicate and interact productively with a diverse and changing workforce and citizenry. This second edition of *Human Resource Management* is designed specifically with these competencies in mind to:

- introduce and explore the fundamental purposes of human resource management in the public service and consider the techniques used to accomplish these purposes;
- provide exercises to give students practice for their skills after being introduced to the theory, foundation, and practices of public and nonprofit sector HRM;
- facilitate instruction of the material by introducing important topics and issues with readings drawn from the professional literature;
- provide information and examples demonstrating the interrelatedness of many of the topics in public sector HRM and the trends shaping public and nonprofit management, especially diversity, ethics, and technology;
- demonstrate and describe differences among HRM practices in public, for-profit and nonprofit organizations, and between the levels of government.

Human Resource Management is organized to provide a thorough discussion of the subject matter, with extensive references to relevant literature and useful teaching tools. Thus, students will consider the issues, purposes, and techniques of HRM and conceptualize how varied their roles are, or will be, whether a personnel specialist in a centralized system or a supervisor managing in one of the increasingly common decentralized systems. Each chapter includes a thorough review of the principles and practices of HRM (including the why and the how), selected readings, important themes, diverse examples, key terms, study questions, applied exercises, case studies, and examples of forms and processes would-be managers will encounter in their roles.

Elizabeth D. Fredericksen is a Professor and the MPA and Nonprofit Administration Director at Boise State University, USA.

Stephanie L. Witt is a Professor of Public Policy and Administration at Boise State University, USA.

W. David Patton, former faculty member at Boise State University and the University of Utah, USA, has directed applied research and technical assistance centers serving state and local governments at both universities.

Nicholas P. Lovrich was the Director of Washington State University's Division of Governmental Studies and Services, USA, for 32 years.

Human Resource Management
The Public Service Perspective

Second Edition

**Elizabeth D. Fredericksen,
Stephanie L. Witt, W. David Patton,
and Nicholas P. Lovrich**

Routledge
Taylor & Francis Group

NEW YORK AND LONDON

First published 2016
by Routledge
711 Third Avenue, New York, NY 10017

and by Routledge
2 Park Square, Milton Park, Abingdon, Oxon OX14 4RN

Routledge is an imprint of the Taylor & Francis Group, an informa business

British Library Cataloguing in Publication Data
A catalogue record for this book is available from the British Library

Library of Congress Cataloging in Publication Data
Fredericksen, Elizabeth D.
  Human resource management: the public service perspective/Elizabeth D. Fredericksen,
  Stephanie L. Witt, W. David Patton and Nicholas P. Lovrich.—Second edition.
  pages cm
  Includes bibliographical references and index.
  1. Civil service—Personnel management. I. Title.
  JF1601.F68 2016
  352.6—dc23
  2015013231

ISBN: 978-1-138-91998-3 (hbk)
ISBN: 978-0-7656-4586-9 (pbk)
ISBN: 978-1-315-68740-7 (ebk)

Typeset in Bembo
by Florence Production Ltd, Stoodleigh, Devon, UK

In Chapter 4, data used in Exhibits 4.1 and 4.2 were drawn from the *Union Membership and Coverage Database*, available at www.unionstats.com. This resource, constructed by Barry Hirsch (Andrew Young School of Policy Studies, Georgia State University) and David Macpherson (Department of Economics, Trinity University), provides private and public sector labor union membership, coverage, and density estimates compiled from the monthly household Current Population Survey using BLS methods. The full citation is included in the relevant Chapter 4 exhibits and in Chapter 4 references.
  In Chapter 5, Excerpt 5.1, "Defining Succession Planning," by Elizabeth D. Fredericksen, is used with permission of Sage Publications. The published version of the article is available on Sage Journals (http://ononline.sagepub.com; doi: 10.1177/0160323X10368518).

Printed and bound in the United States of America by Edwards Brothers Malloy on sustainably sourced paper.

The authors would like to thank the many users of the prior edition, both students and fellow academics. Their suggestions and insightful comments on the 1st edition were a tremendous resource during development of the 2nd edition. We owe them gratitude for this edition. Elizabeth Fredericksen offers thanks in particular to her graduate assistants, Jen Schneider, Leslie Krone, Ryan Linnarz, and Hank Kvamme, who were tireless in tracking details and assisting with the format. Also, her appreciation goes to her co-authors for their willingness to take on a 2nd edition. Most importantly, she offers her love and thanks to her husband, Justin, and children, Morgan, Sydney, and Drew. Their patience and support made her effort possible. Stephanie Witt offers special thanks to Cindy Hendrickson and Chandra Lyles for their support during this edition. David Patton would like to thank his wife, Wendy, and his family for their sacrifice of time and attention on the first go-around of this book. Nicholas Lovrich thanks his *Tres Amigos*, Elizabeth, Stephanie, and David, for their camaraderie on his last book project. He notes that academic careers are wonderful in many ways, but among the absolute very best aspects of such careers is the honor of working with one's students far past the classroom and deeper into their academic careers.

Contents

Exhibits

Excerpts

A Manager's Internet Resources

2010 Model APA
www.uniformlaws.org/
AFL-CIO
www.aflcio.org
American Arbitration Association
www.mediation.org
American Bar Association
www.americanbar.org/groups/dispute_resolution/
American Federation of Government Employees
www.afge.org
American Federation of State, County and Municipal Employees
www.afscme.org/union
Association for Conflict Resolution
www.imis100us2.com/acr/acr/default.aspx
Centers for Medicare and Medicaid
www.cms.hhs.gov
Change to Win
www.changetowin.org/
Employee Benefit Research Institute
www.ebri.org
Federal Chief Information Officer
cio.gov
Government Accountability Project, nonprofit
www.whistleblower.org
International City/County Management Association
www.icma.org
International Public Management Association for Human Resources
ipma-hr.org
International Society for Performance Improvement
www.ispi.org
National Academy of Social Insurance
www.nasi.org
National Labor Relations Board
www.nlrb.gov

Nonprofit Risk Management Center
  www.nonprofitrisk.org
Society for Human Resource Management
  www.shrm.org
Society for Industrial and Organizational Psychology
  www.siop.org/SIOP-SHRM/

1   The Environment and Roles of Public Service HRM

Learning Objectives

- Explore HRM practice and the contemporary demographic and service delivery trends that affect public service HRM.
- Understand the values and goals for public and nonprofit service.
- Review the roles of HRM in organizations.
- Consider the implications of centralization/decentralization of functions and direction.

> Personnelists as we have known them are becoming obsolete.
>
> (Marshall and Whelan 1996/1997, p. 27)

What's in a name? Why is this book entitled *Human Resource Management: The Public Service Perspective* rather than Public Personnel Management? The change in focus from personnel to human resource management (HRM) points to the broadening role that personnel specialists play in an organization. HRM is no longer confined to the narrow set of techniques associated with the old "personnel function." According to Hays (1996, p. 285), "by enforcing torrents of picky rules and regulations, personnelists drove a wedge between the staffing function and line managers. Personnel offices came to be viewed as impediments to be overcome rather than allies in the pursuit of effective management." However, the HRM function is now taking on a "consultative role" to management within the organization, and many established personnel procedures are being abandoned to increase organizational flexibility and provide greater agency-level responsiveness to internal and external clientele interests (Marshall and Whelan 1996/1997). The first part of this chapter will discuss the *internal* changes occurring within the HRM profession. The later portion of this chapter will focus on the *external* changes in the work environment that have an impact on HRM. Contemporary public sector managers need to understand these developments in the HRM area to make proper use of the new dynamism that characterizes this field.

Introduction to the Reading

We use two reading excerpts to illustrate how the HRM profession has evolved and the implications of its influence upon public service. As our opening excerpt by Donald E. Klingner points out, HRM is applied as a concept in different ways and has continuously evolved in the U.S. in response to differing values and pressures (2014). The net result of the combination of foundational roots and change over time is a complex HRM system with multiple, competing values and practices. In other words, HRM is more than just 'personnel'.

In the second excerpt, written decades ago, Mosher argued that the public employees who implement public policies matter greatly in terms of the reality of that delivery of public services. Those who 'implement' the public good may do so as direct service providers, but they may also do so by facilitating the efforts of others in the organization charged with delivering some policy. These professionals matter in terms of the integrity of public service. Those in public service may not be formally elected to office, but serve nonetheless. As you read these excerpts, consider the following questions:

1. What does Klingner observe about changes in societal and governmental values, and how might these lead to changes in how HRM is implemented in either public or nonprofit organizations?
2. Why might we care that the employees in the public or nonprofit realms are demographically representative of those whom they serve?
3. How does Mosher conceptualize 'professionalism', and where does this concept mesh with the precepts of HRM?

Excerpt 1.1 Understanding Public Personnel Management

Public personnel management (also known as human resources management or HRM) can be understood on multiple levels (Klingner, Nalbandian, & Llorens 2010). First, it comprises the four fundamental *functions* (planning, acquisition, development, and sanction) needed to manage human resources in public, private, and nonprofit organizations. Second, it is the *process for allocating public jobs*, including those in private or nonprofit-sector organizations funded through government contracts. . . . Third, public personnel management can be viewed as the continuous interaction among fundamental *values* that often conflict because they reflect key differences over who gets public jobs and how, and over job security. Traditionally, conflict in the U.S. centered around four values [political responsiveness/representation, efficiency, protecting employees from political influence, and social equity]. . . . However, at the end of the 1970s, the political culture began to shift fundamentally toward three nongovernmental values: personal accountability, limited and decentralized government, and community responsibility. . . . Fourth, public HRM can be viewed as *systems*—the laws, rules, organizations, and procedures used to fulfill the four personnel functions in ways that express abstract values. There are four traditional systems—political patronage, civil service, collective bargaining, and affirmative action (AA)—and two nongovernmental systems (privatization and partnerships). . . . The nongovernmental public personnel systems that have developed since the 1980s use the presumed greater efficiency and flexibility of the private sector and community-based organizations to enhance public service delivery. Where public services were still delivered by public agencies, intense pressure to "do more with less" has resulted in increased use of nonstandard work arrangements (NSWAs), including temporary, part-time, and seasonal workers as part of the downsizing, reengineering, and fundamental changes in organizational structure and accountability epitomized by the terms *reinventing government* or *New Public Management* (Battaglio & Condrey 2006; Nigro & Kellough 2006). Although governments have always bought goods and services from private contractors, these pressures also led many governments to deliver services by contract with third-party businesses and community-based organizations (*privatization*). Along with privatization came greater federal and state emphasis on delivering public services through *partnerships* with nongovernmental organizations funded by taxes, user fees, and charitable contributions. Third-party social service provision became more complex with an ideologically driven emphasis that directed contracting strategies toward churches and other faith-based organizations (Lynn & Klingner 2010).

Excerpt References

Battaglio, R. P., & Condrey, S. (2006). Civil service reform: Examining state and local government cases. *Review of Public Personnel Administration, 26,* 118–138.

Klingner, D., Nalbandian, J., & Llorens, J. (2010). *Public personnel management: Contexts and strategies* (6th ed.). New York: Longman/Pearson.

Lynn, D., & Klingner, D. (2010). Beyond civil service: The politics of the emergent paradigm. In S. Condrey (Ed.), *Handbook of human resource management in government* (4th ed., pp. 45–71). San Francisco, CA: Jossey-Bass/Wiley.

Nigro, L. G., & Kellough, J. E. (2006). The states and civil service reform: Lessons learned and future prospects. In J. E. Kellough & L. G. Nigro (Eds.), *Civil service reform in the states: Personnel policies and politics at the subnational level* (pp. 315–324). Albany, NY: State University of New York Press.

Source: Klingner, Donald E. 2014. "On the 75th Anniversary of ASPA: The Congruent Evolution of Civil Rights and the American Society for Public Administration" *Review of Public Personnel Administration* 34 (1): 7–22.

Excerpt 1.2 Implications of the Professions

[W]hen the traditional principles of merit are being challenged, similar forces are undermining the old articles of faith through which administration and democracy were reconciled. . . . [T]he idea of representative bureaucracy has acquired a meaning which is not altogether reassuring to the general public interest. Most of the professions are well represented in their appropriate enclaves, as are most of those growing categories of employees who join in collective organizations . . . But who represents that majority of citizens who are not in any of these groups? . . . The knowledge explosion and the tremendous growth of higher education have greatly enhanced the technical and cognitive capacities of the public service to perform its tasks. At the same time, may they not have weakened its concern for, and competence in, reaching social decisions responsibly with the full polity in view? This is essentially a moral question; indeed it is *the* moral question of the public service in American democracy. . . . The harder and infinitely more important issue of administrative morality today attends the reaching of decisions on questions of public policy which involve competitions in loyalty and perspective between broad goals of the polity (the phantom public interest) and the narrower goals of a group, bureau, clientele, or union. Chester I. Barnard defined administrative responsibility as primarily a moral question or, more specifically, as the resolution of competing and conflict codes—legal, technical, personal, professional, and organizational—in the reaching of individual decisions.[1] . . . [S]tudents of government would add a less definable but nevertheless all-important code—the public benefit. The danger is that developments in the public service may be subtly, gradually, but profoundly moving the weight toward the partial, the corporate, the professional perspective and away from that of the general interest. In this connection a number of developments . . . may be reviewed:

- the tendency of "elite" professions to dominate the governance of bureaus and other public agencies;
- the dominance in matters of recruitment, selection, and advancement of professional groups, both in and outside government, and the declining influence of general government agencies;
- the deepening of professional specializations;
- the development of self-governing professional career systems within public agencies;
- the corporatism of organized public employees, especially those in professional and subprofessional fields.

Excerpt Note

1. Barnard, Chester I. *The Functions of the Executive* (Cambridge, Harvard University Press, 1948), Chapter XVII.

Source: Mosher, Frederick C. 1982. possible pp. 229–231, "Merit, Equity & Affirmative Action" in 2nd ed. *Democracy and the Public Service*. Oxford University Press.

Trends in HRM

A United Nations report identified trends in HRM among the OECD nations that included the following dynamics (The Public Service of 2025):

- hybridization of Public Human Resource Models to include both merit-based, competitive jobs as well as career-based systems;
- reduction of protection, immunity, and privilege for government workers in which 13 countries have changed the status of their civil service systems;
- emphasis on individual performance for evaluation, often tying individual and group compensation to unit and organizational goal achievement;
- decentralization of human resource management policies, including "delegation of responsibility for human resource management to departments and agencies to give managers more flexibility and freedom . . . and simplifying rules and procedures";
- Senior Civil Servant Corps, with development of special leadership programs for top civil servants.

More than a decade ago, the Long-Range Strategic Planning Committee of the International Personnel Management Association identified the major trends affecting HMR (1999, p. 1). Considering the United Nations report in the context of the following trends affirms the significance of HRM in organizations and the continuing emphasis on competencies. The top trends and how their coverage is achieved in this book are summarized in Exhibit 1.1.

Exhibit 1.1 Top HR Trends

1. Information Technology: electronic commerce and communication [throughout book]
2. New Role for HR as Business Partner/Internal Consultant [Chapters 1, 5, and 14]
3. Globalization of HR [throughout book]
4. New Partnerships, Particularly in the Labor Management Relations Area [Chapter 4]
5. Work Life Issues: humanizing the workplace, family leave, flextime, telecommuting [Chapters 9 and 10]
6. Shifting Demographics: diversity, labor pool shortages, shorter tenure of workers [Chapter 2]
7. Leadership Development: employee development, retraining, need for continuous learning [Chapters 10 and 11]
8. Compensation Packages: alternate reward packages, new practices in benefits packages [Chapters 8 and 9]
9. Selection Process and New Values: shift from knowledge, skills, and abilities (KSAs) to behaviors [Chapter 7]
10. Decentralization: shifting decision making closer to the client [Chapters 1, 14]
11. Managing Change: downsizing, accountability, increased politicization, privatization, flexibility in systems, increased deregulation of HR authority [Chapters 1, 2, and 5]

Each of these trends represents a challenge to HR professionals and established practices in personnel management in the public sector. Many of them will require contemporary HR professionals and their successors to develop new skills and perspectives while working in closer coordination with line managers. Additionally, line managers must acquire the skills and knowledge about HRM in the public sector that had been previously shifted to a centralized HR department. The importance of this collaboration and exchange is emphasized throughout the book, and developed in particular detail in Chapter 14.

Sector Differences: Public, Private, and Nonprofit Organizations

Ownership and Profit

HRM in the public sector has much in common with the nonprofit sector, owing to the fundamental role of profit. For the public and nonprofit sectors, there is no 'ownership' expecting a return on investment in the same sense as for a private, for-profit organization. The explicit legal and political differences that establish the significance of a bottom line or profit in the for-profit sector, but with no such corollary for the public or nonprofit sectors, have broad implications for personnel management. For-profit organizations can normally judge their success or failure by the presence or absence of a profit or the proportion of market share they can command. There is no such bottom line in the public or nonprofit sector. The public sector must be responsive to many expectations about performance that are framed by a preference for either efficiency or effectiveness. The management values that drive these expectations range from inclusiveness, equal treatment, and due process to transparency and responsiveness. Meeting these expectations may slow program activities or make them inefficient if measured solely in fiscal terms. Elected officials determine budgets in the public sector, and these officials may increase or decrease budget levels in response to political pressure that may have little connection to expectations about service delivery, efficiency, or policy effectiveness. As in the public sector, nonprofit organizations may have little control over revenue generated or the demand for services in their communities. The expectations that nonprofits face echo those of the public sector. In many ways, success in the public or nonprofit sector will be socially constructed; we do not have the benefit of a tangible, broadly understood measure such as a dollar.

Participation and Scrutiny

Citizens in a democratic society generally expect that government actions will be open to scrutiny by the public (or the press as public watchdog). Consequently, HRM in the public sector is answerable to many more constituencies than HRM staff in the for-profit sector. To some extent, there is scrutiny of the nonprofit sector, but nonprofit organizations may have a bit more discretion over management activities within the organization and potentially less *legal* responsibility to disclose decisions publicly. However, staffing decisions in the nonprofit sector may also be subject to scrutiny by constituents (donors and public agency partners in the main) and decisions made by a board rather than individual managers. Civil service protections simply do not exist in the nonprofit sector. In the nonprofit sector, as in the for-profit sector, due process may be sacrificed at times for managerial discretion. In the public sector, due process is a deeply held value and founds the structure of democratic government in the United States.

Values in Public Service HRM: Influences upon Action

In the midst of so much change and so many competing ideological preferences, what key values inform the practice of HRM in the public and nonprofit sectors? As we see from the recent summary offered by Klingner (2014), scholars have recommended many values as guides for the profession of HRM in general. However, we concur with the judgment of one prominent study that called for renewed attention to issues of accountability, diversity, and justice (Ferris et al. 1999) and set out here the key elements of these core values.

Accountability

With management discretion and flexibility should come strict accountability. Public managers are accountable to a variety of people and institutions, but, unless accountability is defined as both hierarchical and democratic, public managers run the risk of not being as responsive to the citizenry as they should be (King and Stivers 1998).

In the hierarchy of agencies, public managers are directly accountable to their superiors. This reporting relationship is typically formalized in written and verbal reporting mechanisms, and ultimately in a performance appraisal system (Mero and Motowidlo 1995). In the larger picture, however, public managers are accountable to the public through their elected representatives in the executive and legislative branches of government. In many cases, public managers have considerable discretion over the use of their authority and resources and must make decisions based on their own perception of the public good. In these instances, the law and professional codes of ethics guide the manager. Evidence indicates that individuals with discretion tend to focus their work in accord to where they believe they will be held accountable (Tetlock 1992). If one knows she will be tested on the names of South American countries, she is most likely to study South America. The same is true with public sector managers and human resource professionals. By establishing clearer lines of accountability in HRM, we may be able to reconcile the benefits of flexible and responsive public administration with the necessary goals of due process and equity.

Diversity

Most of the attention to issues of diversity has centered on race, gender, and ethnicity. Often, these issues have come to our attention because of documented exclusionary practices of the past and established disparities in employment patterns, promotional opportunities, and occupational representation. Significant effort has been made to address these issues of diversity, but work in this area is far from complete. We may find a more faithful reflection of society in our public workplaces generally than in the past, but this is not yet the case in some levels of management and many professional positions.

Beyond the familiar issues of gender, race, and ethnic diversity, we must consider the broader question of comprehensive diversity in the public workplace. Is it important to have individuals in public service who represent the various races and ethnicities found in society? Should diversity in staffing encompass a broader definition of a diverse work force: range of experience, type of training or academic discipline, religion, culture, or physical ability? In a democratic society, are there proper reasons to seek a diverse workforce, other than satisfying the hope of reflecting the characteristics of a jurisdiction being served?

Many factors enter into the effects of diversity on organizations, including social climate dynamics and the interplay of cultural values of people of differing backgrounds. With the variety of influences present in diverse groups, it is difficult to separate the causes and effects of organizational dynamics. The nature of diversity itself promotes new ways of looking at issues and occasions the consideration of varied cultural perspectives in thinking through workplace problems. Diversity has many dimensions for HRM; consequently, the subject warrants discussion throughout this book.

Justice and Equity

Human resource managers are the guardians of deeply held values in public organizations, including the core values of justice and fairness. In the field of HRM, justice is often perceived as comparability with other employees or organizations. It is important that employees perceive that their work is rewarded fairly as they compare their compensation and their responsibilities with other employees doing similar work. This comparison is a measure of internal equity, from the perspective of the employee. Similarly, employees will look at comparable organizations to determine if salaries, benefits, and working conditions are at parity (external equity). The use of equity in developing compensation systems is discussed in considerable depth in Chapter 8. For example, we often hear about the differences between the public, for-profit, and nonprofit sectors in working conditions and compensation. These perceptions and the implications for HRM will be addressed throughout the text.

The term organizational justice, however, entails more than simply comparing levels of compensation. Human resource managers are responsible to uphold the principles of justice and equity in several aspects of an employee's interaction with the organization. Beginning with the functions of recruitment and selection, human resource managers should be increasingly aware of the need to maintain equity and justice for all applicants, candidates, and newly hired employees with respect to employee development decisions, promotions, and the use of discipline. Employees expect the organization to be fair and just in all of its dealings with them, from the hiring process to providing opportunity for grievance against an action by management (Folger and Cropanzano 1998).

Human resource managers must also be aware of citizen perceptions of organizational equity and justice. The public should perceive the public organization as being fair to its employees and fair to those who would approach government for services. In some cases, the public perception of equity and justice is out of the hands of HRM, such as in the case of public hearings or scheduled deliberations of the legislative body. HRM can set the standard for providing appropriate processes for equity and justice in public organizations.

Ethics and Rules

Every rule was devised for a reason. The rules can become cumbersome, but they are often there to uphold an important principle. As we will discuss in some depth in Chapter 3, civil service rules have been the source of management frustration and the repeated target of reform. We should remember, however, that these rules were put into place for what were considered legitimate reasons at the time of their creation. We have whistleblowing rules because people had been fired for pointing out internal corruption. There are rules to guide how an organization undergoes a reduction in force (RIF) because somewhere, at some time in the past, someone had to decide how to lay off workers in the midst of a financial crisis. Similarly, rules were established for hiring procedures so all applicants have a fair opportunity to compete for public jobs. The most onerous (say many public managers) are the rules created for disciplining or firing public employees. Procedures for disciplinary action or termination were originally put into place to protect competent employees from the political strong-arm tactics of elected officials. Unfortunately, over time, these rules have become quite intricate and cumbersome, severely limiting public managers in their ability to achieve higher productivity in the workplace. As reform efforts expand managerial discretion, we must maintain the balance between flexibility and latitude and the strength of due process rules protecting the values of fairness and consistency. These are pivotal elements of justice in any organization.

The Role and Location of HRM in the Organization

It has been traditional to distinguish between *line* and *staff* positions in an organization. HRM has traditionally been considered a staff function. Line positions are in "the direct chain of command that [are] responsible for the achievement of an organization's goals" (Griffin 1984, p. 283). Staff positions, in contrast, provide "expertise, advice, and support for line positions" (Griffin 1984, p. 293). Line and staff positions often exercise different kinds of authority. Line positions are part of the organization's hierarchy and possess the authority that comes with the chain of command. Staff positions, however, may have only advisory authority (that is, to offer advice), or they may have limited functional authority "which is formal or legitimate authority over activities related [only] to the staff member's specialty" (Griffin 1984, p. 294).

HRM is a classic example of a staff function. Although, in many cases, it has functional authority over types of selection process and procedure for compliance with equal employment opportunity (EEO) law, HRM's authority in strategic planning and other employee-related issues is, typically and exclusively, advisory. Consequently, tension often exists between line and staff positions. Line managers frequently perceive HRM staff to be a threat to their own authority (Griffin 1984, p. 295). In many cases, there are also demographic differences between the two groups. "Line managers tend to be older, to be less well educated, and to have risen through the ranks of the organization" (Griffin 1984, p. 294). Staff specialists generally are younger and better educated and are more likely to have been hired directly into upper-level staff positions. These line–staff tensions contribute to the feeling among many managers that HRM exists outside the mainstream of the organization.

The HRM function can be located in several alternative places within an organization. Many governmental jurisdictions have a central HR agency or HR division within a central administrative services department. In a small jurisdiction, the city clerk or city manager's office is likely to carry out the HR function. Many functional agencies may retain their own HR subdivision rather than deal with a separate agency holding that specialization. For example, a large state department of transportation or health and welfare may have its own HR department within the agency.

When the HR division is distanced from the line manager, this increases the possibility that HR staff become unfamiliar with the work of a unit or department. On the other hand, when HRM is handled by each agency, and no central HR agency, it is more difficult to coordinate (or control) HR activities across the various agencies of the jurisdiction.

The successful reintegration of HRM into the larger organization would solve a longstanding problem linked to the dual roles that the public personnel function has played in the United States. It has a positive role to play—for example, in helping management to select qualified employees. At the same time, however, HRM also plays the role of guardian to the merit system (Shafritz 1991), a function frequently viewed with skepticism by line managers. This gate-keeping role has dominated HRM, leading to Sayre's critique that public personnel administration too often represents "a triumph of technique over purpose" (Sayre 1991). Managers often do not find HRM helpful in successfully meeting management objectives. In fact, managers often characterize the HRM office as an obstacle course of rules and regulations that require circumvention rather than compliance.

Not only is the HR professional expected to be the 'HR expert', that is, acting in the traditional role of merit system protector, but they are also increasingly expected to be the strategic manager as well. Part of being a strategic manager entails becoming a leader in developing staff. Hays and Kearney's 1998 study of personnelists indicated that this function, which includes a priority focus on training and employee development activities, would be the primary concern and most central activity of HRM in the year 2008 (Hays and Kearney 2001). When French and Goodman (2011) replicated the Hays–Kearney study with local government, they found that, although HR professionals must attend to traditional functional activities, reform and new technologies have driven change as "HRM at all levels of government works to supplant outdated systems, overcome staffing shortages, and solve recruitment and compliance challenges" (p. 778). The competency model for HR includes the idea of the personnelist as a "change agent" utilizing a consultative approach (Marshall and Whelan 1996/1997). Taken together, these changes require progressive organizations to de-emphasize the distinction between line and staff, with HRM becoming an important member of an effective management team in common pursuit of a strategic plan of action (Marshall and Whelan 1996/1997). We extend this discussion in Chapter 5 with an overview of HR in the context of organizational strategic planning.

One feature of this transformation from traditional personnel to 'strategic human resource management' is that line managers acquire much more power over personnel decisions. This creates a critical training and development need for supervisory and management personnel, because many line managers have had little formal training in recruitment, selection, and retention practices. The International Personnel Management Association (1998), for example, has developed a guide for HR offices to make available to line managers to help them understand the range of their HR responsibilities. Hays (1996, p. 289) notes that meeting this need in a time when many public sector HR offices have been downsized will be difficult, even though it is of critical importance precisely at such times.

The External Environment of HRM

As public service goals, accountability, diversity, and justice provide a logical impetus for successful HRM to anticipate and cope with a rapidly changing work environment. The four major trends framing contemporary HRM in public and nonprofit organizations are linked to public service organizations' ability to deliver services to the whole of their citizenry in an efficient and effective manner, while attending to due process and equity:

1. *Diversity and the changing work environment*: Demographic shifts in the composition of the workforce include increased numbers of women and minorities, an aging of the workforce, and the resultant challenges of the multigenerational workplace.
2. *The impact of technology*: Technology has transformed the processes of HRM and has altered, with benefits and costs, the manner and substance of what public and nonprofit organizations do to serve the public interest.
3. *Alternative service delivery and HRM*: The implementation systems of government continue to move away from traditional civil service systems. Implementation of public services also features more nontraditional service delivery mechanisms such as privatization (formal service delivery arrangements through nongovernmental actors), alternative employment arrangements such as contract workers, and increased use of performance-based benchmarking.
4. *Downsizing and restructuring*: Beyond shifts in the implementation of services, changes in the economy, including the lingering impacts of the "Great Recession" that began in 2008, lead to demands for greater flexibility in contracting or expanding organizational budgets in response to resources and demands. In conjunction with alternative service delivery models, direct downsizing or reductions in force have been used to decrease the size of the workforce, along with efforts to restructure existing personnel systems.

Each of the trends affects the ability of an organization to recruit, retain, and manage its employees, and the remainder of this chapter is devoted to their consideration.

Diversity and the Changing Work Environment

The environment of the HR professional is greatly shaped by the changing demographics and characteristics of the workforce. As the makeup of the workforce evolves, all aspects of HRM must transform as well. HR planning requires good information about future trends. Recruitment efforts must adapt to new pools of workers and their expectations. Training needs shift as the qualifications of new and continuing workers change. Compensation packaging must meet the needs of workers. As demographics change, the expectations of workers and the needs and motivations that drive them may also change. The environment of the HR manager is not static.

Increased Numbers of Women in the Workforce — *Diversity — reading*

The number of women working outside of the home has increased steadily over the last several decades. In 1960, women comprised 33.4 percent of the U.S. civilian workforce, rising to 46.7 percent of the U.S. civilian workforce in 2010 (U.S. Bureau of Labor Statistics 2014). By 2010, just under 71 percent of women with children under the age of 18 participated in the workforce (U.S. Bureau of Labor Statistics 2013). This has obvious implications for work–life programs and the need for flexible work schedules and for options to deal with childcare responsibilities, as family units may have both parents in the workforce. In fact, 75 percent of working parents said they put family-friendly working hours ahead of other benefits (Ceridian 2004, p. 6).

Although women have made entry to the workforce in increasing numbers, the number of women in top management positions has not increased as rapidly. A 1992 study by the Merit Systems Protection Board noted that, although there are nearly as many women as men in federal white-collar jobs, they constitute only one out of four managers and one out of ten executives (U.S. MSPB 1992). More recently, an analysis of women's workforce participation found that women held 42.7 percent of the senior managerial positions in the United States, a rate just above the OECD average (*Economist* 2014). This is sometimes referred to as the 'glass ceiling' phenomenon. There are a myriad of reasons for this phenomenon, including breaks in career taken for child birth and childcare, lack of experience in traditional male-dominated career paths necessary for promotion, and outright gender discrimination (Barr 1996, pp. 12–17).

Increasing Numbers of Minority Workers — *diversity*

Minorities constituted 18.7 percent of the nation's civilian workforce in 2010 (U.S. Bureau of Labor Statistics 2014). This can be further broken down by Black or African American (11.6 percent of the civilian labor force or CLF), Hispanic (14.8 percent of the CLF), and Asian Pacific Islanders (4.7 percent of the CLF; U.S. Bureau of Labor Statistics 2014). The percentage of Hispanics in the workforce is projected to increase to 18.6 percent by 2020 (Toossi 2012, p. 43). Several states, such as California, Florida, and Texas, have such rapidly increasing percentages of minority workers that soon there will be no 'majority' group in those states. The HR professional should work to encourage tolerance for ethnic, racial, and cultural differences in the workplace. Guy and Newman (1998) point out that this is more than a legal compliance issue (i.e., EEO or affirmative action (AA) laws). The astute human resource manager instead recognizes that a tolerant workplace will best utilize the multitude of talents brought by a diverse workforce (Guy and Newman 2004, p. 76).

The Aging Workforce ✓× *Aging reading*

The percentage of our population comprised of middle-aged individuals will grow with the aging of the baby boom generation. As this large proportion of our population has aged, the median age of our population reached 36 in the year 2000; that is, one-half of the population was older than 36, and one-half was younger. This is the oldest median age in the history of the United States (Johnston and Packer 1987, p. 79). The well-known baby boom generation (1946–1964) has begun to retire, but the full implications of this will be clearer by 2020. The Bureau of the Census estimates that, although the current ratio of over-65 individuals to the working-age adult population (18–64 years old) is 19 per 100 working-age adults, it is estimated to increase to 30 per 100 in 2028 (Ortman, Velkoff, and Hogan 2014, p. 9). There is also evidence that the Great Recession of 2008 has led many workers to delay retirement and stay in the workforce longer (Taylor et al. 2009, p. 2). As we approach 2020, the workforce will be increasingly made up of older workers who will have different needs and benefits preferences than their younger counterparts; for example, there may be an increased focus on retirement planning. A related challenge to HRM arising from the aging of the workforce is the increased need for elder care benefits. A 2004 report indicated that 35 percent of U.S. workers reported they provided regular care for a parent or in-law (Ceridian 2004, p. 6). Employees confronting difficult choices about health and long-term care for aging parents may need benefits structured to provide elder-care options.

Generation X and Millennials

The children of the baby boom generation have been referred to as Generation X. Generation X comprises approximately 52 million people born between 1963 and 1977. Members of Generation X currently form about 34 percent of the workforce (Mauer 1998, p. 19). These workers began entering the workforce in approximately 1992 and will echo the baby boom over the next 20 years. The millennial generation is the name given to the cohorts born in the years since approximately 1980 (Costanza et al. 2012, p. 378). In 2010, millennials constituted about 27 percent of the workforce (Catalyst.org 2012).

Much has been made of the different experiences brought by Generation Xers to the employment marketplace (Tulgan 1995). Having watched firsthand the frequent downsizings of the 1980s and 1990s negatively impact their parents, these workers have lower expectations of staying with one employer and are said to prefer team-based work environments rather than top–down organizations (Guy and Newman 1998, p. 78). A recent study compared Baby Boomers and members of Generation X. Compared with 'Boomers', 'Xers' were more likely to value challenges and the ability to learn from a job over pay. Further, Generation Xers are said to have lower levels of trust in established institutions and are more interested in maintaining a balance between work and family life than Boomers (Mauer 1998, p. 19).

Traditional recruitment techniques may not mesh with Generation Xers, who want to know 'why should I work for your organization?' and who expect to work for any one employer only as long as it meets their personal growth goals. There is some evidence that older workers are resistant to the new attitudes toward work held by many Generation Xers. A study of older small-business owners found that 21 percent said Generation Xers had a poor work ethic; 47 percent said that Generation Xers are less competent than workers from previous generations; 27 percent said that Generation Xers lacked motivation; and 26 percent said that Generation Xers are lazy (Mauer 1998, p. 19).

Millennials are broadly held to have higher levels of social consciousness, and yet to be cynical and narcissistic (Costanza et al. 2012, pp. 375–376). They have been connected to technology their entire lives and are accustomed to being extensively networked (Heathfield n.d.). Millennials are used to working in teams and are purported to require an unusual level of feedback in the workplace (Heathfield n.d.). Millennials are regarded as self-centered, an attitude that is often attributed to having been raised by doting parents (Heathfield n.d.).

HR professionals will need to adapt to the differing values of these younger workers, especially as the number of qualified applicants in the workforce goes down, and employers compete for employees. HR will need to help overcome the resistance of existing, older managers, who may share many of the viewpoints about Generation X and Millennials described above.

The Impact of Technology

Technology changes the nature of work itself and the nature of the relationship between worker and employer. There is now a computer-based application for nearly every HR function described in this book. The pace of change in technology will continuously challenge HRM professionals to 'keep up'. Not only will HR applications come and go, but also the nature of the work described in our classification and compensation systems will change rapidly, challenging our traditional HR processes to stay current.

An example is that advances in technology have allowed line managers to operate outside central personnel offices by advertising widely over the Internet. There are numerous sites listing available jobs in cities (see the City of Seattle Website, for example), counties, and state governments (such as the State of California). The federal government lists jobs on the Internet as well: FedWorld and USAJOBS at the OPM Website list federal government jobs. General job listing sites such as Monster.com and America's Job Bank list for-profit and nonprofit sector jobs as well as public sector jobs. Many public sector professionals belong to 'listserves', where all members share email messages. These are frequently used to advertise jobs specific to that profession. Professional associations also publish their newsletters and job announcements on their official Web page.

The jobs of the future are likely to require increasing levels of technical skills and competencies. Employers are turning to remedial education programs to make up for the deficits new employees have in skills and abilities (Anderson and Ricks 1993). HR managers may have difficulty in finding adequately qualified individuals for jobs and may need to plan for increased training needs for new and existing employees.

Alternative Service Delivery and HRM

As public sector agencies seek alternative mechanisms for delivering public services, these alternative delivery systems will change the role and duties of HRM in public organizations. Although there are many ways to structure the provision of government services, the traditional form where services are delivered exclusively by a government agency staffed by government employees is no longer the predominant structure utilized by governments in the United States. Today, governments use service contracting and privatization as 'tools' to govern and provide services to citizens (Salaman 2002, p. 21). The use of these tools is now so prevalent that some scholars have coined the phrase "hollow state." Milward and Provan (2000, p. 362) define the hollow state as: — *Shadow*

> any joint production situation where a governmental agency relies on others (firms, nonprofits, or other governmental agencies) to jointly deliver public services. Carried to the extreme, it refers to a government that as a matter of public policy has chosen to contract out all of its production capability to third parties.

The chief characteristic of these alternative service delivery systems is, first, that a private sector or nonprofit organization provides the actual service, rather than permanent government employees (Klingner and Lynn 1997). State and local governments have made heavy use of this model of service delivery. Nearly every state, for example, contracts some mental health services with either the for-profit or the nonprofit sectors (Ewoh 1999, p. 11). Such privatization is seen as a way to improve service delivery quality and/or reduce costs. The cost savings are achieved mainly through the reduced salaries and benefits that the for-profit sector provides to the entry-level employees typically involved in privatization (Elam 1997, p. 17). Without the 'constraints' of protections against arbitrary and capricious action, an employer in the for-profit or nonprofit sectors can more easily add or remove employees during peak and off periods of work than can a civil service system. The public agency is also freed from dealing with various personnel concerns, such as employee grievances, complaints, and appeals (Lawther 1999, p. 31). Selection and termination of employees may either be delegated to the employer altogether, or the public jurisdiction may retain some control over those personnel decisions. Retention of control over selection and termination is especially important if the service includes specialized personnel who would be difficult to replace, or whose replacement with lesser-qualified staff would hurt the quality of service provided (Lawther 1999, p. 30). Arguably, contracting offers a means to increase or maintain the level of service provided by the public sector without (at least in appearance) a commensurate increase in staffing.

Nonprofit organizations are often selected to implement public services for three important reasons (Saidel 1989, p. 340). First, nonprofit organizations are often capable of more rapid implementation compared with the public sector, because personnel start-up activities are less cumbersome and the organizations tend to be smaller and able to respond to opportunities more rapidly. Second, the nonprofit organizations can tailor programs in response to community conditions and needs. Third, nonprofit organizations may be able to deliver services to individuals who might not be accessible through direct public administration channels.

Reliance upon the use of nonprofit organizations to deliver services has come under specific critique in terms of tracking accountability and legal responsibility for program delivery and service provision to clientele (Gilmour and Jensen 1996).

Downsizing and Restructuring *— RIF - reduction in force*

Another structural characteristic of the service delivery environment reflects workforce contractions due to downsizing. The intentional reduction of the number of employees in an organization's workforce is referred to as a reduction in force or downsizing. Workforce reduction has become prevalent across job sectors in recent years, as corporations adjust to the competitive global marketplace and governments adapt to periodically tight budgets. The "Great Recession" of 2008 forced many governments, throughout the United States and globally, to reduce their workforce. In some cases, the reductions were quite dramatic. For example, the city of Reno, Nevada cut 24 percent of its workforce in the period between 2008 and 2011 (Witt and Weatherby 2012, p. 143). State governments were also impacted economically by the Great Recession. Overall, the number of state government workers in the United States was reduced by 662,000 positions between 2008 and 2012 (McNichol 2012).

Downsizing is often seen as an end in itself in the public sector, as many believe that a smaller government is better by definition, with the private or nonprofit sector somehow magically 'picking up the service slack'. Politicians who are anxious to demonstrate to voters that they have cut the size and cost of government will often point to smaller numbers of employees to prove their case. Public sector downsizing may be the result of sometimes hostile taxpayers who have passed tax limitation measures, refused to pass bond elections for public facilities, and voted for candidates promising to 'cut the fat' from bloated bureaucracies. Although the evidence indicates the results of organizational downsizing are generally negative or at best mixed (McKinley, Sanchez, and Schick 1995, p. 33), reducing the size of government seems to sell well in political campaigns. Some of the most detrimental effects have been on the employees who remain in the downsized organization and are asked to "do more with less" (Cameron 1994, p. 198). With fewer employees who have to meet heightened demands for services, it is often the HRM professional who is asked to improve morale and make the diminished organization work.

For many nonprofit organizations, RIF is a way of life. Because many nonprofit organizations are heavily dependent upon contracts and grants from government, corporate sponsors, or larger nonprofit organizations (e.g., philanthropic foundations), rapid staffing changes are common. Nonprofit organizations will hire in response to a new grant or contract to inaugurate a new program or enhance existing services. Nonprofits will also lay off these employees if funding is not sustainable.

Civil service systems often have very specific procedures for RIFs. The procedures specify the order in which employees will be laid off from the organization (State of Idaho 2010). The layoffs would begin with temporary employees, then provisional, then probationary, then, finally, permanent employees. The order of layoffs of permanent employees is typically determined by a point system comprised of a combination of years of service and performance indicators. War veterans may receive additional preference points at this point. The employees are then listed in order of points, and those with the fewest points are the first to be laid off. Employees may choose to voluntarily be demoted to a lower classification rather than being laid off. This is referred to as 'bumping' and allows an employee to stay with the organization, albeit in a lower-ranking position than they previously held. Employees choosing such a voluntary demotion are typically granted first rights on reapplication, should their previous position become open. Bumping is often allowed across work groups and causes serious disruption to the organization as a 'chain reaction', wherein bumped employees cascade from position to position.

The major approaches to staffing reductions are summarized in Exhibit 1.2. Many of these strategies are short-term solutions to reducing the overall number of employees in the workforce (for example, attrition or hiring freezes). Other techniques are aimed more at a "work redesign strategy" and involve the elimination of functions, hierarchical levels in the organization, or products, for example (Cameron 1994, p. 198). Although this type of workforce reduction takes more time, it may be more beneficial to the organization in the end.

Although downsizing may bring some short-term cost savings to an organization, studies assessing the effectiveness of downsizing have found that many organizations suffer losses in productivity and employee morale after a downsizing episode (Cameron 1994, p. 189). Several lessons about downsizing emerge. First, downsizing must be coordinated with the long-term strategic planning efforts of the organization (GAO 1996). Short-term RIFs carried out without consideration of the critical KSAs required can be harmful. A properly planned downsizing will begin with an assessment of what types of people (and skill) and how many people the organization needs to end up with after the downsizing is over (GAO 1996, p. 4). Attrition, hiring freezes, and non-targeted early retirement incentives, for example, can result in critical skill shortages. The protocols described above in civil service systems may not allow the HR professional to know whom the organization will be left with after the RIF. Managers may find that all the employees with knowledge of a critical process or procedure have left. Many organizations that have experienced this loss of expertise have found that they had to rehire or replace the employees that had just been separated from the organization (*Newsweek* 2010).

Exhibit 1.2 Approaches to Staffing Reduction

- *Attrition*: reduction in numbers due to resignations, retirements, or death.
- *Hiring Freezes*: prohibition on filling vacant positions.
- *Early Retirement Incentives*: reduction in numbers achieved by offering access to full pension benefits, severance pay, or other monetary reward to encourage early retirement.
- *Job Re-Engineering*: reduction in numbers through elimination of functions and organizational processes.
- *Redeployment and Retraining*: reduction in numbers achieved by shifting employees to positions elsewhere in the organization.
- *Part-Time Employment*: reduction in numbers achieved by converting full-time positions to part time.
- *Involuntary Separations*: reduction in numbers through layoffs and firings.

Source: Adapted from Fisher, Schoenfeldt, and Shaw 1993, p. 735, and GAO 1996, p. 4.

Often, these employees are rehired as consultants at a much higher cost to the organization than when they were permanent employees. Organizational memory and expertise can also be lost (Cameron 1994, p. 198). These problems can be partially minimized by targeting the separation at only particular employees, but collective bargaining agreements and civil service laws and regulations relevant in most public jurisdictions may limit the ability of governmental organizations to target reductions in force. A further step may be to, when possible, ensure that critical skills are backed up by more than one person (GAO 1998). Linking downsizing to the organizational planning process can help with this.

Although organizations may seek to reduce the cost of their personnel by reducing the number of employees, there is often no reduction in the work of the organization. An RIF leaves fewer employees to do more work. As noted above, many of the 'surviving' employees may not have the skills to match the work they are assigned. Organizations will need to plan for training and development to bring the skills of the remaining employees in line with the work.

Reform and Fragmentation in HRM

The preference for alternative mechanisms reflects the goals of increasing flexibility in the delivery of public services as a means to ensure that government is doing what it promised.

However, this preference may be accomplished by restructuring the personnel system within a given organization. Some states have attempted to increase the flexibility of their HR systems by making widespread changes in the way their states' civil service system works. Georgia eliminated its civil service system altogether, and several others, such as Minnesota, Oklahoma, and South Carolina, have made large-scale reforms (Human Resources 1999). Many states have tried to reduce the number of job classifications used in their personnel systems, "because the greater the number of classes, the narrower the focus of the individual job titles and the less flexibility managers have to give adequate raises or shift employees around where they are needed" (Human Resources 1999, p. 25). Increased flexibility has been sought by reducing the requirements for testing for civil service jobs in Wisconsin (Human Resources 1999). This makes it easier to attract and successfully hire good employees in a tight labor market, as well as dramatically reducing the amount of time it takes to hire a new employee. Another example of increased flexibility is allowing managers to select potential employees from a list of the top ten candidates, rather than only the top three candidates (the 'rule of three'). Changes in recruitment and selection techniques are discussed further in Chapter 7. States and local governments also may use some type of pay for performance or enhanced benefit packaging to reward high-performance employees and increase flexibility in civil service compensation systems (Hays 1996, p. 292). Chapters 8 and 9 discuss such innovations in compensation packaging.

Beyond the particulars of a civil service model used in a given jurisdiction, one aspect of the alternative delivery models discussed in the previous section is that, even when the service is provided by an actual public agency, the workers are likely to be contracted, part-time, or seasonal employees, as opposed to permanent civil servants (Klingner and Lynn 1997, p. 161). Using contract or temporary employees may allow an organization to hire much more quickly, and to let the employees go when the demand for work decreases (Klingner and Lynn 1997, p. 161). Also, temporary and part-time workers may be 'cheaper' in the public sector, because they are generally paid less, have fewer benefits than permanent employees, are not entitled to the due process rights of civil service employees, and are seldom part of any collective bargaining agreement (Elam 1997, p. 29; Klinger and Lynn 1997, p. 161). Employees who are exempt from civil service classification systems offer similar advantages to the public sector organization in terms of flexibility. They are generally hired through employment contracts that specify their pay and benefits, as well as their term of employment.

An added advantage is that exempt employees may be discharged "at will," or much more easily than traditional civil service employees (Klingner and Lynn 1997, p. 162).

These fragmented personnel systems can be challenging for HRM professionals and line managers. Having contract employees mixed in among permanent organization employees may lead to confusion over reporting lines, whether or not all organizational due process and grievance procedures apply, and what disciplinary actions are available to managers supervising contract employees. Managing personnel and services in a privatized environment requires HRM professionals to develop and maintain new sets of skills. Ewoh suggests that managers need training on the following areas: "(1) the public–private environment of many public programs, (2) the difficulties of setting performance standards in such a setting, (3) measuring performance in these arrangements and, (4) auditing expenditures and maintaining control in privatized areas of activity" (1999, p. 22).

The Ethics of Change

Transparency through accurate and timely communication may be the most effective way to manage the stress of change for employees in organizations. Because staffing reductions may threaten individual employees' livelihood, spark 'survivor guilt' among those who avoid layoffs, or lead to increased workloads for those who continue in the organizations, it is useful to consider the ethical dimension of this scenario.

Studies of effective downsizing emphasize the importance of communication and point to the ethical dimension in how downsizing is accomplished. An RIF can be traumatic, not only to the employees released from the organization, but to those who remain as well. Open communication between management and employees about the downsizing process can reduce the fear and mistrust sometimes generated by an RIF (GAO 1998, p. 1). Evidence suggests that, when organizations involved employees in the development of and communication about the downsizing process, the organizations retained higher levels of productivity than those without transparency in communication about the RIF (Cameron 1994, p. 202).

Several studies report loss of morale and, consequently, productivity among employees who survive a downsizing (GAO 1996, p. 4). Communication with these employees about the purposes of the RIF, its progress, and anticipated completion can help alleviate the anxiety experienced by survivors. Outplacement and training programs that help employees find new placements not only assist those who have been separated from the organization in their transition, but have been shown to improve the morale and productivity of those who remain (Fisher, Schoenfeldt, and Shaw 1993, p. 740). Although it is certainly legal to proceed with downsizing without communication or outplacement efforts, organizations need to weigh their ethical responsibility to treat their employees with respect. The payback will be in the continued productivity and loyalty of those employees who remain with the organization.

Summary

Organizational change for public and nonprofit agencies has become the norm rather than the exception, and the close linkages that have developed between public and nonprofit organizations as a result are reflected in the focus of this book. The causes of change vary, but include the rapid rate of technological innovations, demands for restructured service delivery, reform–driven experiments in personnel system structures, and the changing nature of the workforce.

The nature of the workforce may drive the greatest demands for reform. The face of government reflects changes in our society. These shifts in age, racial, and ethnic composition further diversify the nation's workforce. More women and minorities populate the workforce than ever before, and the average age of workers is increasing. Public agencies are learning more about employees with disabilities and how best to deal professionally with female and minority coworkers and managers.

Simultaneous citizen demands for better services and restrained public spending also contribute to the changes. As organizations respond with new HR arrangements and alternative service delivery methods, public and nonprofit organizations are working together more closely than ever to serve a shared public interest. Most importantly, the human resource manager is being asked to assist administrators in implementing change in organizations. Thus, HRM must shift from a role of system police to that of helping line managers accomplish the recruitment, selection, retention, training, and compensation tasks required to maintain a quality workforce.

A Manager's Vocabulary

- Accountability
- Diversity
- Equity
- Line vs staff positions
- Centralization vs decentralization of HR
- Temporary or seasonal employees
- Contract employees
- Downsizing
- Reduction in force (RIF)
- Attrition
- Generations in the workplace
- Glass ceiling
- Demographic trends

Study Questions

1. What are some of the key differences between HR in public or private and nonprofit organizations? How do these differences affect the practice of HR in these different types of organization?
2. What are the pros and cons of having a centralized versus decentralized HR office? Of privatizing a governmental function?
3. What are the different perspectives of line and staff managers? How can HR improve its overall relationship with line managers?
4. How will HR functions such as recruitment and benefits administration change with the increasingly diverse workforce?
5. How can public services delivered by broad varieties of employees, some contracted, others appointed, and others perhaps even volunteers, operate in an accountable and stable manner?

Exercises

Exercise 1.1 Training Needs for Decentralized HRM

What are some of the key training needs for line managers in an organization moving to decentralized HRM? Develop a list of new skills those line managers might need to take over certain HRM functions.

*Exercise 1.2 **Contracting Arrangements and HR***

You are the new assistant to the HR director for your city. The city is considering contracting out its garbage collection services to a for-profit company. The employees from the garbage collection services are very nervous about what might happen to them if the change goes through. The city council is hopeful that this move will save money. The HR director has asked you to sketch out the possible impacts on HR from such a move for the next city council meeting. What sorts of issue will you include in your briefing?

References

Anderson, Claire J., and Betty Roper Ricks. 1993. "Illiteracy: The Neglected Enemy in Public Service." *Public Personnel Management* 22 (1): 137–152.

Barr, Stephen. 1996. "Up Against the Glass." *Management Review* 85 (9): 12–17.

Cameron, Kim S. 1994. "Strategies for Successful Organizational Downsizing." *Human Resource Management* 33 (2): 189–211.

Catalyst.org. 2012. "Catalyst Quick Take: Generations in the Workplace in the United States & Canada." New York: Catalyst. www.catalyst.org/knowledge/generations-workplace-united-states-canada (accessed January 8, 2015).

Ceridian. 2004. Surviving and Thriving in the Future World of Work Predictions on Trends in Workforce 2020. Ceridian Centrefile.

Costanza, David P., Jessica M. Badger, Rebecca L. Fraser, Jamie B. Severt, and Paul A. Gade. 2012. "Generational Differences in Work-Related Attitudes: A Meta-analysis." *Journal of Business Psychology Online* 27 (4): 375–394. DOI 10.1007/s10869–012–9259–4.

Economist, The. 2014. "The Glass Ceiling Index." March 8, 2014. www.economist.com/news/business/21598669-bestand-worstplaces-be-working-women-glass-ceiling-index (accessed January 8, 2015).

Elam, L. B. 1997. "Reinventing Government Privatization Style: Avoiding the Legal Pitfalls of Replacing Civil Servants with Contract Providers." *Public Personnel Management* 26 (1): 15–33.

Ewoh, Andrew I. E. 1999. "An Inquiry into the Role of Public Employers and Managers in Privatization." *Review of Public Personnel Administration* 19 (1): 8–27.

Ferris, Gerald R., Wayne A. Hochwarter, M. Ronald Buckley, Gloria Harrell-Cook, and Dwight D. Frink. 1999. "Human Resources Management: Some New Directions." *Journal of Management* 25 (3): 400–405.

Fisher, Cynthia, Lyle F. Schoenfeldt, and James B. Shaw. 1993. *Human Resource Management*, 2nd ed. Boston, MA: Houghton Mifflin.

Folger, Robert, and Russell Cropanzano. 1998. *Organizational Justice and Human Resource Management*. Thousand Oaks, CA: Sage.

French, P. Edward, and Doug Goodman. 2011. "Local Government Human Resource Management Past, Present, and Future: Revisiting Hays and Kearney's Anticipated Changes a Decade Later." *Politics & Policy* 39 (5): 761–785.

Gilmour, Robert S., and Laura S. Jensen. 1996. "Reinventing Government Accountability: Public Functions, Privatization, and the Meaning of 'State Action.'" *Public Administration Review* 58 (3): 247–258.

Griffin, Ricky W. 1984. *Management*. Boston, MA: Houghton Mifflin.

Guy, Mary E., and Meredith A. Newman. 1998. "Toward Diversity in the Workplace." In *Handbook of Human Resource Management in Government*, 1st ed., Ed. Stephen E. Condrey, 75–92. San Francisco, CA: Jossey Bass.

———. 2004. "Women's Jobs, Men's Jobs: Sex Segregation and Emotional Labor." *Public Administration Review* 64 (3): 289–298.

Hays, Steven W. 1996. "The State of the Discipline in Public Personnel Administration." *Public Administration Quarterly* 2 (3): 285–304.

Hays, Steven W., and Richard C. Kearney. 2001. "Anticipated Changes in Human Resource Management: View from the Field." *Public Administration Review* 61 (5): 585–597.

Heathfield, Susan M. "11 Tips for Managing Millennials 4 Tips About What Millennials Need at Work." Human Resources About.Com. http://humanresources.about.com/od/managementtips/a/millenials.htm (accessed January 8, 2015).

Human Resources. 1999. *Governing*, 24–25 February.

International Personnel Management Association. 1998. "Practical Pointers: Interview Guide." *IPMA News* (November): 32.

———. 1999. "Top HR Trends." *IPMA News* (September): 1.

Johnston, William B., and Arnold C. Packer. 1987. *Workforce 2000: Work and Workers for the Twenty-first Century.* Indianapolis, IN: Hudson Institute.

King, Cheryl Simrell, and Camilla Stivers. 1998. "Strategies for an Anti-Government Era." In *Government Is Us*, Eds. Cheryl Simrell King and Camilla Stivers, 195–204. Thousand Oaks, CA: Sage.

Klingner, Donald E. 2014. "On the 75th Anniversary of ASPA: The Congruent Evolution of Civil Rights and the American Society for Public Administration." *Review of Public Personnel Administration* 34 (1): 7–22.

Klingner, Donald E., and Dahlia Bradshaw Lynn. 1997. "Beyond Civil Service: The Changing Face of Public Personnel Management." *Public Personnel Management* 26 (2): 157–174.

Lawther, Wendell C. 1999. "The Role of Public Employees in the Privatization Process: Personnel and Transition Issues." *Review of Public Personnel Administration* 19 (1): 28–40.

McKinley, William, Carol M. Sanchez, and Allen Schick. 1995. "Organizational Downsizing: Constraining, Cloning, Learning." *The Academy of Management Executive* 9 (3): 32–44.

McNichol, Elizabeth. 2012. (June 15) "Some Basic Facts on State and Local Government Workers." Center for Budget and Policy Priorities. www.cbpp.org/cms/?fa=view&id=3410 (accessed January 8, 2015).

Marshall, Sally Kraus, and Marylou Whelan. 1996/1997. "Changing Roles for Human Resources Professionals." *The Public Manager* 25 (4): 27–29.

Mauer, Rick. 1998. "Don't Resist Generation X: Understand and Learn to Manage Them." *IPMA News* (November): 19.

Mero, Neal P., and Stephan J. Motowidlo. 1995. "Effects of Rater Accountability on the Accuracy and the Favorability of Performance Ratings." *Journal of Applied Psychology* 80 (4): 517–525.

Milward, H. Brinton, and Keith G. Provan. 2000. "Governing the Hollow State." *Journal of Public Administration Research and Theory* 10 (2): 359–379.

Mosher, Frederick C. 1982. *Democracy and the Public Service*, 2nd ed. New York: Oxford University Press.

Newsweek. 2010. "The Case Against Layoffs: They Often Backfire." February 4, 2010. www.newsweek.com/case-against-layoffs-they-often-backfire-75039 (accessed January 9, 2015).

Ortman, Jennifer M., Victoria A. Velkoff, and Howard Hogan. 2014. "An Aging Nation: The Older Population in the United States." Current Population Reports P25–1140. U.S. Census Bureau, Washington, DC 2014.

Saidel, Judith R. 1989. "Dimensions of Interdependence: The State and Voluntary-Sector Relationship." *Nonprofit and Voluntary Sector Quarterly* 18 (4): 336–347.

Salaman, Lester M., Ed. 2002. *The Tools of Government: A Guide to the New Governance.* New York: Oxford University Press.

Sayre, Wallace S. 1991. "The Triumph of Techniques over Purpose." In *Classics of Public Personnel Policy*, 2nd ed., Ed. Frank J. Thompson, 154–158. Pacific Grove, CA: Brooks/Cole.

Shafritz, Jay M. 1991. "Position Classification: A Behavioral Analysis for the Public Service." In *Classics of Public Personnel Policy*, 2nd ed., Ed. Frank J. Thompson, 175–190. Pacific Grove, CA: Brooks/Cole.

State of Idaho. 2010. "Division of Human Resources Layoff Information." (September) www.dhr.Idaho.gov/PDF%20documents/Layoff%20information.pdf (accessed January 8, 2015).

Taylor, Paul, Rakesh Kochhar, Rich Morin, Wendy Wang, Daniel Dockterman, and Jennifer Medina. 2009. "America's Changing Work Force Recession Turns a Graying Office Grayer." Pew Research Center. www.pewresearch.org/2009/09/03/recession-turns-a-graying-office-grayer/ (accessed January 8, 2015).

Tetlock, Philip E. 1992. "The Impact of Accountability on Judgment and Choice: Toward a Social Contingency Model." In *Advances in Experimental Social Psychology*, Ed. Mark P. Zanna, 331–377. New York: Academic Press.

Toossi, Mitra. 2012. "Labor Force Projections to 2020: A More Slowly Growing Workforce." *Monthly Labor Review* (U.S. Department of Labor, Bureau of Labor Statistics: January 2012, p. 44) www.bls.gov/opub/mlr/2012/01/art3full.pdf (accessed January 8, 2015).

Tulgan, B. 1995. *Managing Generation X.* Santa Monica, CA: Merritt Press.

U.S. Bureau of Labor Statistics. 2013. "Women in the Laborforce: A Data Book" (Washington, DC: Bureau of Labor Statistics Report 1040). www.bls.gov/cps/wlf–databook–2012.pdf (accessed January 8, 2015).

U.S. GAO 2014. Civilian Labor Force by Sex, Age, Race, and Hispanic Origin, 1960–2010.

———. 1996. *Federal Downsizing: Better Workforce and Strategic Planning Could Have Made Buyouts More Effective.* August 8. Washington, DC: Government Printing Office. GAO/GGD 96–62. govinfo.library.unt.edu/npr/library/gao/gg96062.pdf (accessed January 9, 2015).

———. 1998. "Federal Downsizing: Agency Officials' Views on Maintaining Performance During Downsizing at Selected Agencies (letter report)." March 24. GAO/GGD 98–46. www.access.gpo.gov/su_docs/aces160.shtml (accessed January 8, 2015).

U.S. Merit Systems Protection Board (U.S. MSPB). 1992. A Question of Equity: Women and the Glass Ceiling in the Federal Government (October). Washington, DC: USMSPB.

Witt, Stephanie L., and James B. Weatherby. 2012. *Urban West Revisited: Managing Cities in Uncertain Times.* Boise, ID: Boise State University.

2 Development of Civil Service Systems in the United States

Learning Objectives

- Compare the patronage, merit, and labor relations personnel systems in the U.S. public sector.
- Explore the reform efforts for these systems at the state and local levels.

> What doesn't work and you can't fire it?
> An MX missile? A NASA rocket?
> No, a Civil Service employee.
>
> (Finkle 1984)

Few other occupations have been the objects of as much ridicule as the federal civil servant. The stereotype of the swollen federal agency populated by an abundance of listless and uncaring civil servants is so common it hardly requires illustration. The very word 'bureaucrat' has become an epithet in common parlance. But how much truth is there to the offensive stereotype, and how did it develop? To approach an understanding of these questions, we must examine the evolution of public sector merit systems within the broader political context of the maturation of American government. This section first describes the political environment of public personnel administration in the United States, and then describes the historical development of our country's civil service systems in the federal, state, and local governments. Along the way, we will discover that important parts of the widely shared civil servant stereotype are quite undeserved.

The Context of Public Personnel in the U.S.

Understanding HRM in the public sector is impossible without understanding the governmental context embedding the HR function. The political system determines how many positions there will be in government, the compensation rates for employees, and the manner used to select people for positions. Therefore, an understanding of that system, and how it affects HRM practices, is important. A quite commonly held misperception is that most people who work for government are federal civil servants. In reality, there are a wide variety of governments and types of government employee at the federal, state, and local levels of government. Richard Stillman describes five distinct categories of public employee (1996, p. 187):

- *political appointees*, who serve without job security and are appointed based on party ties and/or personal loyalties to elected officials;
- *professional careerists* who have "specialized expertise in specific fields . . . usually based on advanced professional training";

- *general civil service administrators and workers*;
- *unionized* employees; and
- *contractual* employees.

An understanding of the governmental context not only includes knowledge of the structures and legal powers of government, but also features an appreciation for the variety of shapes, sizes, and missions of governments present within the U.S. governmental scene. The separation of powers, federalism, political parties, a tradition of strong individual rights, and the ubiquitous presence of interest groups all deserve special attention in this regard. These features of the American political setting combine for a highly politicized environment for public personnel administration in the U.S.

Public Sector Workers as Dispersed

Public employees work, not only for the federal government, but also for each of our 50 states and more than 89,000 local and special district governments (U.S. Census Bureau 2012). In fact, by a very large margin, most people who work in the public sector do *not* work for the federal government. From the 1990s through the first decade of the twenty-first century, there were somewhere in the neighborhood of 2.7 million full-time federal employees (U.S. OPM 2012). In 2012, there were 5.3 million state employees and more than 14 million local employees (U.S. Census Bureau 2014). Although state and local government employment grew more rapidly than federal government employment through the 1990s, the "Great Recession" of 2008 hit state and local governments very hard. In fact, the number of state and local government employees fell by an estimated 662,000 positions between 2008 and 2012 (McNichol 2012). Most federal employees do not work in Washington, DC. In fact, only 16 percent of federal employees work in the DC metro area, whereas 84 percent are distributed throughout the United States and, to a limited extent, abroad (Gogovernment.org n.d.).

Contract Workers Are More Common

As noted in Chapter 1, another important characteristic of the public sector workforce is that contract workers, employed by private sector companies or nonprofit organizations, now do an increasing amount of the government's public service work. Some federal agencies employ as many contract employees as they do permanent employees (or more) (Kettl et al. 1996, p. 14). As we will discuss later, this noteworthy development presents a whole host of new challenges for HRM in government.

A final important characteristic of the public sector workforce is that the much-maligned civil service system covers increasingly smaller percentages of the total government workforce. The civil service system, for example, currently covers only 49 percent of all federal employees (Fedjobs.com n.d.). There is also evidence that state governments increasingly use several routes other than their respective civil service systems to recruit, hire, and manage their employees (Jorgensen, Fairless, and Patton 1996, p. 5). Increasing numbers of civil service jobs are being redefined from career service to 'exempt status', making them (political) discretionary appointments that no longer entail job security. The United States uses a substantially higher proportion of discretionary positions and political appointees than any other Western nation (Ingraham 1995, p. xix).

Powers Distributed by Level and Branch Affect Personnel Systems

The separation of powers between our executive and legislative branches means that the president and Congress share responsibility for the management of our federal civil service and most of its public agencies. This authority system applies to governors and legislatures and state personnel systems in each of the 50 states.

Power struggles between the executive and legislative branches can have a major impact on the structure and funding of executive branch personnel systems. Chief executives and prominent members of the legislative branch often disagree on the proper scope of government action in particular areas, especially when they are from different political parties (an increasingly frequent occurrence in our political system). Public employees often find themselves in the middle of heated political battles and need to follow the shifting winds of politics to do their jobs effectively. How personnel systems work in practice in the U.S. public sector is often a reflection of the operating agendas and practices within the political system.

Federalism, or the division of governmental powers by state and substate levels, is one of the most important features of our political system for HRM. The U.S. Constitution enumerates certain powers for the national government and reserves all other powers to the states and the people of the respective states. In practice, the states and the federal government actually share responsibility for most major government programs. Consequently, many public employees work closely with their counterparts at other levels of government. The state and local governments are critical partners in most areas of public policy. From time to time, the federal government places personnel-related requirements on state and local governments, such as AA programs, the implementation of workplace health and safety measures, or minimal wage rates for government contractors. Changes in the nature of government programs, such as when the federal government changed how health care insurance will be provided in the Affordable Care Act, can have far-reaching effects on the HR systems of state and local governments. Particular positions may have to be created, eliminated, or changed. Additional training may be required for existing employees, and funding for appropriate technology may be necessary to help employees do their jobs well.

Changes in our intergovernmental system affect HRM in many important ways. American federalism is changing over time to provide a progressively larger role for state and local government during an era of 'devolution' of governmental responsibilities. The HRM systems of state and local government are experiencing the challenges of recruiting and maintaining effective workforces able to use the high-tech skills needed for contemporary service provision and public policy problem solving in this increasingly decentralized environment.

Constitutional Protections Extend to Public Employees

The U.S. Constitution provides for the protection of individual rights and civil liberties against government action. These protections are contained in the Bill of Rights, or the first ten amendments to the U.S. Constitution. These rights and protections extend to public employees inasmuch as their employers are engaging in 'state action', and therefore public entities are substantially more highly constrained by constitutional limits on government action than are private employers with respect to what latitude they have in the management of employees. Many decisions by the U.S. Supreme Court have outlined specific public sector personnel practices that are permitted and that are forbidden (such as drug testing of public employees), and these decisions and derivative adjudication have greatly shaped the practice of HRM. Some of these important decisions, and the legal rights of public employees derived from them, are described in Chapter 3.

Political Parties and other Interest Groups Affect Personnel Action

Political parties are a singular form of organized interests in the United States with a defined legal role in staffing government. Parties have longstanding ties to public sector HRM and are a key feature of our political system. The practice of patronage, which entails the awarding of government jobs based on membership in, or loyalty to, a political party or prominent elected official, has been a major aspect of our HRM in the United States since the first days of our history as a political community.

Political parties can have an important impact on HRM when different parties control the executive and legislative branches of government; this circumstance is termed 'divided government'. The inevitable differences between the two parties on whether or which government programs should be enlarged, reduced in scale, or eliminated may create uncertainty among government employees. In some settings, this may result in 'cutback management' (a planned reduction in force achieved by not replacing vacancies, encouraging relocation among the workforce, and authorizing early retirement). The prevalence of downsizing and its impacts on the public sector were described in Chapter 1.

A final characteristic of our political system relevant to HRM in the public sector is the presence of a diverse universe of active interest groups. Although these interest groups may not play the same role as political parties, Americans are organized into virtually every conceivable grouping, and many interest groups are concerned with pressuring government for policies that will benefit their particular group. Among the many interest groups seeking influence over public sector personnel policies and practices are public employee unions and their respective lobbying organizations. Although their presence and power varies from state to state, public sector unions and the interest group advocates who represent them are an important part of our political system. The role of unions in public personnel policy development and personnel system operations in the United States is described in Chapter 4.

- Introduction to the Reading - *Pendleton Act of 1883*

The excerpt for this chapter is taken from Paul Van Riper's seminal treatise, *History of the United States Civil Service*, originally published in 1958. The chapter in which this excerpt appeared details the legislative history of the Pendleton Act, the federal legislation that created the merit-based civil service system of the U.S. government in 1883. Substantial parts of that original system remain in place today. The title of this excerpt, "The End of Two Eras," refers to the shift from a more classic patronage system to the populist patronage model articulated through the Jacksonian movement. *Shift from classic to populist Patronage* The 1883 Congress sought the advantages of neutral service and independent expertise over our own patronage-based system of public employment. That Congress, however, resisted importing many aspects of the British system, especially those that reinforced the class distinctions prevalent in British and European society generally at that time. The challenge of finding the way to maximize fairness and efficiency of operation of personnel management systems in government continues to this day. As you read the following selection, please keep the following questions in mind: ✓

1. What were the perceived advantages of the Civil Service Commission over the spoils system?
2. In contemporary discussions, we often hear that 'government should run like a business', yet that would have been of grave concern to the decision makers in 1883. Why?
3. Why might those supporting the Pendleton Act have been concerned about expertise of those in government positions?

Civil Service and Patronage

Understanding the evolution of the federal civil service system is critical, because many of the characteristics of public sector employment described above are either precedents to, or reactions

Excerpt 2.1 The End of Two Eras

Just as 1829 marked the end of the bureaucracy of the Founding Fathers, 1883 marked the first great inroad into the spoils system of the mid-nineteenth century. Twice within a hundred years the American public service had been "reformed." What fundamental contrasts can be drawn between the two movements?

The Jacksonian movement can best be described as a class bursting of bonds. As the new democracy received the ballot—its ticket of admission to participation in government—it insisted on a show to its pleasure. And the cast of characters was adjusted accordingly. American democracy moved by the logic implicit in its premises to a recognition—practical this time, not theoretical—of the implications of both liberty and equality. Public office was to become almost a perquisite of citizenship and "rotation" the watchword. The spoils system provided a system of recruitment for public office very little at odds with the individualism of the day. May the best man win! The whole mechanism reflected the ideals and attitudes of American nineteenth century agrarian democracy.

In the decades immediately after the Civil War, however, individualism seemed to be producing inequality. The "best" men were winning by more of a margin than many people liked to see. And not a few questioned whether those who were winning were actually the "best." What had once been intended as an opening up of public office to the mass of citizens had all the earmarks of becoming the opening up of office to plundering by the politically privileged.

In 1883, contrasted to 1829, there was no new class to turn to, nor any particular desire to turn the clock back to 1829. If democracy was not satisfied with its own product, then it would have to reform itself. There was no one else to do it.

Source: Van Riper, Paul P. 1958. pp. 110–112, "Americanizing a Foreign Invention: The Pendleton Act of 1883" in *History of the United States Civil Service*. Row, Peterson.

Excerpt 2.2 Continuation of Van Riper Content

The invention of the merit system of recruitment for public office by examination made possible a new reformation of a different sort. Essentially a foreign idea, imported from a Europe which had faced similar problems earlier, civil service reform, suitably modified to conform to American ideas of a mobile, classless society, was a scheme brilliantly devised to meet the needs of our version of the modern democratic state.

First, the Civil Service Commission could distribute offices more systematically and rationally than the spoils system had ever been able to do. While the new scheme did not guarantee a partisan apportionment of offices to the party in power, it certainly did not guarantee offices to the opposition. If a compromise had to be reached, political neutrality in the distribution of public office was reasonably acceptable to all concerned.

Second, the merit system provided a remedy for those who objected to the obvious corruption and the oligarchical tendencies of the combination of business and politics into which the spoils system had developed. Civil service reform did again open up many of the public offices to all on a new kind of equal basis;[1] and it provided through a new measure of merit, the examination system, the rewards for individual effort so prized in American life.

Finally, the new reform laid the foundation for the development of that technical expertise crucial to the operation of the modern state. And it reached this goal without offending the democratic sensibilities of the great mass of American citizens. Posing no overt threat to the overpowering individualism of the day, it nevertheless gave implicit promise of other reforms to come. Once again a form of latent antagonism between liberty and equality—potentially so explosive in a democracy—was temporarily pacified.

Excerpt Note

1. As Dorman B. Eaton said in testifying before the Senate Committee considering the Pendleton bill, "This bill assumes that every citizen has an equal claim to be appointed if he has equal capacity." U.S. Congress, Senate Report 576, as cited in footnote 3, p. 6.

Source: Van Riper, Paul P. 1958. pp. 110–112, "Americanizing a Foreign Invention: The Pendleton Act of 1883" in *History of the United States Civil Service*. Evanston, IL: Row, Peterson.

against, the federal civil service system. Most state public personnel systems are modeled on the major aspects of the federal civil service system. Many of the special characteristics and the limitations of public sector employment are rooted in the evolution of the federal civil service system as well. Ingraham correctly notes that civil service systems have three principal purposes (1995, pp. xv–xix): to recruit qualified personnel, to reward and develop that workforce, and to establish the guidelines/rules for orchestrating workforce efforts toward achieving the public interest. Without employees, properly selected and well managed, the governments at each level of government cannot accomplish their work. A well-functioning public service personnel operation is critical to effective governance in any jurisdiction, large or small.

Historical Phases in the Development of the U.S. Civil Service System

Exhibit 2.1 offers a useful list of phases in the development of the public service in the United States. Frederick C. Mosher (1982, p. 52) identified the six initial, distinct phases in the development of the public service in the United States as government by—'Gentlemen', 'the Common Man', 'the Good', 'the Efficient', 'Managers', and 'Professionals'. More recently, scholars are inclined to point to the growing tendency to seek policy implementation through nongovernmental actors. Thus, for Exhibit 2.1, we use Don Kettl's term 'Government by Proxy' (1988), but this concept has been variously described as the 'Hollow State' (Milward, Provan, and Else 1993), 'Third Party Government' (Salamon 1981), 'Shadow State' (Wolch 1990), or 'Shadow of Government' (Light 1999). Contemporary public policy implementation often relies upon a complex orchestration of private and nonprofit contract workers in coordination with public sector employees, all working in concert.

A discussion of each of these phases contributes to our understanding of the merit principle, and portions of each are still prevalent in our system today. Current federal, state, and local public service HRM systems reflect *all* of the historical phases that constitute the legacy of public personnel

---

Exhibit 2.1 Phases in the Development of the U.S. Civil Service

- *Government by Gentlemen (1789–1829)*: The earliest presidents appointed men to the federal public service on the basis of 'fitness of character', determined mostly by family background, education, honor and esteem, and loyalty to the new government. Another name for this phase is government by 'aristocrats'. Tenure in office was assumed for middle- and lower-level officials.
- *Government by the Common Man (1829–1883)*: The beginning of the spoils system, or patronage system, is usually attached to the election of Andrew Jackson in 1829. Selection of public service workers was based upon party loyalty, and government workers turned over with election of a different political party.
- *Government by the Good (1883–1906)*: The Progressive Movement advocated elimination of corruption in government and institution of merit as basis of selection for members of the public service.
- *Government by the Efficient (1906–1937)*: Scientific management swept into industry and government service on the heels of Progressive Era reform. Its emphasis on efficiency, rationality, and the 'one best way' to do things still influences the public service. The emphasis placed on rationality and efficiency paved the way for position classification as the basis for personnel administration and complemented Wilson's politics–administration dichotomy in the development of American public administration thought.
- *Government by Managers (1937–)*: This phase emphasized general administrative skills, advocated responsiveness to executives, and began to question the politics–administration dichotomy.
- *Government by Professionals (1945–)*: The increasing numbers of professionals employed throughout the public service characterized this phase, which included membership exclusions and resistance to control from outside agencies such as civil service commissions or elected executives.
- *Government by Proxy (1980–)*: Nonprofit and private sector workers are more commonly contracted to carry out the work of government.

Source: This box was drawn from Mosher's description of the phases of development of the civil service (1982).

---

administration. In the following sections, we consider additional perspectives on each phase of merit system development.

The Patronage System

As Exhibit 2.1 indicates, the patronage system became prevalent in the United States by the mid-1800s. Patronage refers to the practice of selecting government workers based on their ties to the political party and/or major elected official currently in control of the executive branch of the jurisdiction (e.g. the president, governor, county commissioner, or mayor). A person seeking a public sector job needed a 'patron' within the political party to recommend them for the position in question. The party that secured the presidency (or the governorship or mayorship at the state and local levels) enjoyed the privilege of appointing people (usually political supporters) to many public sector jobs. The patronage system was sometimes referred to as the 'spoils system', as in the common phrase "to the winner go the spoils." Although patronage was initially used to place members of the elite into positions of public trust, its use spread, as political parties extended participation to wider segments of the population via the democratization of American political institutions during Andrew Jackson's presidency (Ingraham 1995, p. viii).

Political parties came to rely heavily upon the systematic disbursement of public jobs to secure loyalty from political party members. Large and internally cohesive partisan political organizations, commonly known as *machines,* built their power with patronage. They rose to prominence in many large urban areas, controlling numerous state and local governments across the country. As George Washington Plunkitt, a leader of the political machine in New York State put it, "How are you goin' to interest our young men in their country if you have no office to give them when they work for their party?" (Riordon 1963, p. 11).

Patronage was effective at ensuring party loyalty; however, it was less effective at placing competent employees in positions of public service. As the scope of government widened, and the work of public agencies became more complex and required higher levels of knowledge, the need for government employees to have strong skills related to their particular jobs became increasingly apparent. This is evidenced in Woodrow Wilson's broadly quoted statement, "It's getting harder to run a constitution than to frame one" (2004, p. 23). In addition to issues of competence and effective operation, the patronage system tended toward corruption (the buying of undue influence in government) as well. Wilson (2004, p. 24) wrote:

> Not much impartial scientific method is to be discerned in our administrative practices. The poisonous atmosphere of city government, the crooked secrets of state administration, the confusion, sinecurism, and corruption ever and again discovered in the bureaus at Washington forbid us to believe that any clear conceptions are as yet very widely current in the United States.

By the late 1800s, pressure began to build among groups interested in reforming this ineffective and too often corrupt system. This coalition of reform-oriented groups active at the end of the nineteenth century is referred to as the Progressive Movement. Among other things, the Progressives were interested in how the newly developing science of administration could bring efficiency and competence to government (Hays 1964). A chief mechanism for improving government was eliminating political considerations from administration, or, as Wilson (2004, p. 28) articulated, "administrative questions are not political questions. Although politics sets the tasks for administration, it should not be suffered to manipulate its offices."

Thus, reforms advocated by the Progressives, such as nonpartisan elections and the council-manager form of local government, were intended to reduce the role of political parties in the administration of local government. The institution of the primary election, a uniquely American institution, was another powerful weapon developed by the Progressives to permit rank-and-file party members to control the choice of candidates for the party, rather than allowing 'party bosses' to control candidacy. This mechanism allowed Progressives such as Woodrow Wilson and Theodore Roosevelt and their followers to gain prominent positions in both the Democratic and Republican parties, respectively, despite the opposition of the party bosses of their day. The Progressive Movement reform most directly relevant to public personnel administration, of course, was the institution of the civil service system.

The Civil Service System

Prior to the passage of the Pendleton Act in 1883, government jobs in our country were generally awarded upon political loyalty, or *patronage*. This landmark legislation created a 'hybrid' system for the staffing of government agency offices, with political appointees retained at the top administrative levels of our agencies, and *civil service* employees below those levels. The civil service system was intended to remove the corruption and political bias often associated with the patronage appointment system, and to increase the competence, fairness, efficiency, and overall effectiveness of government operations. The enactment of the Pendleton Act represented an act of substantial self-limitation on the part of the congressional politicians of the period, akin to contemporary campaign finance reform. Passage was ensured partly by the assassination of President Garfield several years earlier by a disappointed office seeker (Stillman 1996, p. 198). Both Progressive reformers and public administration scholars admired the competency and professionalism of merit-based public personnel systems found at the time in Great Britain and on the continent of Europe. They favored a strong executive able to coordinate and manage the personnel function using a system of merit examinations for the selection and promotion of a politically neutral and loyal workforce competent to serve the public trust, as determined by political superiors (Wilson 2004). By importing portions of these foreign systems, Progressive reformers such as Woodrow Wilson and Theodore Roosevelt believed that the American governmental system would become less corrupt, more professional, and more capable of achieving America's great democratic destiny. Advocates for change recognized, however, that the European systems would have to be adapted to America's distinctly egalitarian political institutions and culture (Wilson 2004). A particular concern to reformers was the class-based nature of European civil service systems, in which only the privileged classes had access to the upper administrative ranks in government (Van Riper 1958, p. 4).

As Van Riper (1958) highlighted in the excerpts for this chapter, the legislative battle fought over the Pendleton Act resulted in a statute featuring elements of the European model of civil service, with important concessions made to American political and social sensibilities. Several forces prompted Congress to accept a public policy that legislators knew would, in time, limit a powerful reelection tool in the Jacksonian Era of the 1830s:

- the pressure of a press "muckraking" for stories on political corruption;
- a substantial presence of Progressive sentiment within both the Republican and Democratic parties at the time; and
- the assassination of a president at the hands of a disappointed patronage seeker.

The Pendleton Act originally applied to only 10 percent of all federal jobs, but provisions of the statute empowered the president to enhance the ranks of the civil service by extension to new areas of coverage on the authority of presidential directives (Ingraham 1995, p. 27). The Pendleton Act required the following:

- competitive exams that were "practical" in content;
- tenure in office;
- political neutrality; and – *nonpartisan*
- the creation of the U.S. Civil Service Commission.

The Pendleton Act established competitive exams for those lower-level administrative jobs in the federal government that were originally covered by the act. However, the American statute, as opposed to the equivalent legislation in European governments, required that the competitive exams would be job-specific rather than test general intelligence and command of language and culture reflective of formal education (Huddleston and Boyer 1996, p. 17). This reflection of the American egalitarian spirit led to the American emphasis on rank-in-position, wherein one's rank is based upon the particular job held. In contrast, rank-in-person systems (such as the military or academia) follow a practice wherein a title stays with a person, regardless of the specific duties he or she performs. Managers filling a position were allowed to select from among the top three scorers on the practical, job-specific exam, also known as the 'rule of three' (Ingraham 1995, p. 27).

The Pendleton Act also features security of tenure in office and political neutrality for government workers, both of which represent ideas adopted from European systems (Huddleston and Boyer 1996, p. 17). Unlike the British and continental European civil service systems, however, which required new administrative personnel to enter at the bottom of governmental organizations, the Pendleton Act reflected the egalitarian ethos of American political life by allowing lateral entry into the civil service at all levels (Huddleston and Boyer 1996, p. 18). In an effort to make the Pendleton Act more palatable to the existing strong party organizations, the scope of civil service positions covered was restricted to the entry- and middle-level jobs of federal agencies. Partisan political appointees would fill the top jobs.

The interests of political appointees, responsible to the executive and sensitive to legislative political currents, are often at variance with those of civil servants who are politically neutral and enjoy permanent status. These differences in basic orientation toward the public interest can make management of agencies in federal, state, and local government most difficult (Ingraham 1995, p. xix). For this reason, the Pendleton Act created a bi-partisan Civil Service Commission, comprised of three full-time members who were to be appointed for indefinite terms by the president (Van Riper 1958, p. 103). Such independent regulatory commissions were favored by the Progressives as vehicles to remove areas of public policy from the political arena and redefine them as *administrative* matters. In this case, personnel practices were removed from the political arena and transferred to the U.S. Civil Service Commission. The Commission became responsible for developing the rules necessary for implementing the new merit system, as well as for investigating any abuses of the merit system that were brought to their attention. These potentially incompatible responsibilities proved troublesome throughout the history of the Commission.

Reform at the Federal Level and Implications for the States

As the civil service system grew in complexity over the years, public sector managers became increasingly frustrated with its rule-driven, inflexible nature. Calls for management discretion and flexibility-oriented reform arose, along with the practice of surreptitious evasion of the civil service system. These two phenomena became oft-repeated themes in the literature of public personnel administration. Calls for major change and systematic reform of public personnel systems have been ongoing ever since personnel systems based on civil service statutes enacted in the federal, state, and local governments were first put into effect. In commenting on a new public personnel textbook in 1948, Wallace S. Sayre critiqued public personnel in a now famous review (p. 137):

> Personnel administration, then, has tended to become characterized more by procedure, rule and technique than by purpose or results. In the public field, especially, quantitative devices have overshadowed qualitative. Standardization and uniformity have been enshrined as major virtues. Universal (and therefore non-arbitrary) methods have been preferred to experiment and variety. From the perspective of the clientele (the public, the managers, and the employees), these traits increasingly connote rigidity, bureaucracy, institutionalism—and they are now

beginning to evoke a reciprocal system of formal and informal techniques of evasion. Among personnel professionals there is an accompanying growth of frustration and a loss of satisfying participation in the real work of the organization.

In 1973, E. S. Savas and Sigmund Ginsburg wrote this of New York City's civil service system (1991, p. 165):

> In trying to prevent public sector managers from doing the wrong things such as engaging in nepotism, filling positions on the basis of political criteria over fitness to serve, displaying racial, gender or other forms of prejudice in the treatment of applicants and employees, exercising favoritism, and permitting corruption (by buying of special favor from government)—the civil service system over time has been warped and distorted to the point where it can do hardly anything at all. In an attempt to protect against past abuses, the "merit system" has been perverted in many respects and for some researchers it has often been virtually transformed into a closed and meritless seniority system. It is argued here that a *true* merit system must be constructed anew; this would be a personnel system that provides the opportunity for any qualified citizen to gain access nonpolitically, to be recognized and fairly rewarded for satisfactory performance, to be secure in continued employment upon the demonstration of satisfactory performance, and even to be replaced for unsatisfactory service after sufficient opportunity has been provided to correct unsatisfactory performance.

Federal Civil Service Reforms

Calls for the modification of the civil service practices created with the Pendleton Act of 1883 have been nearly constant since its passage. Several U.S. presidents convened prominent blue ribbon commissions to study the civil service system and recommend changes for greater executive branch direction of personnel practices, including the Roosevelt administration's President's Committee on Administrative Management of 1937 (commonly called the Brownlow Commission) and the First and Second Hoover Commissions of 1949 and 1955. These commissions were the most noteworthy early efforts of this kind. The federal civil service system had undergone some important changes before 1978, such as the addition of veteran's preference and the implementation of EEO laws. However, the *Reorganization Plan No. 2 of 1978* entailed a thorough overhaul and contained the following important changes to the U.S. civil service system (Campbell 1991, p. 85):

- Divide the Civil Service Commission's responsibilities between two new agencies—the Office of Personnel Management and a Merit Systems Protection Board.
- Create a Federal Labor Relations Authority.
- Create a Senior Executive Service.
- Develop a merit pay system.

Exhibit 2.2 describes the newly created federal agencies established through the reorganization. This change was intended to solve the problem of the conflicting roles given to the old Civil Service Commission. In his testimony before Congress about the 1978 reform act, Alan Campbell, a prominent public administration scholar and longtime member of the U.S. Civil Service Commission, noted (1991, p. 85):

> The Civil Service Commission currently has so many conflicting roles that it is unable to perform all of them adequately. At one and the same time it is expected to serve the President in providing

---

Exhibit 2.2 Agencies Created by the Reorganization Plan No. 2 of 1978

The Merit Systems Protection Board is an:

> Independent, quasi-judicial agency in the Executive Branch that serves as guardian of federal merit systems. Assumed employee appeal functions of the Civil Service Commission. Hears and decides appeals from Federal employees of removals and other major personnel actions . . . Reviews significant actions and regulations of Office of Personnel Management and conducts studies of merit systems . . . The MSPB originally included the Office of Special Counsel that "investigates allegations of prohibited personnel practices."
>
> (U.S. MSPB 2014)

The Office of Special Counsel became independent of the MSPB in 1989.

The Office of Personnel Management (OPM; U.S. OPM 2014) is the "federal government's human resource agency. It administers the federal merit system to recruit, examine and promote employees." OPM also prepares guidance on labor management relations and administers the federal retirement system and federal employee health insurance program.

The Federal Labor Relations Authority (FLRA; Federal Labor Relations Authority n.d.):

> represents the federal government's consolidated approach to labor-management relations. It is 'three agencies consolidated in one' . . . the Authority, a quasi-judicial body that adjudicates disputes concerning the labor relations statute or unfair labor practices, the Office of the General Counsel who investigates unfair labor practice complaints and the Federal Service Impasses Panel that resolves impasses in negotiation between federal agencies and unions.

---

managerial leadership for the positive personnel functions in the Executive Branch—that is, establishing personnel policies and advising and assisting agencies on personnel management functions—while also serving as a "watchdog" over the integrity of the merit system, protecting employee rights, and performing a variety of adjudicatory functions.

In theory, OPM granted the president the "personnel management staff arm" (Campbell 1991, p. 87), with the power to appoint the director of the OPM. Ingraham explained that OPM's creation "marked a turning away from the 'policing' function of the Civil Service Commission to a more proactive planning and support function" (1995, p. 77). Unfortunately, the OPM never fully realized its promise in this regard. As presidents exercised more control over OPM and increasingly relied upon political appointees in the executive branch generally, the OPM's effectiveness has continually decreased since its creation (Ingraham 1995, p. 89).

The FLRA was intended to centralize the federal government's dealings with collective bargaining, which had been handled by several separate agencies. Collective bargaining and the FLRA are discussed in considerable detail in Chapter 4.

The Senior Executive Service (SES) was intended to boost the president's power to coordinate and guide the management of the federal executive agencies. Comprising the top ranks, GS–16, 17, 18 and Executive Ranks IV and V in the General Schedule (GS) system, SES members were envisioned to be available to a president to move across agencies when their expertise was needed (Stillman 1996, p. 187). Merit pay was also enacted to reward these top managers for performance rather than longevity. Initially, more than 90 percent of all the eligible civil servants opted to be a part of the SES merit pay system; by opting in, they were eligible for merit pay, but they were not assured of being in the same position and/or agency, should a transfer be deemed necessary by the OPM. However, by 1983, more than 40 percent of those executives had left government service (Huddleston and Boyer 1996, pp. 109, 112).

State and Local Systems

The Pendleton Act "became the classic model for 'good personnel practices' throughout the nation" (Stillman 1996, p. 199). A number of states and local governments adopted merit systems voluntarily, especially where the Progressives were strong. Many others, however, adopted them only after several federal regulations, such as the Social Security statutes and Intergovernmental Personnel Act of 1970, required them to do so. Many of the states have emulated reforms made at the federal level. For example, twelve states adopted a version of SES that was described in the previous section. This reform reflected an attempt to give their respective governors more flexibility in managing the state's workforce. However, few of the SES-modeled reforms have been successful in their efforts to create a flexible and adaptive senior management corps, responsive to executive leadership, as was intended (1996, pp. 190–191). More recently, even while civil service systems are evolving, the United States Supreme Court has been striking down patronage practices in recent years to hasten the demise of patronage politics in state and local government (see *Elrod v. Burns* 1976 or *Branti v. Finkel* 1980, as described in Stillman 1996, p. 199).

Reflecting the fragmentation inherent in federalism, each state's civil service system is unique, featuring varying levels of combination of civil service sophistication and patronage. Though each state is unique, Battaglio and Condrey (2007, pp. 28–29) observe certain patterns in contemporary reform efforts and translate the varieties of practice into four models used in the states: *traditional, reform, strategic,* and *privatization/outsourcing*. The traditional model reflects classic civil service protocols, with centralized administration, strict procedures and rules, and the agency HR administrator serving as an authoritative enforcer. The reform model decentralizes HR responsibilities and affirms the role of supervisors and organizational mission. The strategic model considers collaborative efforts between HR and supervisors and reframes the HR administrator as a "consultant" who works in concert with managers and supervisors to implement the organization's mission. The privatization/outsourcing model reflects the realities of 'government by proxy', recognizing the preeminence of contracts, efficiency measures, and deliverables.

HRM in the U.S. public sector reflects the variety of experiences, political structures, and interest groups present throughout the country. Hays and Sowa's review of the fifty states' HRM systems revealed four interrelated trends (2006):

1. States are increasingly turning to decentralized models for their HRM systems, doing away with or exempting agencies from central HRM agencies (p. 106).
2. Over half of the fifty states are "uncovering" or declassifying many positions, making them exempt from the civil service systems within the states (p. 108).
3. The increasing numbers of limitations on the due process rights of public employees make it easier to terminate public employees at the state level. For example, twenty-five of the fifty states now restrict grievance rights of state employees by explicit state statutes (p. 110).

4.   At the time of their study, activist governors, who committed to increasing the number of exempt or unclassified positions in their state, as well as limiting the role of public sector unions, were elected in nineteen states (p. 112).

There is tremendous diversity in the ways in which public sector HRM is practiced. Each state and local government will reflect its own unique development and, at the same time, endeavor to keep pace with national trends and developments as they become evident.

Technology and Civil Service

Technology has played an important part in the development of the civil service throughout its history. When the United States first formed, most government jobs were rather uncomplicated, and finding employees capable of performing the tasks required was not particularly difficult. However, the rapid growth of the country in its first 100 years, and the rising complexity of the tasks that government assumed, led to calls for more careful and precise selection methods. As discussed earlier in this chapter, many reformers sought to apply the rigor of science to the study of administration.

The scientific principles that Wilson and other early scholars of public administration sought to apply to administration were rooted in the appeal of the Enlightenment concept of reason. When the Founding Fathers used phrases such as "we find these truths to be self-evident" in the nation's Declaration of Independence, they articulated their belief in the existence of laws of nature that were in the range of human reason to discover and apply toward "building a more perfect union." American political philosophy, from its inception, placed great trust in the potential power of human reason. Indeed, the foundations of our democratic form of government rest on the assumption that the people are capable of self-government, in part because they have the capacity to reason and learn and improve upon the pursuit of happiness in the context of permitting liberty and freedom for all. For civil service reformers, rationalizing governmental organizations through technologies that deconstructed organizational performance was right in line with this American, deeply held faith in human reason's ability to discover "self-evident truths" about how government should be organized and managed. Consequently, classical organization theory hinges upon the importance of bringing rationality to formal organizations, and two general paradigms are associated with this movement—enhanced performance achieved by restructuring either positions or tasks. A focus on macrostructure for the organization considered how authorities and positions were established in relation to one another (Weber 2011), and the notion of systematic position classification flourished within this realm of rationalization. Conversely, Taylor (2011) assessed both task components and task tools in an effort to improve human performance of necessary work tasks. Thus, management used the increasingly science-based technology of the day (the early decades of the industrialization of production processes and global reach of commerce) to exercise centralized control over the HRM process and its organization. This occurred both within the rapidly growing private corporations of the day and the public sector agencies that were coming into prominence within this environment of continental expansion, urbanization, and relentless industrialization.

The classification systems developed early in the twentieth century reflected a need to organize in a systematic way the many jobs that were progressively attached to civil service coverage by succeeding U.S. presidents. The Classification Act of 1923 applied both Weberian organizational logic (bureaucracy as an "ideal type" of organizational design) and Tayloresque scientific management (e.g., time and motion studies to identify the "one best way" to accomplish work tasks) to the federal civil service system by classifying and grading positions according to duties, in ascending order of responsibilities (Ingraham 1995, p. 39). The intent was to ensure that all employees in the classified ranks were being compensated based on their work, regardless of what agency (whether politically favored or disfavored) or what manager (whether friendly or unfriendly) they worked for in the public service. The resulting strict hierarchical system held narrow job descriptions and rigid boundaries between jobs within which every classified service position was to fit (Ingraham 1995, p. 39). The 1923 Act specified five compensation schedules (or services). These were later collapsed into two broad categories in changes in legislation enacted in 1949. Both of these two services were subdivided into grades, and uniform compensation schedules were enacted into law for each grade. Hence, the 'GS', or *general service*, rank refers to federal government jobs (Huddleston and Boyer 1996, 28).

The 1949 Classification Act, developed in response to criticisms of the centralized and complex 1923 system, also returned "extensive classification authority from the Civil Service Commission to the agencies" and "created the first 'supergrade' system at the top of the classified service hierarchy" (Ingraham 1995, p. 39). The agencies still had to comply with the strict, cumbersome personnel rules and procedures that were perceived to tie the hands of managers and make the removal of poorly performing employees difficult, if not impossible (Van Riper 1958, p. 458). Sayre's classic book review title, "The Triumph of Techniques Over Purpose," sums up the great frustration felt by federal managers with the rule-bound classification system that lies at the heart of the civil service system (1948, p. 134).

The impact of technology in today's workplace often has the opposite effect of that witnessed at the time of the original adoption of civil service as a reform of personnel practices. Rather than centralizing control and emphasizing one best way to do nearly all tasks, the diffusion of technology—for example, a personal computer on virtually every desk, smart phones, tablets, and access to all the data that the Internet supplies—encourages the decentralization of control. The rapid pace of change in today's technology and the associated diversification of professional competencies and areas of expertise have led contemporary scholars of public administration to recommend a decentralized approach to administration featuring a high degree of flexibility and pragmatic experimentation, both in job assignment and problem-solving activities. The 'one best way' days of scientific management are largely gone from most public sector agency settings.

Ethics and Civil Service Systems

Ethics is a key part of most public personnel processes. Because we are talking about public employees (as opposed to private sector personnel), it is important to remember that expectations of carrying out duties associated with "the public trust" are generally higher for the public sector. Lewis (1991, p. 17) explained:

> Facing up to the ethical demands on public managers starts with biting the bullet: public service ethics is different from ethics in private life. The reason is that democracy is sustained by public trust, a link forged by stringent ethical standards.

Being ethical in the public sector entails more than being legal. It is possible to be legal but unethical. That is part of the extra burden placed upon public sector employees; the appearance of impropriety or harm to the public interest is enough to cast an ethical cloud over a public agency. Even protocols intended to remove value-based decision making from administrative action warrant analysis from an ethical perspective.

For example, much of the classification system associated with the 1949 Classification Act still exists in the federal government and it has 'first cousins' in most state and local government jurisdictions. Chapter 8, on recruiting and selection, and Chapter 9, on compensation, will consider the implications of classification systems for the other functional areas of personnel. However, the heterogeneity of the approaches used to fashion 'work-arounds' to many problems today (for example, achieving the goal of homeland security without making a mockery of privacy rights) has potential ethical implications. As presidents and federal agency managers became more frustrated with the rigidity of the established classification system, they sought to circumvent procedures viewed as excessively cumbersome. For example, managers use temporary employees to avoid long civil service testing processes and then coach the temporary employees so they do well on the tests required for normal hiring decisions. In some cases, managers attempt to write job descriptions to match only the one person they would like to fill a particular job opening. In addition, special hiring authorities represent exceptions to allow agencies to hire employees outside the classification system's normal testing procedures (Ingraham 1995, p. 40). The increasing use of these special hiring authorities, in part, accounts for the fact that the civil service classification system currently applies to only 49 percent of federal employees (Fedjobs.com n.d.). This declined significantly from the 56 percent reported by Kettl et al. less than a decade earlier (1996, p. 17).

Presidents, governors, mayors, and city managers all, quite logically, want executive agencies to be responsive to their own policy priorities. The inflexibility of the classification system, intended to ensure neutrality, makes the civil service less responsive to political executives than they would like. However, the use of now well-established short cuts and surreptitious practices presents ethical dilemmas for the conscientious public sector and nonprofit sector manager alike.

- Is it wrong for public administrators, who say they are "just trying to get the work done," to find a quicker and possibly more efficient way to select employees?
- Which is the greater good, to obey the spirit and letter of the law or to achieve what may appear to be a greater good for the public by getting the job done expeditiously by 'fudging the rules' from time to time?

Diversity and Civil Service Systems

Diversity can be understood in many different ways. One way that diversity is present in civil service systems is in the variety of personnel systems that exist among our thousands of local governments. As the discussion of historical phases in the development of civil service systems indicated, each phase has added to the diversity of the American public service, and vestiges of each period remain in existing personnel systems today. Scholars of public personnel have identified several different personnel cultures that can be found in the personnel systems in operation at the national, state, and local levels of government in the United States (Klingner and Nalbandian 1998). For example, Freyss's empirical work demonstrated three distinct systems across U.S. local government (1995, pp. 69–93):

- *Merit system culture*: This culture emphasizes competence, political neutrality, and efficient and equitable service to the public, but is associated with rule-driven management and substantial difficulty in getting rid of employees because of strongly protected employee rights. These local governments typically use information-based management practices such as performance appraisals and merit pay, and often make use of HRM innovations such as flexible benefits and employee assistance programs.
- *Collective bargaining culture*: Personnel matters are primarily determined bilaterally with unions and the government in question, with an emphasis being placed on securing and protecting employee rights and sustaining public sector jobs. Recruitment is done by public notices and the use of minimum scores. The culture dictates termination, discipline, and retirement policies,

all of which tend to be highly formalized processes that permit employee groups and their attorneys to represent the interest of employees collectively and individually.

- *Affirmative action culture*: This culture influences hiring processes, with special consideration accorded to race and/or ethnicity in screening job applicants, investing in employee development and training, and assessing promotion. Strong attention is given to having the public workforce mirror the racial, ethnic, and cultural characteristics of the population being served.

According to Freyss, there are regional differences evident in the geographic distribution of these cultures. The collective bargaining and AA cultures are found more frequently in the northeastern and north central states, whereas the merit system culture is more likely to be found in the west and the cities in the industrial states.

Ingraham identifies three "key tensions" present within our public service system (1995, pp. viii–xxi) that pose challenges to establishing and maintaining a well-functioning public personnel management system. They are:

- *Patronage versus merit*: Should jobs be awarded based upon loyalty to political parties, or on the basis of competency and skills tests?
- *Neutrality versus responsiveness*: If civil servants are politically neutral, how can we be assured that they will be responsive to the elected chief executive and/or legislative authorities?
- *Efficiency versus effectiveness*: Public agencies have many goals other than efficiency: for example, a commitment to democratic process may cause public sector agencies to appear to be slow and inefficient. How do we manage demands for efficiency against other worthy goals? How do we measure whether public sector programs are effective, while staying within the bounds of constitutionally permissible, humane, and ethical means?

She observes that these deep-seated tensions are the result of the interplay of our politics, our constitution, our diverse society, and our free market economy (1995, p. vii). The evolution of our public personnel system is rooted in these tensions, and these tensions among conflicting values provide a useful framework for understanding both the historical development and current conditions of public sector employment systems.

Summary

Several forces have combined to lead chief executives and public agency administrators to find ways of getting around the civil service system. The nature of work in today's fast-paced, high-tech, globalized environment is ill suited to a rigid, slow, and legalistic civil service testing and classification system (Kettl et al. 1996, p. 16). Hiring employees outside the cumbersome civil service system can allow a manager greater flexibility in job design, recruitment, task assignment, and compensation. Also, the political neutrality and tenure in office of civil service employees give presidents, governors, commissioners, and mayors the impression (sometimes correct) that civil servants are not particularly responsive to their political goals. The extended use of political appointees and other special hiring authorities allow chief executives and their appointed managers to hire those whom they trust to pursue their political agendas. Finally, harsh budget realities press policymakers to seek the least costly way to continue government service provision. Private sector companies and nonprofit organizations are increasingly perceived to be a viable alternative to direct service provision by government employees. This economic reality, combined with a general political preference in America for smaller government, escalates the use of contract employees in public sector operations. Naturally, these employees are not a part of the civil service system.

A Manager's Vocabulary

- Separation of powers
- Federalism
- Patronage
- Progressive Movement
- Pendleton Act of 1883
- Rank-in-position
- Rank-in-person
- Rule of three
- U.S. Civil Service Commission
- Classical organization theory (Weber)
- Scientific management (Taylor)
- Civil Service Reform Act of 1978
- Office of Personnel Management
- Merit Systems Protection Board
- Federal Labor Relations Act
- Senior executive service
- Merit pay

Study Questions

1. Why do some managers seek to get around the 'rules' of civil service systems?
2. What are the "key tensions" inherent in our public service system as identified by Ingraham?
3. What are the pros and cons of using patronage to fill government positions?
4. What were the key elements of the 1978 Civil Service Reform Act?

Exercise 2.1 Personnel Systems

Choose two cities or two agencies in a state government with which you are familiar. Research the personnel systems prevalent in the respective jurisdictions or agencies and consider the following questions:

1. Are appointments principally made on the basis of merit, as opposed to 'connections' or political loyalties?
2. Is there a strong collective bargaining culture in evidence?
3. To what extent is there evidence of an AA culture actively promoting social equity and diversity in the workforce and among management?
4. What might explain any differences that you identify?

References

Battaglio, R. Paul, Jr., and Stephen E. Condrey. 2007. "Framing Civil Service Innovations: Assessing State and Local Government Reforms." In *American Public Service: Radical Reform and the Merit System*, Eds. James S. Bowman and Jonathan P. West, 25–45. Boca Raton, FL: CRC Press.

Branti v. Finkel, 445 U.S. 507 (1980).

Campbell, Alan K. 1991. "Testimony on Civil Service Reform and Organization." In *Classics of Public Personnel Policy*, 2nd ed., Ed. Frank J. Thompson, 82–104. Pacific Grove, CA: Brooks/Cole.

Classification Act of 1923, ch. 265, 42 Stat. 1488.

Classification Act 1949, ch. 782, 63 Stat. 954.

Elrod v. Burns, 427 U.S. 347 (1976).

Federal Labor Relations Authority (FLRA). www.flra.gov/10.html (accessed June 30, 2014).

Fedjobs.com (undated) "An Introduction to the Excepted Service." www.fedjobs.com/lib/TIP_Excepted_Service.html (accessed June 30, 2014).

Finkle, Arthur L. 1984. "Can a Manager Discipline a Public Employee?" *Review of Public Personnel Administration* 4 (3): 83–87.

Freyss, Siegrun Fox. 1995. "Municipal Government Personnel Systems: A Test of Two Archetypical Models." *Review of Public Personnel Administration* 15 (4): 69–93.

Gogovernment.org (undated) "The Pros of Working in Government." www.gogovernment.org/government_101/pros_and_cons_of_working_in_government.php (accessed June 30, 2014).

Hays, Samuel P. 1964. "The Politics of Reform in Municipal Government in the Progressive Era." *Pacific Northwest Quarterly* 55 (4): 157–169.

Hays, Steven W., and Jessica E. Sowa. 2006. "A Broader Look at the Accountability Movement: Some Grim Realities in State Civil Service Systems." *Review of Public Personnel Administration* 26 (2): 102–117.

Huddleston, Mark W., and William W. Boyer. 1996. *The Higher Civil Service in the U.S.: Quest for Reform.* Pittsburgh, PA: University of Pittsburgh Press.

Ingraham, Patricia W. 1995. *The Foundation of Merit: Public Service in American Democracy.* Baltimore, MD: Johns Hopkins University Press.

Jorgensen, Lorna, Kelli Fairless, and W. David Patton. 1996. "Underground Merit Systems and the Balance Between Service and Compliance." *Review of Public Personnel Administration* 16 (2): 5–20.

Kettl, Donald F. 1988. *Government by Proxy.* Washington, DC: Congressional Quarterly Press.

Kettl, Donald F., Patricia W. Ingraham, Ronald P. Sanders, and Constance Horner. 1996. *Civil Service Reform: Building a Government that Works.* Washington, DC: Brookings Institution Press.

Klingner, Donald E., and John Nalbandian. 1998. *Public Personnel Management: Contexts and Strategies,* 4th ed. Englewood Cliffs, NJ: Prentice Hall.

Lewis, Carol W. 1991. *The Ethics Challenge in Public Service.* San Francisco, CA: Jossey Bass.

Light, Paul C. 1999. *The True Size of Government.* Washington, DC: Brookings Institution Press.

McNichol, Elizabeth. 2012. (June 15) "Some Basic Facts on State and Local Government Workers." Center for Budget and Policy Priorities. www.cbpp.org/cms/?fa=view&id=3410 (accessed June 30, 2014).

Milward, H. Brinton, Keith G. Provan, and Barbara A. Else. 1993. "What Does the 'Hollow State' Look Like?" In *Public Management: The State of the Art,* Ed. Barry Bozeman, 309–322. San Francisco, CA: Jossey-Bass.

Mosher, Frederick C. 1982. *Democracy and the Public Service,* 2nd ed. New York: Oxford University Press.

Pendleton Act. 1883. "An Act to Regulate and Improve the Civil Service at the United States." 22 Stat. 27.

Riordon, William L. 1963. *Plunkitt of Tammany Hall.* New York: E. P. Dutton.

Salamon, Lester M. 1981. "Rethinking Public Management: Third-Party Government and the Changing Forms of Government Action." *Public Policy* 29 (3): 255–257.

Savas, E. S. and Sigmund G. Ginsburg. 1991. "The Civil Service: A Meritless System?" In *Classics of Public Personnel Policy,* 2nd ed., Ed. Frank J. Thompson, 159–168. Pacific Grove, CA: Brooks/Cole.

Sayre, Wallace S. 1948. "The Triumph of Techniques Over Purpose." *Public Administration Review* 8 (2): 134–137.

Stillman, Richard J. 1996. "Inside Public Bureaucracy." In *Public Administration Cases and Concepts,* 6th ed., Ed. Richard J. Stillman, 186–209. Boston, MA: Houghton Mifflin.

Taylor, Frederick Winslow. 2011. "The Principles of Scientific Management." In *Classics of Organization Theory,* 7th ed., Eds. Jay M. Shafritz, J. Steven Ott, and Yong Suk Jang, 65–76. Boston, MA: Wadsworth.

U.S. Census Bureau. 2012. "Statistical Abstract of the United States." www.census.gov/compendia/statab/2012/tables/12s0428.pdf (accessed June 30, 2014).

———. 2014. "Federal, State and Local Government Employment Down Previous Year to 22 Million Jobs in 2012." www.census.gov/newsroom/press-releases/2014/cb14-40.html (accessed June 16, 2015).

U.S. Merit Systems Protection Board (U.S. MSPB). 2014. "About MSPB." www.mspb.gov/about/about.htm (accessed June 16, 2015).

———. 2012. "Historical Federal Workforce Tables." opm.gov/policy-data-oversight/data-analysis-documenta tion/federal-employment-reports/historical-tables/total-government-employment-since-1962/ (accessed June 30, 2014).

———. 2014. "Our Mission Role and History." www.opm.gov/about-us/our-mission-role-history/ (accessed June 16, 2015).

Van Riper, Paul P. 1958. *History of the United States Civil Service*. Evanston, IL: Row, Peterson.

Weber, Max. 2011. "Bureaucracy." In *Classics of Organization Theory*, 7th ed., Eds. Jay M. Shafritz, J. Steven Ott, and Yong Suk Jang, 77–82. Boston, MA: Wadsworth.

Wilson, Woodrow. 2004. "The Study of Administration." In *Classics of Public Administration*, 5th ed., Eds. Jay M. Shafritz, Albert C. Hyde, and Sandra J. Parkes, 22–34. Belmont, CA: Wadsworth/Thomson.

Wolch, Jennifer R. 1990. *The Shadow State: Government and the Voluntary Sector in Transition*. New York: The Foundation Center.

3   Rights, Restrictions, and Laws

- Board of County v. Umbehr
- Rutan v. Republican
- Civil Rights Act Title VII
    www.eeoc.gov/policy/vii.html
- Kristin Marohn

Learning Objectives

- Review the scope of constitutional rights and protections afforded federal, state, and local employees.
- Introduce the major adjudication related to constitutional law and public employment.
- Introduce the major federal laws affecting employment for public and nonprofit agencies.
- Understand the evolution and application of equal opportunity legislation and case law and special consideration of the use of 'affirmative action' in making employment decisions.

Managers often consider the legal status of public employees as one of the most significant differences between public, for-profit, and nonprofit sector employment. The legal environment in which all managers operate is both intimidating and largely misunderstood. The intimidation factor draws strength from the unique and historically deeply rooted legal protections to which public employees are entitled, and the ongoing expansion of those protections over time. Public sector managers more than any others must be aware of the serious implications of the existence of these rights for their employees and be cognizant of employees' legal rights and protections, as well as consider agency responsibilities to act in the public interest.

The legal environment for public sector personnel administration is often misunderstood, because most of us rely upon the interpretation of legislation, judicial rulings, and policy pronouncements offered through informal channels, such as shared horror stories around the proverbial water cooler or inflammatory news headlines. In aggregate, the legal environment surrounding employment, especially in the public sector, tends to frustrate managers when it seems to impede the development and implementation of public policy. However, the old adage 'knowledge is power' holds particularly true in HRM in the public and nonprofit sectors. Public managers must learn about the resources available to assist them as they work within these employee protections to accomplish their goals. This chapter explores the rationale underlying the rights, restrictions, and laws of the public workplace and introduces students to the logic, terminology, and resources available in this important domain of public administration. Understanding the purposes of constitutional and statutory protections and knowing how these apply to public employees, as well as contracted private and nonprofit sector organizations, allow managers to both achieve results and avoid being subject to adverse legal action.

Introduction to the Reading

The following reading from the work of Lee and Rosenbloom (2005) discusses the evolution of judicial interpretation of public employee rights. For most of the history of public service in the

U.S., the nation's federal, state, and local governments managed their employees under the *doctrine of privilege*, a legal principle that working for the government was a privilege granted at the discretion of the employer. Consequently, public employees held no legal right to their jobs and could be hired or dismissed at will. In the famous words of Justice Oliver Wendell Holmes, a public employee "may have a constitutional right to talk politics, but he has no constitutional right to be a policeman" (*McAuliffe v. Mayor of New Bedford* 1892). This disposition toward public employees reflected the *presumption of sovereignty* whereby elected officials exercised unfettered authority, bestowed by 'the People', to manage the affairs of government.

Over time, however, U.S. courts recognized the claim of public employees to constitutional protections against violations of due process and inequitable treatment. American jurisprudence gradually adopted a fairer approach requiring the court to weigh equally the rights of the public employee to due process and fair treatment against the interests of the government in its ability to operate efficiently and in the public's interest in the effective operation of government (*Connick v. Myers* 1983). Public employees do possess certain rights in the public workplace under the Constitution, but these rights cannot unduly interfere with the necessary operations of government. The process of assessing this balance considers first the range of constitutional protections accorded to public employees by the Bill of Rights. These protections are then balanced through competing interests, or, in the words of the court, "a balance between the interests of the employee, as a citizen, in commenting upon matters of public concern and the interest of the State, as an employer, in promoting the efficiency of the public services it performs through its employees" (*Pickering v. Board of Education* 1968). This balancing process requires substantial interpretation of the interests of each party by the courts. Because of this case-by-case assessment of balance, this broad standard of law can lead to considerable inconsistency in subnational court interpretation and, ultimately, to wide variation in management implementation. Fortunately, a large body of state-level legal precedent has developed, providing direction to public sector managers on how courts have struck this balance in prior cases. In reading the Lee and Rosenbloom passage, keep the following central questions in mind:

1. How has the U.S. Supreme Court's approach to defining public employee rights evolved?
2. What interests does the Court 'balance' in cases involving public employee rights?
3. What needs does the government have that could outweigh employee rights?
4. Why might public employees have greater protections in speech, drug testing, and due process than those enjoyed by for-profit or nonprofit sector employees?

Constitutional Rights in Public Employment

The U.S. Constitution—more specifically, the Bill of Rights—was designed to protect citizens from arbitrary and/or malicious actions of government. In a letter to James Madison, Thomas Jefferson expressed his dissatisfaction with an early draft of the Constitution because it did not enumerate specific rights guaranteed to its citizens. "A bill of rights is what the people are entitled to against every government on earth, general or particular, and which no government should refuse, or rest on inference" (Jefferson 1787/1993). Initially, the Bill of Rights applied to people designated as legal 'citizens' in their dealings with the national government. The passage of the Fourteenth Amendment extended these protections to virtually all persons, and to their relationship with their state governments. As the courts generally consider cities and counties as creations of the states (*Clinton v. Cedar Rapids and the Missouri River Railroad* 1868), the protections provided to all persons are nearly all extended to people in relationship to their local governments. In the public setting, the employer is the government. The Constitution restricts all units of American government in their dealings

Excerpt 3.1 The Relationship of the Public Servant to the Constitution

The relationship of U.S. public servants to their government is unique in many ways. The relationship is different from that of ordinary citizens to their government; it is also different from that of private employees to their nongovernmental employers. Years ago, the courts at common law interpreted the relationship between public servants and their governmental employer primarily in terms of the master–servant, or the principal–agent relationship (*McAuliffe v. Mayor and Board of Aldermen of New Bedford* 1892; *Bailey v. Richardson* 1950). In the master–servant relationship, the servant is employed at the pleasure of the master. In a series of decisions in the 1960s and finally in 1972 in *Board of Regents v. Roth*, the Supreme Court discarded that interpretation once and for all *insofar as* it implied that the public servant surrenders constitutionally guaranteed rights to the master in exchange for employment. In one sense, this decision revolutionized the constitutional relationship of U.S. public servants to their government forever; yet in another sense, this decision did not alter much of the classical employment relationship in the master–servant context.

With respect to the Bill of Rights, the Supreme Court believes that public servants do not lose their constitutional rights when they choose to work for government. This does not mean, however, the public servants enjoy the same rights ordinary citizens do. This would be imperialism on the part of public servants. They are hired to perform administrative functions. To perform the administrative functions effectively, public servants must accommodate their constitutional rights to the command of their sovereign employers. Otherwise, no raison d'être is there for their employment.

Accommodation is a balancing act. The Supreme Court recognizes that the government wears two hats, one as a sovereign and another as an employer, just as the public servant wears two hats, one as an employee and another as an individual citizen. The Court reasons that the power of a sovereign over its employee as a citizen is relatively weak as the Constitution clearly limits the breadth of its power. Under the Constitution, as the Court sees it, the government, as sovereign, may not discipline or terminate its "citizen" public servants without constitutionally adequate due process. Nor should the government employer discharge them in retaliation for publicly criticizing an official policy or practice without due process. In business, an employer may fire an employee at any time when he or she publicly criticizes the employer's policy or practice—unless the criticism relates to unlawful business activity (McWhirter 1989).

Yet with the same breath, the Court maintains that the government, as employer, is significantly more powerful over its employees than the government as sovereign is over its "citizen" public servants. As employer, the government has collective action goals to fulfill, so it must have the necessary authority to control and discipline employees. Thus, in *Waters v. Churchill* (1994) the Court held, "The government's interest in achieving its goals as effectively and efficiently as possible is elevated from a relatively subordinate interest when it acts as sovereign to a significant one when it acts as employer" (675).

The public servant also wears two hats: one as employee and the other as an individual citizen. As employees, they are subject to the laws of the workplace: loyalty and the efficient operation of the agency. They may disobey the legitimate command of their superiors only at their peril. They must not divulge confidential information. Nor should they publicly indulge in "personal" criticisms against their immediate superiors that undermine legitimate authority (*Pickering v. Board of Education* 1968; *Connick v. Myers* 1983). Yet they are guaranteed

employee/citizen

constitutional due process protection when their superiors abridge their protected rights (free speech, property interest, privacy, liberty, and equal protection) without constitutionally acceptable reasons. This due process protection enables the employees to participate in the self-correction of agency policy or practice when it strays (*Givhan v. Western Line Consolidated School* 1979).

As the Supreme Court reasons through case law, however, much of the employment relationship in the public sector is fashioned through a balancing act. The balancing act begins with an inquiry as to whether a public servant, who seeks constitutional protection, can demonstrate that he or she actually has the claimed right—such as, the right to free speech, the right to privacy, and the right to equal protection. Without this demonstration, no cause of action exists against the government employer. Even if the right at issue has been established clearly, no relief would be forthcoming unless the government employer fails to articulate a legitimate reason for the underlying action that is strong enough to override the claimed right. In the end, it is clear that the constitutional rights of a public servant are bound and restrained.

The power of the government employer to discipline or terminate an employee, permanently or temporarily, is no less restrained—although it varies a great deal depending on the rights at issue. The government employer might at times have a legitimate reason or a special need to discipline or even terminate an employee. Unlike a private employer, however, a government employer may not do so without complying with a constitutionally adequate procedure. When an occasion for disciplinary action arises, the question of first order is whether the intended action would violate the employee's constitutional or statutory rights. Determination of these rights requires an understanding of constitutional and statutory rights. Analysis may or may not show that the employee at issue has such rights. Even if the existence of particular constitutional rights is clear, the Constitution bars governments from terminating their employees for some reasons such as their race—except in extraordinary circumstances, which are impossible to imagine—and it limits the procedures under which they can discipline or dismiss them for other reasons. At a minimum, the employer must provide advance notice and an opportunity to respond before taking an adversary measure (*Cleveland Board of Education v. Loudermill* 1985). It is fair to conclude that the public employment relationship under the Constitution shapes the delicate contours of rights and obligations for the government employer, as well as for the public employees.

Excerpt References

Bailey v. Richardson, 182 F.2d 46 (D.C. Cir. 1950).
Board of Regents v. Roth, 408 U.S. 563 (1972).
Cleveland Board of Education v. Loudermill, 470 U.S. 532 (1985).
Connick v. Myers, 461 U.S. 138 (1983).
Givhan v. Western Line Consolidated School, 439 U.S. 410 (1979).
McAuliffe v. Mayor and Board of Aldermen of New Bedford, 115 Mass. 216, 29 N.E. 517 (1892).
McWhirter, Darien A. 1989. *Your Rights at Work*. New York: John Wiley & Sons.
Pickering v. Board of Education, 391 U.S. 563 (1968).
Waters v. Churchill, 511 U.S. 661 (1994).

Source: Lee, Yong S., and David H. Rosenbloom. 2005. *A Reasonable Public Servant: Constitutional Foundations of Administrative Conduct in the U.S.*, 232–234. New York: M.E. Sharpe.

with employees, as it does with citizens/residents generally. Public agency managers are acting as the agents of the employing government in a wide variety of employment practices; it follows that constitutional considerations affect almost every aspect of public personnel administration throughout the public service. Employment practices commonly performed in the nonprofit and for-profit sectors may be unconstitutional when carried out by public managers. When nonprofit organizations make use of government grant funds, or when for-profit organizations contract to implement the provision of some public good or some public service, to which access must be provided as government specifies, some of these constitutionally based employee protections may apply as well.

Requirements for equal protection influence the practices used by public sector agencies in the hiring process, recruitment, testing, and selection protocol. The due process provisions of the Fifth and Fourteenth Amendments also cover employee development practices such as training and promotion. The First Amendment guarantees of freedom of association cover union activities and collective bargaining. Requirements for due process have definite implications for employee discipline and termination, giving employees the right to grievance procedures and the right to challenge adverse personnel actions in formal hearing processes and, ultimately, in courts of law beyond the agency. These constitutional protections may make it more difficult to hire a preferred applicant, promote a promising employee, or fire someone viewed as unproductive. These restrictions also prevent government managers from hiring individuals for political reasons, from discriminating based on race, sex, or national origin, or from taking away the livelihood of government workers arbitrarily or for political reasons. The most glaring example of constraint on public sector managers compared with for-profit or nonprofit managers is that of termination. When not limited by public sector contract provisions or collective bargaining agreements, nonprofit or for-profit managers may fire employees for almost any reason—or no reason at all—so long as they are not firing the employee for specifically illegal reasons (e.g., discrimination or an employee's refusal to break the law). In nearly all cases, public managers are required to have a just cause to dismiss an employee and must allow the employee due process in challenging their dismissal, as guaranteed in the Fifth and Fourteenth Amendments. The following discussion of certain provisions in the Bill of Rights illustrates how the enumerated rights of citizens apply in public HRM, and potentially to nonprofit or for-profit entities engaged in substantive public service activities.

Freedom of Speech and Assembly

First Amendment:

> Congress shall make no law respecting an establishment of religion, or prohibiting the free exercise thereof; or abridging the freedom of speech, or of the press; or the right of the people peaceably to assemble, and to petition the Government for a redress of grievances.

Speech

Is it legal for a public employer to dismiss an employee for speaking out against the employer or other government such as the state or federal government? The *Rankin v. McPherson* (1987) case offers a significant baseline from which to consider the notion of restrictions upon free speech exercised by public employees. The U.S. Supreme Court weighed the competing interests of an employee's right to comment on matters of public interest and the employer's need to operate the government agency efficiently. In the balancing process derived from the two-part *Pickering v. Board of Education* test, the U.S. Supreme Court considered whether the comment was a matter of public concern and the manner, time, place, and context of the employee's statement. In this decision, the Court found that the employee was "commenting upon matters of public concern," and that the county government employer produced "no evidence that it interfered with the efficient functioning of the office" (*Pickering v. Board of Education* 1968, p. 568). The latter point related to the particular employee's responsibilities and the level at which they worked (e.g., nonpolicy-making). The right to free speech can be limited only when statements adversely affect the efficient operation of government services *or* when it is reasonable to infer that speech might become disruptive. *Garcetti v. Ceballos* (2006, pp. 160–161) affords:

> employers sufficient discretion to manage their operations. Employers have heightened interests in controlling speech made by an employee in his or her professional capacity. Official communications have official consequences, creating a need for substantive consistency and clarity. Supervisors must ensure that their employees' official communications are accurate, demonstrate sound judgment, and promote the employer's mission.

According to Roberts (2007, pp. 172–173), *Garcetti v. Ceballos* has effectively transformed the ~~*Pickering/Connick*~~ two-part test into the *Pickering/Connick/Garcetti* three-part test. This three-part test involves three questions: *Is speech part of an employee's official duties? Is the speech a matter of public concern?* And, finally, *What is the manner, time, and context of speech?*

[handwritten annotation: *Pickering test*]

Whistleblowing

Given their vantage point within public agencies, as well as proximity to and knowledge of decision making, it seems logical that public employees can shed light on problems therein. Whistleblower protection legislation was first enacted at the federal level, and variations of the idea exist throughout subnational governments in the U.S. (see Exhibit 3.1). The U.S. Office of Special Counsel offers the channel for federal employees to report concerns; that office handles investigations of alleged wrongdoing and enforces protections from retaliation.

According to the National Conference of State Legislatures, as of 2010, thirty-four states had enacted specific state statutes affording whistleblower protections. A number of federal laws, generally administered in aggregate through the Occupational Safety and Health Administration (OSHA), also offer some level of whistleblower protection to both public and private sector employees who report fraud, abuse, violations, and safety issues through official channels.

Does the *Garcetti* position about speech while on the job affect whistleblowers? The Court held, in a five-to-four decision in *Garcetti*, that, "when public employees make statements pursuant to their official duties, the employees are not speaking as citizens for First Amendment purposes, and the Constitution does not insulate their communications from employer discipline" (2006, p. 421). Writing in dissent, Justice Souter explicated a public interest position in suggesting that *Garcetti* might discourage whistleblowing, arguing (*Garcetti v. Cabellos* 2006, pp. 427–444):

> Private and public interests in addressing official wrongdoing and threats to health and safety can outweigh the government's stake in the efficient implementation of policy, and when they do, employees who speak on these matters in the course of their duties should be eligible to claim First Amendment protection.

According to the Court's majority position, existing legislation should be sufficient to ensure that public employees can speak to the public interest. *Garcetti* neither supplanted such laws, nor prevented

---

Exhibit 3.1 Whistleblower Protections for Federal Employees

Whistleblower protection is a particularly complex area of Federal personnel law. As we discussed in this report, the MSPB will not be able to provide relief under the WPA to a Federal employee or applicant who discloses wrongdoing and believes that he or she has been retaliated against for the disclosure, unless all of the following conditions are met:

1. The individual disclosed conduct that meets a specific category of wrongdoing set forth in the law.
2. The individual made the disclosure to the "right" type of party. Depending on the nature of the disclosure, the individual may be limited regarding to whom the report can be made.
3. The individual made a report that is either:

   (a) outside of the employee's course of duties; or
   (b) communicated outside of normal channels.

4. The individual made the report to someone other than the wrongdoer.
5. The individual had a reasonable belief of wrongdoing.
6. The individual suffered a personnel action, the agency's failure to take a personnel action, or the threat to take or not take a personnel action.
7. The individual was able to demonstrate a connection between the disclosure and the personnel action, failure to take a personnel action, or the threat to take or not take a personnel action.
8. The individual sought redress through the proper channels.

Conclusion

Even if an individual establishes all of the above criteria are met, the law states that the relief sought by the individual will not be ordered if the agency can establish by clear and convincing evidence that it would have taken the same action in the absence of the whistleblowing.

Source: U.S. Merit Systems Protection Board. 2010. "Whistleblower Protections for Federal Employees: A Report to the President and the Congress of the United States" (September), pp. 51–52.

---

public employers from maintaining the necessary policies and processes to encourage employees to raise concerns. The logic of the majority decision in *Garcetti* holds that the very obligations public employers have for dutifully seeking efficiency in the workplace would compel employers to maintain such channels for the articulation of noteworthy concerns.

Assembly

The U.S. Constitution, specifically the First Amendment, does not use the phrase 'freedom of association' to establish such a right. However, judicial interpretation articulates it as a logical consequence of First Amendment protections of speech, religious exercise, assembly, and petition.

Can a government employer restrict its employees from joining groups for political or union-related activities? *Shelton v. Tucker* (1960) involved a state law that required teachers in a state-supported educational institution to list all organizations to which they belonged. The intent behind the law was to identify communist sympathizers. The U.S. Supreme Court ruled that such a requirement impaired "that teacher's right of free association" (p. 486) and deprived teachers of "their rights to personal, associational, and academic liberty, protected by the Due Process Clause of the Fourteenth Amendment from invasion by state action" (pp. 484–485). In accordance with this principle, in *Curle v. Ward* (1979), the Court ruled states could not refuse to hire individuals who were members of the Ku Klux Klan, even as correctional officers. In several cases, public employers have tried to prohibit or disqualify employees from joining unions. The Lloyd–Lafollette Act was signed into law in 1912, giving federal employees (specifically postal workers) the right to organize and join unions, so long as those unions prohibited strikes against the federal government. In the case of *Atkins v. City of Charlotte* (1969), North Carolina had adopted legislation prohibiting union membership for full-time employees in police and fire departments. The U.S. District Court declared this broad prohibition to be unconstitutional under the First and Fourteenth Amendments, drawing upon *NAACP v. Alabama* (1958, pp. 460–461) to state:

> It is beyond debate that freedom to engage in association for the advancement of beliefs and ideas is an inseparable aspect of the "liberty" assured by the Due Process Clause of the Fourteenth Amendment, which embraces freedom of speech. Of course, it is immaterial whether the beliefs sought to be advanced by association pertain to political, economic, religious or cultural matters, and state action which may have the effect of curtailing the freedom to associate is subject to the closest scrutiny.

Political Activity

The Hatch Act of 1939 (An Act to Prevent Pernicious Political Activities) was developed to try to ensure the political neutrality of government workers. The Act restricted partisan elected officials from using government employees for political purposes. In theory, the Hatch Act protected public employees from being compelled to carry out politically motivated job actions and, likewise, limited the bureaucracy from exercising influence in partisan political affairs. The 1939 federal law extended to state and local government employees who received loans or grants from the federal government, and emphasized restrictions upon partisan political activity. Nonpartisan political activities were *not* among the restricted political activities. Also, the Act did not apply to federal employees who were lawfully holding patronage appointments, such as federal department heads or officials in the president's Executive Office; however, even patronage employees were not to engage in political campaigns while fulfilling their official job duties. The right to vote was, for all employees, specifically reserved. The U.S. Supreme Court upheld the 1939 Hatch Act, observing (*United Public Workers of America v. Michell* 1947, p. 347):

> If, in [the] judgment [of Congress and the President], efficiency may be best obtained by prohibiting active participation by classified employees in politics as party officers or workers, we see no constitutional objection . . . Congress may regulate the political conduct of government employees "within reasonable limits," even though the regulation trenches to some extent upon unfettered political action.

The Court heard arguments against the Hatch Act again in 1973 and, in *United States Civil Service Commission v. National Association of Letter Carriers* (1973, p. 564), narrowly upheld the precedent established in its initial ruling based on a need for:

balance between the interest of the [employee], as a citizen, in commenting upon matters of public concern and the interest of the [government], as an employer, in promoting the efficiency of the public services it performs through its employees. Although Congress is free to strike a different balance than it has, if it so chooses, we think the balance it has so far struck is sustainable.

Additionally, most states have passed legislation, commonly known as "mini–Hatch Acts," similar in design and intent to the original federal Hatch Acts prohibiting partisan political activity among state and local government workers. Exhibits 3.2 and 3.3 outline a selection of acceptable and prohibited actions published by the U.S. Office of Special Council.

Congress passed major revisions to the Hatch Act in 1993 and in 2012, both with noteworthy implications for state and local employees. In the first case, the Federal Employees' Political Activities Act of 1993 gave many federal government workers expanded rights to engage in political activity. The revision generally allows federal employees to engage in partisan political activity, as long as such action occurs on their own time and not during the scope of their job, a general rule being the avoidance of the perception of undue influence. As Exhibits 3.2 and 3.3 demonstrate, federal and most state/local workers benefiting from federal funds may now participate politically, but they are quite clearly prohibited from using their official authority or public offices to influence elections or influence the participation of individuals who have applied for a government grant, contract, or other government business from their agency. Government employees are specifically prohibited from giving political contributions to their superiors or soliciting contributions from subordinates. In general, the

Exhibit 3.2 Federal Hatch Act: Acceptable Political Activity

When off duty and off site, employees who are not subject to additional restrictions may:	Federal	State
Be candidates for public office in nonpartisan elections?	Yes	Yes
Be candidates for public office in partisan elections?	No	Yes
Register and vote as they choose and assist in voter registration drives?	Yes	Yes
Express opinions about candidates and issues?	Yes	Yes
Contribute money to political organizations, attend political fund-raising functions, and/or join and be an active member of a political party or club, including holding office?	Yes	Yes
Sign nominating petitions?	Yes	Yes
Campaign for or against referendum questions, constitutional amendments, or municipal ordinances?	Yes	Yes
Distribute campaign literature, campaign for or against candidates, and make campaign speeches for candidates in partisan elections?	Yes	Yes
Campaign for or against candidates in partisan and nonpartisan elections?	No	Yes

Federal Hatch Acts apply to state or local employees (and some nonprofit and private sector workers) whose work is financed wholly by federal funds. They may engage in the outlined political activities, unless prohibited by state law.

Source: U.S. Office of Special Counsel. 2005a. "Political Activity and the Federal Employee." www.osc.gov/documents/hatchact/ha_fed.pdf (accessed June 17, 2015), p. 4; U.S. Office of Special Counsel. 2005b. "Political Activity and the State and Local Employee." www.osc.gov/documents/hatchact/ha_sta.pdf (accessed February 4, 2014), p. 4.

Exhibit 3.3 Federal Hatch Act Prohibitions for Federal and Relevant State/Local Employees

Employees may not:

- use official authority or influence to interfere with or affect the results of an election or nomination;
- solicit or discourage political activity of anyone with business before their agency;
- directly or indirectly solicit or receive political contributions (may be done in certain limited situations by federal labor or other employee organizations);
- engage in political activity while on duty, in any government office, wearing an official uniform, or using a government vehicle;
- wear partisan political buttons on duty.

Source: U.S. Office of Special Counsel. 2005a. "Political Activity and the Federal Employee." www.osc.gov/documents/hatchact/ha_fed.pdf (accessed June 17, 2015), p. 4; U.S. Office of Special Counsel. 2005b. "Political Activity and the State and Local Employee." www.osc.gov/documents/hatchact/ha_sta.pdf (accessed February 4, 2014), p. 4.

---

restriction applies to all civilian employees (full and part time) in the executive branch (except the president and vice president), postal employees, and certain contract or state local employees. Certain federal employees are subject to additional restrictions, depending upon the agency in which they are employed. For example, employees with the Federal Elections Commissions, most agencies dealing with safety and security (such as the FBI, CIA, or NSA), and career members of the senior executive service may still engage in a variety of political activities, such as voting, joining political organizations, and expressing opinions. They may not, however, engage in partisan campaigns or their management, nor may they express political positions at work. With the passage of the Hatch Act Modernization Act of 2012, most state and local government employees may now run for partisan political office, if their own salaries are not funded entirely by federal loans or grants, but this allowance does not override state and local limitations.

Political Patronage

Chapter 2 described how the staffing of government has evolved from a pure patronage system into a modern civil service system. A series of decisions by the U.S. Supreme Court, in particular *Elrod v. Burns* (1976), *Branti v. Finkel* (1980), and *Rutan v. Republican Party of Illinois* (1990), reflect the marked shift away from the patronage system in the U.S. at all levels of government service. In *Rutan,* the Court ruled that government agencies may not hire, promote, transfer, recall, or dismiss public employees solely on the basis of their political affiliation or activity, unless party affiliation is shown to be a legitimate requirement for the job.

The First Amendment and Nongovernmental Employees

In two noteworthy cases, the U.S. Supreme Court expanded to private and nonprofit service providers on government contracts the principle that freedom of speech protections extend to them as well as to public employees (Koenig 1997). In *Board of County Commissioners, Wabaunsee County, Kansas v. Umbehr* (1996), the public contract of a government contractor was canceled after he publicly criticized county policies and the county's commissioners; the contractor sued for breach of contract. The courts ruled that the government could not place conditions on someone's rights under the Constitution and reinstated the compensation owed the contractor. In *O'Hare Truck Service, Inc. v. City of Northlake* (1996), a towing company was deleted from the listed contractors used by a municipality because it had supported the mayor's opponent and refused to contribute to the mayor's electoral campaign. The Court ruled that terminating a government-issued contract for political reasons violated First Amendment rights.

Nonprofit sector employees are not specifically subject to Hatch provisions, but nonprofit employee political activities are often limited by IRS regulations. As a general rule, 501c(3) organizations (nonprofits organized for charitable and religious purpose) may jeopardize their

---

Exhibit 3.4 The Right to Bear Arms?

"A well regulated Militia, being necessary to the security of a free State, the right of the people to keep and bear Arms, shall not be infringed."

Generally, the Second Amendment to the U.S. Constitution does not have a featured spot in public personnel administration textbooks. In any place of employment, one might usually find an array of items that could be used as weapons, such as scissors, letter openers, or cutlery. Often, formal organization policy might not even speak to whether employees are approved or forbidden to carry weapons. The nature of certain public sector organizations may prescribe the use of weaponry, but, in general terms, the presumption is that one's coworkers are not armed. However, public safety organizations use various processes to authorize employees to carry weapons in the course of their responsibilities.

High-profile attacks in elementary, secondary, and postsecondary educational sites have raised questions about whether such authorization should be limited to public safety organizations, and exactly who can be armed, in what venues, and under what circumstances. Should elementary, junior high, and high school teachers be trained to respond to such attacks? Should these teachers be armed to do so? Should teachers or staff be allowed to carry weaponry as a right? At the postsecondary level, should faculty and/or students be allowed to carry firearms while on campus? Should, or can, universities ban firearms in one part of campus (e.g, a residence hall), but allow them in a different location (e.g., the classroom)? If teachers, students, or university faculty are allowed to carry weapons, either concealed or otherwise, what regulations should guide such scenarios?

Notably, system-wide bans upon weaponry in public education sites have been overturned in the courts, on the logic that, although states may regulate firearms (in terms of use and sale), such regulation falls short of categorically banning firearms. The National Conference of State Legislatures (2014) reports that seven states (Colorado, Idaho, Kansas, Mississippi, Oregon, Utah, and Wisconsin) permit students/faculty to carry concealed weapons on public college or university campuses. Each of the fifty states does allow citizens to carry concealed weapons per the specific statutes of each state.

Source: See Chapter 3 References.

nonprofit

tax-exempt status if the "substantial part of the activities of such organization consists of carrying on propaganda, or otherwise attempting to influence legislation" (26 USC §501). In fact, nonprofits receiving federal funds (and some states require this as well) are asked to sign compliance forms indicating that they limit the 'cost' of information dissemination to policymakers to an amount below some set proportion of their budget/funding and generally refrain from using public funding for policy advocacy purposes.

Privacy and Unreasonable Search and Seizure

Fourth Amendment ✓

> The right of the people to be secure in their persons, houses, papers, and effects, against unreasonable searches and seizures, shall not be violated, and no warrants shall issue, but upon probable cause, supported by Oath or affirmation, and particularly describing the place to be searched, and the persons or things to be seized.

One of the most controversial issues related to search and seizure in public employment is the question of drug testing. Here, the difference between the principal employment sectors is very important, indeed. For-profit and nonprofit sector employers are not bound by the limitations of the Fourth Amendment. The warning against violating the people's right to be secure in their persons applies to actions taken by the government, not private parties. In the case of drug testing, the government is limited in its ability to test for drug use by its employees. There must be a prevailing public service interest to override the individual's protection of privacy. For example, in *National Treasury Employees Union v. von Raab (1989)*, the U.S. Supreme Court ruled that the U.S. Customs Service could require a urinalysis test for employees actively involved in drug interdiction and/or those who were required to wear firearms. However, the Court directed that this case did not extend drug testing on other employees. The justices reiterated that, without probable cause or reasonable suspicion, no such testing is permitted. The compelling government interest need not include suspicion of individual misconduct if other public interests outweigh an individual's expectation of privacy; they opined in this regard:

> Government's need to discover such latent or hidden conditions, or to prevent their development, is sufficiently compelling to justify the intrusion on privacy entailed by conducting such searches without any measure of individualized suspicion. We think Government's need to conduct the suspicionless searches required by the Customs program outweighs the privacy interests of employees engaged directly in drug interdiction, and those who otherwise are required to carry firearms.

> (*National Treasury Employees Union v. von Raab* 1989, p. 1384)

What about ISP?

U.S. Courts have generally sustained the power of public employers to require persons in safety-sensitive positions, such as police officers (*Copeland v. Philadelphia Police Department* 1988), firefighters (*Seelig v. Koehler* 1990), prison employees (*McDonell v. Hunter* 1987), and public health workers (*AFGE v. Skinner* 1989), to submit to urinalysis where there is a reasonable basis to suspect drug use. Random testing of non-safety employees is normally impermissible (*NTEU v. Yeutter* 1990).

Another privacy or illegal search issue hinges upon the government's ability to search employee offices and their desks. In *O'Connor v. Ortega* (1987), the U.S. Supreme Court held that a public employer could search an employee's office, files, or desk, without a warrant, whenever their offices are so accessible to other employees or the public that there is no reasonable expectation of privacy;

public employees may have a reasonable expectation of privacy, however, if they are able to lock their doors or cabinets. Even when there is a reasonable expectation of privacy, however, the Court called for a case-by-case assessment of the balance between "the invasion of the employees' legitimate expectations of privacy against the government's need for supervision, control and the efficient operation of the workplace" (*O'Connor v. Ortega* 1987, pp. 719–720). Such searches must meet a *reasonableness* standard; a search could occur, for example, to locate a needed item in an employee's office (such as a client file) and, significantly, when there is a reasonable suspicion of evidence of work-related misconduct in the employee's office or files.

Technology and the Constitution in the Public Workplace

Digital technology is a key element of a twenty-first-century workplace; Internet use in the workplace is virtually a universal norm. In 1996, Dichter and Burkhardt reported that employees in the U.S. spend an average of 1.2 hours per day on email. In 2012, employees averaged 28 hours online in a combination of email, research, and collaborative efforts (Chui et al. 2012, p. 1). The McKinsey Global Institute (Chui et al. 2012, p. 6) commented upon the diffusion of technology adoption, noting the following: "It took commercial television 13 years to reach 50 million households and Internet service providers three years to sign their 50 millionth subscriber, it took Facebook just a year to hit 50 million users. It took Twitter nine months."

The expansion of the virtual world, our collective engagement with it, and a general societal expectation of immediacy has both good and bad news for productivity, as well as weighty implications for rights and restrictions in the public sector workplace.

> Work and workplace processes have been fundamentally transformed with the rise of mobile communication . . . a most notable change is the blurring of the boundary between work and the private sphere. While permanent connectivity allows work to spill over into homes and friendship networks, it is also likely that personal communication will penetrate the formal boundaries of work.
>
> (Castells, Fernandez-Ardevol, Qiu, and Sey 2004, p. 82)

Both the scope of technology to date and the infinite possibilities in the future demand attention to the protections and restrictions linked to speech, association, privacy, and the like. Not surprisingly, in *City of Ontario v. Quon*, the U.S. Supreme Court took a cautious stance on prescribing standards in judicial interpretation for emerging technologies:

> The Court must proceed with care when considering the whole concept of privacy expectations in communications made on electronic equipment owned by a government employer. The judiciary risks error by elaborating too fully on the Fourth Amendment implications of emerging technology before its role in society has become clear . . . Rapid changes in the dynamics of communication and information transmission are evident not just in the technology itself but in what society accepts as proper behavior . . . at present, it is uncertain how workplace norms, and the law's treatment of them, will evolve.
>
> (2010, pp. 2629–2630)

Technology allows us to converse through a variety of devices with colleagues and friends and exchange all sorts of information, both that directly related to our work and content that is entirely personal in nature. The research capabilities alone are stunning: we can find information on virtually any topic, from both legitimate and undocumented sources, with the click of a mouse. Not only can employees access information, but so too can citizens and clients being served. Access is no longer limited to the eight-to-five, Monday-through-Friday workweek, phone conversations, or office visits. In fact, information (and communication) often is systematically logged, date/time-stamped, and archived for subsequent retrieval. The nearly immeasurable expansion of information raises opportunities in productivity, but also comes with many unsettling issues. For example, in a legal sense, there exists a vast amount of information that might be of use to litigants—email, databases, texts, posts to social media of all types—and this information may be 'discoverable' in a legal proceeding. In fact, there are organizations devoted to studying the best emerging strategies for doing so (Electronic Discovery Institute 2014).

Soylu and Campbell (2012) remind us that expanded technology is associated with increased workplace stressors, cautioning organizations to consider the legal implications of greater expectations for employee use of computers and cell phones, both in and out of the office setting. Clearly, this set of considerations has implications for OSHA-type protections of employee workplace health and safety. However, for the purpose of the Constitution and employee rights discussion, the accessibility afforded by cell phones and tablets is entirely relevant when the line between personal time and work time blurs so greatly compared with long-established boundaries and practices. Technology has definitely expanded the realm of political participation, offering individuals many more platforms on which to offer information and opinion and to advocate. For example, anyone with a phone, tablet, or laptop and Internet access can instantly take a position on any number of political issues, and broadcast such a stance broadly. And, just as instantly, their geographic position, the exact language used, the day/time, and scope are readily captured and documented. Not surprisingly, violations of the Hatch Act now may include social media posting and sharing, such as tweets, Facebook posts, and the like, when done while on duty or at a clearly designated worksite (U.S. Office of Special Counsel 2014).

In light of the expanded use of the Internet, how much of our use of ubiquitous electronic equipment is private as opposed to work-related? In the *City of Ontario v. Quon* (2010), the Court considered whether an employee could presume privacy for an employer-issued pager, finding that a municipality's review of the texts did not violate employee privacy, because the transcripts made of the texts stored in the pager were duly generated in the context of a "reasonable, work-related search." A government employer generally may read employee email without that employee's permission, when such content is either generated upon or received by government-owned computers. In fact, government can review the sites their employees visit on the Internet while working on their government jobs. Most jurisdictions use a variety of mechanisms to notify employees (and citizens generally, for public-use venues such as libraries) that they have no reasonable expectation of privacy. Under current U.S. law, an email sent on an employer's computer, even to a third party and regardless of the content, is essentially the property of the employer. *City of Ontario v. Quon* (2010) neither revoked this interpretation, nor determined a separation line between private or public communications in the context of government-issued communication devices. Monitoring of such communications is, arguably, attributed to a recognized legitimate need to ensure productivity and oversee employee performance and conduct. The courts have generally ruled in favor of the employer's right to search employee messages, saying there is no reasonable expectation of privacy in email communications (*Bourke v. Nissan Motor Corp.* 1993; *Smyth v. The Pillsbury Co.* 1996). The rationale of suspending a reasonable expectation of privacy is consistent with other court rulings allowing an employer to search through office desks and files, if the search is reasonably done. Although public employers are restricted by the Fourth Amendment, courts have permitted searches of employees' workplace and communications, if the purpose is either to satisfy the government's interest in efficient operation or proper supervision of its employees (*O'Connor v. Ortega* 1987).

Due Process of Law

Fifth Amendment

"No person shall be . . . deprived of life, liberty or property, without due process of law."

Fourteenth Amendment —

"No State shall make or enforce any law which shall abridge the privileges or immunities of citizens of the United States; nor shall any State deprive any person of life, liberty, or property, without due process of law."

The Lloyd–Lafollette Act (1912) gave federal employees the right to petition government for redress of employment-related grievances, implying a property interest in their jobs. For public employees, the granting of tenure or "permanent status," a formal contract, or clearly implied promises of continued employment establish a property interest (as distinct from a privilege) in one's government position. Property interests are not limited to formal written agreements, but may be established through existing rules or understandings between employers and employees. "Classified" or "permanent" employee status, or the passage of probationary status, may be required to establish a property interest that cannot be dismissed without *due process of law*.

Federal and state laws and administrative rules provide for *procedural* due process, whereas the Fifth and Fourteenth Amendments to the U.S. Constitution guarantee *substantive* due process. The concept

---

Exhibit 3.5 Administrative Procedures Act of 1946

At the federal level, the Administrative Procedures Act of 1946 (APA) establishes a kind of residual body of procedural rules that become pertinent if rules of any given agency are insufficient. Managers could consider this as a type of baseline. Administrative procedures, whether in the 1946 federal version, those versions already in place in the states, or the newest Model APA developed by the National Conference of Commissioners on Uniform State Laws, are designed to promote due process and consideration for fully disclosing all relevant information to all stakeholders. Thus, sections of APA 1946 require publication of information regarding agency structures, rules, regulations and procedures, written records and justification of decisions on the record, and separate adjudicative and prosecutorial functions within each agency. According to APA 1946, the components of a hearing might include:

- timely and adequate notice;
- disclosure of evidence;
- confronting adverse witnesses;
- cross-examining adverse witnesses;
- oral presentation of argument;
- presentation of evidence (written record);
- right to *retain* an attorney.

Source: Pub. L. 79–404, 60 Stat. 237 (June 11, 1946), Title 5 of USC, Section 500; www.uniformlaws.org/

of due process is, essentially, a government's obligation to be fair. Thus, due process of law requires that actions constituting a loss of a property interest "be preceded by notice and opportunity for hearing appropriate to the nature of the case" (*Board of Regents v. Roth* 1972; *Boddie v. Connecticut* 1971; *Mullane v. Central Hanover Bank & Trust Co.* 1950, p. 313). When employees have a property interest in their employment, they are entitled to an opportunity to present reasons why the proposed action against them should not be taken, before such action occurs (*Cleveland Board of Education v. Loudermill* 1985). The courts have stated that such hearings need not be elaborate: "something less than a full evidentiary hearing is sufficient prior to adverse administrative action" (*Mathews v. Eldridge* 1976, p. 431). Nonetheless, some official and systematic hearing process must be in place, and an official record emanating from it must be generated. This record is often the basis for subsequent appeals made to trial courts when employees seek relief from alleged illegal or arbitrary wrongful treatment or discharge.

The logic of procedural due process in application to employee discipline and redirection will receive additional attention in Chapter 12, on discipline and dismissal. However, it is useful to note that the *Mathews v. Eldridge* decision (1976, p. 431) outlined three significant factors in cueing the formality of due process in administrative procedures:

> first, the private interest that will be affected by the official action; second, the risk of an erroneous deprivation of such interest through the procedures used, and probable value, if any, of additional or substitute procedural safeguards; and finally, the Government's interest, including the function involved and the fiscal and administrative burdens that the additional or substitute procedural requirement would entail.

Equal Protection and Its Applications

Thirteenth Amendment

"Neither slavery nor involuntary servitude, except as punishment for crime whereof the party shall have been duly convicted, shall exist within the United States, or any place subject to their jurisdiction."

Fourteenth Amendment

> All persons born or naturalized in the United States, and subject to the jurisdiction thereof, are citizens of the United States and of the State wherein they reside. No State shall make or enforce any law which shall abridge the privileges or immunities of citizens of the United States; nor shall any State deprive any person of life, liberty, or property, without due process of law, nor deny to any person within its jurisdiction the equal protection of the laws.

Although the implications of the First Amendment are pivotal, the protection offered by the Fourteenth Amendment warrants special attention. In addition to defining citizenship and extending comparable constitutional protections to citizens in their relationship with state government as held in relation to the federal government, this amendment extends constitutional protections, not just to citizens, but also to *persons* residing in the U.S. From the beginning of American history, people from virtually all parts of the world have suffered the prejudice of the majority and have been denied the right to work and live on an equal basis with others in our society. In response to such inequity, and playing a major role in the American Civil War, the government and its courts have taken forceful actions to make unfair discrimination illegal.

In combination, the Thirteenth and Fourteenth Amendments and the Civil Rights Acts of 1866 and 1871 intended both to prohibit racial discrimination and to enforce lawful equal employment rights, especially in relation to public sector employment. These constitutional amendments and federal statutes, guaranteeing fundamental rights to citizens, encompassed both women and minorities. Despite these legal protections, however, discrimination persisted throughout the country, and a second wave of civil rights activity gained great momentum in the early 1960s, eventually resulting in significant new laws guaranteeing a broader range of civil rights.

Equal protection under the law was specified in the Civil Rights Act of 1964 (CRA) and later amendments to that statute. Exhibit 3.6 outlines various CRA iterations. Title VII of the CRA is specific to EEO. The law prohibits discrimination in the terms and conditions of employment (including recruitment, selection, promotion, training, pay, benefits, discipline, and termination), when such discrimination is based on race, color, religion, sex, or national origin. Title VII applies to virtually all nonprofit and for-profit organizations (with fifteen or more employees) and public organizations, including state and local governments (except elected officials and their staff), as of 1972. The Equal Employment Opportunity Commission (EEOC) was established to oversee compliance with these equal employment statutes and rules, and it tends to be the principal investigative and enforcement entity for a large segment of U.S. 'anti-discrimination' laws. Although the EEOC handles a number of employment-related statutes, responsibility for enforcement is distributed among federal agencies, including the Department of Labor (DoL), the National Labor Relations Board (NLRB), the Department of Health and Human Services (DHHS), the Office of Special Counsel (OSC), the Merit Systems Protection Board, the U.S. Department of Defense (DoD), and the U.S. Department of Justice (DoJ).

Laws protecting specific classes of individuals have followed the CRA of 1964 and provide protection against discrimination for specific groups or on bases not included in the original legislation (e.g., age, disability, or genetic information). In addition, laws protecting employees as they blend personal and professional obligations (e.g., the Family Medical Leave Act) have had significant import in the workplace. More discussion about specific, noteworthy laws establishing benefits for employees will be set forth in Chapter 9. Although the federal government establishes a minimum baseline through these laws, states have the latitude to extend, amplify, or detail protections. A state cannot exclude a protected category from protection, but it can enhance protections (e.g., applying legislation to smaller companies or organizations than those covered by federal law). States, and even some cities and counties, often have established such entities to oversee employment discrimination within their own jurisdictions.

Harassment as Discrimination

Harassment is (U.S. EEOC 2014a):

> unwelcome conduct that is based on race, color, religion, sex (including pregnancy), national origin, age (40 or older), disability or genetic information. Harassment becomes unlawful where 1) enduring the offensive conduct becomes a condition of continued employment, or 2) the conduct is severe or pervasive enough to create a work environment that a reasonable person would consider intimidating, hostile, or abusive.

Law in terms of protected class defines harassment as discrimination. Harassment *without* reference to protected class might be addressed through OSHA (Yamada 2000). Although the EEOC discounts "petty slights, annoyances, and isolated incidents (unless extremely serious)," we do discuss various forms of workplace aggression considered actionable in Chapters 10 and 11.

Exhibit 3.6 Federal Laws Related to Employment

Statute	Provisions	Enforcing Agency
Civil Rights Act of 1866	Affords all citizens the right to make contracts	n/a
Civil Rights Act of 1871	Gives all citizens the right to sue if their constitutional rights are infringed	n/a
Equal Pay Act of 1963	Prohibits discrimination in pay on the basis of sex for work of equal skill, effort, responsibility, and similar working conditions (not necessarily the same job)	EEOC
Civil Rights Act of 1964 (and as amended in 1972)	Prohibits discrimination on the basis of race, color, religion, sex, or national origin. This Act is the fundamental law for civil rights legislation in the U.S. and, as amended in 1972, extended protection to states and local levels and to education	EEOC & DoJ
Age Discrimination in Employment Act of 1967 (and as amended in 1974, 1978, & 1987)	Establishes age as a protected class by prohibiting employment discrimination against applicants and employees who are 40 years of age or older	EEOC
Occupational Safety and Health Act of 1970	Establishes guidelines covering the private sector (except for self-employed, family farms, and entities protected through other legislation) and federal government workers. Standards address issues ranging from blood-borne pathogens, confined spaces, or hazardous materials to fire prevention	DoL/OSHA
Vocational Rehabilitation Act of 1973	Requires employers with federal contracts to take affirmative action toward workers with disabilities by seeking out qualified applicants with disabilities and making reasonable accommodations to their needs in the workplace	EEOC, DoL, & DoJ
Pregnancy Discrimination Act of 1978	Amended the Civil Rights Act of 1964 to prohibit discrimination by excluding pregnancy and childbirth in medical insurance and sick leave policies	EEOC
Immigration Reform and Control Act of 1986	Prohibits employers from knowingly hiring illegal aliens. Employers must determine the legal status of job applicants and complete the I-9 form required under this Act	OSC
Whistleblower Protection Act of 1989	Protects federal employees or applicants from retaliatory personnel action by agency authorities in response to whistleblower complaints of law, rule, or regulatory violations, gross mismanagement or waste of funds, abuse of authority, or substantial and specific dangers to public health/safety	OSC
Americans with Disabilities Act of 1990 (and as amended in 2008)	Applies broadly to the terms, conditions, and privileges of employment and prohibits discrimination based on disabilities that substantially limit major life activities of qualified individuals. The 2008 amendment clarified congressional intent on definitions of such disabilities	EEOC & DoJ

continued . . .

Exhibit 3.6 Continued

Statute	Provisions	Enforcing Agency
Civil Rights Act of 1991	Prohibits discrimination on the basis of race, color, religion, sex, or national origin as even a contributing fact in employment actions; shifts the burden of proof to the employer in cases of disparate impact and allows punitive damages for intentional discrimination	EEOC
Government Employee Rights Act of 1991	Prohibits discrimination based on race, national origin, color, gender, religion, age, or disability	DoL
Family Medical Leave Act of 1993	Permits employees to take up to 12 weeks of unpaid leave during any 12-month period to tend to family needs	DoL
Uniformed Services Employment and Reemployment Rights Act of 1994 (and codified as amended at 38 U.S.C. §§ 4301–4335)	Protects civilian job rights/benefits for military veterans and reserves including expectations about reasonable accommodation for disability, and protection of seniority, status, compensation/benefits upon a veteran's return to the civilian workforce	DoJ
National Defense Authorization Act (NDAA) of 2008 (and as amended)	Expands FMLA for military families	DoD
Genetic Information Nondiscrimination Act of 2008	Prohibits discrimination against either employees or applicants because of genetic information and limits the disclosure of such information (including family medical history)	EEOC, DoL & DHHS

Source: Varied; see Chapter 3 References.

The term discrimination does not, by itself, connote evil, unfairness, or injustice; after all, to discriminate is a key part of managing in any organization. Managers must discriminate between job applicants who are qualified and those who are not. Discrimination is required when one employee is promoted over other candidates. In performance appraisal, the supervisor must assess the quality of an employee's work and distinguish between exceptional, acceptable, and inadequate performance. Unfortunately, this obligation of management to discriminate is oftentimes illegally biased when ethnic, religious, and racial groups are judged, intentionally or through longstanding practices, on their appearance, physical characteristics, ancestry, or beliefs, rather than on their qualifications and performance. Illegal discrimination happens in the workplace when employers and coworkers unfavorably differentiate employees and applicants in statutorily protected classes owing to factors unrelated to the job. Various civil rights laws, beginning with the CRA of 1964, have identified specific groups as protected classes based on a characteristic of that group, such as their age, race, color, religion, sex, national origin, disability, or veteran status—characteristics that have been subject to historically documented disadvantage in employment considerations. Persons who qualify as being in a "suspect classification" vis-à-vis protected class status have legal standing to make complaints to the courts for redress of illegal discrimination allegedly based on that classification. Unless a characteristic is a bona fide occupational qualification (BFOQ), necessary for the business to conduct operations or an organization to fulfill its mission, using such a factor in personnel actions is illegal.

Demographic changes in the workforce have dramatic implications for equal protection. As noted in Chapter 1, the U.S. population is aging at a rate disproportionate to the population as a whole, and both organizations and individuals may increasingly face somewhat different expectations than the norms of recent decades regarding retirement, career duration, and active work life. An aging population offers a variety of advantages in the workplace in terms of institutional knowledge (as we will discuss in Chapter 5), but may likewise bring new challenges and opportunities in terms of disability, reasonable accommodations, and workplace access.

Exhibit 3.7 Implications of Demographic Shifts: Equal Protection and Age

In public sector organizations, as well as those private and nonprofit entities with twenty or more employees, and unions with more than twenty-five members, employees over 40 years of age are protected under the Age Discrimination in Employment Act of 1967 (ADEA). Originally, the protections were capped, first at 65 and then at 70; however, a maximum age for protection under the Act was removed in 1987. The Supreme Court ruled in 2000 that the ADEA's abrogation of state immunity under the Eleventh Amendment exceeded Congress's authority (*Kimel v. Florida Board of Regents* 2000). Notably, *this ruling* does not seem to extend to private for-profit, nonprofit, or federal employees or to local government employees. It appears, then, that age is not provided the same protection as other protected classes such as race, color, sex, and national origin, and that states may discriminate on the basis of age, if the age is rationally related to a legitimate state interest. Furthermore, EEOC rules articulate a "reasonable factor other than age" as a basis for disparate treatment, rather than "business necessity," based upon the Court's holding in *Smith v. City of Jackson* (2005). The burden of proof for age-based practices rests with the employer.

Source: See Chapter 3 References.

Exhibit 3.8 Implications of Demographic Shifts: Equal Protection and Disability

Those with disabilities are protected under the Rehabilitation Act (1973) and the Americans with Disabilities Act (ADA; 1990).

Americans with Disabilities Act of 1990

ADA is administered by the EEOC and it expands upon the basic provisions of the Vocational Rehabilitation Act by prohibiting discrimination based on an individual's disability for all firms and agencies employing fifteen or more personnel. The general rule of the Act is as follows:

- No covered entity shall discriminate against a qualified individual with a disability because of the disability of such individual in regard to job application procedures, the hiring, advancement, or discharge of employees, employee compensation, job training, and other terms, conditions, and privileges of employment.
- The definitions of the terms "disability," "qualified," "reasonable accommodation," and "undue hardship" are critical to complying with ADA and are defined in the Act:
  - *Disability*: the term "disability" means, with respect to an individual (a) a physical or mental impairment that substantially limits one or more of the major life activities of such individual; (b) a record of such an impairment; or (c) being regarded as having such an impairment.
  - *Qualified individual with a disability*: the term "qualified individual with a disability" means an individual with a disability who, with or without reasonable accommodation, can perform the essential functions of the employment position that such individual holds or desires. For the purposes of this title, consideration shall be given to the employer's judgment as to what functions of a job are essential, and, if an employer has prepared a written description before advertising or interviewing applicants for the job, this description shall be considered evidence of the essential functions of the job.
  - *Reasonable accommodation*: the term "reasonable accommodation" may include (a) making existing facilities used by employees readily accessible to and usable by individuals with disabilities; and (b) job restructuring, part-time or modified work schedules, reassignment to a vacant position, acquisition or modification of equipment or devices, appropriate adjustment or modifications of examinations, training materials, or policies, the provision of qualified readers or interpreters, and other similar accommodations for individuals with disabilities.
  - *Undue hardship*: in general, the term "undue hardship" means an action requiring significant difficulty or expense.

Source: See Chapter 3 References.

Legal and Ethical Protections for Transgender and Sexual Orientation

A number of local jurisdictions have acted to recognize civil rights for homosexual and transgendered individuals by including sexual orientation and transgender status in their civil rights statutes. From the standpoint of HRM, concerns range from the reality or perception of discrimination due to sexual orientation or transgender in personnel practices to the very tangible implications of defining employment benefits such as health insurance and retirement by virtue of whether or not parties have a legally recognized marriage. Transgender individuals face further complexity as, in addition to legal protections, they must deal with a variety of organizational policies and procedures, ranging from dress codes to compatible locker room and restroom access (Colvin 2007). The Human Rights Campaign (2014) reports that twenty-one states and the District of Columbia (Washington, DC) prohibit discrimination based on sexual orientation (generally for both public and private sector employees), and seventeen of those states and DC extend protection based on gender identity. According to the National Gay and Lesbian Task Force, 156 local governments across the U.S. have enacted nondiscrimination ordinances that extend to transgendered individuals working in those governments (2012). With respect to federal government employees, Executive Order 13087 prohibits discrimination associated with sexual orientation, and the EEOC decision in *Macy v. Holder* clarified that Title VII prohibitions on sex discrimination extend equally to transgender persons (Mottet 2013). Same-sex harassment is also deemed illegal (*Oncale v. Sundowner Offshore Services, Inc.* 1998). Although the executive orders and the decision in *Macy v. Holder* apply specifically to federal employees, the data from the Human Rights Campaign and the National Gay and Lesbian Task Force suggest local and state governments are equally as, if not more, progressive in this regard. Although the U.S. Supreme Court has precedent on government employers taking adverse actions against homosexuals, in the *Padula v. Webster* (1987) case it cautioned that all discrimination against homosexuals would not necessarily be unacceptable as state action. However, any discrimination against homosexual individuals that does occur must pass the rational basis test of the equal protection clause—that is, there must be a compelling legitimate government need to discriminate.

Sex Discrimination and Sexual Harassment

The shifts in the proportion of men and women in the workplace and in particular occupations have significant implications for this discussion. An important dimension of Title VII is the major issue of employment discrimination based upon sex and the related cases of sexual harassment. A traditional view of sexual harassment was that the mix of women and men in the workplace set the stage for sexual harassment. In this traditional view, men were depicted as the likely harassers, and women were depicted as the likely victims. A much more complex reality is that, although statistically the odds continue to favor the traditional scenario, the contemporary U.S. workplace increasingly defies such traditionally defined roles. When it comes to harassment in the workplace, equal opportunity is increasingly the reality. We will address gender-based inequities in terms of compensation in Chapter 8. Early cases dealing with gender justice include *Diaz v. Pan Am* (1970) and *Dothard v. Rawlinson* (1977), which articulated the scenarios wherein gender might or might not serve as a legitimate BFOQ in the workplace. However, in *Barnes v. Costle* (1977) sexual harassment was included as a form of unlawful discrimination on the basis of sex. Since then, the courts have interpreted sexual harassment as illegal discrimination based on sex under Title VII of the CRA of 1964 (*Harris v. Forklift Systems* 1993; *Meritor Savings Bank v. Vinson* 1986). Sexual harassment, thusly classified under the law, is defined as:

Bona fide Occupational Qualification

Unwelcome sexual advances, requests for sexual favors, and other verbal or physical conduct of a sexual nature constitute sexual harassment when this conduct explicitly or implicitly affects an individual's employment, unreasonably interferes with an individual's work performance or creates an intimidating, hostile or offensive work environment.

(U.S. EEOC 2014b)

For sexual harassment to be actionable, it must be sufficiently severe or pervasive "to alter the conditions of [the victim's] employment and create an abusive working environment" (*Henson v. City of Dundee* 1982, p. 904). Views of sexual harassment have evolved to the extent that victimization may extend beyond direct parties involved, and harassers may include, not only direct supervisors, but also coworkers or even non-employees. Victims are not necessarily women and need not be of the opposite sex (*Oncale v. Sundowner Offshore Services, Inc.* 1998).

Employers are liable for sexual harassment perpetuated in the organization (*Burlington Industries, Inc. v. Ellerth* 1998; *Faragher v. City of Boca Raton* 1998). Ideally, organizations must prevent, rather than react to, these scenarios.

Affirmative Action

The term "affirmative action" was first used by President Kennedy in Executive Order 10925 (1961) in application to contracting arrangements with the federal government. Four years later, President Johnson announced Executive Order 11246 (1965), reiterating the concept of AA in contracting arrangements, and denounced sex discrimination in contracting arrangements in Executive Order 11375 (1967). President Johnson's commencement speech at Howard University articulated his position on AA, and this statement continues to serve as an important rationale for its application:

Thus, it is not enough just to open the gates of opportunity. All our citizens must have the ability to walk through those gates. This is the next and the more profound stage of the battle for civil rights. We seek not just freedom but opportunity. We seek not just legal equity but human ability, not just equality as a right and a theory but equality as a fact and equality as a result.

(Johnson 1965)

AA has been the subject of much divisive debate in the U.S., and the definition and purpose of AA have become rather obscured. AA does not normally require quotas or forcing employers to hire or promote unqualified people, although these drastic steps were taken in some specific court decisions where institutionalized discrimination against persons in protected classes was proven. Generally, it simply means that organizations should take 'positive steps' to ensure that everyone, including historically disadvantaged groups, has the opportunity to apply, be interviewed, and be hired for public employment. Once hired, everyone should enjoy an equal opportunity to be fairly considered for opportunities and career advancement in the workplace, including promotions. The debate about AA occurs over what these positive steps should be and how long corrective actions should be in force.

Disparate Treatment or Impact?

The wording of the equal protection clause, although direct and clear, has been subject to diverse interpretation in connection with CRA Title VII. Two forms of illegal discrimination are at issue in application to EEO laws and AA. When policies or longstanding practices are essentially neutral, but have differing effects upon protected classes, the term "disparate impact" applies. The employer has the burden of proof to establish that its policies and procedures are appropriate in these cases and genuine efforts have been and are being made to recruit underrepresented persons. When such discrimination is intended to differently affect a protected class, the term "disparate treatment" applies.

The hierarchy of law in the U.S. is such that, although states and local jurisdictions may vary widely in the content of their laws and ordinances, federal action trumps that taken at the state and local level. Judicial interpretation by the U.S. Supreme Court supersedes all interpretation of lower courts. There has been some inconsistency of court rulings over the years when dealing with EEO and AA cases, but one trend is clear—namely, the U.S. Supreme Court generally has been unwilling to overly constrain the authority of public sector managers. Its decision in *Garcetti v. Ceballos* (2006) to consider whether speech is job-related is clear on this point; so too is the Court's decision in *Engquist v. Oregon Department of Agriculture et al.* (2008) to reject the 'class-of-one' theory of equal protection. The premise of that theory of equal protection is that an employee can claim equal protection from a status as an individual rather than as a member of a particular group. In rejecting this theory per the Title VII litigation, the Court was further affirming its unwillingness to micromanage public sector employment.

The path to remedying *unintentional* discrimination, while avoiding the use of *intentional* discrimination to do so, remains a difficult one to navigate for courts. Most recently, Peffer (2009) related an analysis of *Ricci v. DeStefano* (2009) in which the Court held against a municipality's attempt to remedy apparent disparate impact by dismissing some putatively valid employment tests. She argues, "the decision may . . . [mean that] employers are left with little guidance on how to avoid discrimination under Title VII and . . . must choose between being sued for disparate-treatment discrimination or disparate-impact discrimination" (p. 402).

The U.S. DoL requires all organizations that contract with government, having fifty or more employees or receiving $50,000 or more in federal funding to have an affirmative action program (AAP). Exhibit 3.9 depicts significant court cases that have contributed to best practices in this area. Judicially approved AA plans meet the *two-prong standard of strict scrutiny* established in *Wygant v. Jackson Board of Education* (1986). Plans must satisfy a compelling governmental interest (such as correcting the effects of past discrimination or a significant imbalance among protected categories in specific job categories), and they must be *narrowly tailored* to address the problem. AA should entail a variety of mechanisms to challenge 'but-that's-the-way-we've-always-done-it' modes of conducting personnel actions. Actions taken may include enhanced recruitment, selection, training and promotion of qualified individuals from historically underrepresented groups, as well as the explicit removal of employment protocols that serve as demonstrable barriers to protected groups (e.g., height requirements for police). In general, voluntary AAPs are more likely to withstand judicial scrutiny if they are temporary, intended to eliminate a 'manifest' and documented racial imbalance, apply to nontraditional jobs, and do not require terminating or freezing the normal advancement of other employees. AAP templates are available online from reputable sources, including the Society for Human Resource Management (www.shrm.org) and the U.S. DoL (www.dol.gov).

State-Level Referenda, Citizen Initiatives, and Affirmative Action

In 1996, California voters passed Proposition 209 prohibiting preferential treatment to individuals or groups due to race, color, sex, ethnicity, or national origin in public education, employment, and contracting. Washington followed in 1998 with Initiative 200. Oklahoma and Arizona voters approved legislative referenda in 2010 and 2012 to prohibit preferential treatment using the same general parameters as those enacted in California and Washington. The State of New Hampshire added the category of sexual orientation to the longstanding categories of race, color, sex, ethnicity,

Exhibit 3.9 Significant Affirmative Action Case Law

Griggs v. Duke Power Co. (1971)	Job requirements must have a "demonstrable relationship to successful performance" and "artificial, arbitrary, and unnecessary barriers to employment [that] . . . operate invidiously to discriminate on the basis of racial or other impermissible classification" must be removed (pp. 429–433)
University of California Regents v. Bakke (1978)	This case established the concept of "reverse discrimination" as a consequence of adopted AA programs and disallowed the use of separate candidate pools. Minority status could be taken into account in calculating admission scores if racial and ethnic diversity was believed to promote educational purposes
Steelworkers v. Weber (1979)	Title VII neither requires any employer to grant preferential treatment, nor prohibits voluntary race-conscious AA. In the case of *Steelworkers*, the Court noted: "the plan is a temporary measure, not intended to maintain racial balance, but simply to eliminate a manifest racial imbalance" (pp. 208–209)
Firefighters Local Union 1784 v. Stotts (1984)	A seniority-based layoff system (last hired, first fired) could take precedence over a voluntary AA plan, even though it had an adverse effect on recently hired black firefighters
Wygant v. Jackson Board of Education (1986)	"Strict scrutiny" should be applied to preferential consideration of minorities and women. Racial classification must be justified by a compelling governmental interest, and the methods used must be narrowly tailored to the achievement of that goal (p. 273)
United States v. Paradise (1987)	The Court upheld a U.S. federal district court's imposition of promotion quotas for qualified black candidates (when available) owing to a "compelling governmental interest" in eliminating persistent discrimination, and that the remedy developed was narrowly tailored to address the deficiency in the upper ranks
Johnson v. Transportation Agency (1987)	The court upheld a hiring under a local government's voluntary AA plan in which race and sex were considered as one of many factors in the qualification of the applicants, because the plan reflected a moderate, flexible, case-by-case approach toward gradual improvement in a conspicuous imbalance in identified job categories and did not trammel the rights of male employees
Richmond v. J.A. Croson Co. (1989)	There was no compelling governmental interest justifying a set-aside plan (e.g., a 30% quota for minority business) when no past discrimination in the industry was found to exist for minorities affected by the plan. In this case, the plan was not narrowly tailored, as any minority business from anywhere in the country could benefit from the plan
Wards Cove Packing Co. v. Atonio (1989)	Demonstrating a prima facie case of disparate impact requires an appropriate comparison between at-issue jobs and the qualified labor force population. Simple comparisons with the general population are not sufficient. Those claiming discrimination must show a disparate impact in hiring outcomes *and* must identify specific employment practices that have caused the disparate impact

continued . . .

Exhibit 3.9 Continued

Adarand Constructors Inc. v. Pena (1995)	The Fifth and Fourteenth Amendments protect persons, not groups. AA plans are constitutional, but governmental action based on race should apply strict scrutiny to ensure the protection of individual rights
Grutter v Bollinger (2003)	Although "race or ethnicity [cannot be] the defining feature," their use as a variable augmenting some set of characteristics or skills is acceptable (p. 322)
Gratz v. Bollinger (2003)	An admission system should treat applicants as individuals rather than employing a point system that offers an automatic advantage

Source: See Chapter 3 References.

and origin, and explicitly prohibited discrimination or preferential treatment in public sector personnel actions and college admission. Nebraska's Initiative 424 focused upon AA in postsecondary education. States continued the trend against AA in college and university admissions, with the adoption of California's "Four Percent Plan," Florida's Executive Order 99–281 "One Florida" in 1999, and the Texas's "10 Percent Plan" (passed in 1997 and amended in 2009). Only Colorado's voters defeated a comparable anti-affirmative measure. In June 2014, the U.S. Supreme Court ruled to uphold Michigan's Proposal 2, a measure similar to the others mentioned, which focuses on public education, employment, and contracting.

Because of the hierarchy of law in the U.S., the Supremacy Clause of the U.S. Constitution would, in theory, circumvent state action that countered Executive Orders 10925, 11246, and 11375. However, the composition of the U.S. Supreme Court has changed since these Executive Orders were declared by U.S. presidents, and the Court may well reconsider precedents set in earlier cases as it hears a series of state-level challenges to AA.

Those who oppose AA typically emphasize individual liberty in their comments, believing that the rights guaranteed in the Constitution are individual rights, whereas AA addresses group rights. Although there is precedent for protecting group rights (Fourteenth Amendment), most of the liberties and rights we enjoy are individual protections. For those arguing against AA, discrimination against members of unprotected categories (often white males) cannot be justified as a remedy for past discrimination against members of protected categories. In reviewing U.S. Census data, Kogut and Short (2007, p. 205) found:

> The good intentions of the federal government to obtain equality of opportunity in federal employment for all persons have actually resulted in the implementation of AAPs that may have institutionalized preferential hiring in federal employment; that is, some minority groups appear to be receiving the benefits of federal jobs at the expense of other minority groups.

Full–Spectrum Diversity

An argument gaining growing support across the nation is that the AA approach has focused too narrowly. *Diversity* can be conceived of as being much broader in scope than ethnicity, race, and gender. AA plans in force usually do not address a 'manifest imbalance' in the number of Muslims or refugees from some troubled area of the world employed in an organization compared with the number of qualified Muslims and refugees present in the local work force. Similarly, AAPs do not single out persons by their sexual orientation, age, or whether they trace their national origin to Denmark, Honduras, or Canada. The argument for a more diverse workplace envisions a workforce reflecting "proactively the gender, cultural and ethnic complexity of each local community as well as the American society" (Slack 1997, p. 76).

Although laws designed to promote equality in the workplace spurred AA, diversity can be motivated in good measure by economics, along with a preference for inclusiveness. A diverse workforce revitalizes organizations by providing resources capable of enhanced creativity and innovative problem solving (Cox and Blake 1991, pp. 45–56). The benefit of 'full spectrum diversity' is that employees from diverse backgrounds and heritages can contribute to a richer dialog on how an agency can better address the needs of clients or customers.

Summary

No longer are public employees considered privileged to work for government and, consequently, work at the will and whim of elected officials. Because their employer is the government, public sector employees warrant protections from government (state) action, as do citizens generally per the U.S. Constitution. Much of the employment law detailed in this chapter applies to private and nonprofit sector employees as well; however, public sector employees face many unique protections and prohibitions. Personnel managers must keep pace with new laws and court interpretations granting special rights or new benefits to employees. They must monitor federal and state court decisions on employment law and determine if they have application to employees under their jurisdictions. This is an onerous task without sound legal advice; lawyers who specialize in employment law keep up with changes in the law, administrative regulations, and court decisions and are called upon to periodically update supervisors, managers, and HRM specialists. Unfortunately, the great complexity of employment law and the rapidity with which it can change make personnel practice particularly challenging for small, nonprofit organizations and the many public jurisdictions lacking access to specialists.

Federal offices, such as the Office of Special Council, EEOC, and the Wage and Hour Division of the DoL have responsibility to enforce some of these laws, and likewise to assist public organizations to comply with the requirements of the law. State and local government also have specialists assigned to enforce and advise public agencies as to their responsibilities under these fair employment practice laws. Their services may be able to keep public organizations from experiencing unpleasant and costly lawsuits by helping the agency-based personnel administrator maintain up-to-date practices.

A Manager's Vocabulary

- Affirmative action
- Americans with Disabilities Act of 1990
- BFOQ
- Disparate impact versus disparate treatment
- Disability
- Doctrine of privilege versus at-will service
- Due process of law (procedural and substantive)
- Equal employment opportunity

- Equal protection clause
- Hatch Act and "Mini-Hatch Acts"
- Hostile environment (sexual harassment)
- Procedural versus substantive due process
- Reasonable accommodation
- Title VII, Civil Rights Act of 1964

Study Questions

1. How are public employees viewed differently from private sector employees under the Constitution?
2. Should public employees be more or less limited in their right to participate in political activity? If yes, to what degree?
3. What responsibility do public agencies have to address sexual harassment?
4. What would be a reasonable accommodation for an obese employee? A diabetic employee? For someone who identifies as an alcoholic? For a near-sighted employee?
5. What are the differences between an affirmative action plan and a diversity program?

Exercises

Exercise 3.1 You Rule! McMillan v. NMSU

Bill McMillan accepted a 1-year appointment as a nontenured track lecturer in the Department of Political Science at Northern Minnesota State University. He worked hard during the semester, preparing and teaching three classes and working on publications. He commented to his departmental colleagues on multiple occasions that he thought the college dean could do a better job at allocating teaching loads. He also observed that faculty salaries were not up to par with those of other state universities. He thought things were going well. However, on January 23, as the spring term began, he received official word that the university would not review his contract for the next academic year. No explanation was given. Disappointed, angry, and having just taught a course on the Constitution and Bill of Rights, Professor McMillan sued the university. He claimed the administration had infringed on his First Amendment right to free speech and his Fourteenth Amendment rights to due process, because he did not receive reasons for the contract nonrenewal and was not afforded an administrative hearing to challenge the action.

1. If you were a judge hearing this case, how would you rule?
2. What rights does an untenured professor have to employment with the state?
3. Is there reason to believe that Professor McMillan's right to free speech was violated?
4. Is the university obligated to provide procedural due process to Professor McMillan?

Exercise 3.2 You Rule! U.S. Customs Service v. Agnes Jones

After careful study of the validity and reliability of drug testing techniques, the Commissioner of the U.S. Customs Service announced a new drug-testing program utilizing urine sampling (UA). Any applicant for, or incumbent of, specific positions that meet one or more of the following criteria would be required to submit to UA testing: (1.) the position involves drug interdiction or enforcement; (2.) the employee is required to carry a firearm; or (3.) the employee handles 'classified' material.

Customs employees who test positive for drugs and can make no satisfactory explanation are subject to dismissal. The union, on behalf of Ms. Jones, agrees that there is a legitimate government interest in a drug-free workplace, but argues that this drug-testing program was overly intrusive and violated the employees' right to privacy. Furthermore, they point out that this program lacked either stipulation of probable cause or reasonable suspicion.

1. Does requiring a urine sample constitute a search?
2. Are such searches warranted in the case of U.S. Customs agents?
3. Should the employees in all three categories listed be subject to the drug-testing program?

References

Adarand Constructors Inc. v. Pena, 515 U.S. 200 (1995).

AFGE v. Skinner, 885 F.2d 884 (D.C. Cir. 1989).

Atkins v. City of Charlotte, 296 F. Supp. 1068 (W.D.N.C. 1969).

Barnes v. Costle, 561 F2d 983 (1977).

Board of County Commissioners, Wabaunsee County, Kansas v. Umbehr, 518 U.S. 668 (1996).

Board of Regents v. Roth, 408 U.S. 564 (1972).

Boddie v. Connecticut, 401 U.S. 371, 379 (1971).

Bourke v. Nissan Motor Corp., No. BO68705 (Cal. Ct. App. 1993).

Branti v. Finkel, 445 U.S. 507 (1980).

Burlington Industries, Inc. v. Ellerth, 524 U.S. 742 (1998).

Castells, Manuel, Mireia Fernandez-Ardevol, Jack Linchuan Qui, and Araba Sey. 2004. *Mobile Communication and Society: A Global Perspective*. Cambridge, MA: MIT Press.

Chui, Michael, James Manyika, Jacques Bughin, Richard Dobbs, Charles Roxburgh, Hugo Sarrazin, Geoffrey Sands, and Magdalena Westergren. 2012. "The Social Economy: Unlocking Value and Productivity through Social Technologies, Executive Summary." McKinsey Global Institute. www.mckinsey.com/insights/high_tech_telecoms_internet/the_social_economy (accessed February 26, 2014).

City of Ontario v. Quon, 130 S.Ct 2619, 560 U.S. (2010).

Cleveland Board of Education v. Loudermill, 470 U.S. 532 (1985).

Clinton v. Cedar Rapids and the Missouri River Railroad, 24 Iowa 455 (1868).

Colvin, Roddrick A. 2007. "The Rise of Transgender-Inclusive Laws: How Well Are Municipalities Implementing Supportive Nondiscrimination Public Employment Policies?" *Review of Public Personnel Administration* 27 (4): 336–360.

Connick v. Myers, 461 U.S. 138 (1983).

Copeland v. Philadelphia Police Department, 840 F. 2d 1139 (3d Cir. 1988).

Cox, Taylor H., and Stacy Blake. 1991. "Managing Cultural Diversity: Implications for Organizational Competitiveness." *Academy of Management Executive* 5 (3): 45–56.

Curle v. Ward, 46 N.Y.2d 1049 (1979).

Diaz v. Pan Am, 311 F. Supp. 559 (S.D. Fla 1970).

Dichter, Mark S., and Michael S. Burkhardt. 1996. "Electronic Interaction in the Workplace: Monitoring, Retrieving and Storing Employee Communications in the Internet Age." The American Employment Law Council, Fourth Annual Conference, October.

Dothard v. Rawlinson, 433 U.S. 321 (1977).

Electronic Discovery Institute. 2014. www.ediscoveryinstitute.org (accessed February 14, 2014).

Elrod v. Burns, 427 U.S. 347 (1976).

Engquist v. Oregon Department of Agriculture et al., 478 F. 3d 985 (2008).

Executive Order No. 10925, Pres. Kennedy, 3/6/61, "Establishing the President's Committee on Equal Employment Opportunity." 13 C.F.R. (1960).

Executive Order No. 11246, Pres. Johnson, 9/24/65, "Equal Employment Opportunity."

Executive Order No. 11375, Pres. Johnson, 10/13/67, "Amending Executive Order No 11246 Relating to Equal Employment Opportunity."

Executive Order No. 13087, Pres. Clinton, 5/28/98, "Further Amendments to Equal Employment."

Faragher v. City of Boca Raton, 524 U.S. 775 (1998).

Firefighters Local Union 1784 v. Stotts, 467 U.S. 561 (1984).

Garcetti v. Ceballos, 547 U.S. 410 (2006).

Gratz v. Bollinger, 539 U.S. 244 (2003).

Griggs v. Duke Power Co., 401 U.S. 424 (1971).

Grutter v. Bollinger, 539 U.S. 306 (2003).

Harris v. Forklift Systems, 510 U.S. 17 (1993).

Hatch Act Pub. L. 76–252 (1939).

Hatch Act Reform Amendments Pub. L. 103–94 (1993).

Hatch Act Modernization Act Pub. L. 112–230 (2012).

Henson v. City of Dundee, 682 F.2d at 904 (1982).

Human Rights Campaign. (2014). "Statewide Employment Laws and Policies." http://hrc.org/resources/entry/maps-of-state-laws-policies (accessed March 4, 2014).

Jefferson, Thomas. 1787/1993. "Letter from Thomas Jefferson to James Madison, December 20." In Richard B. Bernstein and Jerome Agel, *Amending America*. New York: Times Books.

Johnson, President Lyndon B. 1965. "To Fulfill These Rights." Commencement Address at Howard University. www.lbjlib.utexas.edu/johnson/archives.hom/speeches.hom/650604.asp (accessed February 27, 2014).

Johnson v. Transportation Agency, 480 U.S. 616 (1987).

Kimel v. Florida Board of Regents, 528 U.S. 62 (2000).

Koenig, Heidi. 1997. "Free Speech: Government Employees and Government Contractors." *Public Administration Review* 57 (1): 1–3.

Kogut, Carl A. and Larry E. Short. 2007. "Affirmative Action in Federal Employment: Good Intentions Run Amuck?" *Public Personnel Management* 36 (3): 197–206.

Lee, Yong S., and David H. Rosenbloom. 2005. *A Reasonable Public Servant: Constitutional Foundations of Administrative Conduct in the U.S.*, 232–234. New York: M.E. Sharpe.

Lloyd–Lafollette Act of 1912 Stat 539. 5 U.S.C. §7513.

McAuliffe v. Mayor of New Bedford, 155 Mass. 216 (1892).

McDonell v. Hunter, 809 F.2d 1302 (8th Cir. 1987).

Macy v. Holder USEEOC complaint, appeal #0120120821, agency # ATF-2011–00751 (2011).

Mathews v. Eldridge, 424 U.S. 319 (1976).

Meritor Savings Bank v. Vinson, 477 U.S. 57 (1986).

Mottet, Lisa. 2013. "Movement Analysis: The Full Impact of the EEOC Ruling on the LGBT Movement's Agenda." http://thetaskforceblog.org/2012/10/05/movement-analysis-the-full-impact-of-the-eeoc-ruling-on-the-lgbt-movements-agenda/ (accessed June 18, 2015).

Mullane v. Central Hanover Bank & Trust Co., 339 U.S. 306 (1950).

NAACP v. Alabama ex rel. Patterson, 357 U.S. 449 (1958).

National Conference of State Legislatures. 2010. "State-level Whistleblower." www.ncsl.org/research/labor-and-employment/state-whistleblower-laws.aspx (accessed February 12, 2014).

———. 2014. "Guns on Campus: Overview." www.ncsl.org/research/education/guns-on-campus-overview.aspx (accessed March 8, 2014).

National Gay and Lesbian Task Force. 2012. "Fact Sheet: Jurisdictions with Explicitly Transgender-Inclusive Nondiscrimination Laws." www.thetaskforce.org/static_html/downloads/reports/fact_sheets/all_jurisdictions_w_pop_10_11.pdf (accessed June 29, 2015).

National Treasury Employees Union v. von Raab, 489 U.S. 656 (1989).

NTEU v. Yeutter, 918 F.2d 968 (D.C. Cir.1990).

O'Connor v. Ortega, 480 U.S. 709 (1987).

O'Hare Truck Service, Inc. v. City of Northlake, 518 U.S. 712 (1996).

Oncale v. Sundowner Offshore Services, Inc., 523 U.S. 75 (1998).

Padula v. Webster, 822 F.2d 97 (D.C. Cir. 1987).

Peffer, Shelly L. 2009. "Title VII and Disparate-Treatment Discrimination Versus Disparate-Impact Discrimination: The Supreme Court's Decision in *Ricci v. DeStefano*." *Review of Public Personnel Administration* 29 (4): 402–410.

Pickering v. Board of Education, 391 U.S. 563 (1968).

Rankin v. McPherson, 483 U.S. 378 (1987).

Ricci v. DeStefano, 557 U.S. 557 (2009).

Richmond v. J.A. Croson Co., 488 US 469 (1989).

Roberts, Robert. 2007. "The Supreme Court and the Deconstitutionalization of the Freedom of Speech Rights of Public Employees." *Review of Public Personnel Administration* 27 (2): 171–184.

Rutan v. Republican Party of Illinois, 497 U.S. 62 (1990).

Seelig v. Koehler, 76 N.Y.2d 87, 556 N.E.2d 125 (1990).

Shelton v. Tucker, 364 U.S. 479 (1960).

Slack, James D. 1997. "From Affirmative Action to Full Spectrum Diversity in the American Workplace." *Review of Public Personnel Administration* 17 (4): 75–87.

Smith v. City of Jackson, 544 U.S. 228 (2005).

Smyth v. The Pillsbury Co., 914 F. Supp. 97 (1996).

Soylu, Ali, and Stefanie Snider Campbell. 2012. "Physical and Emotional Stresses of Technology on Employees in the Workplace." *Journal of Employment Counseling* 49 (3): 130–139.

Steelworkers v. Weber, 443 U.S. 193 (1979).

United Public Workers of America v. Michell, 330 U.S. 75 (1947).

United States v. Paradise, 480 U.S. 149 (1987).

United States Civil Service Commission v. National Association of Letter Carriers, 413 U.S. 548 (1973).

———. 2014a. "Harassment." www.eeoc.gov/laws/types/harassment.cfm (accessed February 27, 2014).

———. 2014b. "Facts About Sexual Harassment." www.eeoc.gov/eeoc/publications/fs-sex.cfm (accessed February 27, 2014).

U.S. Merit Systems Protection Board. 2010. Whistleblower Protections for Federal Employees: A Report to the President and the Congress of the United States (September), pp. 51–52.

U.S. Office of Special Counsel. 2005a. "Political Activity and the Federal Employee." www.osc.gov/documents/hatchact/ha_fed.pdf (accessed June 17, 2015).

———. 2005b. "Political Activity and the State and Local Employee." www.osc.gov/documents/hatchact/ha_sta.pdf (accessed February 4, 2014).

———. 2014. "Federal Employee Violates Hatch Act Through Twitter." https://osc.gov/News/pr14_03.pdf (accessed June 18, 2015).

University of California Regents v. Bakke, 438 U.S. 265 (1978).

Wards Cove Packing Co. v. Atonio, 490 U.S. 642 (1989).

Wygant v. Jackson Board of Education, 476 U.S. 267 (1986).

Yamada, David C. 2000. "The Phenomenon of 'Workplace Bullying' and the Need for Status-Blind Hostile Work Environment Protection." *Georgetown Law Journal* 88 (3): 475–536.

26 U.S.C. § 501 Exempt from Tax on Corporations.

4 Management–Employee–Citizen Relations

Learning Objectives

- Introduce the history of unionization for public and private sector employees.
- Introduce unionization rates and rationales pro and con.
- Explain collective bargaining processes and objectives.
- Discuss negotiation styles, including adversarial and collaborative approaches.

Most people would describe labor relations as confrontational, adversarial, and unpleasant. We tend to envision smoke-filled rooms where angry men face each other across a table. They are inclined to take unreasonable positions and question the opposing side's integrity and parentage. This image, reflective of a largely bygone era, is less and less in evidence in the public service today. Nonetheless, unions are widely perceived to be difficult to work with, inclined to challenge any kind of managerial action taken to discipline employees, and nearly always opposed to changes in the workplace that will improve productivity. Likewise, on too many occasions, managers have proven to be everything the unions want to fight—engaging in unilateral adverse actions, practicing favoritism, or according arbitrary and unfair treatment to their employees. Thus, on occasion, both labor and management in government and nonprofit settings play to the stereotype of bitter enemies battling over control of employees and influence regarding the work of the organization. It is indeed true that conflict can be useful as a means to clarify problems, develop and articulate contrasting views, and establish group unity around shared meaning (Coser 1956; Fisher and Ury 1983). However, it is likewise true that unmanaged conflict, when unaddressed by conflict resolution processes, can be unproductive, damage essential workplace relationships, and lead to manifest inefficiency and public opprobrium.

Discussions about the relative health of labor unions in the U.S. echo Mark Twain's quip, "The report of my death was an exaggeration" (Twain 1897). In recent decades, membership in labor unions has declined considerably, and, as a consequence, some commentators have predicted the end of organized labor (Engvall 1995). However, many employees continue to organize and seek representation in their dealings with employers. The traditional rationales for labor organization—improved salaries and more healthful and secure working conditions—are still significant factors for many employees. Moreover, in the current era of public sector reform and downsizing, public employees increasingly seek a stronger voice in the transformation of their workplace. Through this vehicle, public employees add their input along with the many competing interests lobbying state and local government officials for a share of public resources. Finally, one of the basic reasons for employees to organize is to gain protection from unjust decisions by management. As much as we would like to believe that all managers are well trained, well intentioned, and competent, far too many exercise poor judgment or operate outside organizational policy.

The Rise and Fall of Union Membership

Probably the most significant contribution to the decline in union membership has been the change in the structure of the U.S. economy in recent decades (Kochan, Katz, and McKersie 1986). When manufacturing plants dominated the economies of cities, large groups of employees could be organized with relative ease. Factories were often dangerous places, where labor was often viewed as merely a necessary cost of production. Very often, employees needed someone to represent their interests to factory owners, whose actions appeared arbitrary and uncaring in many cases. During the early stages of the labor movement, the employees in question were often poorly educated and unskilled and largely had limited ability to relocate for other work. Today, many of these conditions have changed, owing in part to previous union activity but also because of government regulation of the workplace with respect to health and safety and prohibitions on illegal discrimination (Nelson 1997).

Demands for better wages and working conditions, once the battle cry of the union movement, have often been met or guaranteed through labor law and regulation. In a good many respects, government, through labor laws and employer regulations, has become somewhat of a substitute for unions. Wages and hours have improved and become standardized to an extent, through federal laws such as the Fair Labor Standards Act. Safety and health concerns have been mitigated through improvements in the workplace mandated by law and enforcement by federal, state, and local government regulators. The economy has shifted to a service orientation that features a strong preference for information-intensive, knowledge-based jobs. Workers are more geographically dispersed, and hence more difficult to organize. A spirit of union solidarity, or a common belief in a union cause, is lacking in the contemporary setting, and unions are simply not as popular with the general public as they were decades ago. Farber (1990) notes such reasons for the decline of unions and adds that there is an increase in employer resistance to unionization resulting from heightened market competitiveness. He notes as well that news stories about union corruption and the involvement of union money in political campaigns have negatively affected public perceptions of unions.

Because labor law treats public and private sector employees differently, both nonprofit and for-profit organizations should be considered the 'private sector' for the purposes of discussion in this chapter. In the private sector, union membership, as a proportion of overall sectoral employment, has declined in recent years. According to the BLS, 7.3 million private sector employees belong to unions, compared with 7.2 million public sector union members (U.S. Department of Labor, Bureau of Labor Statistics 2014a, p. 2). However, in comparison with overall employment levels (with private sector employment being far greater in aggregate), public sector employees are unionized in greater proportion than are private sector employees. As Exhibit 4.1 demonstrates, unionization rates (or density) in the public sector were 36.7 percent in 1983, compared with 16.3 percent for the rate of unionization in the private sector in that year (Hirsch and Macpherson 2014). By 2013, public sector union membership density, though decreasing slightly to 35.3 percent, still exceeded that of the private sector at 6.7 percent almost fivefold.

Within the public sector, statistics archived by Hirsch and MacPherson (2014) illustrate some variation, as depicted in Exhibit 4.2. In 1983, postal employees unionized at a rate of 74.2 percent, compared with all other federal employees at 19.4 percent. Local employees, in cities, counties, and special districts, unionized at the rate of 42.2 percent of total employed, whereas state workers unionized at a rate of 28.2 percent. By 2013, nearly all categories of public employees registered slight declines, while still being higher in proportion compared with private sector workers, excepting state employees. In 2013, union membership among postal employees dropped to 62.7 percent, which represented a far greater decline than that of other federal workers (17.8 percent). Even local employees declined slightly as a proportion of the total employed workforce at that level to 40.8 percent. However, state employee unionization density grew slightly to 30.9 percent.

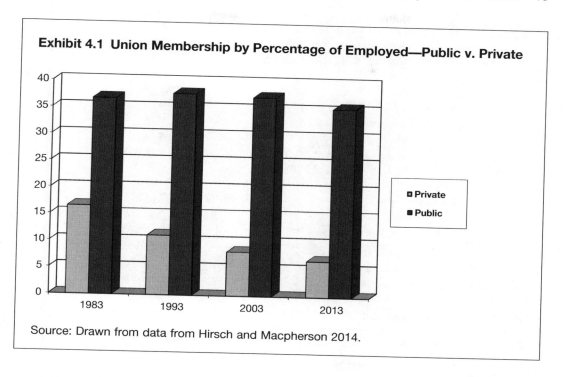

Exhibit 4.1 Union Membership by Percentage of Employed—Public v. Private

Source: Drawn from data from Hirsch and Macpherson 2014.

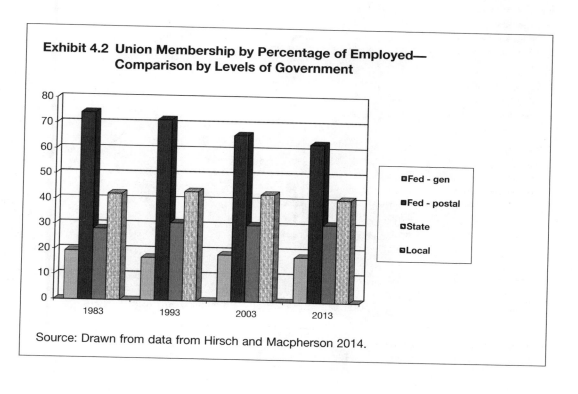

Exhibit 4.2 Union Membership by Percentage of Employed— Comparison by Levels of Government

Source: Drawn from data from Hirsch and Macpherson 2014.

Age, gender, race, and type of job all play a role in the decision as to whether to join or not to join unions. In general, minority employees are more likely to be union members than are nonminority workers in the federal government (Rubin 2011), but there are noteworthy differences in unionization rates between different minority groups, as illustrated in Exhibit 4.3. The percentage of employees who belong to unions increases with age, with those 55–64 years of age having the highest percentage of membership in unions. More men are members of unions than are women. An in-depth review of the BLS report shows that men, across ethnic/race categories, are generally more likely to be members of unions than are women, except for Asian men (U.S. Department of Labor, Bureau of Labor Statistics 2014a, Table 1). Although both Hispanic men and women have the lowest aggregate percentage of membership in unions at 9.4 percent, Asian men unionize at 8.9 percent, compared with Asian women at 9.9 percent in 2013. Black men had the greatest percentage of union membership (14.8 percent). The occupational category of farming, forestry, and fishing had the lowest percentage of union members, followed by the technical/sales and managerial/professional categories. Public employees had the highest rate of union membership. The reasons behind union membership in each category deserve further research attention.

Exhibit 4.3 Percentage of Union Members, by Selected Characteristics: 2013

Characteristic	Percent of Total Number with this Characteristic who are Union Members
Age: 16–24	4.2
Age: 25–34	9.8
Age: 35–44	12.5
Age: 45–54	14.0
Age: 55–64	14.3
Sex: women	10.5
Sex: men	11.9
Race: Hispanic	9.4
Race: White	11.0
Race: Black	13.6
Part-time workers	6.0
Full-time workers	12.5
Occupation:	
– Farming, forestry, fishing	2.1
– Sales and office occupations	6.6
– Management	4.1
– Community and social service	16.0
– Education, training & library	35.3
– Transportation	16.6
Sector:	
– Private	6.7
– Public	35.3

Source: U.S. Department of Labor, Bureau of Labor Statistics 2014a.

Why Employees Join Unions

Employees likely weigh the cost of joining unions against the benefits. The greatest benefits for most employees are economic—namely, the prospect of higher salaries and improved fringe benefits and greater safety provisions in the workplace achieved through collective bargaining (Fossum 1991). Unions also offer the employee greater job security benefits through bargaining for grievance procedures that allow the employee to have a voice in actions taken against him or her and to receive professional representation during these procedures (Webb and Webb 1965). Some people enjoy the social benefits of joining with others to improve working conditions and participate in social association with the group. Unions offer employees the opportunity to engage at many levels and attain leadership skills by rising through union ranks. Finally, public employees are also attracted to unions by political benefits, with the opportunity to influence the political environment in which they work (Olson 1971, p. 68).

Public unions often form political action arms or political action committees (PACs) to influence the political process. Unions employ professional lobbyists who work with Congress, with state legislatures, and with local governments to advocate for favorable legislation and administrative regulations in the union membership's interest. Many large unions conduct research and provide information on documented methods for improving working conditions. Public sector unions may also influence public policy by organizing in cooperation with specialized client groups that are served by government agencies (Devinatz and Kennedy 1995; Johnston 1994, p. 28). In addition, union membership may provide the opportunity to exercise political power within one's own agency through participation in the collective bargaining process. Some employees may seek influence in the policies and procedures of the organization, or in the terms and conditions of employment. Rubin (2011) found that, when federal employees feel management is fair, they are less likely to join a union; however, if they sense unfairness, they favor union representation.

In contrast to the benefits of union membership, there are also noteworthy costs. Again, the greatest cost in the minds of most employees is economic—namely, the union dues to be paid. Dues and various fees associated with representation may exceed $1,000 per year for many public sector employees, and members might be expected to pay dues to national, state, and local organizations simultaneously. In addition to dues, members may be asked to pay into a PAC as a vehicle for contributing to political campaigns. Another economic consideration is the cost to each employee if an unresolved dispute arises between management and labor. Picketing can involve extra time, contract impasses can postpone wage increases, and even work stoppages (and paycheck stoppages) are possible when unions and management hit an impasse in negotiations. Union membership can have social and political costs as well. Some employees may perceive a loss of personal identity within a union, some do not like unions per se, and some might prefer to handle their employment issues themselves, rather than having a union negotiate on behalf of their bargaining unit. In some states, employees are required to pay union dues (or a service charge to the union), even if they do not wish to belong to a union.

Finally, many employers deal with their own employees somewhat differently when a union is involved. Relationships can become strained when unions and employers come into dispute over issues for which resolution is difficult, and an atmosphere of conflict and adversarialism sometimes pervades the unionized workplace, to the detriment of all concerned (Moe 2009).

A Short History of Labor Relations

Although the demise of unions tends to be exaggerated, the work environment is indeed changing in ways that make public sector unions' goals and objectives more difficult to attain today than was true in the past. Employers, employees, and their representatives are facing a shift away from manufacturing toward service provision, information exchange, and technology-intensive enterprises and associated jobs. Increased global competition and heightened consumer expectations require higher quality and lower costs in virtually all sectors of the economy, including governmental enterprises. As discussed in Chapter 1, in the contemporary U.S. workforce, many workers are more highly educated than was the case in the past, and they desire more individual input into management decisions. Unions and employers have been somewhat resistant to adjust to these changes, and they too often continue to conduct labor relations largely under the adversarial model established in far different circumstances, more than seventy years ago. Dramatic changes in the marketplace and work environment are not limited to the private sector: the public sector work environment is equally affected. Citizens today demand more services for their tax dollars, even while they endorse legislation and support public referenda to decrease the taxes received by their governments. Public services are often delivered through contracts with private sector entities, and intergovernmental competition grows in response to citizen demands for lower taxes and more services—often leading to smaller local government workforces.

Higher-level government officials often act unilaterally to address these problems, while public employees with arguably the greatest direct knowledge about public services are too often left out of the discussion. Management and labor still too often display suspicion and distrust in their relations. This adversarial framing of labor relations is associated with the industrial revolution and later national global economic primacy in the 1950s and 1960s. Although once a reasonable approach, adversarial employee relations may be particularly counterproductive, as today's employers and employees in both the public and private sectors face the challenges of the global economy and the modern, progressively knowledge-driven workplace (Patton 1994).

As early as the 1860s, national organizations of labor began to coalesce in the United States, and the first major coalition, the Knights of Labor, was established in 1869 (Patton 1996). This coalition emphasized political action, education, and arbitration to replace increasingly common strikes. The Knights of Labor was a collection of many different, often-competing trades and occupations, a fact that led to its ultimate demise in the 1890s. The American Federation of Labor (AFL) was organized by a group of craft unions in 1886 and used collective bargaining to improve the working conditions of its membership of skilled workers. Rapid industrialization in the United States created large numbers of unskilled or semi-skilled industrial workers. In 1938, unions composed of these workers formed the Congress of Industrial Organizations (CIO).

As the American economy grew rapidly after the end of World War II, unionism reached a peak when more than one-third of the nonagricultural American workforce belonged to unions. Over time, it became clear that competition between the two major labor organizations hampered the union movement, and the AFL–CIO was created in 1955 (Paradis and Paradis 1983). The AFL–CIO represents a large number of unions and more than 12.5 million workers (AFL–CIO 2014). In 2005, four rather large unions, including the Teamsters and the Service Employees International Union, broke away from the AFL–CIO and formed the *Change to Win Alliance*. Exhibits 4.4 and 4.5 provide an overview of the specific unions affiliated under the respective umbrellas of either the AFL–CIO or the Alliance. The percentage of employees in the nation's workforce belonging to unions has steadily declined, from a peak of 35.5 percent in 1945 to only 11.3 percent of total employment in 2013 (U.S. Department of Labor, Bureau of Labor Statistics 2014b; Hirsch and Macpherson 2014).

The Legal Environment of Unions

From the earliest days of the conspiracy and anti-trust doctrines, existing laws and court rulings suppressed union organizing in the U.S. Employers used the legal doctrine of *criminal conspiracy* to

Exhibit 4.4 Selection of AFL–CIO Unions

More than fifty unions are under the AFL–CIO umbrella: public sector employees potentially join the following:

- Air Line Pilots Association (ALPA)
- Amalgamated Transit Union (ATU)
- American Federation of Government Employees (AFGE)
- American Federation of School Administrators (AFSA)
- American Federation of State, County and Municipal Employees (AFSCME)
- American Federation of Teachers (AFT)
- American Postal Workers Union (APWU)
- California School Employees Association (CSEA)
- Communications Workers of America (CWA)
- International Association of Bridge, Structural, Ornamental and Reinforcing Iron Workers (Ironworkers)
- International Association of Fire Fighters (IAFF)
- International Association of Machinists and Aerospace Workers (IAM)
- Transportation Communications International Union/IAM (TCU/IAM)
- International Brotherhood of Electrical Workers (IBEW)
- International Federation of Professional and Technical Engineers (IFPTE)
- International Union of Operating Engineers (IUOE)
- International Union of Police Associations (IUPA)
- Marine Engineers' Beneficial Association (MEBA)
- National Air Traffic Controllers Association (NATCA)
- National Association of Letter Carriers (NALC)
- National Nurses United (NNU)
- National Postal Mail Handlers Union (NPMHU)
- Office and Professional Employees International Union (OPEIU)
- Professional Aviation Safety Specialists (PASS)
- Utility Workers Union of America (UWUA)

Source: AFL–CIO 2014.

Exhibit 4.5 Change to Win Coalition

- International Brotherhood of Teamsters (IBT): www.teamsters.org
- Service Employees International Union (SEIU): www.seiu.org
- United Farm Workers of America (UFW): www.ufw.org
- United Food and Commercial Workers International Union (UFCW): www.ufcw.org

Source: www.changetowin.org/ (accessed March 21, 2014).

prevent employees from striking. Collective action that harmed others was considered unlawful at that time, and the courts generally prohibited strikes on these grounds (Patton 1998). By the middle of the nineteenth century, however, the conspiracy doctrine began to falter, as judges ruled that the objectives of the collective activity had to be explicitly forbidden by law for an action to be considered an unlawful conspiracy. In *Commonwealth v. Hunt* (1842), the Massachusetts Supreme Court ruled in favor of shoemakers who had struck over the hiring of nonunion shoemakers. In that case, the court ruled that the strike had no illegal purpose and was, therefore, not an unlawful conspiracy. The anti-trust approach emerged in the early twentieth century, when the U.S. Supreme Court sided with business owners in the famous *Danbury Hatters Case*, arguing that unions impeded commerce (*Loewe v. Lawlor* 1908). During this time, organized labor had scant legal protection, and many businesses engaged in 'union-busting' practices to try to keep employees from organizing. With industrial relations weighted so heavily on the side of the employer, labor unrest increased. Federal and state legislatures began to look at the balance of power between labor and employer and nervously observed labor-supported social movements gaining ground worldwide. The Great Depression brought further labor unrest, along with nationwide calls for laws to limit the power of businesses to impede employee organization.

Shortly after the *Loewe v. Lawlor* decision (1908), the legal environment began a shift in favor of organized labor. A series of noteworthy federal statutes significantly altered the labor-management relationship in the U.S. and opened the door to a rapid increase in the ranks of organized labor. In 1912, Congress passed the Lloyd–Lafollette Act allowing some federal workers the right to form and join unions, with the proviso that the union would not be permitted to strike against the U.S. government. The Railway Labor Act (1926) gave railway workers the right to organize into unions and engage in collective bargaining and, when negotiations broke down, even the right to strike. The Norris–LaGuardia Act (1932) limited the ability to stop collective labor actions by court injunctions and prohibited employers from entering into agreements with employees where workers agree to refrain from joining a union as a condition of employment (known as yellow-dog contracts). The most important piece of labor legislation in the history of the United States was the National Labor Relations Act (1935; NLRA), also known as the Wagner Act. The NLRA gave all private sector, nonagricultural employees the right to organize and engage in collective bargaining and the right to strike. The Wagner Act did not apply to public employees, although many of its provisions have been adopted in state labor laws, and the decisions of the NLRB are commonly used as precedent in public sector labor relations.

Wagner Act (NLRA)

The NLRA established the NLRB to administer the provisions of the act. It defined employees as nonsupervisory and nonmanagerial workers, prohibited the use of unfair labor practices for management, and established the scope of bargaining as wages, hours of employment, or other conditions of employment. The NLRA set guidelines for the determination of employee bargaining units within an organization and made provision for the right of election of exclusive employee representatives for bargaining units. The Act established the following as unfair labor practices for management:

- interfering with the right to organize, bargain collectively, or engage in collective action;
- interfering with any labor organization or influencing employees to join or not join a particular labor union;

- refusing to bargain in good faith with the elected representative of each bargaining unit;
- discriminating against any employee because of any union-related action under the NLRA.

The Wagner Act redefined the balance of power away from management and reinforced the bargaining position of labor. As a result, labor organizing activity and collective bargaining expanded: by 1946, more than 50,000 collective bargaining agreements were in place across the nation (Patton 1998). The Act decreased strikes over union organizing, but likely had the effect of increasing strikes over compensation and working conditions (Taylor and Whitney 1983).

Taft–Hartley Act

Because of the increase in strikes and the fear that labor unrest might harm the national economy, Congress enacted the Labor Management Relations Act (1947), which was popularly known as the Taft–Hartley Act. Taft–Hartley was intended to bring balance into labor relations by banning certain unfair labor practices by *unions*, protecting the rights of employees and employers vis-à-vis unions, and setting guidelines for the peaceful resolution of strikes(particularly those involving national security (Taylor and Whitney 1983, pp. 229–235). The labor unions were prohibited from the following specific actions:

- restraining or coercing employees in the exercise of their collective bargaining rights;
- causing an employer to discriminate against an employee to affect union membership;
- not bargaining in good faith with employers;
- calling some types of strike *boycotts*, if the purpose of the job action was to force an employer to join a labor or employer organization or stop dealings with another employer (*secondary boycott*); compel recognition as the exclusive bargaining agent without NLRB certification; or compel an employer to assign particular work assignments;
- charging excessive or discriminatory union dues;
- attempting to cause an employer to pay for services not actually rendered by the union (referred to as *featherbedding*).

The Taft–Hartley Act prohibited *closed shops*, where all workers have to be union members at the time they are hired. Taft–Hartley allowed states to pass labor laws related to union security known as *right-to-work laws*, preventing *union shop* provisions in labor contracts requiring employees to be union members to keep their jobs. The Act permitted payroll dues check-off deductions for union dues only if the employee authorizes the deduction in writing. Employees were also given the right to present grievances directly to the employer, without the union deciding on the merit of the grievance. The Taft–Hartley Act also allowed employers to express their opinions regarding union representation to their employees, so long as they did not attempt to interfere with union representation elections by threatening reprisals or promising benefits. Employers could also call for representation elections, refuse to bargain with supervisors' unions, and file unfair labor practices complaints against unions with the NLRB. Finally, the Taft–Hartley Act was also designed to protect national security. If the U.S. president determines that a strike seriously threatens national health or safety, the strike could be suspended for up to 80 days. This 'cooling-off period' is designed to protect the public and allow time to mediate a settlement. The Act also established the Federal Mediation and Conciliation Service (FMCS) to help employers and unions resolve disputes without resorting to strikes, and established steps to keep industries operating when strikes created national emergencies (Taylor and Whitney 1983).

Public Sector Labor Relations

Public employees were excluded from the two important labor relations statutes enacted into law in the 1930s and 1940s (Hunt 1988, p. 117). The reasons for their exclusion were primarily legal. In the early decades of the twentieth century, the federal government believed it was severely limited in its power to regulate activities occurring in the states (Tenth Amendment), and the courts ruled that public employees could be prohibited from joining unions under the doctrine of sovereignty. The argument went something like this: despite the right of employees to freely associate, there was no constitutional right to government employment, and the government's need (or the public interest) to maintain public services without interference outweighed the employees' right to associate (Hanslowe 1985, pp. 33–35). This line of argument was widely accepted; Calvin Coolidge was propelled into the national spotlight in 1919, when he took a strong stand as governor of Massachusetts against striking Boston police and declared an absolute moratorium on the rights of public safety personnel to strike. Coolidge and his supporters believed public sector unions would interfere with the sovereign right of governments to represent the people in formulating and implementing public policy. Collective action by public unions might, in theory, place undue pressure on public policy decisions, leaving citizens with relatively little voice. As discussed in Chapter 4 and its attendant reading, public employees were seen as enjoying the 'privilege' of working for government and had no property rights to their jobs. Further, public employees were involved in police and fire protection activities: any strike by public employees could directly endanger the public safety of all citizens.

In reality, the government in its sovereign power can allow for discussions with its employees over working conditions and can likewise bargain collectively with employee representatives. The government is not compelled to agree to union demands nor forced to take any actions as a result of collective bargaining. The governing body must always approve and place into statute or ordinance any agreements arrived at through the bargaining process. Today, the sovereignty doctrine is no longer used as a legal prohibition against union organizing in the public sector.

No nationwide labor relations law governs the union activities of public sector unions, nor have labor organizing activities been protected by law. In fact, they are still prohibited in some areas of the country. In this regard, President Kennedy issued E.O. 10988, entitled "Employee-Management Cooperation in the Federal Sector" to allow federal workers limited rights to organize and bargain. This initial step was followed by additional related executive orders issued by Presidents Nixon (Executive Order 11491) and Ford (Executive Order 11838). In 1978, Congress passed the Civil Service Reform Act, a statute that replaced these executive orders and established a *limited right to organize and collectively bargain* for federal workers as a matter of federal statutory law.

The landscape for federal labor relations evolved even further under President Clinton with the issuance of Executive Order 12871 establishing the National Partnership Council, with the goal of reducing the adversarial elements of labor relations and increasing the collaborative aspects of labor relations. However, President George W. Bush summarily dissolved the Council with his issuance of Executive Order 13202 and further weakened the fledgling federal workforce labor movement with a series of administrative actions exempting some types of employee from collective bargaining (Ferris and Hyde 2004; Thompson 2007; Tobias 2004). Generally speaking, federal employee unions are restricted in their scope of bargaining, being largely prohibited from bargaining over wages and benefits, and they are universally prohibited from engaging in strikes. Labor disputes that inevitably arise are settled with the help of the FMCS or the Federal Impasse Panel.

Exhibit 4.6 State Collective Bargaining Practices

States allowing some form of bargaining or conference for state employees

Alaska, California, Colorado, Connecticut, Delaware, Florida, Hawaii, Illinois, Iowa, Kansas, Maine, Maryland, Massachusetts, Michigan, Minnesota, Missouri, Montana, Nebraska, New Hampshire, New Jersey, New Mexico, New York, North Dakota, Ohio, Oregon, Pennsylvania, Rhode Island, South Dakota, Vermont, Washington, West Virginia

States allowing some form of bargaining for local government employees

Alabama, Alaska, California, Connecticut, Delaware, Florida, Hawaii, Illinois, Iowa, Kansas, Maine, Maryland, Massachusetts, Michigan, Minnesota, Missouri, Montana, Nebraska, Nevada, New Hampshire, New Jersey, New Mexico, New York, North Dakota, Ohio, Oklahoma, Oregon, Pennsylvania, Rhode Island, South Dakota, Vermont, Washington, West Virginia

States allowing some form of bargaining for Police (P), Firefighters (F), or Teachers (T)

Alabama (P, F, T), Alaska (P, F, T), California (P, F, T), Connecticut (P, F, T), Delaware (P, F, T), Florida (P, F, T), Georgia (F), Hawaii (P, F, T), Idaho (F, T), Illinois (P, F, T), Indiana (T), Iowa (P, F, T), Kansas (P, F, T), Kentucky (P, F), Maine (P, F, T), Maryland (T, P), Massachusetts (P, F, T), Michigan (P, F, T), Minnesota (P, F, T), Missouri (P, T, F), Montana (P, F, T), Nebraska (P, F, T), Nevada (P, F, T), New Hampshire (P, F, T), New Jersey (P, F, T), New Mexico (P, F, T), New York (P, F, T), North Dakota (P, F, T), Ohio (P, F, T), Oklahoma (P, F, T), Oregon (P, F, T), Pennsylvania (P, F, T), Rhode Island (P, F, T), South Dakota (P, F, T), Texas (P, F), Utah (T), Vermont (P, F, T), Washington (P, F, T), West Virginia (P, F, T), Wisconsin (P, F, T), Wyoming (F)

States not allowing public sector bargaining

Arizona, Arkansas, Louisiana, Mississippi, North Carolina, Oklahoma, South Carolina, Tennessee, Virginia, Wisconsin

Source: Adapted from Kearney and Mareschal 2014, Table 2.2 "Bargaining Status, Political Ideology, and Union Density, 2013", pp. 31–33.

The Case of State and Local Government

State and local government workers are faced with a confusing mixture of labor relations laws, varying from state to state (Kearney and Mareschal 2014, pp. 31–33). Only thirty-one states require state and local governments to bargain with legitimate employee representatives; thirty-seven states explicitly prohibit strikes by their employees (p. 244). Some states allow some types of employee to bargain collectively (primarily teachers and firefighters) by means of enabling legislation for each specific group, but prohibit other public workers from exercising the same rights in the absence of such legislation. Exhibit 4.6 shows the states that allow collective bargaining (or 'meet and confer' arrangements) for public employees, and those that limit the right of public workers to bargain collectively (Kearney and Mareschal 2014, pp. 31–33).

The true scope of collective bargaining activity in the states and local governments is difficult to ascertain, given that employees can be covered by collective bargaining agreements even when they are not formal members of the relevant union. As Exhibits 4.7 and 4.8 suggest, there are a large number of employees who benefit from union activity, although they do not participate as members. This is true of both public and private sector workers.

As Richard Kearney and Patrice Mareschal argue in the following excerpt from their book, the public sector unions of today face fiscal, structural, public policy, and strategic challenges. The following passage focuses upon the structural challenges that they identify, as these issues echo many of the trends identified in this book. As you read this passage, keep the following questions in mind:

1. How does the trend toward contracting and privatization affect unions?
2. What challenges and opportunities derive from the shifting demographics in the workplace?
3. What are the implications of emerging technologies for the unions in the public sector workplace?

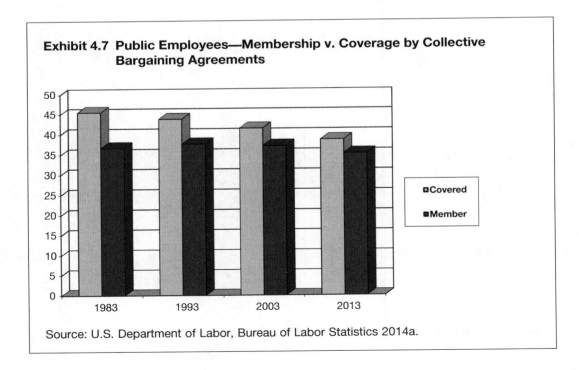

Exhibit 4.7 Public Employees—Membership v. Coverage by Collective Bargaining Agreements

Source: U.S. Department of Labor, Bureau of Labor Statistics 2014a.

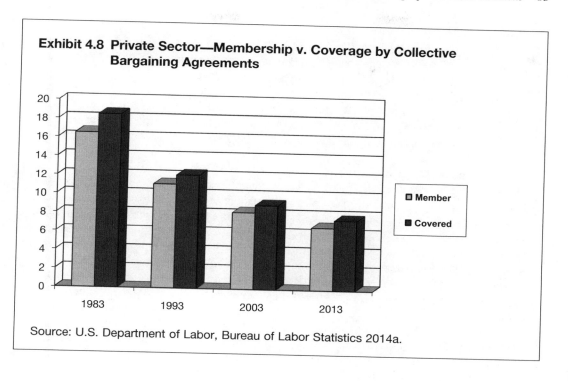

Exhibit 4.8 Private Sector—Membership v. Coverage by Collective Bargaining Agreements

Source: U.S. Department of Labor, Bureau of Labor Statistics 2014a.

Excerpt 4.1 Challenges for Public Employee Unions: Structural Challenges

Like the business sector, the public sector is experiencing new global economic, political, and social forces. Among the most critical of these forces for public employees and their unions are technological change, the attractions of a market economy that has produced a resource shift from government to the private sector, and the new demographics of the workforce.

Public employee unions enjoyed some of their greatest early success in organizing blue-collar and office workers who discharged job tasks that essentially replicated those in the private sector. Gradually, however, technological innovations have made it increasingly feasible to replace such employees with machines or software. The character of much government work (e.g., police and fire protection, classroom teaching, and social service casework) makes technological substitution for labor problematic. But new technology and software have supplanted some public employees, in areas such as printing and production, HR and financial, data entry, and sanitation collection. Some governments have outsourced data entry, call centers, and other mundane activities to India and other countries. There are many other examples of technologically driven attrition, and additional ones will emerge. For unions to maintain their levels of membership and financial resources, members displaced by technology must in turn be replaced by signing up new members or establishing new bargaining units for previously nonrepresented workers.

A second structural threat to unions is a shift in ownership, management, financing, or control of public services from government to the private economy. A multiplicity of forces, including tax resistance, negative public opinion toward government, public worship of the private marketplace, and the NPM movement, are conspiring to transfer government functions and activities to the private and nonprofit sectors. These powerful forces, augmented by the common perspective that, at least in theory, nearly all of the work of government could be accomplished by private and nonprofit service providers, represent a serious threat to public employee unions.

The negative effects of privatization and outsourcing on public employee unions are obvious. Privatization depresses public employment and union membership. Many of the jobs being outsourced are those of direct service providers such as counselors, caseworkers, laborers, and corrections officers. Other common examples of contracting out are water services and sanitation. As a result, the relative proportion of predominantly nonunion professional and administrative positions is growing. Privatization's effects are registered with every public job lost to a private or nonprofit provider. For example, several states have turned over various components of welfare program administration to private contractors, placing at risk an estimated quarter of a million government social service jobs. In the embattled public education community, thousands of teaching jobs have been lost to private schools as voucher plans are adopted. Despite such general affection for privatization, there is little evidence of genuine cost savings. For instance, a recent meta-analysis of 38 studies on water provision and solid waste collection services "does not reveal a systematic relationship between cost savings and private production" (Bel, Fageda, and Warner 2010).

A third structural problem is a human capital challenge. It is common knowledge that the U.S. labor force is becoming increasingly female, older, Latino, African American, Asian, and foreign-born, and these trends are projected to extend into the foreseeable future. Some of these new workers require special accommodations by employers and unions. The culture of work is undergoing dramatic change, with important implications for interpersonal, interorganizational, and supervisor–subordinate relations.

Unions are struggling to clearly define their role in attracting and representing this socially diverse workforce. Their organizational health and well-being depend greatly on how effectively they respond to employment issues associated with demographic and sociocultural changes in the labor force. To remain viable organizations, unions must convince the new workforce that they can effectively represent the interests and concerns and job-related needs of these workers.

As demonstrated by largely unsuccessful efforts to organize Southern workers and recruit new members from the expanding information technology (IT) sector, the unions' record is mixed. In general, out of necessity, public sector unions have chalked up a much better record of incorporating women and minorities into union affairs and leadership positions than private sector unions. The American Federation of State, County, and Municipal Employees (AFSCME), the National Education Association (NEA), the American Federation of Teachers (AFT), and SEIU report substantial numbers of women in their ranks, including top leadership positions. AFSCME has aggressively pursued discrimination complaints and filed lawsuits to force employers to adopt comparable worth policies. Public employee unions have also promoted and bargained for more flexible and family-friendly benefits.

Research indicates that nonunion workers in government tend to exhibit an affinity for collective representation, and most would join a union if they could. Pro-union sentiment is most pronounced among African American and Latino workers; women's desire for unionization is about the same as that of men. It would seem, then, that in those unorganized public jurisdictions in which the legal environment permits union recognition and collective bargaining, women and minorities are waiting for unions to provide them with tangible and compelling reasons to join. Among the possible avenues for unions to demonstrate their relevance to these workers is through negotiated benefits such as health-care and wellness programs, family-friendly benefits, specialized training and education opportunities, purchase discounts, property and vehicle insurance, and even favorable rates on union-sponsored credit cards.

As if these other structural challenges were not daunting enough, the baby-boom retirement bulge presents another. With an increasing proportion of today's baby boomers eligible for retirement with each passing year, unions are staring in the teeth of a significant loss of staunch union advocates and leaders. The need to turn their unwavering attention to young labor force entrants is patently obvious.

Excerpt Reference

Bel, Germá, Xavier Fageda, and Mildred E. Warner. 2010. "Is Private Production of Public Services Cheaper than Public Production? A Meta-Regression Analysis of Solid Waste and Water Services." *Journal of Policy Analysis and Management* 29(3): 553–577.

Source: Richard C. Kearney and Patrice M. Mareschal 2014. *Labor Relations in the Public Sector*, 5th ed., 344–353. New York: CRC Press.

Public versus Private Sector Labor Relations

The public sector labor relations model has closely followed the private sector model, although there are some quite important economic, legal, and political differences between the two. Shafritz et al. (1992, pp. 322–326) describe four such important features of private sector labor relations that differ from those of the public sector.

1. The parties to collective bargaining are more or less equal in the private sector.
2. Private companies and unions are constrained by market forces, whereas public sector labor relations are dominated by politics.
3. Economic issues are distributive in the private sector—in other words, wages, capital, and profits all come from the firm's earnings, and the issue is how these earnings are distributed. A gain by the union usually means a loss in the amount distributed to investment or profits.
4. In the private sector, economic disputes can be settled by strikes, lockouts, and other job actions, whereas these labor actions are illegal under most circumstances in the public sector.

These differences bring into question the appropriateness and effectiveness of traditional forms of collective bargaining in the public sector. Most public sector labor laws place management and labor in unequal positions. The government is not neutral in its decisions about public sector labor relations:

government is the employer in the public sector and defines its own provisions for labor relations. Government defines the scope of bargaining, identifies management rights, and determines the methods of dispute resolution to be employed. It can outlaw strikes and specify what it considers unfair labor practices. By definition, government can define its labor relations policy by law. In the federal government, unions cannot bargain over wages, hours, budgets, or management rights to operate. State and local labor relations laws often restrict the right of public employees to exercise many of the bargaining rights commonly found in the private sector. These laws limit which public employees have the right to bargain. For example, in some jurisdictions, firefighters can bargain, but police cannot. Teachers may be given the right to bargain, whereas university professors may be denied that right. State laws can limit what issues may be discussed, and what recourse may or may not be taken in the event of an impasse. Most states prohibit strikes by public employees.

The second difference noted is also significant. The government is not as susceptible to market forces as is the private sector, in that the economic power derived from employees organizing for collective action is not as significant to financial profitability in the public sector as it is in the private marketplace. In most cases, the absence of the right to strike removes the strongest potential economic weapon from public unions. Boycotts are seldom effective, because governments provide essential services and they operate as monopolies over public services. Picketing is sometimes an option in the public sector, but its impact is not economic as is the case in the private market. Instead, public actions such as picketing and demonstrations are most commonly used primarily for public relations and information dissemination purposes.

The public sector depends on tax dollars and voter support, not company earnings. When union demands are considered by public officials, the decision is not whether to direct more of the company's earnings to employee pay or benefits; instead, the decision may be whether to reduce the level of a government service or increase taxes. In difficult economic times, public employers have had to make the decision to reduce the number of public employees in order to continue to meet the payroll for the remaining employees. Unfortunately, police, firefighters, and teachers in districts, counties, and municipalities often comprise the larger categories of local government employees, and citizens are generally unwilling to sacrifice public safety or the quality of public education. In an environment where citizens tend to feel they are already paying too much in taxes, the decision to raise taxes to pay for employee raises is becoming less of an option for elected officials. The balance is often nearly impossible to negotiate. As one author aptly described the difference between public and private labor relations, "Collective bargaining in the private sector is about economics; in government, it is about politics" (Kearney 1992, p. 134).

The ultimate weapon of private sector unions is the strike, but, as noted, this weapon is usually not a viable option for most public employees in most of our states. In some cases, such as teacher unions, public officials have allowed a strike-like action, even if it was technically illegal, in order to promote labor peace. However, this occasional forbearance is no guarantee that technically illegal work stoppages will continue to go unpunished. The famous PATCO strike by air traffic controllers and President Reagan's termination of those workers taught a lasting lesson to public employees attempting to use the illegal strike as a tool of labor relations.

Without the right to strike, how do public sector unions have leverage in collective bargaining? What substitute for a strike could compel a legally sovereign government to address employee workplace issues? A source of power not available to private sector unions, but a potent tool for public sector unions, is the ability to influence the makeup of management in public office. Unions have been a strong lobbying force, both in influencing labor legislation and regulation in the public sector, and in contributing to the political campaigns of sympathetic candidates running for political office in local, state, and federal elections. Through this power to participate in elections and influence governmental decision-making, public sector unions have the ability to address employee workplace issues in a way that may be even more powerful than the traditional actions available to private sector unions.

Discrimination in Labor Relations

Most of us are aware that civil rights legislation has focused on the employment practices of public and private employers. Interestingly, the Civil Rights Act of 1964 and other laws since have also targeted labor unions in their efforts to eliminate discriminatory practices in the workplace. The Civil Rights Act of 1964 holds in part:

> (c) It shall be an unlawful employment practice for a labor organization: (1) to exclude or to expel from its membership, or otherwise to discriminate against, any individual because of his race, color, religion, sex, or national origin; (2) to limit, segregate, or classify its membership or applicants for membership, or to classify or fail or refuse to refer for employment any individual, in any way which would deprive or tend to deprive any individual of employment opportunities, or would limit such employment opportunities or otherwise adversely affect his status as an employee or as an applicant for employment, because of such individual's race, color, religion, sex, or national origin; or (3) to cause or attempt to cause an employer to discriminate against an individual in violation of this section.

Prohibitions against discrimination by labor unions illustrate the close linkage between labor unions and the workplace. Labor organizations cannot discriminate against their members or applicants for membership because of race, color, religion, sex, or national origin. They may not classify their membership by these criteria, nor limit employment opportunities based upon these protected classes. These restrictions apply to all common union practices such as negotiations and representation. In collective bargaining negotiations, unions cannot classify one of the protected groups for different benefits. Similarly, in the case of grievance or other forms of representation, a labor organization cannot fail to represent a member filing a grievance because of that person's race, color, religion, sex, or national origin.

Public Labor Organizations

Recall the union lists from Exhibits 4.4 and 4.5. There are many public sector labor organizations representing public employees at all levels of government. The federal government lists dozens of unions that represent federal workers, ranging from the National Association of Aeronautical Examiners to the West Point Elementary School Teachers Association (Center for Partnership and Labor-Management Relations 1997). Most of these unions are affiliated with the AFL–CIO. The largest public employee union is AFSCME. Part of the AFL–CIO coalition, AFSCME (2014) represents more than 1.6 million working or retired public employees. Another large public employee union is the high-profile American Federation of Government Employees, representing approximately 650,000 employees in 2014 (AFGE 2014). The National Treasury Employees Union has approximately 150,000 federal employees as members (NTEU 2014). By contrast, the entirety of the Change to Win (2014) alliance mentioned in a previous section is reported to exceed 5.5 million workers, including a significant number of public employees.

Union Certification and Recognition in the Public Sector

Most public jurisdictions have modeled their labor relations laws after the Wagner Act and the Taft–Hartley Act. Public labor laws or implementation policies usually contain guidelines or procedures for union certification and representation of employee bargaining units. When a group of employees seeks union representation, they must complete the certification process, which typically entails an election conducted by an independent, specialized public agency. The certification process formally begins when authorization cards are distributed to all employees in the proposed bargaining unit. These signature cards authorize a specific union to be the exclusive bargaining agent for that employee. These alone do not constitute an election for a union. Typically, at least 30 percent of the affected employees must sign the authorization cards before a recognition election can take place. If authorized, employees seeking representation petition the government body for a recognition election. That agency then designates the extent of the bargaining unit and conducts an election. A bargaining unit description determines who is eligible to join a prospective union and what the commonality of interests is for that group of employees, and denotes the principal groupings of employees within the unit by wages, skills, and working conditions. An election can be held with one or more unions competing for representation, along with the option for no union representation. The choice receiving the majority of votes wins the election. If no single choice receives a majority vote, a run-off election is held, with the majority electing the winner. In the event a union (or guild, association, brotherhood, etc.) is elected by a majority of employees in the bargaining unit, that particular employee organization becomes the exclusive bargaining agent, and management must bargain in good faith with that entity—*and only that entity*. Historically, just under 50 percent of elections result in employees selecting a union, and often such elections are decided by fewer than ten votes (Kearney 1992, p. 34).

As is the case with the National Labor Relations Act, state and local labor laws prohibit unfair labor practices by both management and unions during bargaining agent election campaigns. These laws also restrict other potentially biasing activities related to union certification elections. Both employees and employers are allowed to express their views and opinions regarding the election, so long as there are no threats of retribution made or promises of reward offered for voting a certain way in the election. Employers can inform employees of their opinion as to the costs and benefits offered by unions, and employees can advertise the expected benefits of union membership in their advocacy. Employers may restrict union organizers from contacting employees at the workplace, so long as reasonable access to employees is possible through advertisement or meetings away from the workplace, and equal treatment of other non-employees who may also desire access to employees at the work location or facility is provided. Employees may campaign at the workplace, but are restricted to times when they and other employees are not working and in locations away from work areas. In the same way that certification elections take place, employees may petition the NLRB to hold a *decertification* election. In these cases, employees may seek to discontinue having a union represent them in negotiations with management. According to data available from the NLRB Website (National Labor Relations Board 2014), there have been 6,175 petitions filed for decertification elections since fiscal year 2004. Of these, 3,035 elections occurred, and 61.98 percent were lost by the unions, resulting in decertification.

Collective Bargaining

Good Faith Bargaining

Under most state labor laws, the employer has a duty to bargain in good faith exclusively with a legally elected employee representative. The duty to bargain in good faith "requires active participation in negotiations with a sincere effort to reach an agreement" (Kearney 1992, p. 137). According to

D'Alba (1979), good faith bargaining means conducting negotiations under rules of fairness; these rules usually include these seven elements:

1. a time frame for beginning and conducting negotiations;
2. making information available that is relevant to negotiations;
3. not bypassing the official bargaining representatives by discussing bargaining issues with the other side rather than through the bargaining team;
4. not making unilateral changes in working conditions while negotiations are being conducted;
5. not engaging in a strike during negotiations (if allowed by law), and following formal procedures for impasse resolution;
6. willingness to put a negotiated agreement in writing and execute the agreement;
7. not engaging in insincere bargaining as demonstrated by delaying the bargaining process, failing to offer legitimate proposals or counterproposals, or refusing to make any concessions.

The exclusive bargaining representative has the right to negotiate a binding contract with management for employees in the bargaining unit over specific permissible issues, referred to as the scope of bargaining. Negotiations are normally permitted for rates of pay, wages, hours of employment, or other conventional conditions of employment. Collective bargaining in the public sector generally does not take the form of the traditional across-the-table, confrontational, stressful process; instead, it tends to be approached in an organized, professional way, with parties seeking to agree upon a contract that elected officials will be likely to endorse.

The Collective Bargaining Process

There are at least eleven commonly noted phases or processes in the cycle of labor negotiations: initiation, preparation, internal negotiations, informal discussions, preliminary negotiations, issue identification, problem solving, impasse resolution, settlement, ratification, and contract management.

Step 1: Initiation

In most public jurisdictions, legislation authorizing collective bargaining requires either party to a labor contract to notify the other party of their desire to open negotiations within a specific number of days prior to the expiration of the labor contract in current force. For example, a city ordinance may require the union and city officials to notify each other within 60 days prior to the expiration of the existing contract if either side intends to renegotiate. The NLRA requires a 60-day notice before the contract expires if either party wishes to open negotiations. This time frame allows the two sides sufficient time to prepare for negotiations.

Step 2: Preparation

The organization's long-term goals are the first consideration in negotiations for management and employees alike. Negotiations should be aimed toward satisfying shared goals for the organization. Tactical planning involves determining how negotiations will be conducted, what issues will be introduced into the negotiations, and what the desired objectives might be for each issue. The natural tendency to succumb to 'group think' when working in a setting of 'us versus them' negotiations demands caution. It is often helpful to have one or two people involved in tactical planning who can offer genuine insight into how the other bargaining team and their constituents will react to issues proposed for negotiations, prior to face-to-face bargaining.

Exhibit 4.9 Questions to Ask in Preparation for Negotiations

Administrative Arrangements

- What is the commitment of upper-level management to the bargaining process?
- How united is the governing body in supporting the bargaining effort?
- What human and time resources will be committed to the bargaining process?
- What style of bargaining is to be used? When would this style change during negotiations?
- Who will lead the negotiations?
- What personnel will be assigned to act as the bargaining team and advisors to the team?
- What is the reporting relationship to the governing bodies involved in making administrative decisions during the bargaining time period?
- How will tactical decisions be made throughout the bargaining period?
- What will be done in the event of job actions during negotiations or at impasse?
- Who should work with the media, and what should be said?

Issue Analysis

- What are the specific issues to be proposed for negotiation?
- What is the priority ranking for each issue?
- What are the current trends in the industry regarding this issue?
- What is the history of this issue in previous negotiations?
- What is the range of acceptable solutions for each issue?
- What are the costs and benefits across the range of acceptable solutions?
- Can contract language be prepared reflecting acceptable solutions to important issues?
- What are the acceptable and expected outcomes of negotiations for each issue?
- What is the alternative to negotiated settlement on each issue? Is it acceptable?

Understanding the Opposite Bargaining Team

- Who will be on the negotiating team?
- Who will be their chief spokesperson?
- What are the political interests and needs of the negotiating team?
- What is their expected negotiating style?
- What are the expected issues from the other group?
- What are their individual interests regarding bargaining issues?
- What are their likely goals for settlement?
- What level of support do they have from their constituents?
- What decision-making authority do they have?

Source: Authors.

Each issue is defined in terms of the interest it serves, or what the underlying goal is that is desired by introducing this issue. During the process of negotiations, solutions are likely found that may satisfy your interests, even though your team never considered them. A negotiating position should not interfere with a legitimate solution to your interests. The negotiating team should establish objectives for each issue anticipated in negotiations. For example, the issue may be to revise the grievance procedure. Say your team believes the process takes too long; the objective might then be to reduce procedural steps from five to three, hence shortening the process.

Procedural planning involves identifying the assignments for members of the bargaining team, including those of chief spokesperson, personnel policy advisor, budget advisor, legal advisor, and subject matter specialist for issues related to the bargaining unit. Decisions on how the team will report to their administrative oversight group and the articulation of preferences for bargaining ground rules are often decided at this early stage of the negotiation process.

Step 3: Internal Negotiations

Sometimes, the most difficult part of collective bargaining is the negotiating process that takes place within your own organization. It is unwise to assume that the conflict over interests will begin once you meet at the bargaining table, against the opposite side. Political ambition might create conflict between rival elected officials, or competition among rival administrators may lead to disagreements about bargaining strategies to be employed. In almost every case, personalities in conflict intrude into the planning and conduct of collective bargaining. Union organizations also experience similar internal conflict. Factions within the union may vie for leadership and control of the union. Often, the interests of new employees who seek to increase wages clash with those of more experienced employees who tend to prioritize issues relating to job security, health insurance, and retirement benefits. The bargaining unit negotiating team should be prepared to deal with these varied internal interests of the union membership.

Step 4: Informal Discussions

Experienced negotiators frequently contact the leader of the opposite team prior to formal negotiations, and at critical points during the bargaining, to discuss the ground rules and mutual expectations and explain actions that will take place or have already happened at the bargaining table. Although developing solutions to specific issues during these informal sessions can be dangerous, these discussions often establish the framework for more formal conversations and reduce tensions arising from differences brought to the negotiation. In the later stages of negotiations, informal discussions ('sidebars') can help create a plan for resolving issues.

Step 5: Preliminary Negotiations

Before grappling with the issues to be negotiated in the formal bargaining sessions, the negotiation teams must establish the rules under which negotiations will take place. Ground rules are usually agreed to in the first sessions of any negotiation, and these often include such items as a schedule and location for negotiating sessions, the list of participants and the roles they will play, identification of a chief spokesperson, expectations on recording sessions and the information available to both groups during negotiations, and a media relations plan.

Step 6: Issue Identification

During the issue identification phase, the bargaining teams present their issues, proposals, or demands to the other side. This is often done briefly, presenting the topic to be discussed without going into much detail at first, until all the individual issues are on the table. Once both sides have heard all the issues to be discussed, they typically retire, or 'caucus', to discuss how they will approach each issue. Some subjects are mandatory subjects of bargaining, others might be permissible, and some may be illegal. This phase establishes the scope of bargaining, articulating the legal restrictions of what may and may not be discussed in collective bargaining. Legislation authorizing collective bargaining specifies what types of issue can be discussed.

Mandatory issues must be negotiated by both parties in good faith if either side desires to bring up such an issue. However, this does not mean that either party must agree or settle the issue. Mandatory issues usually include wages, hours, or conditions of employment. These three categories may include fringe benefits, overtime hours, pay scales, management rights provisions, union security and union rights provisions, grievance procedures, safety, and other conditions of employment.

Permissive issues can be negotiated if both parties agree to discuss them, but they are not required to bargain over these issues. If both parties agree to negotiate permissive issues, but an agreement cannot be reached over these issues, it is illegal to pursue the issue to the point of impasse. Permissive issues include management or union operations such as budgeting procedures or service levels, and can include items not normally covered by a contract such as retiree benefits. Neither labor nor management can bring illegal issues to the bargaining table. These would include such topics as discrimination in hiring and promotion, management financial support for the union, or salary increases in return for political contributions.

Wages are the most familiar issue brought to the bargaining table. Unions negotiate for higher average wages to keep pace with inflation in the region or to bring salaries and wages up to the level of comparable public entities. They may negotiate for higher wages than other surrounding communities if they feel their work requires a higher standard. Unions also negotiate for predictable incremental wage increases, usually to compensate for an employee's seniority, rather than increases subject only to management discretion such as performance or productivity. Management in many jurisdictions is moving toward more open pay scales, with increases in salaries and wages awarded on the basis of individual performance. During negotiations, the parties may decide to defer compensation or put potential wage increases into enhanced benefits. Deferred compensation plans are becoming increasingly popular, as baby boomer-aged employees are increasingly interested in enhanced retirement benefits. Unions often face quite competing demands from their constituents when they make demands for better fringe benefits. Younger employees tend to favor improvements to medical and dental insurance plans, whereas older workers are more interested in pension plan enhancements. Chapters 8 and 9 will consider the issues surrounding compensation packaging and employee preferences in detail.

Contract negotiations often include issues dealing with job security, work rules, and grievance procedures. Most contracts also include a statement of management and union rights. Negotiations may include issues that seek to establish rules in the event of layoffs and grievance procedures for ensuring due process in cases of employee discipline or dismissal. With the increased attention to contracting-out and privatization, negotiations frequently include issues related to subcontracting. Management articulates its rights in organizational operations, decision-making, or service levels. Reserved rights, all rights not specifically granted to the union as a part of the contract, are common. For their part, unions also desire a statement of their rights under the contract and often bring issues into negotiations to amend this statement of rights. Union security issues are often negotiated, where the union is compensated for its representation by all employees in the bargaining unit, whether members of the union or not. There are several options for union security arrangements. The least controversial and commonest union security provision is dues check-off. The employer deducts dues automatically from the employee's pay, until the employee specifically requests in writing that payments be stopped. Union shops require all employees covered in the bargaining unit to join the union within a specific number of days after they are hired. An agency shop does not require membership in the union, but all nonmembers must pay a representational fee to the union for services rendered as the exclusive bargaining agent of the bargaining unit. This fee is usually equal to or only slightly less than the dues paid by members of the union. The closed shop is illegal under the NLRA and all other public labor laws. A closed shop required membership in the union before consideration to be hired to a position within the bargaining unit. Many states have passed right-to-work legislation to outlaw all forms of union security provisions except dues check-off.

Step 7: Problem Solving

Once the issues have been identified, the negotiating teams can begin working on the problems on the table. During the problem-solving phase, the two sides develop ideas, proposals, and counter-proposals, with the objective of resolving the issues at hand. Subcommittees are sometimes formed to work on specific issues and to craft suggested resolutions. Special guests may be called in to testify or provide expertise on specific issues.

Step 8: Impasse Resolution

If a settlement is not reached, guidelines in the relevant labor law may require impasse resolution steps. For example, the NLRA requires notification of the FMCS if negotiations have not produced an agreement within 30 days of the initial notification of intent to renegotiate an existing contract. Many public sector jurisdictions have incorporated similar provisions in public labor laws. Also, the negotiating parties may extend the contract, even after its previously negotiated expiration date. If there is no progress, and settlement does not appear to be forthcoming, the parties are at an *impasse* and may need to seek outside assistance or try to apply extraordinary pressure to settle the contract issues in dispute. In private sector negotiations and some public jurisdictions, employees are allowed to strike, and employers are allowed to lock out employees after the expiration of the labor contract. These actions can place major strain on all concerned. Strikes and lockouts are an open conflict, with the outcome usually determined by the side that can afford to suffer losses the longest. Strikes receive a lot of media attention, but occur in relatively few negotiations, and their incidence is steadily declining over time; Exhibit 4.10 demonstrates that decline graphically. According to the Department of Labor (U.S. Department of Labor, Bureau of Labor Statistics 2014b), 1953 witnessed 437 work stoppages involving 1,623,000 workers and resulting in 18,130,000 idle days (only 0.14 percent of working time), whereas 2013 featured only fifteen work stoppages involving 55,000 workers and resulting in 290,000 idle days (0.005 percent of working time).

Management and labor use a number of methods to assist them in the settlement of labor disputes that have reached impasse. It is useful at this point to consider the level of assertiveness (and potential for collaborative conflict resolution) along a continuum, ranging from mediation, fact finding, mediation–arbitration, and conventional arbitration, to final offer arbitration.

Mediation consists of a third party to assist the union and management negotiators in reaching an agreement. A mediator has no authority to compel agreement, but rather facilitates it by working to keep communication channels open between the two parties, transmitting proposals from one party to the other, suggesting ideas, and generally keeping the talks going by summarizing discussions

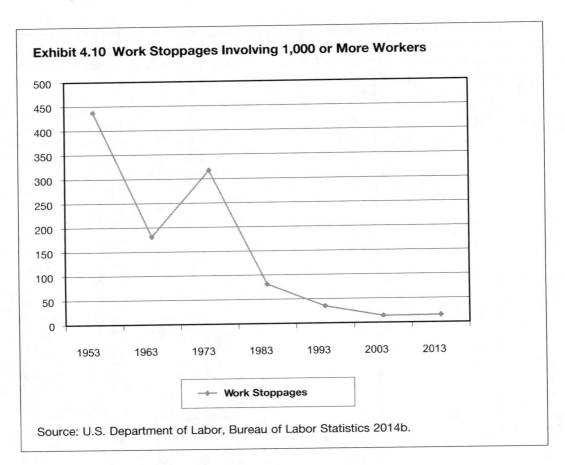

Exhibit 4.10 Work Stoppages Involving 1,000 or More Workers

Source: U.S. Department of Labor, Bureau of Labor Statistics 2014b.

and agreement points. Mediators are often skilled at facilitating 'interest-based' negotiations, a process that involves keeping interests in the forefront, while encouraging the negotiating parties to avoid taking hardened positions.

Fact finding is more formal than mediation and can consist of one neutral third party or a panel of individuals, where one is selected by the union, a second is selected by management, and a third is selected by those two persons. As the name implies, fact finders use formal hearings, call witnesses, research pertinent documents, and often consult similar settlements from outside the organization to determine the facts relevant to negotiations. The fact finders then prepare a report that can feature a recommendation for settlement. The report is not binding, but does place additional pressure on the negotiating parties to reach a settlement along the lines suggested.

Arbitration is a formal process where the settlement decided by the arbitrator is binding on both parties. The arbitrator is usually a professionally trained attorney, judge, or conflict resolution expert who holds formal hearings to hear the facts of the negotiation. The parties to the negotiation present their arguments to the arbitrator, who then prepares a written decision. In conventional arbitration, the arbitrator uses the evidence and the written positions presented during the hearings to craft a fair settlement. A different form of arbitration, called final offer arbitration, has fewer negative consequences than conventional arbitration. In final offer arbitration, the two parties to the negotiations present their final offers to the arbitrator, who then selects one offer or the other. Depending on the type of arbitration described in the particular labor laws, final offers may be in the form of an entire package, including all the outstanding issues in negotiations, or final offers by each separate issue, where the arbitrator selects the final offer issue by issue.

Mediation–arbitration, or the 'med–arb' process, represents a combination of these two forms of impasse resolution. A third party is called in to mediate negotiations for a limited time. If no settlement is reached during that specified time, the mediator switches roles to that of an arbitrator and imposes a settlement for all remaining issues in dispute. Med–arb is a simplified version of impasse resolution, reducing the number of people involved and the time taken to settle the dispute.

Arbitration has a number of advantages. Like other forms of impasse resolution, a neutral third party conducts arbitration. The outside perspective is useful in calming emotions and getting to the facts in dispute. The primary goal of arbitration is to prevent labor conflict in the form of a strike by imposing a prima facie fair settlement. In situations where a strike may be illegal and endanger the public safety of citizens, arbitration gives the union an alternative where its arguments can be given a fair hearing and it will not be entirely subject to management's will. Arbitration can also be a political safety valve for elected officials, who can claim a hard-line approach during negotiations, but must abide by the decision of the arbitrator.

The first problem with arbitration is the chilling effect it can have on the conduct of normal negotiations. At times, negotiators bargain toward arbitration instead of toward settlement. In other words, the parties position themselves to look good before an arbitrator, instead of working together to reach an agreement acceptable to both sides. The second problem is related to the first: arbitration can become 'habit-forming' for the parties. Management and union negotiators can lose their ability to work out solutions for themselves in anticipation of arbitration. It is also a natural tendency for arbitrators to find something for both sides of the conflict, and they often 'split the differences' between the two parties. This tendency discourages meaningful bargaining, as both sides know they should take a somewhat extreme position during negotiations. Finally, and particularly important for politically elected public officials, arbitration turns decision-making authority over to an unelected and practically unaccountable third party. Arbitrators make decisions directly affecting public policy and public funds, but they are neither elected nor are they bound to the consequences of their decisions.

Final offer arbitration reduces some of the negative aspects of conventional arbitration. Negotiators must seriously bargain before the case goes to the arbitrator, so that their final offers will be judged the most acceptable. Negotiators often reach a settlement when getting to their final offers, thereby promoting problem solving rather than deferring it. Arbitrators cannot 'split the difference' between management and labor positions, and there are no incentives to take extreme positions. Finally, the settlement comes from the final offers as determined by the negotiating parties, not a settlement imposed by a third party.

Step 9: Settlement

As negotiations wend toward conclusion, either by resolution of the issues identified or as the expiration of the previous contract approaches, the negotiation teams must determine the likelihood of settlement. A third party, such as a mediator, fact finder, or arbitrator, may be required by the applicable legislation, or a mediator may be requested to assist the negotiating teams in reaching a final settlement.

Step 10: Ratification

Once the two negotiating teams have reached an agreement on the issues, the package must be presented to the members of the bargaining unit for ratification. A negotiated agreement is neither permanent nor legally binding until ratified by both the union membership and the governing body of the public jurisdiction. After the governing bodies of both the union and employer have voted upon and approved the key elements of the agreement, they must be incorporated into a new contract. The process of preparing language for inclusion in the contract can be almost as painstaking as the actual negotiation. Typically, the specific implementation language for each issue is negotiated during the bargaining process, but there is often the need to alter language in other parts of the contract to mesh with other changes that may have been made in a different section as a result of negotiations. The lead negotiators and their legal representatives meet to finalize the contract language before it goes forward for final approval. In state and local government settings, the agreement and contract must be ratified by legislative action. In cases when the members of the governing body do not approve the agreement, the negotiating teams must reconvene to find a new solution to the issues still in contention.

Step 11: Contract Management

Collective bargaining often entails an open and informative exchange between management and labor. Unfortunately, at times there can be acrimony that can scar working relationships. The sustaining of positive communication and a trusting relationship throughout negotiations is important to both labor and management for two reasons. First, the interested parties will come together again when the new contract expires; second, they must meet together often to clarify contract language and resolve contract disputes that arise during the term of the contract.

As soon as the new contract is ratified, and formal negotiations have ended, the process of contract management begins. Throughout the life of the contract, issues will arise either that are not covered in the contract or where the contract is not sufficiently specific. In these cases, informal discussions between management and labor can address the majority of such matters. Some questions must be left for resolution at the bargaining table when the contract expires, and some interpretations of contract language or disputes about performance under the contract must be managed through a quasi-legal process. A contract grievance procedure is incorporated into most contracts as a means to resolve disputes arising from the interpretation of the contract or a claim that the rights of an employee under the contract have been violated. The objective of the grievance procedure is to resolve the dispute at the lowest possible level, before involving upper management or resolution through a third-party arbitrator. The vast majority of such grievances are settled before going to the final steps of the process.

The first step in the contract grievance procedure in most contracts is for an employee to take a complaint to their immediate supervisor. This is usually done informally where the employee, possibly accompanied by a union representative, meets with the supervisor to discuss the problem in question. According to the terms of the grievance procedure established in the contract, the supervisor has a specified amount of time to respond to the issue raised. If the employee and/or union representative view the response to the complaint as unsatisfactory, the grievance is formalized into writing and submitted to the next level of management for potential resolution. During a timeline specified in the contract's grievance procedure, the manager must submit a written response to the grievance. Again, if the response is judged to be unsatisfactory, the grievance can be appealed to the next level, usually upper management or the chief executive. In some cases, the response of the chief executive is the final step in the procedure. Many contracts, however, allow for binding arbitration as the final step in the grievance procedure for certain types of major grievance. In most cases where grievance arbitration is allowed, the contract specifies how the arbitrator will be selected. The FMCS or the American Arbitration Association can provide a list of qualified arbitrators and their histories for selection by the union and management, who share the cost of the arbitrator.

Bargaining Style

In practice, the conflict of interests between management and employees has led to an inclination to develop an adversarial relationship, resulting in a typically contentious bargaining style being taken on by both sides. Given a competitive global marketplace environment, and given the advent of significant pressure to economize, downsize, and privatize in the public sector, both management and labor have found it beneficial in many jurisdictions to work together to improve their organization's competitive position. Common interests for both management and organized labor in many governmental jurisdictions have given rise to a more collaborative bargaining style.

Distributive versus Integrative Bargaining Style

The distributive bargaining style is characterized as adversarial. The inherent conflict between labor and management can devolve to an adversarial bargaining style. One reason for the open animosity and lack of trust in so many labor–management relationships is the zero–sum game perspective (victor/loser dichotomy) of the parties, wherein the parties to the negotiation believe that, for one to gain, the other side must lose. Participants may believe that, at times, it is more beneficial for one side to 'defect' or intentionally harm the other side when it is perceived that retaliation is not possible. Trust is frequently fragile, and either side stands ready to revert to traditional, adversarial bargaining, should trust be replaced by suspicion among negotiators.

An alternative practice in labor relations negotiations is based on the development of capacity for cooperation and trust between parties in dispute. Management and union negotiators are instructed to bargain over interests, not positions. At every step of negotiations, cooperation builds, and each side opens itself up to the other to reach mutually beneficial agreements, or 'win–win' solutions. Kearney (2006) suggests that labor relations are witnessing a trend toward less confrontational negotiations. Win–win negotiation was popularized in the early nineties (Fisher and Ury 1983; Fisher, Ury, and Patton 1991; Ury 1991). Collaborative negotiators learn to: (1.) differentiate between people and the problem; (2.) focus on interests, rather than emphasize positions; and (3.) create options that result in mutual gain. Although integrative bargaining has helped negotiations become more congenial in a good number of cases, it does not provide a solution to all possible bargaining situations. In areas where mutual gain is a possibility, and the needs of both sides can be served, 'principled' or 'interest-based' bargaining has been used quite successfully. When the interests of the bargaining parties are diametrically opposed, labor negotiations often revert to traditional adversarial bargaining and frequently result in impasse (Lewicki, Saunders, and Minton 1999a, 1999b).

Ethics and Negotiation Tactics

Ethical considerations in negotiations often relate to a problem of self-interest versus cooperation. For example, the union negotiators may personally be better off by agreeing to a two-tiered wage increase (where senior employees are given a larger wage increase than new hires), but the union might suffer overall. Another theory of bargaining is based on the relative power of each party to the negotiation. Power can be understood as the ability to withstand the costs involved in ongoing negotiations (Chamberlain and Kuhn 1965). Costs may be inflicted on one side by the other, or costs may be incurred by one side as a result of the decisions they make. The typical economic costs to management are job actions by union members such as a strike, work slow-down, or boycott. In the public sector, most of the traditional economic costs do not exist. Political costs might include media reporting and public opinion, loss of votes in the next election, a decrease in public services, or an increase in taxes, if union demands are agreed upon. Union costs include lost or delayed wages, a possible loss of jobs due to layoffs, and dissatisfaction of members resulting in loss of membership or the possibility of losing the next union leadership election. Power in bargaining is also realized when one party has more venues for bargaining or influence than does the other side (Bacharach and Lawler 1981). Options for public employee unions include lobbying public decision makers at all levels of government where public labor relations policy is made. Unions are also involved in election campaigns, raising campaign funds, and mobilizing members to work in political campaigns and get-out-the-vote efforts. Finally, unions and management may see some dispute resolution mechanisms as alternatives to bargaining.

Summary

Labor–management relations in the public sector continue to evolve. For most of the history of this nation, unions were considered a conspiracy of workers who posed a threat to sovereign government. As public employees were paid from tax dollars and worked for the public, a government job was viewed as a privilege. The threat of a strike by public employees was quasi-treasonous, as the employer, in essence, was the citizenry. This reasoning may have been derived from the practice of political patronage, where public employees often obtained their jobs in return for their support and assistance given to elected officials. The thought of employees needing to bargain collectively about wages, benefits, and conditions of employment seemed inconsistent in the context of jobs distributed as a reward. As Chapter 2 illustrated, merit systems at all levels of government established a professional tone, employees began to voice concerns about their treatment in the workplace, and discrepancies emerged between private and public sector workers, who sometimes performed essentially the same job. Labor relations in the public sector took on many of the same characteristics as in union–management relations in the private sector. Public employees held elections for union representation, began collective bargaining, and either ratified contracts or took job actions. The adversarial format of public sector negotiations tended to assume the same tenor as that of private companies and their employees (Patton 1994).

However, history teaches that the nature of labor relations is quite different in the public sector. In reflection of this difference, a variety of alternative methods of negotiating and settling disputes are more commonly found in public sector settings. Labor relations and, specifically, collective bargaining practices are evolving toward a more cooperative style of negotiation at all levels of government in the U.S. The traditional adversarial style will persist in conditions where trust has not developed between labor and management, but, increasingly, public agencies and unions are recognizing mutual interests and are discovering the short- and long-term benefits of collaboration.

A Manager's Vocabulary

*   Arbitration - *Binding, Voluntary*
*   Mediation - *impartial mediator facilitates negotiation*
*   Bargaining ground rules -

- Bargaining unit and exclusive bargaining agent
- Closed shop
- Collective bargaining
- Distributive (adversarial) bargaining
- Integrative (cooperative) bargaining
- Good faith bargaining
- Mandatory versus permissive issues
- Scope of bargaining
- Unfair labor practices
- Union certification/decertification
- Wagner Act (National Labor Relations Act)
- Taft–Hartley Act (Labor Management Relations Act)

Study Questions

1. What are the advantages and disadvantages to adversarial labor negotiations? Is it to the advantage of management and labor to adopt a more cooperative approach to negotiations?
2. What are the major barriers to establishing labor–management cooperation?
3. Should there be a national labor relations law for all public employees, similar to the Wagner Act? What would be the major advantages and disadvantages of such a law?
4. Do the political strategies available to public sector unions offset their restrictions to strike?
5. Should public employees be allowed to strike?
6. When would a distributive negotiation style be preferable to an integrative negotiation style?
7. How would arbitration as an impasse resolution strategy cause a 'chilling effect' on the conduct of negotiations? How could this problem be overcome?

Exercises

Exercise 4.1 Organizing a Graduate Assistant Bargaining Unit

Assuming that collective bargaining for university personnel is permitted in your state, prepare a campaign for organizing graduate assistants (graduate teaching and research assistants). Consider what union might be the best 'fit' for graduate assistants and decide on a strategy for organizing.

Exercise 4.2 Negotiations between Students and Faculty

Consider the possibility of negotiations between students of your program and the faculty of that program to consider course offerings, schedules, and the types of assignment to be given. What ground rules would you ask for before discussions on the issues actually begin?

References

AFGE. 2014. "AFGE at a Glance." www.afge.org/?Page=AboutUs (accessed March 24, 2014).

AFL–CIO. 2014. "About the AFL–CIO." www.aflcio.org/About (accessed March 22, 2014).

AFSCME. 2014. "We are AFSCME." www.afscme.org/union/about (accessed March 22, 2014).

Bacharach, Samuel B., and Edward J. Lawler. 1981. *Bargaining Power, Tactics, and Outcomes*. San Francisco, CA: Jossey-Bass.

Center for Partnership and Labor-Management Relations. 1997. *Union Recognition in the Federal Government*, 10–26. Washington, DC: U.S. Office of Personnel Management.

Chamberlain, Neil W., and James W. Kuhn. 1965. *Collective Bargaining*, 2nd ed. New York: McGraw-Hill.

Change to Win. 2014. "About Us." www.changetowin.org/about (accessed March 22, 2014).

Civil Service Reform Act 1978.

Commonwealth v. Hunt, 4 Metcalf 3 (1842).

Coser, Lewis A. 1956. *The Functions of Social Conflict*. New York: Free Press.

D'Alba, Joel A. 1979. "The Nature of the Duty to Bargain in Good Faith." *In Portrait of a Process*, Eds. Muriel K. Gibbons, Robert D. Helsby, Jerome Lefknowitz, and Barbara Z. Tener, 149–172. Fort Washington, PA: Labor Relations Press.

Devinatz, Victor G., and Wayne Kennedy. 1995. "AFGE Local 2816 and 'Community Unionism': A New Conception of Public Sector Unionism." *Journal of Collective Negotiation* 24 (2): 121–132.

Engvall, P. Robert. 1995. "Public-Sector Unionization in 1995 or It Appears the Lion King Has Eaten Robin Hood." *Journal of Collective Negotiations in the Public Sector* 24 (3): 255–269.

Executive Order No. 10988, Pres. Kennedy, January 17, "Employee–Management Cooperation in the Federal Sector" (1962).

Executive Order No. 11491, Pres. Nixon, October 29, "Labor–Management Relations in the Federal Service" (1962).

Executive Order No. 11838, Pres. Ford, February 6, "Amending EO11491, 11616 and 11636" (1975).

Executive Order No. 12871, Pres. Clinton, October 1, "Labor–Management Partnerships" (1993).

Executive Order No. 13202, Pres. George W. Bush, February 17, "Preservation of Open Competition and Government Neutrality Towards Government Contractors Labor Relations on Federal and Federally Funded Construction Projects" (2001).

Farber, Henry S. 1990. "The Decline of Unionization in the United States: What Can Be Learned from Recent Experience?" *Journal of Labor Economics* 8 (1): 75–105.

Ferris, Frank, and Albert C. Hyde. 2004. "Federal Labor–Management Relations for the Next Century—Or the Last? The Case of the Department of Homeland Security." *Review of Public Personnel Administration* 24 (3): 216–233.

Fisher, Roger, and William Ury, 1983. *Getting to Yes*, 1st ed. Boston, MA: Houghton Mifflin.

Fisher, Roger, William Ury, and Bruce Patton. 1991. *Getting to Yes*, 2nd ed. Boston, MA: Houghton Mifflin.

Fossum, John A. 1991. *Labor Relations: Development, Structure, and Process*, 5th ed. Homewood, IL: Irwin.

Hanslowe, Kurt L. 1985. "The Emerging Law of Labor Relations in Public Employment." In *Labor Relations Law in the Public Sector*, 4th ed., Eds. Harry T. Edwards, R. Theodore Clark Jr., and Charles B. Craver, 33–39. Charlottesville, VA: Michie.

Hirsch, Barry T., and David A. Macpherson. 2014. *Union Membership and Coverage Database*. www.unionstats.com (accessed March 20, 2014).

Hunt, James W. 1988. *The Law of the Workplace: Rights of Employers and Employees*, 2nd ed. Washington, DC: Bureau of National Affairs.

Johnston, Paul. 1994. *Success While Others Fail: Social Movement Unionism and the Public Workplace*. Ithaca, NY: ILR Press.

Kearney, Richard C. 1992. *Labor Relations in the Public Sector*, 2nd ed. New York: Marcel Dekker.

———. 2006. "The Labor Perspective on Civil Service Reform in the States." In *Civil Service Reform in the States: Personnel Policy and Politics at the Subnational Level*, Eds. J. Edward Kellough and Lloyd G. Nigro, 777–793. New York: State University of New York.

Kearney, Richard C., and Patrice M. Mareschal. 2014. *Labor Relations in the Public Sector*, 5th ed. New York: CRC Press.

Kochan, A. Thomas, Harry C. Katz, and Robert B. McKersie. 1986. *The Transformation of American Industrial Relations*. New York: Basic Books.

Labor Management Relations Act of 1947, 29 U.S.C. §§ 141–197 (1947) (Taft–Hartley Act).

Lewicki, Roy J., David M. Saunders, and John W. Minton. 1999a. "Negotiation (Section Three)." *Strategy and Tactics of Distributive Bargaining*, 3rd ed. Boston, MA: McGraw-Hill.

———. 1999b. "Negotiation (Section Four)." *Strategy and Tactics of Integrative Negotiating*, 3rd ed. Boston, MA: McGraw-Hill.

Lloyd–Lafollette Act of 1912, Stat. 539. 5 U.S.C. §7513.

Loewe v. Lawlor, 208 U.S. 274 (1908).

Moe, Terry M. 2009. "Collective Bargaining and the Performance of the Public Schools." *American Journal of Political Science* 53 (1): 156–174.

National Labor Relations Act of 1935, 29 U.S.C. §§ 151–169 (1935).

National Labor Relations Board. 2014. "Decertification Petitions—RD." www.nlrb.gov/news-outreach/graphs-data/petitions-and-elections/decertification-petitions-rd (accessed March 24, 2014).

Nelson, Daniel. 1997. *Shifting Fortunes: The Rise and Decline of American Labor, 1820s to Present*. Chicago, IL: Ivan R. Dee.

Norris–La Guardia Act of 1932, 29 U.S.C. §§ 101–115 (1932).

NTEU. 2014. "About NTEU." www.nteu.org/NTEU/ (accessed March 24, 2014).

Olson, Mancur. 1971. *The Logic of Collective Action: Public Goods and the Theory of Groups*. Cambridge, MA: Harvard University Press.

Paradis, Adrian A., and Grace D. Paradis. 1983. *The Labor Almanac*. Littleton, CO: Libraries Unlimited.

Patton, W. David. 1994. "Teaching Labor Relations: A Choice between Paleontological and Contemporary Approaches." *Review of Public Personnel Administration* 14 (4): 52–65.

———. 1996. "Labor Unions." In *Ready Reference: American Justice*, Ed. Joseph M. Bessette, 455–458. Pasadena, CA: Salem Press.

———.1998. "Labor Law." In *Magill's Legal Guide: Federal Judicial System—Principals and Agents, vol. 2*, Ed. Timothy L. Hall, 503–505. Pasadena, CA: Salem Press.

Railway Labor Act of 1926, 45 U.S.C. §§ 151–188 (1926).

Rubin, Ellen V. 2011. "Exploring the Link Between Procedural Fairness and Union Membership in the Federal Government." *Review of Public Personnel Administration* 31 (2): 128–142.

Shafritz, Jay M., Norma M. Riccucci, David H. Rosenbloom, and Albert C. Hyde. 1992. *Personnel Management in Government: Politics and Process*, 4th ed. New York: Marcel Dekker.

Taylor, Benjamin J., and Fred Whitney. 1983. *Labor Relations Law*, 4th ed. Englewood Cliffs, NJ: Prentice Hall.

Thompson, James R. 2007. "Federal Labor–Management Relations Reforms Under Bush: Enlightened Management or Quest for Control?" *Review of Public Personnel Administration* 27 (2): 105–124.

Tobias, Robert M. 2004. "The Future of Federal Government Labor Relations and the Mutual Interests of Congress, the Administration, and Unions." *Journal of Labor Research* 25 (1): 19–41.

Twain, Mark. 1897. Note to London Correspondent of the *New York Journal* (June, 1).

Ury, William. 1991. *Getting Past No*. Boston, MA: Houghton Mifflin.

U.S. Department of Labor, Bureau of Labor Statistics. 2014a. "Union Members—2013." www.bls.gov/news.release/pdf/union2.pdf (accessed March 20, 2014).

———. 2014b. "Major Work Stoppages in 2013." www.bls.gov/news.release/archives/wkstp_02122014.htm (accessed June 27, 2015).

Webb, Sidney, and Beatrice Webb. 1965. *Industrial Democracy*. New York: Kelly.

5   Strategic HRM

Learning Objectives

- Understand the basic steps in strategic planning and the tenets of strategic HRM.
- Explore the rationale for succession planning and the ramifications of failing to plan.
- Review the common barriers to planning in public and nonprofit sector organizations and methods to overcome these.

HR departments are responsible for both control and support operations. Consideration of HR in planning activities sometimes occurs only when the HR department is asked to forecast staffing needs (e.g., generated from retirements, turnover, or growth) or to conduct skill inventories to identify noteworthy deficits. Very often, discussions about planning in HR texts focus upon different models used for forecasting or on illustrating the staffing issues that warrant consideration. In earlier chapters, we discussed the contemporary context of HR activities for public and nonprofit organizations. Obviously, the present context for public and nonprofit organizations is very important in formulating appropriate staffing considerations. However, the very high degree of socio-economic and political turbulence of the contemporary environment facing public and nonprofit organizations warrants a substantial discussion of strategic planning in this text.

The HR function is a pivotal part of strategic planning and actions to follow. Effective planning, however, requires more than formulaic workforce calculations. It requires the integration of HR into the larger organizational planning process to achieve organizational objectives. Though integrating strategic thinking by HRM into all aspects of policy-making is an appropriate ideal, in practice, its integration ranges the full spectrum from absolute to tangential. Centralized HR departments may be fully integrated, with executive-level decisions in some cases. Conversely, if HR responsibilities are decentralized to line supervisors and tend to be viewed as tangential to decision making, then in planning activities HR issues are weighted with the same level of importance as any other area of operation, and strategic, long-term planning takes a backseat to preoccupation with ongoing operations.

In this chapter, we focus upon organizational planning and strategy, and explore the implications these concepts have for HRM. We begin with a review of some basic definitions of planning, with attention being directed to strategic planning and its specific application to traditional workforce or succession planning. After a brief exploration of strategic planning initiatives in state governments, we discuss difficulties commonly associated with strategic planning in public and nonprofit organizations and address the limitations of an uncritical application of private sector planning templates to the public sector. Next, we outline a general strategic planning script. Although the outline of strategic planning will serve as a review for students familiar with planning efforts, the brief discussion of the strategic planning script serves to illustrate the challenges associated with recommending the 'one-best-way' strategic planning process in public and nonprofit organizations. Finally, we consider strategic HRM—HRM as *partner* versus advisor or compliance officer in the development of organizational strategy.

Introduction to the Reading

Planning as a straightforward forecast of staffing levels for production or succession is no longer adequate for many contemporary public and nonprofit sector organizations. In the following reading, Elizabeth Fredericksen considers the importance of comprehensive succession planning at this critical time in public service. Although certain issues raised in the reading may not be of direct concern in all jurisdictions or to nonprofit organizations, the implications for leveraging organizational effort warrants serious consideration in nearly all public and nonprofit agency settings, because of the potential to invigorate and sustain organizations through strategy-driven succession planning. However, she cautions us about the attendant managerial and structural impediments to effective succession planning commonly encountered. Consider the following questions:

1. In the coming decade, what challenges face public organizations in staffing government?
2. This article focuses on state and local governments. Are there unique implications for the federal government on these points? What about nonprofit organizations?
3. Why should a service delivery network care about succession planning efforts among its members?

Excerpt 5.1 Defining Succession Planning

Kim (2003, 533) defers to the National Academy of Public Administration to define succession planning as "an ongoing process of systematically identifying, assessing and developing organizational leadership to enhance performance." The essential task of public policy implementation demands that we consider succession for multiple positions, not just for senior management (Conger and Fulmer 2003, 78), but also for areas devoted to mission-critical efforts of the organization, or that serve as conduits for intra- and intergovernmental relationships (Kim 2003, 535; Lukensmeyer and Hasselblad Torres 2006). To cope with workforce reductions, and an aging and more diverse workforce, agencies need key employees with aptitudes and knowledge that differ from the traditional skill set for executive leadership (Mills 2001; Riccucci 2002). Clearly, a different expertise for leadership and mission-critical positions may be needed than might have been the case even a decade ago. Those leading the delivery of public goods and services may not be public sector employees, but rather may be part of a collaborative service delivery network, consultants, or contractors. Succession planning must consider these arrangements. . . .

[S]uccession management entails more than simply filling empty seats with the first available individual (Kim 2003). . . . [P]ublic administrators must attend to public service goals such as achieving a fair and representative workplace . . . [and] without formal processes, managers may unconsciously default to what is familiar and comfortable. . . .

Decisions at one level of a state or local agency may result in a cascade of ethical effects within and across organizations. When dealing with internal succession, the promotion of one person may signal that a new opportunity is available for other employees. Likewise an unintended deference to one group at the expense of another may have ramifications for subsequent decisions. Also, losing experienced personnel has additional intangible implications for ethical culture in state and local organizations . . . Simply filling an open position with available internal or external applicants who lack such experience, even if these applicants have other qualifications, may not allow agencies to perform effectively on the ethical front. The pending demographic shifts mean that succession management is no longer a simple formula with initial recruitment, work for some number of years, and subsequent retirement. Ultimately, to achieve public service goals, fulfill an agency's mission, and implement policies, an organization must reconsider whom they recruit, how those new employees are managed and ways to encourage employees with critical knowledge and skills to stay in or re-enter public service. . . .

Table 2 summarizes barriers to workforce planning generally that were reported by practitioners in various studies drawing upon both public and private sector organizations. Not surprisingly, resources, prioritization and the legal structures within which public organizations operate are central.

Table 2 Barriers to Succession Planning

Resource availability	• Development and succession programs are resource intensive (Hopen 2005; Johnson and Brown 2004; Pynes 2009) • Human resource efforts have focused on staff reductions and budget problems (Johnson and Brown 2004)
Perception of need	• Not a priority of senior management (Johnson and Brown 2004) • Planning is not critical need; immediate agency priorities supersede planning efforts (Hopen 2005; Johnson and Brown 2004; Pynes 2009) • Staffing has not been a problem in the past; plenty of applicants for positions; existing approaches will suffice (Johnson and Brown 2004)
Structural issues	• Time horizon of elected and appointed officials is short (Johnson and Brown 2004) • Personnel systems preclude flexibility in succession programs (Johnson and Brown 2004)

Note: The barriers are drawn from surveys reported by Hopen (2005, p. 5) and Johnson and Brown (2004, pp. 382, 386), as well as general observations from Pynes (2009).

Excerpt References

Conger, Jay A., and Robert M. Fulmer. 2003. Developing your leadership pipeline. *Harvard Business Review* 81:76–84.

Hopen, Deborah. 2005. Succession planning facts and fantasies. *The Journal for Quality and Participation* 28(3):4–6.

Johnson, Gilbert L., and Judith Brown. 2004. Workforce planning not a common practice, IPMA–HR study finds. *Public Personnel Management* 33:379–388.

Kim, Soonhee. 2003. Linking employee assessments to succession planning. *Public Personnel Management* 32:533–547.

Lukensmeyer, Carolyn J., and Lars Hasselblad Torres. 2006. Today's leadership challenge: Engaging citizens. *The Public Manager* 35:26–31.

Mills, Claudia. 2001. Workplace wars: How much should I be required to meet the needs of your children. *Philosophy & Public Policy Quarterly* 21:15–20.

Pynes, Joan E. 2009. Strategic human resources management. In *Public human resource management: Problems and prospects*, ed. Steven W. Hays, Richard C. Kearney and Jerrell D. Coggburn, pp. 95–106. New York: Longman.

Riccucci, Norma M. 2002. Managing diversity in the government workplace. In *Public Personnel Management*, ed. Carolyn Ban and Norma M. Riccucci, pp. 85–94. New York: Longman.

Source: Fredericksen, Elizabeth D. 2010. pp. 50–60. "When the Music Stops: Succession Is More than Filling Seats." *State and Local Government Review*, 42(1): 50–60. Excerpt drawn from pp. 52–55.

Introduction to Planning

The word *plan* serves as both noun and verb. As noun, a plan denotes "a method of doing or proceeding with something formulated beforehand" or "a project or definite purpose" (*Random House Dictionary* 1980, p. 670). As verb, the action of planning suggests both foresight and intention. Simply stated, planning is the nexus of knowledge and intention.

People plan every day. On a basic level, when we decide what to prepare for a meal or how to study for an exam, we are engaged in planning. We develop sequences of activities that occur in response to certain stimuli. Sometimes, our plans become a matter of habit, no longer requiring much conscious thought or decision. This auto-response approach to decisions has been termed "cybernetic decision-making" (Steinbruner 1974). In most cases, we do all of these things without great contemplation. However, if we begin to select between multiple courses of action using some relevant criteria (e.g., speed versus safety, cost versus convenience, ease versus carbon footprint on the environment) to develop responses to new or unique situations, then we engage in a considerably more complex level of planning. In response to fresh data, or an unexpected opportunity or threat relating to our preferences or values, we apply more information to our situation and consider different combinations of actions and resources. For example, you may wish to add a quick errand prior to arriving at class, to save yourself time later in the evening, or you might consider the possibility of construction delays on your usual route and adjust your timing or selection of avenues accordingly.

Workforce and Succession Planning

For many years, textbooks in personnel administration identified planning as a centralized forecasting function maintained in a personnel department. For example, Coleman (1973) offered a seminal argument for the importance of the personnel department for 'manpower' planning beginning in the 1950s. Despite calls for more sophisticated, comprehensive plans throughout the U.S. states, comparatively few have been developed (Johnson and Brown 2004, p. 380). Many public jurisdictions do not engage in formal succession planning. As the reading for this chapter suggests, neglecting such planning has clear negative consequences beyond the ability to address immediate agency needs.

In traditional workforce planning processes, HR analysts typically examined the levels of staff, considered the number and types of positions that might be added or reduced in number, noted the projections for retirement, and applied historical turnover rates to develop a formula that projects future staffing level needs. Projected staffing levels would prompt responses from other functions in personnel, and eventually from other organizational departments. In theory, workforce forecasts should drive all subsequent HR activities. If, for example, analysts determined that the agency would need additional engineers because of retirements or pending projects, specialists in job analysis and classification would identify the responsibilities for potential new employees and assign each of them to a classification level commensurate with the required KSAs. The classification level in turn would frame the compensation package. Recruiting specialists would use the resulting position descriptions and compensation package to seek out appropriate applicants. Selection would occur in response to a sufficient pool and in consideration of criteria generated by job analysis and classification.

Succession in organizations was often viewed as a simple matter of identifying upcoming retirements and considering possible successors from among the eager entry- and mid-level managers. In many cases, senior management might identify certain individuals as being likely candidates and steer them onto particular promotional tracks to provide informally the necessary experiences believed to be relevant (Baker Tilly 2011). Although the hierarchy in an organization suggests some path to promotion (e.g., from assistant director to associate director to director), much of the logic of succession and promotion appeared to be linked to informal organizational culture and legend. Some career paths were more likely than others to lead to higher management positions (e.g., fiscal and production types of activity were more often the path than 'softer' managerial activities such as HR). These informal approaches are no longer either adequate or legal, as discussed in Chapter 3.

Perceived barriers to formal succession planning are linked to limited access to resources, traditional management practices reflecting informal candidate preparation and advancement, and the longstanding structural differences between public, nonprofit, and private sector organizations. Prioritizing resources for planning efforts that are sometimes viewed as rather speculative may be difficult when agency 'politicos' have had to focus on reducing staff owing to the budget challenges facing nearly all jurisdictions during the past decade. However, it is these very concerns for predictable cycles of shortfalls and relative abundance in public sector revenues and nonprofit fundraising fortunes that demand attention to strategic HRM, according to Perry (1993). Contemporary public and nonprofit organizations must manage rapid changes in the knowledge and skills required for different positions, despite their often tenuous financial fortunes. The present-day workforce is diverse in many more respects than was once the case. The ideal of the stereotypical 'organizational man' of the 1950s, prepared to enter into a uniform, highly predictable, deeply patterned, male-centered organization, has been replaced with a prevailing view of employees as people who are trying to balance the competing demands of their professional and highly varied personal lives (Anyim, Ekwoaba, and Ideh 2012). Traditional succession planning also presumes long-term alliances between organizations and their employees. As discussed in Chapter 1, the majority of today's employees may not be planning on a 20- or 30-year commitment to the organization in which they gain employment. Succession planning can no longer be a relatively simple matter of having an employee 'pay his or her dues' by moving up through the organizational hierarchy, step by step.

Although simple staff forecasting influences activities throughout the organization, more sophisticated HR planning efforts have extended the reach of planning to the maintenance of an 'inventory' of the skills (current and potential) possessed by the current workforce (Southern 2012). Furthermore, as we will discuss in Chapter 11, the systematic identification of gaps in skills, either for promotion or for new projects and agency programs, prompts training in deficiencies.

Strategic Planning

Use of the term *strategic* in combination with the word *plan* is somewhat like saying 'planned planning'. However, in application, strategic planning has come to denote a systematic process for orchestrating organizational direction through individual action, after a careful, simultaneous evaluation of an organization's external environment and its internal capacity. Arguably, planning by definition should entail considering both the organization's resources and the context in which it endeavors to fulfill its mission, and a specification of goals and objectives for achieving a preferred future state of operations.

As Denhardt has observed: "Strategic planning helps an organization match its goals and capabilities to the anticipated demands of the environment to produce a plan of action that will assure achievement of goals" (1991, p. 235). Essentially, planning in an organization entails developing a guideline or 'game plan' to accomplish organizational goals. This guideline could range in detail from a relatively simple statement of goals and general organizational direction to a complex document with a hierarchy of goals, objectives, tasks linked to timelines, and observable evaluation criteria. Whether the end product is simple and succinct or highly complex and richly detailed, the process of strategic planning and the preparation for a planning effort require the development of an agency-wide awareness of how different decisions, structures, goals, and values can influence ongoing organizational efforts and activities into the future.

Strategic planning is distinguished from other more general planning activities in three principal ways—an emphasis is placed upon active implementation, a detailed assessment of the organization's internal and external environments is conducted, and some degree of stakeholder participation is

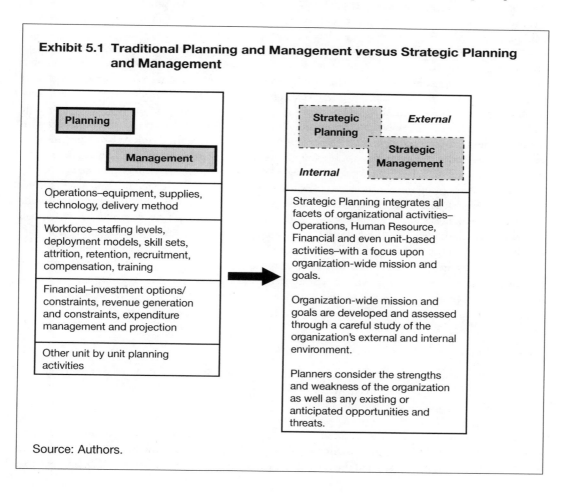

Exhibit 5.1 Traditional Planning and Management versus Strategic Planning and Management

Planning

Management

Operations–equipment, supplies, technology, delivery method

Workforce–staffing levels, deployment models, skill sets, attrition, retention, recruitment, compensation, training

Financial–investment options/ constraints, revenue generation and constraints, expenditure management and projection

Other unit by unit planning activities

Strategic Planning — External

Strategic Management

Internal

Strategic Planning integrates all facets of organizational activities–Operations, Human Resource, Financial and even unit-based activities–with a focus upon organization-wide mission and goals.

Organization-wide mission and goals are developed and assessed through a careful study of the organization's external and internal environment.

Planners consider the strengths and weakness of the organization as well as any existing or anticipated opportunities and threats.

Source: Authors.

incorporated into the process in a substantive way (Bryson 1995, p. 1; Denhardt 1991, pp. 235–236). Each organization, whether public, private, or nonprofit, has a unique environment. The characteristics of particular importance in this environment can be categorized as social/demographic, political/legal, geographic, and economic/technological. These categorizations do overlap to some extent. For example, demographic considerations such as the aging of a population could prompt economic concerns (e.g., a retiring workforce) or be linked with geography (e.g., aging populations may be more concentrated in certain sunbelt regions). Environmental changes require special attention from managers as a means to improve organizational performance (McEnery and Lifter 1987, pp. 62–63). Strategic planning implies that organizations carrying out this process will be *mission-driven*—with goals, objectives, and eventual actions identified through a careful analysis of the organization's environment. Later in this chapter, we will examine a general script for strategic planning as it has been developed over the course of the past decade in countless federal, state, local, and nonprofit agencies.

The organizational context, coupled with the impetus for the initiation of strategic planning within the agency, determines the most appropriate methods to employ (Bryson 1995, pp. 18–19, 104–129). For example, planning may occur in response to anticipated change. In this scenario, organization members may have greater control over the process used and outcome aimed at than if reacting to a particular dramatic (or tragic) event, such as a natural disaster or a man-made tragedy such as a workplace eruption of violence or discovery of illicit drug use.

However the need may arise for strategic planning, organization members often are moved to plan in response to some pivotal incident or pending dramatic change in 'business as usual' looming on the horizon. Depending upon the nature of the event or pending challenges, organization members may need to change direction and organizational activities rather quickly in response to community-based demands or changes in how their services are going to be provided in the future. In the public and nonprofit sectors, at times, catalytic events trigger community concern that the organization is not responding effectively to a problem. In many cases, a public 'failure' needs to be addressed, such as a school shooting or an outbreak of violence between gangs. Strategic planning under these circumstances can be very challenging, as many organization members will exhibit defensiveness, and responses to community critiques and possible press coverage of changes being planned will enhance the stressfulness of the work to be achieved. Strategic planning requires organization-wide cooperation and necessitates a genuine commitment to the planning process and its subsequent implementation. Unfortunately, employees in organizations planning under duress often feel neither cooperative nor committed; in such cases, professional assistance from experienced facilitators is usually brought in to initiate the process and move it along toward a more hopeful future. When organization members are not being driven by anticipated threats in their environment or by some specific event, but rather wish to plan in response to opportunities, it is often possible for a leadership team within the agency to initiate and carry the strategic planning process.

Strategic Planning in the Public or Nonprofit Sector

Planning in times of certainty, with full knowledge about the implications of different options, can occur comfortably, with small, incremental shifts from the current situation in response to new conditions (Lindblom 1992, pp. 233–234). However, for employees in public and nonprofit organizations, persistent uncertainty appears to be one of the most certain aspects of their work. Managers in organizations generally attempt to manage uncertainty by assembling an image of an environment derived from a composite of organizational functions, the medium or domain within which the organization operates, and the organization's clientele (Thompson 1967, p. 27). The external

41517

environment for nonprofit and public sector organizations is generally relatively turbulent, reflecting changing expectations from clientele and other stakeholders, fluctuating resource levels, and increasingly blended roles for public, private, and nonprofit organizations working in networks—sometimes referred to as 'communities of practice'—and dealing with interrelated problems or the same persons and/or families and businesses on a regular basis. McCann and Selsky (1984) offer an interesting discussion of organizational response to what they term "hyperturbulence" as organizations face demands from their environments that threaten to overwhelm their ability to respond. As illustrated in previous chapters, calls for reform, new approaches to delivering public goods, shifting workforce demographics, and evolving technology all require organizations to prepare for change on an ongoing basis. Within those organizations, managers and line supervisors, either those holding primary HR responsibility or those working in conjunction with an HR department, can instigate and manage necessary adaptation through the combination of efforts of skilled, effective employees and carefully calibrated employment practices.

As effective strategic planning actively engages the source of authority for an organization and the employees carrying out the work of the agency in collaboration, these planning efforts vary considerably by organization and sector with respect to the form they take. For public sector organizations, *the citizenry*, through their designated legislative body, must play a role in strategic planning processes; this normally takes the form of one or more members of a city council, county commission, or state legislature being an active participant in the strategic planning process. For nonprofit organizations, the service constituency and directing board must contribute their time to the planning process. Effective strategic planning in public and nonprofit organizations is highly participatory in nature, with staff and client participation and insight from multiple levels and functional areas within the organizations being brought into active involvement with condition assessment and plan development (Bryson 1995; Denhardt 1991). Within community-centric organizations such as government agencies and nonprofits, strategic planning must involve many individuals at many levels. Effective change in organizational practices or policy direction is most readily accomplished by involving anyone who will be affected by the change. This frequently means including outside 'stakeholders', the service providers who will work directly with these stakeholders, and the internal staff who will be supporting organizational efforts. Democratic administration requires *working with* rather than administering over citizens, and it necessitates changing procedures that hamper this collaborative effort (King and Stivers 1998, pp. 195–202).

Ethical Issues

Ethical considerations in strategic planning for public and nonprofit organizations parallel other issues raised throughout this text. As planners examine the organizational environment and anticipate social trends, they should be aware of how their personal values may shape their analysis and color their perceptions. Stereotypes used to support prejudicial assessments of the capacity or interests of others can detract from the integrity of the planning process and inhibit the proper inclusion of all stakeholders. In addition, planning for the sake of generating a document in response to a legislative or board mandate may backfire when agencies engage in a strategic planning process as a matter of form, or give only superficial attention to genuine stakeholder participation. Most agency staff who provide their input expect that it will matter in some way. People resent efforts that simply result in the collection of data—opinions and attitudes—without any sincere assessment of their contribution in developing an organizational direction. Community members experience participant fatigue when agencies invite feedback only to ignore community recommendations at the final stages of the process. Agencies may not implement all community recommendations, but all issues identified through public processes warrant due consideration and sincere respect for the citizens who donated their time to engage in a democratic process. Given these dynamics related to heightened citizen expectations, successful strategic planning processes involve an active outreach element in the implementation phase designed to demonstrate how citizen input was acted upon in some concrete and meaningful way.

How Common Is Strategic Planning in Government?

It is somewhat difficult to assess the extent, effectiveness, and administration of strategic planning efforts in government. Federal agencies have been developing formal strategic plans linked to annual budgets and performance benchmarks ever since the Government Performance and Results Act (1993). More than half of the U.S. municipal governments surveyed by Poister and Streib (2005) indicated that they engaged in strategic planning on an ongoing basis. Some research on state-level planning efforts suggests that many state agencies are engaged in some type of strategic planning effort equivalent to that of the federal agencies. Berry and Wechsler found that approximately 60 percent of responding agencies indicated the use of some type of strategic planning exercise (1995, p. 160). Most typically, the planning efforts undertaken were initiated by agency leadership rather than imposed by legislative or executive mandate (p. 160). Conversely, Selden, Ingraham, and Jacobson (2001) looked at states generally and found that central HR departments from more than thirty states reported either no planning or only a limited degree of basic workforce planning was taking place, and only five states (Illinois, New Jersey, North Carolina, Washington, and Vermont) had integrated workforce planning with overall strategic planning in what would be considered best practice. In contrast, the integration of these two dimensions of organizational strategic planning has been more commonplace in private sector firms that have adopted a total quality management (TQM) approach to organizational operations (Briggs and Keough 1999).

Perceived Barriers to Strategic Planning in the Public and Nonprofit Sectors

Wolch (1990) suggests that there are three major barriers to planning in nonprofit organizations; these may likewise pose difficulties for public sector strategic planning efforts as well. These barriers include the skill level of managers charged with planning, the diversity of agendas for the various stakeholders, and concerns about the rigidity of formal plans (pp. 222–223).

First, staff may be relatively unskilled in planning/management techniques (Wolch 1990, p. 222). Just as workforce or succession planning efforts were often relegated to centralized HR departments, other planning efforts might be compartmentalized, delegated as the domain of a particular department in an agency, or retained at a certain level of organizational decision making. Under these circumstances, little active participation would be required from line supervisors, whose formal preparation may not feature any elements of planning. However, with the strategic planning process, succession planning is integrated with all other aspects of operations and in consideration of other environmental factors. This means that line managers, as well as HR specialists, need to be familiar with strategic planning generally and equally attuned to the issues attendant on succession and recruitment. Targeted training in the techniques of planning and in environmental assessment methods is necessary. Even if employees (and outside participants) are familiar with the general concepts of strategic planning, the complexity of the data to be considered may be overwhelming without some prior training in how to frame that information. Complex modeling programs to manage all of the detail about the organization's environment, staffing levels and characteristics, range of project types, varying timelines, and diverse benchmarking criteria are commonly used in larger agencies;

in smaller agencies, software programs are now increasingly available that provide some of the same types of data to relatively small public and nonprofit agencies. The printouts and visual displays of graphs and charts could hinder active participation by those unfamiliar with, or intimidated by, statistical analysis, in the absence of appropriate training.

Second, the diversity of goals, values, and interests of the people associated with the organization can often make planning difficult (Wolch 1990, p. 223). Bringing out the perspectives of clients, donors (taxpayers), volunteers, agency staff, and board members (political decision makers) can be quite challenging. Meshing these views may require some degree of vagueness in goals and objectives to limit internal conflict between organization stakeholders. Unfortunately, the ambiguity in goals and objectives sometimes necessary to achieve consensus makes it difficult to develop a tangible implementation protocol. The very nature of 'ownership' in the public and nonprofit sector can complicate an already complex process. In the private sector, ownership and direction are quite a bit easier to ascertain for planning purposes. For the public sector, agencies are responsive to citizens indirectly, as citizens select the representatives comprising the legislative bodies that authorize and fund the agency, and directly, when the citizens are members of the constituency served by the agency's mission. For nonprofit organizations, 'ownership' can be just as complex, with a directing board, agency clientele, donors, contracting agencies, and granting foundations each claiming some say over a piece of the nonprofit agency's activity. For both public and nonprofit organizations, typically the only virtual certainty is that demand for services exceeds resources.

Third, in nonprofit sector organizations, staff members and volunteers may resist planning because it seems a bit too corporate or businesslike, rather than client-responsive (Wolch 1990, p. 223). They echo concerns frequently expressed by public sector administrators, arguing that formal plans have the potential to limit flexibility of action, or alternatively impose 'bureaucracy' on activities that must be adaptive and/or innovative to be impactful for clients (Kanter and Summers 1987). Within public agencies or nonprofit organizations, line managers and personnelists alike must adhere to professional tenets and to the legal constraints of civil service systems. At times, the strategic planning process places great pressure on these individuals to modify their activities in ways that might run contrary to civil service and/or employment contract provisions. If the plan does not consider all of these diverse perspectives, it likely will not work as hoped.

Additional problems with strategic planning may stem from previous efforts that were not implemented well. Unfortunately, public managers sometimes find themselves buffeted by 'flavor of the week' management trends (Frederickson 1992, p. 13). Strategic planning has often been treated as one such faddish effort. Picture this: Without warning, an agency is asked to develop a plan by a legislative body or executive branch official. Consultants are hired, committees are formed, and daylong work sessions are scheduled. Mid-level managers are thrown together with a sprinkle of line-level supervisors to develop a mission statement, goals, and objectives in an 8-hour retreat. The comments are scribbled on large pieces of paper for the group to see and then carefully transferred to a document that will become *The Strategic Plan of Agency X*. Copies of this document are distributed to managers throughout the agency and made available to appropriate political decision makers.

This rapid-fire approach to strategic planning is quite common and typically results in considerable difficulty in implementation (Vinzant and Vinzant 1996, pp. 139–157). Often, the haste of plan development precludes a careful assessment of organizational resources and environmental concerns or opportunities. Even if managers attempt to implement some objectives within the plan, ill-considered issues frequently harm their efforts. In addition, if participation in plan development is limited, then the important perceptions of other employees and of the organization's external stakeholders may not be represented. The practical disadvantages that this entails parallel the ethical considerations raised earlier. The 'buy-in' or commitment by employees and stakeholders is diminished.

Most employees and many citizens, if asked, will offer both input and commitment to planning and organizational change. However, if the employees make an investment in a planning activity and see no effort to implement or believe that their input was not valued, then participation fatigue sets in, and they will become increasingly cynical and detached from these efforts.

Another problem, at the other end of the spectrum, is that of over-planning. The highly detailed scheduling of implementation efforts or the development of overly structured plans can often impede organizational responsiveness. Some individuals do invest heavily in the written plan and limit their activities to only those specifically detailed, thereby limiting innovation. The organization's environment will still be fluid even after a plan is in place, and so a general focus on goals and a willingness to let the organization respond to environmental cues are important (Stilwell 1996, pp. 6–8). Managers should have the latitude to respond to shifts and be comfortable with change and variety, while recognizing that even small decisions can lead to larger outcomes, for good or ill (Stilwell 1996, p. 8).

Strategic Planning Script

Although failing to plan can have serious consequences, sloppy planning efforts may be even more threatening—lulling managers into a false sense of security. A plan that is thrown together without adequate research and analysis likely will not be implemented successfully. A plan drafted in the context of addressing an organizational failure or seeking to adapt to a rapidly changing environment developed without representation from all key organization personnel will not be implemented successfully, nor will a plan to integrate community members or policy constituents be successfully implemented unless representatives from those groups have had the genuine opportunity to participate. Strategic planning in public or nonprofit sector organizations serves as a critical mediating activity—blending people, information, and organizational direction into a collective effort of coordinated activities. The general template that we offer for planning has three main steps—preparation, data collection and analysis, and development of the plan, as illustrated in Exhibits 5.2–5.4.

Nevertheless, it is important to acknowledge the limitations of any general strategic planning template. In planning, there is no magic formula, nor does one format work for every organization; this is the case for several reasons. Organizations differ greatly in terms of their legal or social mandates. For example, a police department may be expected to protect and serve the public by apprehending offenders; a nonprofit organization dedicated to youth advocacy may have an entirely different mandate and working relationship with juvenile offenders. Both mandates are compelling and binding in terms

---

Exhibit 5.2 Steps in the Preparation Phase

- Identify organizational leadership.
- Train organizational leadership.
- Identify the planning team.
- Train the planning team.
- Identify participating organizational members.
- Identify participating community members.

Source: Authors.

of the employees and stakeholders for those organizations, and both mandates will ultimately guide individual and organizational action. Organizations will differ as well in terms of any prior actions associated with their statutory or charter-based charge. Relationships with other agencies will also vary. Finally, the people in an organization differ in terms of their prior experience, aptitude, and skills. These differences should be considered as critical resource issues in the design of strategic planning efforts.

Stage 1: Preparation

Organization members should prepare, following the steps outlined in Exhibit 5.2. It is common, though not critical in many cases, to bring an outside facilitator into an organization to assist with first-time planning efforts. The facilitator can work with organizational leadership to adapt the planning effort to the needs of the organization. Core managers who will lead planning efforts should be identified and trained in all key aspects of planning. These planning leaders would identify a list of employees who would comprise the *planning team.*

The planning team should include managers and representatives from all facets of the organization. These individuals may or may not hold formal leadership or managerial roles in the organization, but they must have demonstrated *informal leadership.* Employees sought out for advice and counsel by others are the ideal members for a planning team. The planning team should draw widely upon expertise within the organization. Technical specialists with knowledge about HRM issues and financial management are critical, as are community members and representatives of other agencies. The planning team may include members from the community, or outside organizations, who can also identify others (community and interorganizational) who should play an advisory role as the planning process unfolds.

Stage 2: Data Collection and Analysis

In the second stage of planning depicted in Exhibit 5.3, organizational members identify and systematically gather data. One of the primary steps in strategic planning is an assessment of the

---

Exhibit 5.3 Data Collection and Analysis

1. Identify and gather relevant data:

   - Assess organizational capacity (internal documents, employee focus groups, surveys, etc.)
   - Assess the organization's environment (SWOT analysis, community documents, surveys, focus groups, etc.)
   - Develop summary report/supporting documentation for planning process.

2. Review data:

   - Identify issues.
   - Consider alternatives.

3. Develop summary of issues and key findings.

Source: Authors.

organization's environment in terms of *strengths*, *weaknesses*, *opportunities*, and *threats*. This is commonly known as the SWOT analysis. Environmental data can be categorized in a number of ways. Categorizing data in terms of sources—those internal to the organization and all things external—can offer a useful, commonly shared baseline picture of the organization. Careful analysis of the organizational structure is quite useful to identify agency culture and to note access points for citizens. The degree of formalization in policies, procedures, and communication lines is also important to assess as part of that agency culture conceptualization. Another internal dimension of the organization has to do with the internal distribution of personnel, programs, and organizational responsibilities.

Data can also be sorted into broad categories of geographic, social/demographic, economic/technological, and political/legal. Although these categories depict the external environment for an organization, the strengths, weaknesses, opportunities, and threats identified as part of the external environment usually are reflected internally. For example, an organization may have developed (or need to develop) policies to respond to a shift in the population requesting services or may need to rethink recruiting practices in response to a dearth of qualified applicants in a given geographic region.

Social/Demographic Environment

The unique social environment for a particular community, and the diversity of cultures within that community shape the community and employee preferences for the direction an organization will take. The community in which an organization functions has a great influence. The extent to which there is a great deal of agreement or disagreement upon community priorities and methods of addressing policy priorities will also shape the tensions that will arise in the planning process. Significantly, demographic trends have enormous implications for succession planning, an important aspect of *strategic* HRM that can involve significant conflict between different generations within the agency and within and among the communities being served by the agency.

Political/Legal Environment

The political/legal environment can be defined in terms of the process used to distribute resources or public goods and the policy or law to proscribe such distribution. If we define public safety as a social good, then political decision making regarding budget caps for a given level of public safety is a relevant concern in strategic planning. Also, the means or process by which a community is willing to achieve a certain level of public safety is an important political issue, with great political import for the planning process.

Formal parameters codified in law institutionalize the types of issue raised in the political arena. Community values and priorities are often defined in terms of legal versus illegal actions. For example, one community may consider graffiti to be the pinnacle of evil, whereas another community is preoccupied with drug use among teens.

Economic/Technological Environment

The scope of the economic/technological environment ranges from the types of employment opportunity and business development issue faced by a community, to the relative ability of a region to address fiscal issues from population growth and residential and neighborhood infrastructure demands. Planning efforts must consider the fiscal resources required to sustain a given level of service established by the political process. For example, in the area of public safety, a strict enforcement of traffic safety (e.g., seatbelts, child restraints, cell phone use, impaired driving active enforcement, etc.)

commands an appropriate level of staffing and assignment to shifts and must recognize the links to other infrastructure demands in a community—such as schools, recreation facilities, and educational programs.

What technology is available for use to achieve the mission of the nonprofit or public agency? Do we rely upon sophisticated computer systems, personal tablets, and cell phones—or can we do our work without such 'gadgets' and their associated technical support staff? What type of communication system supports our efforts? What science informs our deliverables? What expectations might citizens, legislators, directing boards, or clients hold about the use of the most appropriate technology?

The E-Government Act (2002) provides ample evidence of the startling transformation in government over the past decade with respect to how citizens interface with public agencies and the nonprofit organizations frequently associated with them. This federal law illustrates how planning in this realm is not only critical, but is likely to be challenging, given the rapid rate of change in communication technology and associated electronic devices capable of connecting to the Internet. The digital exchange between the citizenry and their government, as well as in intergovernmental relationships, greatly enhances information sharing and acquisition. The nature of these exchanges may include everything from electronics as mundane as telephones to sophisticated surveillance mechanisms to ensure security or mechanisms to provide services more efficiently. Aside from the public policy and potentially troublesome personal privacy implications, at a fundamental level, U.S. governmental agencies at all levels must have personnel with the knowledge to handle the rapid changes and nuanced political and legal issues attendant on advances in technology and their myriad applications to public and nonprofit sector work.

Geographic Environment

According to the old adage in real estate, buyers and sellers should concentrate on 'location, location, location'. This holds true for planning, as well. The geographic environment of a particular community includes the natural lines of demarcation that may exist (hills and waterways), as well as climate and proximity to natural resources. Natural geography and that created by architecture and roadways or transformed by landscaping affect public decision making. The physical environment influences both service demands and implementation options. For example, if a community decentralizes the police department to establish a geo-based service provision structure, then the layout of the city will matter greatly in terms of the optimal organizational procedures and practices adopted to maximize coverage and provide flexibility to address 'hot spots' where public order is most often compromised. Staffing arrangements must follow policy directives for effective implementation. Even a small change in policy could ripple through the position descriptions, classification systems, compensation packaging, and performance measurement systems.

Stage 3: Development of the Plan

When the planning team has finished generating and assessing external environmental data and internal organizational data, it may begin drafting the major elements of the plan. Sometimes, organizations rush to this step at the expense of the preplanning and data collection phases. However, this phase benefits from a careful selection of planning participants and thorough data collection and analysis. Oftentimes, an experienced consultant is called in at this point to offer independent commentary and suggest priority concerns to be addressed in the strategic plan.

Technology and Data Analysis

The implications of technology transcend simply informing the plan and also include the use of technology in the development of the strategic plan itself. The explosion of data that can now be compiled with even the most basic of computer applications offers both great opportunity and challenge (Ripley 1995). Potentially, managers could track a wealth of data, including, for example, the training backgrounds of employees, their preferred career paths, education levels, and other demographic characteristics. This information could be employed with modeling software to predict skill needs for particular projects or timelines or even to manage a work team from afar—an entire work team could telecommute (Ripley 1995, p. 84). However, along with greater access to information come predictable frustrations. As planning group members aggregate and analyze data, they should consider a few precautionary notes.

First, as we employ more data and rely heavily upon automation to gather and compute them, we do raise the specter of accuracy. As Ripley (1995, p. 89) cautions us:

> Don't forget that every number the system produces, except for today's actual data is a guess— a very good guess; perhaps, but still only that. In addition, the longer the projection, the more the data degrade. Building an automated system that defines future gaps or surpluses in very specific detail implies a degree of precision that simply does not exist.

Second, as we consider more variables in planning, we are also expected to employ those data to develop contingency responses to imagined scenarios. This raises the possibility that data could impede rather than enhance planning. How do managers sift through a cascade of noise to determine what is most relevant? Managers are understandably frustrated by their inability to manage the growing volume of information. So, too, might the speed of technological change intimidate even the most computer-savvy person. As sophisticated modeling techniques become more widely available in strategic planning to address succession planning and general staff forecasting, there is a propensity to defer analysis to those persons most comfortable with those programs. Too often, critical evaluation by line managers does not occur. Decision making about staffing may become increasingly disconnected from line managers, simply because of the medium of the information. In some ways, the potential for specialization of planning with technology echoes Sayre's dour pronouncement— namely, a case of "triumph of technique over purpose" (1991).

Diversity in Analysis and Planning

Diversity in an organization brings a wealth of viewpoints and interpretations to bear on data. Contending analysis and alternative solutions drawn from different perspectives are among the advantages of a diverse organization. However, contrasting viewpoints may also spark unresolved conflict, and the resulting frustrations in the workplace could impede strategic planning efforts. This can be particularly dysfunctional when the differing views of organizational members and stakeholders crystallize into 'us versus them' disputes. Cox and Finley (1995) note that diversity in an organization does not simply rest with characteristics such as gender or ethnicity, but may also rest with differences derived from functional roles in the organization and professions. For this reason, most general strategic planning processes encourage *comprehensive representation* (across departments and decision-making levels and from inside and outside the organization) to ensure broad participation and representation of different functional perspectives in the development of the plan.

The strategic plan usually includes a mission statement, goals, objectives, and derivative action steps. During its development, the planning team should consult frequently with advisory members

---

Exhibit 5.4 Steps in Developing the Plan

1.   Write the mission statement.
2.   Develop goals, objectives, and action steps.
3.   Integrate the plan into ongoing operations by:

   •   identifying unit responsibility;
   •   designating communication lines;
   •   establishing performance expectations; and
   •   documenting contingency conditions.

4.   Do contingency planning to determine what happens if . . .?
5.   Implement the plan.
6.   Evaluate the plan, process, and outcome by:

   •   examining the planning process using the criteria established during preliminary, preplanning activities;
   •   assessing the resulting performance of the organization using the criteria established through the mission, goals, and objectives.

Source: Authors.

---

of the organization and the community of interests being served. The general procedural activities are outlined in Exhibit 5.4 and reflect the usual general components that should be addressed— mission/goals/objectives/activities, operations integration, contingency assessment, implementation, and evaluation.

Mission Statement

A mission statement offers direction. Ask an organization for its mission statement and you may receive a lengthy list of missives, complete with elaborate statements about organizational values and trendy words such as 'empower', 'collaboration', and 'commitment'. Too often, however, employees in the organization either have no idea what the formal mission statement is, or they point to a framed document on a wall—the meaning of which they would be hard-pressed to explain. Like constitutions and charters of government, mission statements (and strategic plans generally) should be simple, brief, and clear. For mission statements, less really is more. The mission statements in a public sector or nonprofit agency should convey a common purpose to inspire employee commitment to service.

Goals, Objectives, and Action Steps

A goal is a general statement of intent. Goal attainment relies upon the completion of the more detailed objectives and tasks embedded within each goal. Objectives identify more specific activities, often by organizational unit, that will contribute to the overarching goal. For each objective, action steps are specific segments of activity assigned to an identified organizational unit to implement some action within a specified time frame. Action steps could also be characterized as specific tasks, with deadlines and an assignment of responsibility. Both objectives and action steps should include assessment criteria relating to goal accomplishment.

Operations Integration

After the team drafts the basic outline of the plan, members should work with others in the organization to identify appropriate unit responsibilities and the established performance expectations. As we discussed earlier, the environment is not static. Planning team members must consider what actions would be taken if critical assumptions about either the external environment or the internal setting (e.g., an unexpected retirement or separation of a key employee) warrant revision.

Contingency Planning

No organization can be entirely certain of the environment. Thus, planning team members must address contingency planning, that is, what actions would be taken if critical assumptions about the environment had to be revised. Contingency planning can be either comprehensive or of limited scope, depending on the amount of predictability being experienced by the agency (Morais 2010).

Evaluation

Unfortunately, in our excitement over finally completing the planning document, we often do not consider the importance of revisiting the efforts to be certain that we are proceeding appropriately. The performance goals that are established and the assignation of responsibilities require periodic review. An evaluation component in the strategic plan is an important mechanism to be used to ensure that performance goals are met and responsibilities assigned have been acted upon.

Evaluation requires the organizational leadership and planning group to identify some criteria for each objective and action steps in order to assess whether the mission, as well as subordinate goals, was achieved as planned; where there are gaps, decisions are then made regarding whether to revise the plan or devote more resources to bridge the gaps noted. In addition, evaluation may require a constant assessment of the availability of resources, and environmental change. Evaluators should also consider whether the completion of an action was instrumental in, rather than tangential to, goal attainment. Reliable evaluation benefits from utilization of both quantitative and qualitative methodologies—that is, performance data must be monitored, and the people carrying out the work in question should be systematically asked about their perceptions and sentiments regarding their work stemming from the strategic plan.

Strategic HRM

Thorough strategic planning efforts incorporate the specific actions necessary to bring organizational goals to life. Thus, effective plans draw guidance from a detailed assessment of the organization's internal and external environments and the participation of interested parties from the organization and its service community. John Bryson (1995, p. 1) echoes other theorists in arguing that public and nonprofit organizations face chronically turbulent environments, necessitating a great deal of coordinated action.

Organizational leadership must think in terms of internal operations and external environments to translate potential organizational responses into goals that are indeed coordinated and serve to mesh organizational efforts with environmental demands in a timely manner. Leadership must extend this effort beyond general goals to action necessitating an assessment of organizational capacity and concern with the ability of the organization to respond to a mix of constant and changing environmental cues (Bryson 1995; McCann and Selsky 1984; Vinzant and Vinzant 1996). Good examples of recently completed strategic HR plans can be found with relative ease on the Internet via simple google searches. For a federal agency example, the executive summary of the Smithsonian Institution's plan can be found by searching Smithsonian Institution Human Capital Strategic Plan FY 2011–2016; for a state government example, the State of Vermont Department of Human Resources Strategic Plan, 2011–2015 serves as a good source; for the county level of government, the Multnomah (Oregon) County Central Human Resources FY 2014–2016 Executive Summary provides a representative example; and, for the municipal level, the City of Seattle Personnel Department Strategic Plan 2013–2015 provides a useful example.

The rationale underlying the growing importance of strategic planning in public and nonprofit organizations gathers momentum as we note that the distinctions between different arenas of authority—public, private, and nonprofit—have become increasingly blurred in recent years (Bryson 1995, pp. 3–4; Light 2003). In an era of privatization and public–private partnerships, the delivery of certain public goods may no longer be the routine or exclusive domain of the public sector (Francisco and Singer 2010).

Strategic HRM requires that HR departments move beyond the conventional, limited roles of facilitator or advisor to an integration of HRM activities into strategic planning, ongoing management, and systematic coordinated action. Strategic HRM is "the pattern of planned HR deployments and activities intended to enable an organization to achieve its goals" (Wright and McMahan 1992, p. 298). Strategic HRM occurs when the HR unit recasts itself as part of the decision-making team rather than an agent primarily of internal accountability and control.

Considering HR efforts in the context of organization-wide strategic planning reflects the acknowledgment of the key role that employees play in organizational success. Linking HR practices and strategic management to accomplish organizational goals and objectives requires close coordination of HR practices with organizational mission development and implementation (Wright and McMahan 1992, p. 298). Strategic HRM becomes relevant for other organizational actors when it is intimately linked to the enhancement of organizational capacity and the ongoing monitoring of accomplishments and critical assessment of instances of failure to achieve anticipated results. Lacking such a close linkage, line managers are unlikely to accord much priority to HR development initiatives or supportive services (Ospina 1992, p. 53).

Unfortunately, if HR activities are not integrated into organizational strategy, or if strategic planning is simply left to HR departments as one more management fad to be borne, then decisions made in the HR department or by other agency units assigned related work could be ill considered. Ospina cautions us that exclusive focus on short-run problem solving can lead to systematic suboptimization and larger-scale organizational problems experienced over the long run (1992, p. 62).

What might occur if staffing became entirely ad hoc? What if, in response to a perceived shortage, managers added personnel without regard to civil service procedures? Potentially, such actions could disrupt salary levels and raise equity issues. Agency career ladders could become convoluted and unpredictable, leading to employee morale and motivation concerns down the road. Key employees could leave for organizations with greater structure and more career predictability in terms of career path progress and clearer expectations about job responsibilities along the way, thereby raising problems with employee retention and motivation. "Quick fix solutions to human resource problems that arise in the normal course of work will often have unanticipated and negative consequences that are costly to the agency" (Ospina 1992, p. 64).

Summary

Performance in the public sector and in those nonprofit organizations that deliver public goods and services hinges upon the effective management of people to accomplish organizational goals. In this regard, traditional conceptions of HR planning and the role played by HR departments in organizations are inadequate for meeting the challenges of contemporary public sector management. Strategic HR management and planning in the public sector cannot be accomplished with a narrow focus upon each individual, traditional HR function conceived of as distinct from the 'harsh realities' of line management and public service delivery systems. Rather, agency strategic planning efforts require active collaboration between HR specialists and line managers. Without this level of organization-wide planning, adaptation to changing expectations of citizens, to different means of evaluating performance, or to different demands for service delivery from new and nontraditional clientele will be exceedingly difficult. As the various resources available to the HRM unit are identified, the planning process can respond effectively to the expectations arising from agency clientele and political decision makers. Strategic HRM offers a powerful way to enhance productivity and build organizational capacity for the future.

A Manager's Vocabulary

- Contingency planning
- Economic/technology environment
- Goals
- Implementation
- Mission
- Objectives
- Political/legal environment
- Social/demographic environment
- Strategic planning
- Strategic human resource management
- Succession planning
- SWOT analysis
- Workforce planning

Study Questions

1. How might traditional workforce or succession planning differ from strategic planning?
2. How might planning activities differ between public, private, and nonprofit sector organizations?
3. What factors are likely characteristics of the external environment for a nonprofit organization? And for a public sector organization?
4. How should we evaluate planning efforts in public sector organizations? And in nonprofit organizations?

Exercise 5.1 Dissecting an Organization

Select a public or nonprofit sector organization for discussion. As you consider this organization today, address the following questions:

- What is its mission?
- What are the organization's principal strengths? And its noteworthy weaknesses?
- What opportunities are available to the organization? What threats must it endure?

Now jump forward 10 years to project:

- What may change?
- What may stay the same?
- How do you know?

References

Anyim, Frances C., Joy O. Ekwoaba, and Dumebi Anthony Ideh. 2012. "The Role of Human Resource Planning in Recruitment and Selection Process." *British Journal of Humanities and Social Sciences* 6 (2): 68–78.

Baker Tilly, LLP. 2011. "Succession Planning in Government: Why is it Still Relevant?" *State and Local Government Industry Insights* (August): 1–4.

Berry, Frances Stokes, and Barton Wechsler. 1995. "State Agencies' Experience with Strategic Planning: Findings from a National Survey." *Public Administration Review* 55 (2): 159–168.

Briggs, Senga, and William Keough. 1999. "Integrating Human Resource Strategy and Strategic Planning to Achieve Business Excellence." *Total Quality Management* 10 (4–5): 447–453.

Bryson, John. 1995. *Strategic Planning for Public and Nonprofit Organizations*. San Francisco, CA: Jossey Bass.

Coleman, Charles J. 1973. "Personnel: the Changing Function." *Public Personnel Management* 2(3): 186–193.

Cox, Taylor H., Jr., and Joycelyn A. Finley. 1995. "An Analysis of Work Specialization and Organization Level as Dimensions of Workforce Diversity." In *Diversity in Organizations*, Eds. Martin M. Chemers, Stuart Oskamp, and Mark A. Costanzo, 62–88. Thousand Oaks, CA: Sage.

Denhardt, Robert B. 1991. *Public Administration: An Action Orientation*. Belmont, CA: Brooks/Cole.

E-Government Act of 2002. Pub.L 107–347 116 Stat. 2899 44 U.S.C. §101.

Francisco, Laura, and Paula Singer. 2010. "Workforce and Succession Planning: No Longer a Zero-Sum Game." *IPMA HR News* (September): 7–8.

Fredericksen, Elizabeth D. 2010. "When the Music Stops: Succession Is More than Filling Seats." *State and Local Government Review* 42 (1): 50–60.

Frederickson, H. George. 1992. "Painting Bull's-Eyes Around Bullet Holes." *Governing* 6 (1): 13.

Government Performance and Results Act of 1993. S.20, 103rd Cong.

Johnson, Gilbert L., and Judith Brown. 2004. "Workforce Planning Not a Common Practice, IPMA-HR Study Finds." *Public Personnel Management* 33 (4): 379–388.

Kanter, Rosabeth Moss, and David V. Summers. 1987. "Doing Well While Doing Good: Dilemmas of Performance Measurement in Nonprofit Organizations and the Need for a Multiple-Constituency Approach." In *The Nonprofit Sector: A Research Handbook*, Ed. Walter W. Powell, 154–166. New Haven, CT: Yale University Press.

King, Cheryl Simrell, and Camilla Stivers, Eds. 1998. *Government Is Us*. Thousand Oaks, CA: Sage.

Light, Paul C. 2003. "The Illusion of Smallness." In *Classics of Public Personnel Policy*, 3rd ed., Ed. Frank J. Thompson, 157–177. Belmont, CA: Wadsworth.

Lindblom, Charles E. 1992. "The Science of 'Muddling Through'." In *Classics of Public Administration*, 3rd ed., Eds. Jay M. Shafritz and Albert C. Hyde, 224–235. Pacific Grove, CA: Brooks/Cole.

McCann, Joseph E., and John Selsky. 1984. "Hyperturbulence and the Emergence of Type 5 Environments." *Academy of Management Review* 9 (3): 460–470.

McEnery, Jean M., and Mark L. Lifter. 1987. "Demands for Change: Interfacing Environmental Pressures and the Personnel Process." *Public Personnel Management* 16 (1): 62–63.

Morais, Rowena. 2010. "The Critical Nature of Strategic Workforce Planning: It's Not About Planning for Every Job, it is Planning for Critical Ones." *HR Matters* (October). www.hr.matters.info/feat2010/2010.Oct10.htm (accessed April 19, 2014).

Ospina, Sonia. 1992. "When Managers Don't Plan: Consequences of Nonstrategic Public Personnel Management." *Review of Public Personnel Administration* 12 (1): 53–64.

Perry, James L. 1993. "Strategic Human Resource Management." *Review of Public Personnel Administration* 13 (4): 59–71.

Poister, Theodore H., and Gregory Streib. 2005. "Elements of Strategic Planning and Management in Municipal Government." *Public Administration Review* 65 (1): 45–56.

Random House Dictionary. 1980. New York: Random House.

Ripley, David E. 1995. "How to Determine Future Workforce Needs." *Personnel Journal* 74 (1): 83–89.

Sayre, Wallace S. 1991. "The Triumph of Techniques Over Purpose." In *Classics of Public Personnel Policy*, 2nd ed., Ed. Frank J. Thompson, 154–158. Pacific Grove, CA: Brooks/Cole.

Selden, Sally Coleman, Patricia Ingraham, and Willow Jacobson. 2001. "Human Resource Practices in State Governments: Findings from a National Survey." *Public Administration Review* 61 (5): 598–607.

Southern, Craig. 2012. "Strategic, Workforce, and Succession Plans: Organizational Success All Rolled Into One." *HR News Magazine* (September): 10–11, 14.

Steinbruner, John D. 1974. *The Cybernetic Theory of Decision: New Dimensions of Political Analysis*. Princeton, NJ: Princeton University Press.

Stilwell, Jason. 1996. "Managing Chaos." *Public Management* 78 (9): 6–9.

Thompson, James. 1967. *Organizations in Action*. New York: McGraw-Hill.

Vinzant, Douglas H., and Janet C. Vinzant. 1996. "Strategy and Organizational Capacity: Finding a Fit." *Public Productivity & Management Review* 20 (2): 139–157.

Wolch, Jennifer R. 1990. *The Shadow State: Government and Voluntary Sector in Transition*. New York: The Foundation Center.

Wright, Patrick M., and Gary C. McMahan. 1992. "Theoretical Perspectives for Strategic Human Resource Management." *Journal of Management* 18 (2): 295–320.

6 Job Design, Analysis, and Classification

Learning Objectives

- Understand the difference between job analysis and job design, and their respective applications in organizations.
- Explore the challenges associated with identifying a comprehensive inventory of job tasks and prioritizing and valuing job tasks.
- Appreciate the influence of analysis, evaluation, and classification on virtually all functional areas of personnel administration.

In a strategic management paradigm, decisions about positions in an organization, the requisite skills and knowledge for employees, and the structure of their work should be as consistent as possible with the organization's mission and goals. Anyone who has worked with a large organization probably has seen an outline of what they are responsible for doing in their position, or they have looked at a schedule of salary ranges to identify what they were being paid relative to others. However, these small snapshots of an organization may or may not make very much sense in the context of organizational goals. For example, if we use a construction analogy, we might view planning activities as the blueprint for structure. However, the foundation, upon which this building would rest, is composed of the design, analysis, and classification of positions. Much of what we will discuss in later chapters on recruitment and selection, compensation, and performance management hinges upon the analysis, classification, and evaluation of work performed in a particular position. Job analysis— and the resultant classification and evaluation of organizational positions—is fairly simple in concept, but tends to be quite complicated in actual application.

The dependence upon classification systems in the public sector and in larger nonprofit organizations is a very important factor in differences that arise between line supervisors or managers and HR support staff. Many managers and supervisors express frustration as they try to obtain an additional employee to respond to demands made upon their work unit or attempt to reclassify an existing member of their work team who is capable of taking on additional responsibility. Immediate personnel needs that managers try to articulate to HR staff often have to be translated into a complex, comprehensive system that is rigidly dependent upon hidden formulas and often-obtuse task definitions. Additionally, job evaluation and classification for any particular jurisdiction is constrained by merit system practice, constantly evolving labor law, and the usual public sector due process expectations. Complete textbooks devoted to job analysis and position classification cannot capture the full range of nuances of the various approaches in common use across the country. In this chapter, we will provide an overview of job analysis, evaluation, classification, and design and offer a working knowledge of common practices, key terminology, and principal issues in controversy.

Let us assume for the sake of argument that a job is a collection of tasks and duties associated with a particular activity in an organization. The intent behind job analysis is to identify exactly what those tasks are, the ramifications to the organization (or work group) of performing those tasks, and the skills and knowledge required to perform the identified tasks competently. Once these tasks are specified, it is possible to forecast the importance, difficulty, or relative contribution of the competently performed job to the overall organizational effort. After specifying the tasks and the implications of those tasks for the organization, the analyst would next consider the skills or knowledge necessary to perform the tasks and fulfill the duties of the position in question. From such a job analysis, position descriptions are developed that typically identify the overall rationale/objective for the position and list the specific tasks that are required and the requisite skills or knowledge that must be possessed by the applicant. Evaluation of jobs allows them to be grouped in classes and be assigned relative worth. Classification is the process of grouping similar jobs together—usually to develop uniform compensation levels and to establish appropriate recruitment strategies. The logic of job analysis in an organization presumes that it is possible to identify, clearly and completely, the tasks and duties associated with a particular position.

Analysis, evaluation, and classification constitute a complex and time-consuming process intended to ensure equity and consistency in practice. Because of the substantial resources that are consumed in this exercise, it is more common in very large organizations, and the degree of sophistication varies greatly across organizations. Very small nonprofit organizations or public sector jurisdictions may dispense with many of the activities outlined in this chapter, although they are advantageous from a legal and economic perspective. Instead, such organizations may consider position descriptions (without the preliminary stages of analysis and evaluation) to be adequate for their purpose. In very small organizations, employees may often work without any formal position definitions or established job parameters, and may experience a degree of expansion in job duties as they gain experience in the organization.

Introduction to the Reading

Because job analysis is a basic first step in recruitment and selection, performance management, and compensation packaging, it is vital that the KSAs required for positions be evaluated without deliberate error or unintentional bias. As you read Guy, Newman, and Mastracci (2008), keep the following questions in mind:

1. What do the authors mean by "theories of caring"?
2. What are the implications of conceptualizing responsiveness versus efficiency, and then prioritizing these respective values in public or nonprofit work?
3. According to the authors, what are the commonest job characteristics of a position that requires emotional labor? What others might exist as well?
4. What types of common error may exist in our assessment of the merits of one job over another?
5. Why might some jobs be considered more important than others in achieving organizational goals?
6. What does the potential for measurement error and bias in job analysis and evaluation have for discussions about workplace diversity?
7. Capturing the role of judgment and discretion in a position can be a complicated undertaking. Does the framework in this excerpt simplify or add to this challenge?
8. What is, per the authors, the *citizen–state interchange*, and why should this concept be integrated into analysis and classification?

Excerpt 6.1 Emotional Labor

Emotion work is instrumental in bridging the "how" and the "what" of government. It turns our attention to the _caritas_ function that is at the heart of public service, and the means by which this work is performed. . . .

The focus on caring illuminates the disconnect between the actual performance of public service and the theoretical development of public administration. While a framework of caring is implied (indeed essential) in an understanding of the practice of public administration, it is not articulated. Instead, twin values of rationality and efficiency predominate. With the notable exception of the recent work of Camilla Stivers, Cheryl King, O. C. McSwite, and a handful of others, there is a vacuum in the literature on both the theory of caring and on the value of service and relational tasks. Caring as a value has not moved into the mainstream of public administration discourse. Without a place in the paradigm, the concept of relational work and its essential component, emotional labor, is absent. . . .

The void in the public administration literature on the _caritas_ function and the concept of emotional labor as a theoretical construct stands in marked contrast with the rich treatment of "caring" in other disciplines. Most fundamentally, this research stream has addressed the dichotomy between the "rational" aspects of organizations and the role of emotion in organizing, developing, and leadership. . . .

Stivers makes reference to leadership as having become public administration's "Phlogiston—the mysterious substance that, prior to the discovery of oxygen, was believed to be the ingredient in substances that made them burn" (2002, p. 62). The same term can be accurately applied to the concept of emotion work. Most public service jobs require interpersonal encounters, often in emotionally wrenching circumstances. . . . Relational skills are essential for job completion but have only recently come under scrutiny as prerequisites that make a difference in the performance of public programs (Guy and Newman 2004, p. 289). Emotional labor requires that workers suppress their private feelings in order to show the "desirable" work-related emotion. Unlike physical labor, this "invisible" work: it is not measurable and it can rarely be seen, touched, or heard. Jobs that require emotional labor have three distinct characteristics in common: first, they require person-to-person contact with the public; second, they require workers to manage the emotional state of another person; and third, they allow the employer to exercise a degree of control over the emotional activities of employees (Hochschild 1983, p. 147). In short, the focus is on an emotional performance that is bought and sold as a commodity. . . .

Our understanding of what it means to work derives from our disciplinary roots, and is founded on Wilsonian, Tayloristic, and Weberian assumptions. For the most part, theories of work and caring are treated as unrelated concepts. According to Himmelweit, "The dichotomized picture—which places home, care, and women on one side and the workplace, paid labor, and men on the other—needs adjusting to remove the distorting dualism that leaves no room for care to cross the boundary into the workplace" (1999, p. 28). . . .

[T]he market's "objective" approach to task elements and to performance evaluation rests on an ideology of work that is buttressed by norms suited to industrial but not service jobs. Traditional administrative language is the language of scientific management—span of control, hierarchy, authority, and division of labor. A conception of administration practice that is relational rather than controlling has a very different vocabulary. . . .

[W]orkers are called upon to exercise various forms of emotion work, ranging from practicing common courtesy to calming people who are agitated or upset to intense degrees of guiding people through trying circumstances. How does such work affect their workday? The answer is that it requires workers to perform not only the cognitive tasks required by their job but also the emotional labor tasks. More challenging than these requirements is the task of suppressing one's own feelings while expressing a different feeling. . . . Dwight Waldo noted that the issues public administration practitioners and scholars wrestle with are issues of "human cooperation." There are few, if any, questions in public administration that are simply technical (Stivers 2000, p. 135). A social worker comforts a frightened child, a paralegal calms a teenage client, an investigator becomes a chameleon in order to gain the trust of informants, a public attorney engages in crisis intervention, an administrator rallies her staff, while another acts as a surrogate mother to her charges. Theirs is not the work of a "neutral expert" simply "doing the job" as a technician. Their work is relational in nature and involves considerable emotional labor demands. Yet much of their work, and that of others who engage in emotional labor and caregiving, is treated informally[;] . . . it is not part of any formal job description, nor does it appear on performance evaluations. Nor is this work measurable or documented. Much of the work in the caring relation is "uncharted."

Excerpt References

Guy, Mary E. and Meredith A. Newman. 2004. "Women's Jobs, Men's Jobs: Sex Segregation and Emotional Labor." *Public Administration Review* 64(3): 289–298.

Himmelweit, Susan. 1999. "Caring Labor." *Annals, AAPSS* 561 (January): 27–38.

Hochschild, Arlie. 1983. *The Managed Heart: Commercialization of Human Feeling*. Berkeley, CA: University of California Press.

Stivers, Camilla. 2002. *Gender Images in Public Administration: Legitimacy and the Administrative State*. 2nd ed. Thousand Oaks, CA: Sage.

———. 2000. *Bureau Men, Settlement Women: Constructing Public Administration in the Progressive Era*. Lawrence, KS: University of Kansas Press.

Waldo, Dwight. 1948. *The Administrative State: A Study of the Political Theory of American Public Administration*. New York: The Ronald Press Company.

Source: Guy, Mary E., Meredith A. Newman, and Sharon H. Mastracci. 2008. "The Disconnect Between Public Administration Theory and Practice." In *Emotional Labor: Putting the Service in Public Service*, excerpt from pp. 38–55. Armonk, NY: M.E. Sharpe.

Analysis and Classification in Context

Much of contemporary job analysis and classification is founded in Progressive Era calls for the replacement of spoils system political appointees with neutral, competent public servants, detailed in Chapter 2. Competence rather than patronage predicated the logic of the Pendleton Act. Thus, a means to identify necessary competencies for a given position in government was a critical first step for civil service reform. Civil service reform and the notion of equity in compensation provided fertile ground for what we know today as contemporary analysis, description, evaluation, and classification. These personnel activities suggest that patronage defers to competence, as analysis and

Exhibit 6.1 Analysis and Classification: Context and Development

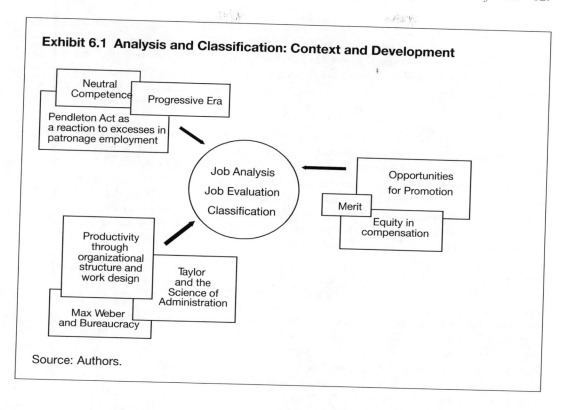

Source: Authors.

classification specifically define positions in terms of necessary competencies rather than the possession of political ties.

In parallel with concerns in the political arena about neutrality and competence in government, a collection of early-twentieth-century organization theorists studied the implications of organization structure and procedure for productivity; these practice-oriented scholars are often collectively referred to as the classical school of organization theory. The classical school of organization theory is predicated upon the belief that it is necessary to control the irrationality of humans to improve organizational effort (Fry 1989, pp. 3–5). Two major approaches are associated with classical organization theory. The science of administration approach holds that human beings can be controlled to improve organizational outcomes through the development of appropriate authority structures. Scientific management, in contrast, focuses concern upon control over behavior exercised through the structure of tasks associated with the positions within organizations.

Structuring the Organization for Efficiency

Max Weber's depiction of the ideal structure of bureaucracy is the cornerstone of the science of administration movement. Weber, a German sociologist, believed that a particular organizational structure could improve the rationality of the collective efforts of human beings, reducing the likelihood of arbitrary and capricious action (1987, pp. 81–83). This structure—the bureaucracy—hinges upon the division of labor and hierarchical authority relationships that are explicitly detailed in organizational policies and rules. In *The Wealth of Nations*, originally published in 1776 and quite influential to the founders, Adam Smith posited the importance of the division of labor to the efficient use of resources and the generation of wealth (1987, pp. 30–35). Weber counted on the craft and professional specializations that would emerge in industrializing countries to argue that organizational productivity required a high degree of division of labor, giving structure to uniform work processes and outcomes. The division of responsibility for particular tasks presumes a clear distribution of authority and a limited span of control to ensure direct supervision of subordinates throughout a bureaucracy.

Authority as commensurate with the narrow responsibilities associated with a particular job tends to be centralized and reflective of a monocratic hierarchy. In bureaucratic models, individuals holding positions in the structure are selected according to their ability to perform the defined job. This concept is critical in public administration, given the logic of a merit-based system. Authority rests with the position and remains fixed to the location of the position in the hierarchy. Authority does not rest with individuals, and jobs do not belong to people. Employees can move in and out of different positions with no discernible affect upon the organization. In this sense, all employees are, *by design and intention*, interchangeable and replaceable.

Structuring the Job for Efficiency

For scientific management theorists such as Frederick Taylor, the position (rather than the organizational authority structure) can be shaped to achieve productivity, and jobs can be reduced to a collection of small, repeated tasks. Productivity can be improved and sustained through identification of the most efficient way to perform each of these tasks. Taylor believed there was "one best way" to complete every meaningful task, and that people, properly motivated with the right incentive, would work to optimum indefinitely (1987, pp. 66–81.) The tenets of scientific management emphasize technical efficiency to enhance organizational activity. However, analysts focus upon the task or job characteristic as the unit to consider in building a position, or in deconstructing an organization, then a department, then a position, and ultimately the tasks therein.

Analysis and Classification in Human Resource Management

The practice of administration, as prescribed through classical organization theory, means that some method is required to study and categorize positions embedded within organizations and those positions we anticipate adding. If the goal is to enhance efficiency for the organization and to deal with employees on a merit-centric basis, then decisions should hinge upon competence in task rather than upon personal characteristics. As Guy, Newman, and Mastracci (2008) caution us, even if efficiency is a goal, we still must consider that it is neither the only characteristic of a job, nor the fundamental organizational objective in public or nonprofit organizations.

Contemporary job analysis, evaluation, and classification should address multiple factors, including concerns about subjectivity, relationships, responsiveness, equity, merit, and efficiency. Such analysis and categorization functions are fundamental to established personnel systems in the public, private for-profit, and not-for-profit sectors. The structural linkages between the various technical activities of analysis, evaluation, and classification and other personnel functions are detailed in Exhibit 6.2. The functional activities detailed in Chapters 5–13 of this text are based upon decisions made during analysis, evaluation, and classification. In fact, decisions made decades ago may drive contemporary management options to a significant extent.

Analysis, evaluation, and classification link directly to compensation packaging (Pettibone 2013). As discussed in Chapters 8 and 9, salaries and wages should be based upon fair compensation for the

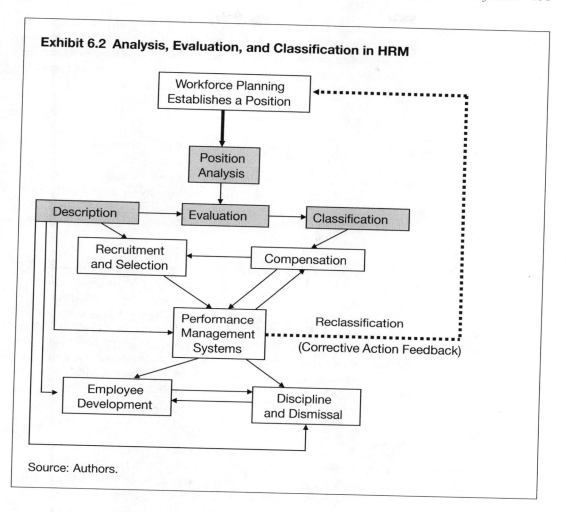

Exhibit 6.2 Analysis, Evaluation, and Classification in HRM

Source: Authors.

tasks accomplished or services provided by the employee. Employees are recruited and selected using a job description that outlines the general responsibilities and duties and requisite qualifications. In a performance management system, the position description suggests baseline expectations for an employee's performance. In combination, analysis, evaluation, and classification activities support employee development activities. Employees can assess their skills and knowledge and their responsibilities in terms of the expectations for a related position or a position to which they aspire. The position description outlines the appropriate scope of a position for an employee. The responsibilities and duties outlined in the job descriptions provide some guidance to an employee and their employer as to the minimum expectations about performance for a position. Disciplinary action must be consistent with guidelines established about employee responsibilities and behavior. The policies and procedures used to ensure continuity, stability, and uniformity may hinge upon decisions about what tasks constitute certain positions and how these positions relate to one and other in organizational production and communication patterns.

A component of the organization's strategic planning effort should entail the identification of the types of activity that an organization is performing currently, as well as those that may be necessary in the short-term and longer-term future. Moreover, we have to make these decisions in the context of a budget, as well as the political demands upon our organization for action. Current and pending needs, coupled with environment constraints, merge to prompt several questions:

- What types of job will we have in an organization?
- What jobs we will need in the future?
- What skill sets, educational backgrounds, aptitudes, or capacities will people require to fill those jobs?
- How much of the budget can we allocate to hire people to perform certain activities?
- What salary or benefits must we offer to recruit and retrain employees with the knowledge and skills that we need?
- How much should (or can) we invest in the training and development of existing employees to acquire needed knowledge and skills?

In addition to ongoing mundane budgetary and political considerations, the nature of work itself is changing rather dramatically—along with people's expectations about how their jobs fit into their lives. Even the same basic position becomes revised, reconceptualized, and retitled during the course of a decade, as we will see later in this chapter when considering an entry-level clerical/secretarial/administrative position. The use of technology, communication skills, language versatility, equity, and access, and even the physical environment of work, affect employee and management attitudes toward different positions. The dynamics of organization effort and the evolving scope of many traditional jobs affect the expectations that employers have about minimum qualifications and performance levels for different jobs.

Job Analysis

The premise behind job or position analysis is relatively simple. Job analysis identifies the tasks necessary for a competent performance of a particular activity. The person who holds the job under scrutiny is usually called the job incumbent. To develop a complete picture of what a particular job may entail, the analyst may interview the job incumbent, their supervisor, and often others with whom this person works. The analysis must focus upon the tasks and duties affiliated with a particular position, not upon the particular person in the position or any unique contribution he or she brings to the work to be accomplished in that position.

A job analyst will determine the specific duties associated with a particular position and identify the amount of time associated with each major duty. It is customary to identify the tangential positions associated with a particular job. What levels of supervision occur, and what kinds of decision does the job incumbent have authority to make? Does the job incumbent have to perform their job in conjunction with others, such as a supervisor or as a peer? For each task, the job analyst must identify the KSAs required.

The knowledge required for a position suggests that a person is informed about the body of organizational procedures, channels of communication, and techniques associated with a particular area of activity. Skills and abilities are somewhat similar in meaning. Ability suggests the potential or capacity to perform, whereas a skill may be the more specific mastery of a technique or tool. The job analyst must also identify any formal training or education necessary to certify those elements of KSA. For example, what is necessary to manage a particular computer-related task—an engineering degree or select courses in a specific software application?

It is very important, as we will see in later chapters, that the tasks be logically linked to a particular job, and the qualifications (e.g., education or training) be related to the tasks. Tasks should be legitimately associated with a position, and the qualifications should be commensurate with the required KSAs. In addition to training or education, there may be additional qualifications necessary for a particular position. Questions include:

- Are there legal requirements for licensure, as in the case of the medical profession?
- Does the job incumbent need to operate machinery that may require licensure or a particular permit?
- What are the physical and operational parameters of the position?
- Does it require that the job incumbent work shifts in the evening? Morning? On rotation?
- Does the job incumbent work outside or in an office setting?

Strategic job analysis requires a consideration of the demands or requirements of a position over time, rather than through a static assessment of the tasks at one point in time (Schneider and Konz 1989). Managers seeking a new position or a reclassification of an existing slot need to consider carefully the position in context—over time, in comparison with like positions in different units, and with regard to organizational goals. For analysts, the focus is often upon how the job may evolve in the future in response to the work environment, changing technology, or different mandates specified for public sector organizations. Both managers and HR specialists must recognize the practical, legal, and political constraints facing the organization in terms of an existing structure or personnel system, if the political will necessary to revise an existing classification system does not exist.

Technical considerations in job analysis also warrant attention. Two procedures are commonly used to conduct job analyses: the task inventory procedure (TIP) and the position analysis questionnaire (PAQ). Many permutations of these two general methods exist, and substantial research time has been devoted to developing these broadly applied procedures. Job analysis can be a very complicated specialty within HRM.

Task Inventory Procedure

Although there are variations in the implementation of TIP, generally the job incumbent would identify the list of tasks he or she performs as a starting point (Mitchell and Driskill 1996). The job incumbent then assesses the relative difficulty of each task and reports how often she or he performs the tasks identified (Sanchez and Levine 1989). Job incumbents may also be asked to assess the difficulty of *learning* a particular task relative to other job-related activities. Incumbents may be asked to assess the importance of the task in terms of their other activities, as well as to the organization as a whole. In some cases, agency supervisors are asked to assess the difficulty, frequency, and importance levels that employees assign (Clifford 1996).

Job incumbents tend to rate as higher in importance those tasks that are difficult to perform and difficult to learn, rather than those that are relatively more time-intensive or associated with greater responsibility (Sanchez and Levine 1989, p. 339). There appears to be an acceptable level of inter-rater validity in the TIP process: incumbents tend to be consistent in how they assess different tasks for many of the difficulty, frequency, and centrality scales to be applied (Sanchez and Fraser 1993). Interestingly, researchers who found evidence of some variability in the assessment of different tasks attributed the variation to personal characteristics of the incumbent, rather than actual variations present between positions. "Such idiosyncratic perceptions of job tasks might in turn be moderated by differing degrees of job experience or educational level or perhaps by true differences in the manner in which comparable jobs are performed" (Sanchez and Fraser 1993).

Exhibit 6.3 outlines a sample of task dimensions. In this sample, tasks are differentiated in terms of difficulty and relative significance to the organization. Difficulty and significance may be established from multiple perspectives (e.g., significance could be time spent, task criticality, or inherent task importance). A simple list of tasks does not capture the relational aspects of the position such as responsibilities to coordinate information or prioritize correspondence and reaction to queries from other organizational units or from outside the organization. The task list similarly does not establish job context with respect to the level of authority, noise levels, or frequency of interruptions.

Position Analysis Questionnaire

The PAQ, developed by Ernest McCormick and his associates over the course of several years, presumes that a job can be broken down into "discrete job variables" that could then be "identified and quantified as they relate to individual jobs" (McCormick, Jeanneret, and Mecham 1972, p. 348). PAQ distinguishes between job variables that are technical kinds of skill, such as may be identified in task inventories, and those that relate to the interpersonal and behavioral nature of work (McCormick 1959). The PAQ contains questions designed to generate data for differentiating positions according to the global categories of information input, mediation processes, work output, interpersonal activities, work situation, job context, and a catch-all for miscellaneous aspects (McCormick, Jeanneret, and Mecham 1972, p. 349). A list of these categories, along with sample job elements for the PAQ, is located in Exhibit 6.4. The job elements normally would be assessed according to the frequency of occurrence or perhaps the level of importance of the job element to the overall position. The PAQ attempts to identify the behaviors necessary to complete a particular task, rather than identify the discrete task.

Limitations of Job Analysis

Both TIP and PAQ are used to analyze jobs in preparation for subsequent personnel process activities. The procedures identify slightly different types of information. The TIP focuses on the aggregation of tasks necessary for a job, whereas the PAQ includes behavioral and interpersonal activities. The choice of job analysis method could result in a different snapshot of the same position, with implications for other personnel activities within an organization.

To illustrate the potential for problems with a focus upon tasks, consider a familiar position. The position of secretary or administrative assistant has changed over time, but is arguably one of the most critical and demanding jobs in any organization. The position title alone has changed to reflect the integral nature of the position to administrative processes from 'secretary' to 'administrative assistant'. These positions often serve a central coordinating function in work units, and quite commonly are responsible for the overall flow of administrative operations. Using TIP, we might identify several activities, including word-processing, scheduling, photocopying, or transcription, as well as activities that may or may not have lingered in the contemporary organization, such as dictation and shorthand, among other things. How have these tasks evolved in the last decade?

Applications in technology and software have changed simple typing to word-processing and desktop publishing. Scheduling may require the mastery of complex software and an ability to link multiple operating sites on intranets and, potentially, using Internet-based systems. Documents have become graphic masterpieces using basic word-processing software. In the past, document development of this nature was the bailiwick of graphic arts or printing specialists, rather than the department's administrative assistant. Photocopying now presents a dizzying array of choices, from paper size or color scale to decisions about scanning, collating, stapling, or duplexing. Dictation may

Exhibit 6.3 Sample Dimensions of Task

Task Dimension	In Application:
Time spent	The amount of time spent by the job incumbent upon on a task relative to other tasks in a job
Task difficulty	The difficulty of performing the task perceived by the incumbent relative to other tasks in the job
Task criticality	The degree to which incorrect performance of the task by the incumbent would result in negative consequences relative to other tasks in a job
Difficulty of learning the task	The amount of time and effort that the incumbent believes they exerted to learn the task relative to all other tasks in a job
Task responsibility	The degree of responsibility that the incumbent holds for completing a task without supervision, relative to all other tasks in a job
Overall task importance	The overall importance that the incumbent perceives the task to hold relative to all other tasks in a job

Source: The task dimensions are drawn from Sanchez and Levine 1989, p. 337.

Exhibit 6.4 Position Analysis Questionnaire

General Categories	Subdivisions of Activity	Job Element
Information input	Sources of job information	Use of written materials
	Discrimination and perceptional activities	Estimating speed of moving objects
Mediation processes	Decision making and reasoning	Reasoning in problem solving
	Information processing	Encoding/decoding
	Use of stored information	Using mathematics
Work output	Use of physical devices	Keyboard
	Integrative manual activities	Handling objects
	General body activities	Climbing
Interpersonal activities	Communications	Instructing
	Interpersonal relationships	Coaching
	Supervision and coordination	Level of supervision received
Work situation and job context	Physical working conditions	Low temperature
	Psychological and sociological aspects	Civic obligation
Miscellaneous aspects	Work schedule	Irregular hours
	Job demands	Specified/controlled work pace
	Responsibility	Responsible for the safety of others

Source: The PAQ is drawn, with certain job elements adapted for clarity, from McCormick, Jeanneret, and Mecham 1972, p. 349.

be obsolete with the latest in voice recognition software. Scanners can translate handwritten documents into digital files. Clearly, the position is driven, shaped, and constrained by technology as we progress through the second decade of this century. What might we expect in the near and longer-term future?

Now consider the categorization of activities and elements in the PAQ depicted in Exhibit 6.4. In addition to the problems introduced with task identification, we must also consider that work behaviors and relational aspects in the workplace are typically fluid. As responsibilities evolve and people develop new skills sets, relationships and interpersonal demands will also change. As we will discuss later in this chapter and revisit in Chapter 10, the structure of organizations and the location in which people will do their work are likewise in flux. Assessing behaviors and interpersonal activities becomes an even more complex undertaking when we are studying a position that may interact with a work team that is fluid in composition, drawn from across departments, and composed of some members who are physically present and others who are located in a different office, city, state, or country.

Traditional job analysis focuses on a snapshot of the tasks or work behaviors at the moment of study. For this reason, the rapid changes in the work environment and in the character of work make it difficult to maintain up-to-date job analysis data. Strategic job analysis requires a consideration of the demands or requirements of a position in the future, rather than a static assessment of the tasks today (Schneider and Konz 1989). Managers are concerned with how a job may evolve in the future in response to the work environment, changing technology, or different mandates for public and nonprofit organizations. Analysts in strategically adaptive organizations must share this focus.

Position Description

A position description is drawn from the job content analysis. Thus, any limitations or errors that are introduced during job analysis will be transferred to the job description. A position description should offer a summary of the general responsibilities and feature the specific duties associated with a particular position in an organization. Most job descriptions are meant to be somewhat generic to describe a type of position, rather than being tailored to a unique type of job or set of professional characteristics possessed by an individual. As these descriptions are quite time-consuming to develop, they tend to outlive the contemporary realities of the work in a given position. Position descriptions usually include a general statement about the objectives of the position. In addition, there may be a general summary of the environment and overall obligations of the position. The essential job duties are usually listed specifically, a requirement of the ADA (1990). Finally, most position descriptions include a section identifying the specific KSAs required. Position descriptions should identify the mechanisms by which a person can demonstrate that she or he has the appropriate knowledge; a specific degree or training program, or a specified amount of related job experience may be stipulated.

Sometimes, position descriptions and the data generated from the job analysis reflect social norms in a particular community, and they can even reflect social biases, as we saw with the reading for this chapter (Erez 2010). Problems with position descriptions can also occur as expectations change about different jobs, and as the tools for performing the job change. When the tasks or tools change, public and nonprofit organizations should revise the requisite KSAs associated with their positions. If the organizational mission changes, might this also be cause for a revision of position descriptions? Sometimes, to consider the various contingencies that will arise for different positions, the position description is written to be rather general and, thereafter, is applied to a wider variety of similar jobs. Yet, a very general position description may be almost as inappropriate as one that is too specific. If we look to the position description to guide employees in what to do and to serve as the basic unit in job evaluation and classification activities, then descriptions that are either too general or too specific can be counterproductive. Ideally, position descriptions should establish the parameters of the position, offer a link to performance management systems, and communicate standards for performance as well as priorities for activities.

The language used in a position description can have serious implications during the job evaluation stage. The valence of information (positive or negative) and its placement in the position description affects the later assessment of job worth. "Positive information placed at the beginning of a description tends to increase its evaluation, whereas negative information placed at the beginning tends to lower the evaluation" (Smith, Hornsby, and Benson 1990, p. 305). The sensitivity of position description language serves as a warning that the 'objectivity' of the classification system is at least somewhat tenuous.

Job Evaluation

After jobs have been analyzed for content, and a position description has been generated, an evaluation is conducted of different jobs to assess their relative worth to the organization in question. Consistent with Weber's caution that authority rests with the position rather than the person, organizations should consider the worth of a position as separate from the qualities of any person who might occupy the job. The position should be evaluated in terms of its value to an organization when performed at a minimally competent level. After the relative value of a particular job to the organization has been assessed, similar jobs are grouped or classed together and eventually assigned to a specific compensation level.

Job evaluation has important implications for subsequent personnel activities. As the job is evaluated in terms of the work environment and demands of the position, then recruitment and selection strategies will be driven by assumptions about the relative value of the skills necessary in a particular position, as well as the characteristics of the job. This evaluation process establishes the salary range, a critical component in recruitment and hiring negotiations. Assumptions about the nature of a position and the relative hazards or expectations about minimum performance have substantial implications for managing performance, employee motivation, and the KSAs held by supervisors.

Employee Motivation and Job Evaluation

Two perspectives upon motivation are important to consider before we look at the different methods that may be employed to assign worth to jobs. You will recall that expectancy theory suggests that an individual's motivation is linked to whether what they expect to occur in response to their effort actually does take place, and whether they are looking forward to that outcome (Vroom 1964). Equity theory, in contrast, suggests that people pay close attention to the relationship between the effort they expend and the outcome realized, but also consider the effort expended by others and the outcome that they receive for their contribution to the organization (Adams 1965).

Job evaluation efforts should consider the motivational effects of different assessments. Internal equity suggests that the preparation required for the position (the KSAs), the demands placed upon the worker (whether physical, intellectual, or emotional), and the significance of the position in terms of organizational activities should be commensurate with the assessed worth of the job to organizational members. External equity would draw a similar analogy, except that jobs would be compared between organizations (e.g., the State of California versus the State of Texas) or job sectors (private, nonprofit, or public).

Point-Factor Evaluation

Job evaluation methods vary, from very simple ranking of positions according to some set of criteria, to very complex weighted-factor systems involving multiple characteristics with variable weights attached to each. One of the more common methods in current use is point-factor evaluation. (You will learn a bit more about one popular variation of point-factor evaluation, the Hay factor method, in application to compensation systems in Chapter 8.) The point-factor evaluation relies heavily upon an assessment of the content of jobs. Although point-factor approaches vary to some degree, most include the following essential steps.

1. The evaluator gathers data about the jobs under scrutiny. Sometimes, the evaluator will categorize jobs generally in terms of whether they are management, supervisory, or line positions.
2. The evaluator will next identify factors to be used in a study of the different jobs.
3. Jobs are examined in terms of the factors used to develop a point total for each job.
4. Evaluators assess the relative weight of the job factors and the points assigned to different degrees of applicability within the job factors.

The factors may be general variables, such as knowledge, supervisory responsibility, or working conditions. Within each of these factors, the evaluator may have different degrees to assess relative positioning within the factors. For example, what range of knowledge is required? What type of information or experience is necessary? How many individuals are supervised? How much discretion do the subordinates exercise? Percentage or point weights may be assigned to each factor as a whole, with those points then being distributed to the degrees within the factors. Factors that are more critical warrant more weight. Within the factors, higher degrees of knowledge or discretion would warrant a greater value than others. Organizations may group similar jobs, in terms of the point total, for the purpose of compensation ranges or recruitment strategies.

In Exhibit 6.5, we illustrate the logic of a point-factor system with a sample instrument drawn from a study by Davis and Sauser (1993). For the purpose of this example, we assigned the weights and developed the degrees for accountability as a means to illustrate the logic of a point-factor evaluation. In this example, we are weighting the job factor "accountability," at 17, as having greater import in the organization than other job factors (e.g., job scope at 16, communication exchange at 14, or tax calculation complexity at 11). Note also that the degrees within the factor will vary in 'value' according to the manner in which this job factor applies to a particular position. Although every job is evaluated using "accountability," in some positions, "decisions/errors have a significant impact upon the organization," and, in other positions, "decisions are not made" and "errors would be barely noticeable in the context of operations."

Suppose we examined a position and found that a person holding that position would make decisions that reflected limited authority, and the consequence of errors was limited to the scope of the work group. In our evaluation of that job, we might assess the relative degree of accountability as low as 2. We would then multiply the weight for "accountability" (17) by the degree to which accountability was evidenced in the position (2). That score (34) would be noted, and then we would continue assessing the job in terms of the remaining factors to develop an overall score for the job. In the case of the instrument in Exhibit 6.5, the maximum score would be 1,000, and the minimum would be 0. Collectively, all positions would be scored, ranked, and have value assigned.

Exhibit 6.5 Sample Point-Factor Instrument

Factors	Weight 100-pt Scale	Definition of Factor
Accountability	17	Impact of decisions and errors
Job scope	16	Standardization of duties and closeness of supervision received
Communication exchange	14	Frequency, importance, and complexity of interpersonal communication
Job preparation	13	Education, training, and/or experience required
Task variety	12	Diversity of duties performed
Task complexity	11	Technical complexity and uncertainty
Work conditions	8	Work environment and conditions such as noise levels, temperature, lighting, required exertion
Job pressure	9	Demands upon the incumbent, including time pacing, deadlines, physical and emotional hazards

Factor 1: Accountability (17) Degrees	*Degree Points*
Decisions/errors have a significant impact upon the organization	10
Decisions/errors have an impact upon the work unit	5
Decisions reflect limited authority. Errors are managed within a work group	2
Decisions are not made. Errors would be barely noticeable in the context of operations	0

Source: The factors for both tables were drawn from those studied in Davis and Sauser 1993, pp. 95–96.

Considerations in Job Evaluation

It is clear from the foregoing that a process that appears to be a rigorously quantitative process on the surface actually features quite a bit of room for subjectivity and value-based assessment throughout. Potentially, job evaluation is subject to bias in terms of the evaluator's assessment of job factors dealing with the capacity of the employee to perform certain tasks at an acceptable level (Erez 2010; Tompkins 1988). For example, the relative merits of experience versus education have been hotly debated in many public sector hallways since the advent of civil service. Is speed more important than accuracy? How can we identify the necessary degree or experience that will capture some level of interpersonal skills? What are interpersonal skills? What are adverse working conditions—constant interruptions, or the low thrum of a copy machine next to one's desk? How do we capture job factors related to physical threat or danger—proximity to certain machines or exposure to disease? What about the dangers a department secretary faces from desperate students who cannot find a professor for a critical signature? Even the valuation that we assign to job factors is problematic. As Tompkins (1988, p. 7) notes:

Weights will incorporate effects of any discrimination existing in the marketplace. Such biases may reflect historical systematic under-valuation of female-dominated jobs based on stereotypes regarding the value of work; the traditionally weaker union power of women; the location of jobs in the competitive economic sector; purposeful gender discrimination; and other determinants of compensation not associated with job content, such as seniority and supply and demand.

In a study of employees who evaluated a diverse set of jobs, Davis and Sauser found that the weighting schemes differed when the employees believed that they were evaluating male-dominated jobs versus the schemes assigned to female-dominated jobs (Davis and Sauser 1993). Male-dominated jobs received a generally higher overall valuation (p. 99). Observers concerned with external equity suggest that job sector (public, private, nonprofit) or location may have more to do with an assessment of job worth than any type of objective analysis (Bellak, Bates, and Glasner 1983). Even the most technically pristine approach to job classification and evaluation is still predicated upon social valuation of certain types of work (Grandey and Diamond 2010). Treiman and Hartmann (1981, p. 422) indicate:

> We make no ultimate judgments here regarding the relative value of jobs to employers or to society or the appropriate relationships among the pay rates for various jobs. The concept of intrinsic job worth—whether there is a just wage—has been a matter of dispute for centuries. We do not believe the value—or social worth—of jobs can be determined entirely by scientific methods. The hierarchies of job worth are always, at least in part, a reflection of deep-seated values about which people disagree.

Other methods of assessing and categorizing jobs link to the skills and characteristics of the employees rather than the position. In 'rank-in-person' systems, the unit of analysis is the individual. Promotion and compensation are based upon individual qualifications, not career classification patterns. This approach may be more common when there is a clear protocol for assessing the skills demanded of the job occupant. For example, rank-in-person is common in public sector settings where the rank is less a matter of placement in the hierarchy but more likely to be drawn from experience, education, or achievements. For instance, in academic settings, the instructor's rank (assistant professor, associate professor, or full professor) is a matter of the person's experience, level of education, publication record, or aggregated accomplishments in teaching or community service.

Ethical Considerations: Equity or Efficiency

Job analysis and position description serve as the basis for many types of personnel action, including cases where historical patterns of discrimination based on suspect classifications have been established, and AA is taken to address such bias. If, as Treiman and Hartman suggest, we continue to observe the intrusion of social values that place less importance upon positions that are commonly held by women versus men, then the decisions about the weights of job factors in evaluation are especially worthy of close scrutiny. Is it incumbent upon public sector organizations to make a special effort to compensate for social inequity of this type? Should public sector organizations simply be bound by the market, or are social equity goals part and parcel of personnel work? Should we consider the possible gender bias implicit in job evaluation to be comparable with external equity issues generally? Does it matter if we are comparing like positions, but in different geographical areas? These questions arise for every jurisdiction in government, and they require that HR specialists frame these issues as clearly as possible and place them before politically accountable authorities for their determination of policy.

On a different ethical note, we can look at job design to consider the implications of characteristics for facilitating ethical conduct. Piccolo et al. (2010, p. 259) argue that:

> Leaders with strong ethical commitments who regularly demonstrate ethically normative behavior can have an impact on the . . . [job] elements of task significance and autonomy, thereby affecting an employee's motivation (willingness to exert effort), which in turn will be evidenced by indications of enhanced task performance and organizational citizenship behavior.

Thus, positions can be analyzed to discern both leadership characteristics and those characteristics that may signal the importance of ethical behaviors and decision making. Also, jobs can be designed to emphasize such elements as well.

Job Classification

Federal legislation, such as the Federal Classification Act of 1923 and the Classification Act of 1949, served as pioneer activity in public sector job evaluation and classification. In response to provisions in the Pendleton Act, which established the foundation of the federal civil service system (see Chapter 3), it became apparent that some means was necessary to establish accountability in the compensation of government employees. Classification presumes a comprehensive system of "formal job descriptions that organize all jobs in a given organization into classes on the basis of duties and responsibilities for the purpose of delineating authority, establishing chains of command, and providing equitable salary scales" (Shafritz 1991, p. 175). Positions were categorized—that is, *classified*—based on duties. Salaries were established to correspond with classification.

Classification, once seen as the mainstay of public sector HRM, is definitely on the decline. According to Hays and Kearney, position classification is going to be increasingly less important in the next decades as a process for connecting persons to jobs in the public sector (2001). This erosion may be due to concerns that rigid classification systems impede the ability of management to respond to performance demands, and do not fully apply to contemporary organizations experiencing rapid change. Shafritz (1991) has long argued the growing obsolescence of classification systems in the public sector, because they presume the accuracy of classical organization theory assumptions about workers and their roles in the organization, noting that public sector classification systems were established as mechanisms to prevent patronage abuse rather than manage employees. Cipolla suggests that, "classification has always been viewed as a 'personnel' program or system and will continue to be unless managers are put in control of work distribution and assignments without being restricted by artificial positions controls and grade-level distinctions" (1996, p. 18).

In some cases, the technical nature of analysis and classification may take precedence—the structure itself may serve to shape the behavior of employees, rather than support their ability to perform their work (Shafritz 1991). Efforts to manage HR despite the constraints of the classification system erode the rationale for their inception—rewarding merit without regard to personal characteristics or political affiliation. There may even be perverse incentives in the classification schema to reduce productivity and efficiency (Penner 1983).

Calls for the reform of civil service often focus upon the classification system. Because classification, analysis, and evaluation require a substantial investment of time, effort, and technical skill, revision of these systems is no small matter. At times, the complexity of reform efforts overwhelms jurisdictions, resulting in disjointed and episodic microadjustments of positions here and there. Unfortunately, piecemeal reclassification, while a means to remedy a problem in one area or work unit, results in even more inconsistencies. These attempts to restructure classification systems are confounded by political and economic constraints in different jurisdictions.

One rather popular alternative to the more detailed classification systems commonly used is known as broadbanding—that is, the collapsing of several related classifications into a smaller number of classes with substantially broader ranges of compensation within these classes. Although the number of states considering the use of broadbanding classification systems has increased, this sign of relatively intense professional interest has not translated into widespread political adoption. The number of jobs subject to classification decreased in thirty states, but not everyone is engaging in broadbanding efforts, as jobs subject to classification increased in fifteen states (Selden, Ingraham, and Jacobson 2001, p. 604). Broadbanding systems are showing a great deal of promise in compensation packaging schemes in the public sector, particularly in flatter, less hierarchical organizations engaged in high-tech activities and multi-agency collaborative work. In other states, administrators are responding to concerns about the need for greater flexibility by decentralizing authority for classification. In Georgia, for instance, each state agency is responsible for its own classification process (Selden, Ingraham, and Jacobson 2001, p. 604). Broadbanded systems and the role of classification systems in employee compensation packaging will be explored in considerable detail in Chapters 8 and 9.

Implications of Job Analysis, Evaluation, and Classification

As we attended to each particular segment of this chapter—analysis, evaluation, or classification—we have discussed some of the issues that may result from the techniques and practices in the public sector generally or in larger nonprofit organizations. Now, we turn to a discussion of broader concerns that may transcend the particulars.

Technology: Terror or Tool

Only a few years ago, if we wanted to share a document with a colleague in another community, we mailed it and patiently waited for delivery and reply—without express (pony or otherwise) mail options. In due time, the fax became a new tool for the rapid transfer of printed information. Documents and draft materials were furiously pumped through telephone lines to be printed at the other end. Now, such documents can be "attached" to our email and instantly deposited into a waiting PC. With advancements in workplace technology, the pace of work and communications has changed dramatically, as have the tools and processes that must be mastered to take advantage of the power of technology. Notably, we may consider that the rapidity of technology change has accelerated, meaning that issues that might have played out over a year or two now reveal themselves within days. This list is suggestive of the dramatic changes in the way that work is done today, and posits that escalating demands will likely be placed upon employees in the future, as technological change continues to accelerate and complicate our workplace lives. Tasks, skills, and requisite knowledge change rapidly in response to evolving technology; the tools and practices of HRM must keep pace, or organizational effectiveness will doubtless suffer.

Certainly, a good deal of the frustration that supervisors and unit managers report in their interaction with HR specialists may also find root in advancing technology. Computer software advances in data management and statistical analysis have made it possible to tabulate the responses for a job analysis instrument quickly and accurately. This approach to analysis becomes increasingly dependent upon often-mysterious formulas that are derived and applied without a human assessment of each particular job. Furthermore, many of the tools used for HRM work are becoming highly sophisticated in appearance and presentation, which may serve as a barrier to the many individuals who do not have the requisite skills or equipment to use them for their own benefit.

Diversity: Assessing Difference

The practice of job analysis and the development of classification spring from the belief that there is an accurate and unbiased means to assess the tasks associated with a particular position, without regard to the person holding that position. These objective assessments are intended to grant some security for individuals who worry about whether salary levels are being determined for reasons other than merit, or whether job qualifications are genuinely essential, or are really established to exclude some people. If the position analysis is accurate, and the resulting position description is unbiased, then individuals of differing personal qualities or backgrounds would not be held hostage by assumptions about what they can or cannot do.

In a different vein, Cox and Finley (1995) examined the role that organizational level and work specialization had on attitudes toward work and other indicators of workplace adaptation. They anticipated that work specialization and organizational level shaped the experiences that employees had and shaped the perceptions that employees held about their own work and their own role in the organization. The latter dimension is particularly of interest for employees who are 'minorities' within their organization—that is, either in less-common occupations (e.g., a community relations outreach specialist in a civil engineering unit) or in demographic groups that are less well represented. They found that, although gender, race, and age tend to matter in terms of job performance, compensation satisfaction, and allegiance with organizational identity (1995, p. 83), these findings were compounded by degree of work specialization and level of hierarchy. "Different specializations or levels may represent different work cultures . . . differences in rates of promotion and in job performance ratings may be attributable to different opportunity structures and different performance expectations across groups" (Cox and Finley 1995, p. 83).

Hierarchy and job classification can serve to alienate groups of workers from one another in a way similar to gender and race (Erez 2010). Consequently, one important task for HRM is the promotion of activities such as strategic planning to reinforce the realization that organizations reflect collective efforts to accomplish shared goals, and those goals are most effectively approached by organizations wherein inclusiveness, trust, and mutual support are broadly practiced norms of conduct.

Job Design

Job design reflects a slightly different focus in perspective than 'classic' analysis, description, and evaluation. Recall our earlier discussion about organization theory and the structuring of the organization or the position to achieve efficiencies or a certain level of performance. By contrast, job design is a bit more organic, meaning adaptive and flexible in nature. Jobs are designed in consideration of the organization's goals and resources as well as the individual's goals and resources. The resulting job would be some composite, reflecting the best fit for both the organization and the individual.

As organizational structure becomes flatter, and work groups evolve and become increasingly project-driven, jobs have changed in accord. In the area of job design, the analysis begins with what needs to be done (hence, the close connection between strategic planning and job analysis). After determining who will do the work (recruitment and selection), the designer would determine the processes and the locations where work should be accomplished. Job design entails framing work and tasks in the context of overall organizational goals and in concert with stakeholder interests in the organizational environment. The design of some aspects of the job may even be further adapted to mesh with the characteristics or needs of the employees performing the work (for example, providing accommodations for employees with disabilities). As we noted in Chapter 1, the work environment has changed quite dramatically over the past three decades. For this reason, Hays and Kearney (2001) call for increased focus on innovative approaches to job design in the coming decades—especially with regard to job sharing, job enlargement, and job rotation.

Flex-design for jobs, in terms of location (flexplace or telecommuting) or scheduling (flextime or job sharing), has become increasingly common. More than half of the cities responding to a survey of alternative work arrangements reported using some form of alternative scheduling (Wadsworth, Facer, and Arbon 2010). Telecommuting may improve employee productivity in a variety of settings, but Shockley and Allen (2007) found differences in the perceived utility reported by employees of either flexplace or flextime, noting that the value of the flex-design approach depended upon the potential conflict (e.g., family versus other factors).

Flexibility in scheduling can be a significant advantage of a particular job. In a study of municipal employees, Facer and Wadsworth (2008) reported that flexible scheduling (in this study, a 4/10 workweek) led to employee perceptions of improved productivity, greater effectiveness in working with citizens, and reduced work–family conflict. Flex-design can also aid organizations as they accommodate employees in the context of ADA.

Job design strategies such as job enlargement can be used to encourage employees to develop additional skills that the agency needs. Job enlargement occurs when employees have the opportunity to take on tasks in tangential positions (horizontal job enlargement) or to learn tasks associated with positions holding a higher rank in the organization (vertical job enlargement). Devaro (2010) suggests that job design offers an important variable in retention and motivation generally, arguing that employers "can design the relational architecture of the workplace as a means of motivating workers, thereby putting in place the conditions that motivate workers to care about making a prosocial difference by helping others" (p. 281).

Summary

Job analysis serves to frame almost all subsequent personnel activities. As you read about recruitment and selection in Chapter 7, you will understand how important a clear and accurate position description becomes in the search and selection of new employees. The proper valuation of the position as you attempt to recruit employees to critical positions in a seeker's market illustrates the importance of carefully assessing the necessary KSAs and then offering appropriate compensation packages to those employees whose KSAs are needed. If job analysis is inaccurate, there may be serious implications related to equity and comparable worth for the workforce.

The position description is a critical baseline document in any performance management system. If employees are to learn what is expected of them in a given position, and if they are to understand what they might need to know to be promoted, then appropriate job classification offers an important tool for developing HR. Finally, the position description offers an outline for employees to identify the critical tasks and, if necessary, may be used by managers to address performance problems. Job content analysis plays a pivotal basic role in contemporary personnel systems. Unfortunately, job analysis is very complex and fraught with all of the same types of measurement bias that tend to exist when we endeavor to assess human activity. A thoughtful, objective, accurate assessment of the tasks associated with a particular position and the appropriate evaluation of the worth of those tasks to an organization lie at the very heart of the legitimacy of a merit-based personnel management system.

The nature of the work done in and by government and the expectations held about public sector jobs are changing. Public goods and services are increasingly delivered through grant and contract arrangements by nongovernmental organizations, and this development signifies change for public sector jobs and the means for assessing the worth of particular activities. Traditional approaches to job evaluation will be at least partially inappropriate. Job analysis per se as a function of HRM may become less important to an organization than the ability to outline the scope of a grant or contracted project, assess any required technical competencies/licensure requirements associated with service delivery, and set the compensation levels for the project team in terms of the prevailing market for similar activities.

Audiomatique Vol 2.0 Dgital Edition

A Manager's Vocabulary

- Broadbanding
- Emotional labor
- Job analysis
- Job classification
- Job design
- Job evaluation
- Job incumbent
- Position description
- Task inventory procedure
- Position analysis questionnaire
- Point-factor evaluation

Study Questions

1. How might changing technology influence your work in the next year? And in the next decade?
2. What might we need to consider as we design alternative work arrangements for employees?
3. How might organization theories that address individual and group behavior influence job analysis and classification schemes?

Exercise 6.1 Devolution and Descriptions

Identify two position descriptions. These are readily available through the central HR office of the university or through a government Website such as the central personnel site for the state. After two position descriptions have been identified, the class could divide into teams to deconstruct the position descriptions in the context of the task inventory approach to job analysis discussed in this chapter.

- Using the position description, identify the tasks that would be performed by the job incumbent. Identify only tasks that are readily discerned from the position description.
- Are all the tasks that one might assume to be part of what the job incumbent would do apparent from the position description? What noteworthy tasks might be missing?
- Select five of the tasks that were clearly identifiable through the position description and develop a rank order of the five tasks performed by the job incumbent according to the level of difficulty (e.g., 5 is most difficult and 1 is least difficult).

- Develop a second rank order of the same five tasks according to the relative frequency with which the task is performed.

References

Americans with Disabilities Act of 1990 (ADA), 42 U.S.C., ch. 126.

Adams, J. Stacy. 1965. "Inequity in Social Exchanges." In *Advances in Experimental Social Psychology*, Ed. L. Berkowitz, 267–300. New York: Academic Press.

Bellak, Alvin O., Marsh W. Bates, and Daniel M. Glasner. 1983. "Job Evaluation: Its Role in the Comparable Worth Debate." *Public Personnel Management* 12 (4): 418–424.

Cipolla, Frank P. 1996. "Human Resources Management in the Federal Government: A Retrospective." *The Public Manager* 25 (1) 17–20.

Classification Act of 1923, Mar. 4, 1923, ch. 265, 42 Stat. 1488.

Classification Act of 1949, Oct. 28, 1949, ch. 782, 63 Stat. 954.

Clifford, James P. 1996. "Manage Work Better to Better Manage Human Resources: A Comparative Study of Two Approaches to Job Analysis." *Public Personnel Management* 25 (1): 89–102.

Cox, Taylor H., Jr., and Joycelyn A. Finley. 1995. "An Analysis of Work Specialization and Organization Level as Dimensions of Workforce Diversity." In *Diversity in Organizations*, Eds. Martin M. Chemers, Stuart Oskamp, and Mark A. Costanzo, 62–88. Thousand Oaks, CA: Sage.

Davis, Kermit R., Jr., and William I. Sauser Jr. 1993. "A Comparison of Factor Weighting Methods in Job Evaluation: Implications for Compensation Systems." *Public Personnel Management* 22 (1): 91–106.

Devaro, Jed. 2010. "A Theoretical Analysis of Relational Job Design and Compensation." *Journal of Organizational Behavior* 31 (2/3): 279–301.

Erez, Miriam. 2010. "Culture and Job Design." *Journal of Organizational Behavior* 31 (2/3): 389–400.

Facer, Rex L., and Lori Wadsworth. 2008. "Alternative Work Schedules and Work–Family Balance: A Research Note." *Review of Public Personnel Administration* 28 (2): 166–177.

Fry, Brian R. 1989. *Mastering Public Administration*. Chatham, NJ: Chatham House.

Grandey, Alicia A., and Jennifer A. Diamond. 2010. "Interactions with the Public: Bridging Job Design and Emotional Labor Perspectives." *Journal of Organizational Behavior* 31 (2/3): 338–350.

Guy, Mary E., Meredith A. Newman, and Sharon H. Mastracci. 2008. *Emotional Labor: Putting the Service in Public Service*. Armonk, NY: M. E. Sharpe.

Hays, Steven W., and Richard C. Kearney. 2001. "Anticipated Changes in Human Resource Management: Views from the Field." *Public Administration Review* 61 (5): 585–597.

McCormick, Ernest. 1959. "The Development of Processes for Indirect or Synthetic Validity: Application of Job Analysis to Indirect Validity." *Personnel Psychology* 12 (3): 402–413.

McCormick, Ernest, Paul R. Jeanneret, and Robert C. Mecham. 1972. "A Study of Job Characteristics and Job Dimensions as Based on the Position Analysis Questionnaire (PAQ)." *Journal of Applied Psychology* 56 (4) 347–368.

Mitchell, Jimmy L., and Walter Driskill. 1996. "Military Job Analysis: A Historical Perspective." *Military Psychologist* 8 (3): 119–142.

Penner, Maurice. 1983. "How Job-Based Classification Systems Promote Organizational Ineffectiveness." *Public Personnel Management* 12 (3): 268–276.

Pettibone, Craig. 2013. "What Would GS System Pay Reform Look Like?" *Public Manager* 42 (2): 9–11.

Piccolo, Ronald F., Rebecca Greenbaum, Deanne N. Den Hartog, and Robert Folger. 2010. "The Relationship between Ethical Leadership and Core Job Characteristics." *Journal of Organizational Behavior* 31 (2/3): 259–278.

Sanchez, Juan I., and Scott L. Fraser. 1993. "On the Choice of Scales for Task Analysis." *Journal of Applied Psychology* 77 (4): 545–553.

Sanchez, Juan I., and Edward L. Levine. 1989. "Determining Important Tasks Within Jobs: A Policy Capturing Approach." *Journal of Applied Psychology* 74 (2): 336–342.

Schneider, Benjamin, and Andrea M. Konz. 1989. "Strategic Job Analysis." *Human Resource Management* 28 (1): 51–63.

Selden, Sally Coleman, Patricia Ingraham, and Willow Jacobson. 2001. "Human Resource Practices in State Governments: Findings from a National Survey." *Public Administration Review* 61 (5): 598–607.

Shafritz, Jay M. 1991. "Position Classification: A Behavioral Analysis for the Public Service." In *Classics of Public Personnel Policy*, 2nd ed., Ed. Frank J. Thompson, 175–190. Pacific Grove, CA: Brooks/Cole.

Shockley, Kirsten M., and Tammy D. Allen. 2007. "When Flexibility Helps: Another Look at the Availability of Flexible Work Arrangements and Work–Family Conflict." *Journal of Vocational Behavior* 71 (3): 479–493.

Smith, Adam. 1987. "Of the Division of Labour." In *Classics of Organization Theory*, 2nd ed., Eds. Jay M. Shafritz and J. Steven Ott, 30–35. Chicago, IL: The Dorsey Press.

Smith, Brian N., Jeffrey S. Hornsby, and Philip G. Benson. 1990. "The Effects of Job Description Content on Job Evaluation Judgments." *Journal of Applied Psychology* 25 (3) 301–309.

Taylor, Frederick Winslow. 1987. "The Principles of Scientific Management." In *Classics of Organization Theory*, 2nd ed., Eds. Jay M. Shafritz and J. Steven Ott, 66–81. Chicago, IL: The Dorsey Press.

Tompkins, Jon. 1988. "Sources of Measurement Error and Gender Bias in Job Evaluation." *Review of Public Personnel Administration* 9 (1): 1–16.

Treiman, Donald J., and Heidi I. Hartmann, Eds. 1981. *Women, Work and Wages: Equal Pay for Jobs of Equal Value*. Washington, DC: National Academy Press.

Vroom, Victor H. 1964. *Work and Motivation*. New York: Wiley.

Wadsworth, Lori L., Rex L. Facer, and Chyleen A. Arbon. 2010. "Alternative Schedules in Local Government: Cui Bono?" *Review of Public Personnel Administration* 30 (3): 322–340.

Weber, Max. 1987. "Bureaucracy." *In Classics of Organization Theory*, 2nd ed., Eds. Jay M. Shafritz and J. Steven Ott, 81–87. Chicago, IL: The Dorsey Press.

7 Recruitment and Selection

Learning Objectives

- Understand the importance of the job description to recruitment and selection.
- Explore the various approaches to a search process to find the best match between employee skills and a position.
- Consider the legal constraints to, and guidelines for, conducting recruitment activities.

In a seminal discussion on the role of professionals in the public service, the venerated scholar Frederick Mosher (1991, p. 35) asked: "How can we be assured that a highly differentiated body of public employees will act in the interests of all the people, will be an instrument of all the people?" A simple response is that, "we identify, choose, retain, develop, and reward the right people." Though simple in concept, the reality of implementation is surprisingly complicated.

Essentially, we staff positions in government in four main ways—by elections, through political appointments (including patronage systems), via civil service systems, and by means of contracts/grants. Some of those employed by government are elected to office by the citizens they serve. Others are appointed through partisan patronage arrangements, usually to senior-level, policy-making executive positions. The focus of this chapter is upon the recruitment and selection of those employees who fall in the remaining categories of employees (e.g., neither elected nor appointed by an elected official). Other persons may be hired within civil service systems and are, in theory, employed by government because their KSAs match the needs of positions sanctioned either directly or indirectly through legislative action at the national, state, or local levels. The remainder may be hired through contracts or grants by supra-fiscal authorities (e.g., the U.S. Department of Agriculture receives an allocation from Congress that stipulates it must pass through funds to county extension agencies) or in response to temporary service demands (as in the case of seasonal firefighters or emergency response).

Recruitment is the process of finding and attracting the best people to fill vacancies in new or existing jobs within any type of organization, including nonprofit and every level of government. The scope of recruitment, either from a pool of existing employees or from outside the organization, is driven by the nature of the job at the microlevel and by government's goals in staffing at the macrolevel. The selection process has a long-term impact on the performance of the organization. Despite the clear significance of recruitment and selection, surprisingly little attention is devoted to these procedures in many organizations. Common mistakes range from illegal application forms and faulty interviews to unclear job requirements, unreliable screening mechanisms, and even the abject failure to follow through diligently on something as basic as reference checks.

Government's recruitment and selection process has a reputation for inflexibility; it is often described as being aggravatingly slow, in addition to requiring many steps from application to selection.

Of course, this negative overall perception may not be true for all (or even most) public agencies. Many jurisdictions have enacted significant HRM reform to improve performance in the recruitment and selection areas (Ritz and Waldner 2011; Trahant and Yearout 2006). Moreover, a good number of states and local governments are using some innovative techniques, such as skills assessment, job simulations, and video testing, for selecting employees (Choudhury 2007; Hays and Sowa 2010; Llorens and Kellough 2007). Ban (1997) observes that a range of federal-level reform efforts have targeted speeding up the recruitment and selection process and facilitating recruitment to find the most qualified persons for job vacancies. These reform movements include:

- improving access to employment by minorities and others who are not sufficiently informed of public service opportunities;
- decentralizing and streamlining the recruitment and selection processes;
- promoting public agency responsiveness;
- giving managers more discretion in the hiring process to permit more effective teambuilding at the operations unit level of public agencies.

Still, despite real progress having been made, government personnel systems have persisting reputations of being overly rigid and painfully inefficient.

Ban (1997) writes that the slowness and rigidity of traditional civil service systems are an unfortunate result of noble intentions. Government's recruitment and selection processes were designed to ensure equal access on the part of citizen applicants and to prevent favoritism or political patronage from affecting the hiring process. However, the rules established to prevent abuse have had unintended consequences. As a result, some managers have found ways of thwarting the rules by entering a personnel "nether world" of dubious practices (Shafritz 1974). In some cases, managers hire employees as 'temporary' workers and later convert these employees to permanent status (Jorgensen, Fairless, and Patton 1996). Similarly, employees may be hired as contract workers and are later brought under direct government employment. One method used frequently is to design a unique job that only a desired applicant is qualified to perform (Savas and Ginsburg 1973). At other times, a manager may 'coach' an applicant so they place among the top candidates on the job register of qualified applicants. Another practice entails asking the top candidate to decline a job offer so a preferred candidate can be offered the position. These practices are, arguably, unethical, if not illegal, but frustration in filling critical job vacancies too often leads to 'creative' behavior on the part of line managers who are directly responsible for producing outcomes in the form of public goods or services. In many cases, it is a matter of the good ends being used to justify the dubious means. The harmful results of these practices include poor morale, the proliferation of job titles, and contribution to the fundamental unfairness of the selection process.

Overview of Recruitment and Selection

Without question, one of the most important activities of management is the selection of skilled and capable employees. The quality of performance of any organization depends heavily on the skills, character, and level of commitment of its people. The most direct way of ensuring excellence in performance is to hire highly talented and enthusiastic employees. The first step in the hiring process is to attract the attention of such applicants, and the second step is to select the most qualified individual from among highly qualified candidates. A number of important objectives and principles can be followed to select the best job candidates, but the overriding principle guiding ethical and effective hiring is to base all recruitment information, tests, and selection decisions on the specific requirements of the particular job to be done. Factors unrelated to the job, such as political affiliation, personal appearance, common school ties, or friendship, have no place in the process. The recruitment process ends with the consummation of an employment contract and employee 'onboarding' activities. In the event of legal challenges, a critical component of public sector recruitment and selection entails documenting every step of the process, including the development of the job description, all relevant employment announcements and advertising, all applicants, the selection criteria applied, the selection methods used, and the evaluation results for each qualified candidate.

Recruitment

Recruitment is the process of finding and attracting the best people to fill vacancies in new or existing jobs within the jurisdiction or organization. Internal recruitment is done among existing employees within the jurisdiction's workforce. External recruitment goes outside the workplace. The nature of the job determines the extent of the search process used.

Adequate recruitment, though critical, can be quite costly. Resources must be devoted to the development and posting of announcements, as well as related advertising to ensure an applicant pool of diverse, well-qualified candidates. Staff time must be dedicated to managing the recruitment process and evaluating candidates. Substantial effort is needed to interview candidates, and those candidates (or potentially the interviewing panel) might need to travel to and from the interview site. Higher-level, professional positions will cost more for recruitment and will require more lead time.

Who Is Responsible for Recruitment?

In the absence of an HRM director or personnel department, in most cases the city manager, county executive, or the head of the department with the job opening in question handles recruitment. Whoever does the hiring should work closely with the direct supervisor of the position. The supervisor is one of the best sources of information about the KSAs needed to fill the vacancy. However, the supervisor's understanding of the open position should be based on a carefully researched job analysis.

The recruitment process encompasses several administrative tasks, such as developing and purchasing advertisements, compiling a set of recruitment files, and systematizing the files. The recruiting administrator needs to establish a secure location for the applicants' documents and to plan for the additional work the hiring process may require from him or her and from administrative support personnel.

If the administrator establishes a search committee to do the recruitment and hiring, that committee should include the direct supervisor of the open position. A search committee is indicated when a position entails working with two or more units of the organization and the job incumbent needs to be accepted by all significant administrators in those units. The search committee requires the same administrative support already noted: staff time, access to a telephone, Internet/email, and a secure place (either physical or virtual) where the search materials generated by the search process can reside. Developing a recruitment information system and single point of contact is useful for candidates who seek information about where they stand in the selection process and with whom they should communicate during the search.

Regardless of who is placed in charge of the recruitment process, the EEO/AA officer should be included in planning for the recruitment effort. If the city, county, or state agency does not have such a staff person, the legal counsel of the jurisdiction should review the process for compliance with anti-discrimination requirements.

From Job Analysis to Job Announcement

The best tool to begin the recruitment process with is a recently completed job analysis (see Chapter 6). The job analysis identifies the KSAs required for the opening, the nature of the work, and the essential and secondary tasks the job incumbent must complete, specifies the experience and/or education required, and identifies the placement of the incumbent in the organization's chain of command. When contemplating recruitment, the organization should determine whether an accurate and up-to-date job analysis exists for the position in question. The emergence of a vacancy in an established position may provide an opportunity to update a job analysis.

After conducting a job analysis, the organization can determine the requisite KSAs required to perform the duties. For example, the job of police officer includes the enforcement of laws. To fulfill the expectations of the position, the officer must possess driving and weapons skills, have the ability to handle difficult people and situations, and hold a working knowledge of criminal law. This KSA set is added to those from other aspects of the law enforcement position to establish what KSAs are needed to do the job successfully.

Minimum qualifications describe the *essential* KSAs necessary to function at the basic, minimum level of performance. Usually, minimum qualifications include knowledge of the general principles related to the scope of work, experience doing similar work, and any skills specifically needed for the position. Each qualification must be a valid indicator of performance.

Law or public policy might be another source of some minimum qualifications, and organizations commonly add distinct additional qualifications that may relate to their agency mission. For example, child labor laws apply to all government employment, but professional certifications and licensure may be required by statute for particular jobs and/or administrative positions. Residency requirements might also be among legitimate minimum qualifications; for example, some local jurisdictions require that employees live in the city in which they are employed. Employers may also include a list of preferred or desired qualifications that transcend the minimum qualifications. These could be used to differentiate further between a pool of otherwise qualified candidates. For example, prior experience at a similar job may not be a requirement for consideration, but could be used to help differentiate among qualified applicants.

At times, employers specify as minimum qualifications some characteristics or prior achievements that are not clearly the minimum necessary, nor are such qualifications labeled as preferred or desired. For example, employers may use a college degree as a minimum qualification for a job, without stopping to consider whether possessing a BA or BS degree is directly related to the performance of a specific job. Although the employer may view the college degree as a proxy for some KSA set, it may not be the only way to ascertain whether a job candidate can perform. A candidate may acquire (and demonstrate) the knowledge needed to perform a job through experience, or a combination of education and experience. Thus, unless an employer can demonstrate that the duties of the job require a particular level of formal education, it would be unlawful to require a high-school diploma or more from an applicant (Balbresky 1993).

Once the KSAs and minimum and preferred/desired qualifications are determined and approved, the employer can generate the detailed job description, along with additional documentation to support placement of the job within an organization's overall hierarchy of positions, and detail job duties and qualification. Because employers should ask for only those skills, education, and prior experience necessary for the successful performance of the job, basing the recruitment efforts on the job analysis avoids possible legal concerns later.

As we will discuss in Chapters 8 and 9, the compensation range of a new position should be based upon the previous salary offered to the last occupant, the KSAs needed by the job, and pay scales relevant to those KSAs in other similar jobs within the area, and the relevant regional or national external market.

Internal versus External Recruiting

Once the job announcement has been developed, managers should decide whether to recruit from inside the organization or from outside. Using external recruitment methods may bring new ideas into an organization and avoid picking among internal candidates with established networks and obligations. In contrast, hiring from within (internal recruiting) signals a high degree of confidence in the workforce and often permits the promotion of persons who have demonstrated loyalty to the organization and commitment to the agency mission.

Internal recruiting is nearly always less expensive and takes significantly less time than external recruiting. When existing employees are likely to have the requisite skills, then internal recruiting is a logical and appropriate approach. An added advantage is that the employees' strengths and weaknesses are known to the organization, and the employee applicants are likely to know the goals and objectives of the unit doing the hiring.

For an internal recruitment effort, the organization places the job announcement in its newsletters and on physical and electronic bulletin boards and announces the posting through email and any venues specific to the relevant collective bargaining units. Interested employees can apply directly for the opening. Providing feedback to employees who apply, but who are not selected, reinforces the fairness and transparency of the selection process (Fisher, Schoenfeldt, and Shaw 1996, p. 232).

Internal recruiting must comply with existing civil service procedures, with collective bargaining agreements in force, and with other personnel rules under which the jurisdiction may be operating. The collective bargaining agreement and personnel rules often prescribe the procedures to be used in filling many types of opening. Seniority is often an overriding principle in such agreements, and protecting seniority is commonly a point of central focus for unions and employee organizations. In some cases, the rules of selection require that the employee with the most seniority has the first claim to an open position, even if that person is only minimally qualified. The administrator in charge of the hiring or the search team needs to consult these documents (and the legal counsel) to ensure that the recruitment process adheres to all requirements stipulated in the personnel policy document and existing labor agreements.

External recruiting draws upon applications made from virtually anywhere outside the organization. The administrator must determine the proper pool of candidates, based on the nature of the job to be filled. For example, a national search for a receptionist position is unnecessary; the local labor market is likely to have many applicants with the necessary KSAs for the job and many more like it. An advertisement in the local newspaper will probably generate an adequate number of applicants. Other positions, however, such as state agency director, county engineer, or city manager, will require either a regional or national search, depending on the size of the organization. Generally, the higher the salary, the longer it takes to fill the position. Costs associated with external recruitment include advertising the position, long-distance telephone calls to check references, and travel expenses if the organization invites candidates for in-person interviews.

University internship programs may be an important resource for finding paraprofessional or young professional workers. Internships are especially suited for short-term projects for which permanent staff are unavailable. However, interns require supervision and opportunities for learning more about the larger issues of management and operations facing the whole organization. Moreover, significant staff time needs to be set aside for their proper supervision and evaluation, and for communicating back with the college or university providing the intern.

Management recruitment firms are available in a number of areas to assist in locating professional employees. For a fee, the consultant locates professionals who meet the job description and have established a good track record in a similar position. Local governments considering this option should investigate the cost carefully. Fees for such services may be a substantial percentage of the open position's salary, often as high as one-third. The cost of a recruiter may be justified, because most public organizations underestimate the indirect costs incurred when staff members handle the search from beginning to end (Rush and Barclay 1995). In fact, external recruiters may complete a search more quickly than can an internal committee, whose members all have "full-time jobs" to which to attend (Rush and Barclay 1995, p. 21). Organizations should exercise due care in choosing an external recruiter, opting for recruiters who have experience with the relevant sector, public or nonprofit. In addition, the recruiter must understand the jurisdiction's commitment to AA and any other relevant organizational priorities relating to diversity in the workforce.

Advertising for the Job Opening

The targeted nature and size of the applicant pool should drive decisions about where and how to advertise. Organizations interested in diversifying their workforce may face considerable challenges in particular locales. Advertisements in local or regional newspapers may suffice for entry-level positions, or organizations might use the local state unemployment office. Positions that are more specialized require advertisement in national publications. Most professions offer journals, newsletters, and online services targeted at their respective association memberships. Usually, positions more elevated in status or those prompting a greater degree of specialization will require a regional or national search for candidates to locate the most qualified individual.

Innovative advertising techniques include direct mail to professional associations and schools and drawing upon outplacement firms or contacting employers that have recently laid off large numbers of employees. For example, if the city or county is attempting to attract more minority applicants, it should consider placing advertisements in neighborhood weeklies based in ethnically diverse areas or contacting placement offices at colleges and universities with large minority student populations, such as historically black colleges. Thinking creatively about new outlets for the recruitment ads developed can increase the diversity of the applicant pool substantially.

The advertisement can serve an initial screening function, to attract applicants with the right skills and deter those who lack the appropriate skills. It should be specific enough to attract interest, but not so specific (e.g., regarding levels of compensation) as to obligate the jurisdiction to contractual arrangements prematurely. The advertisement should have many of the same details as the job announcements for internal recruiting. An effective ad should include the following key components:

- job title, code, or other identifying information;
- education or experience required or preferred;
- skills, certifications, or licenses required or preferred;
- the materials needed to apply (for example, diplomas, certificates of study, or college transcripts);
- address or contact information to indicate where and to whom the candidates should submit application documents;
- a statement of the jurisdiction's compliance with the ADA and EEO laws or any other clauses required in a particular state statute or local ordinance;
- the application deadline or date used to signal that review of applications will begin.

Like the position announcement, the qualifications set forth in the advertisement must match the KSAs needed for the job per the job analysis. When advertisements are distributed outside the organization's geographic area, it is good practice to include general information about the jurisdiction or community—including the size, range of amenities, and other locational characteristics that might attract interested applicants.

All advertising (plus application, testing, and selection procedures per discussion later in this chapter) must comply with all legal requirements, including AA and EEO laws. Unless characteristics listed are considered to be BFOQs for a job, the advertisement should not include references to requirements or preferences relating to gender, race, religion, age, ethnic origin, or physical capabilities.

All organizations must make reasonable accommodations for applicants eligible for such under the 1990 ADA. Title II of the ADA requires compliance from local governments with more than fifteen employees to ensure that personnel actions are disability-neutral to a maximum extent possible. Advertisements may alert potential applicants of specific selection procedures to be used (e.g., pen-and-paper or computer-based testing, or physical-agility testing). This notice allows applicants who seek reasonable accommodation under ADA sufficient time to make the request and comply with the job search timelines.

Technology and the Recruitment and Selection Process

Governments use technology in a wide array of personnel functions, including recruitment and selection. The Internet offers a relatively inexpensive means for organizations to advertise positions and for candidates to submit application materials. Application files may be retained in electronic form and, potentially, made readily available for review by the recruiting offices and selection teams. Large databases can hold resumes and formatted application content, and managers seeking qualified candidates can acquire and review an eligibility list through a variety of filters. Social media sites such as LinkedIn allow applicants to place portfolios and other work products online for prospective employers to review.

Probably the most widely used technological resource for traditional HRM functions is that of access to jobs at all levels of government posted on the Internet. Although there are a variety of job board services (e.g., Monster.com and others), governments rely upon programs developed in house as well as contracted services to deal with the often-unique issues attendant on public sector employment. Online resources are available to those seeking employment and those jurisdictions and organizations that have positions to fill. These include the state, municipal, and county Websites that list employment opportunities. The International Public Management Association for Human Resources (2014) offers a job listing service to members and nonmembers for a nominal fee. Online services and technical support are also available for other staffing needs, such as assessment. For example, at the federal level, the U.S. Office of Personnel Management (2014) features a variety of high-tech-based approaches to recruiting and staffing, as well as assessment mechanisms such as USA HIRE[SM]. The Society for Human Resource Management (2014) has a variety of online resources, ranging from spreadsheets and calculators to online talent assessments.

Additional online tools may allow organizations to search the Internet for possible candidates, especially for high-level positions featuring rather unique KSAs, even though the individuals may not be actively seeking employment (Schweyer 2004). As Exhibit 7.1 suggests, public and nonprofit organizations can make a few small changes to their websites and gain considerably greater recruiting impact. In articulating a typology for technology adoption and recruitment, Llorens (2011, pp. 412–413) comments upon the rapid expansion of resources available using the Internet, noting that:

> Taking advantage of overall increases in the computing and processing power of modern computers and mobile computing devices, employers are now able to utilize a host of more interactive tools in recruiting candidates. Leading organizations in the area of e-recruitment can

---

Exhibit 7.1 Basic Best Practices for Recruitment Using Technology

Organizations should include the following elements on Websites:

- links from their Web pages especially to career options on the home page and any division or department pages;
- routing for candidates for all postings on external job boards and newsgroups through a single 'career' page for application, with the ability to apply online;
- the URL on all print-based postings;
- information on benefits, work–life policies, training/education, and advancement opportunities;
- a separate page/site tailored for students and recent graduates;
- job descriptions and salary range;
- a job-fit portal developed with mechanisms for applicants to store application profiles/resumes/letters for future use by the job seeker and to allow applicants to register for automated job alerts when new positions open that might be of interest to the applicant; organizations might include prescreening questionnaires at the individual job posting level to help screen candidates and assist them in determining their fit for positions;
- a privacy policy and statement for candidates.

Organizations should send personalized email acknowledgments to applicants.

Source: The preceding was adapted from Schweyer 2004, pp. 40–41.

---

now post streaming videos of employees working in their office environments, advertise vacancies on social networking sites and, in the case of extremely innovative organizations, conduct virtual job fairs where potential candidates are not even required to leave the comforts of their home to interact with a recruiter.

Selection Process

Whether the selection process is brief or lengthy, internal or external, every organization follows the same basic steps to find qualified employees:

1. Use the position description/announcement derived from the job analysis to delineate the minimum qualifications and differentiate these qualifications from those preferred or desired.
2. Determine who will contribute to the selection and hiring of the best candidate.
3. Determine the selection method(s) best suited to the position.
4. Apply the selection method, using the criteria drawn from the qualifications, to the application materials provided by the candidates.
5. Conduct reference checks and any background investigations warranted by the job description.
6. Hire the candidate who best meets the requirements and begin the process of bringing the new employee into the organization.

Compiling the Qualifications

Because the primary goal of a selection process is to find the individual who can perform most successfully in a specific position, the first step in this process actually begins during the recruitment phase that we have discussed in the preceding pages. Thus, the selection process should be open to anyone who feels qualified to apply. The methods applied to assess and select the best candidate should provide each applicant who reaches this stage of the application process with the same opportunity to demonstrate his or her abilities.

Employers who understand the fundamental elements of the job can compile a screening list of qualifications that can be used to make the final hiring decision. Just as in the recruitment process, an important principle to follow throughout the selection process is to base all selection protocol elements and decisions on the specific requirements of the job and requisite KSAs, *not* factors such as political affiliation or friendship. Political affiliation may be relevant for patronage appointments, but not for the vast majority of public sector positions. The courts have determined that, for selection criteria to be valid, they have to be job-related as documented by the job analysis.

Contributors to the Hiring Decision

In most organizations, a number of people may be involved in the selection process. Clerical employees may receive and review applications for completeness; personnel specialists may screen applications for minimum qualifications and prepare a list of qualified or eligible candidates. Managers from each of the departments affected by the work done in the position will want to interview or test the candidates.

Considerations in Selection

The selection process is designed to gather information about applicants in order to make good hiring decisions. Most organizations use several selection tools in sequence, such as application forms, tests (written and performance), personal interviews, assessment centers, and reference or background checks. Multiple methods are ideal as a way to cross-check information, perceptions, and observations about the suitability of candidates. Each of the selection instruments developed must be designed to measure an applicant's abilities as they relate to actual job requirements, and should not disqualify candidates because of factors not related to the job.

Organizations must be able to defend the selection methods as being both job-related and equitably administered. To meet the first criterion, each method must measure factors related to specific requirements of the job the prospective employee is expected to perform. To meet the second criterion, the method or instrument must be applied consistently from applicant to applicant. At every step of the hiring process, the manager should be asking, "Is this question job-related? Am I being consistent with all candidates?" Resources are available to assist managers in developing defensible selection protocols. The Uniform Guidelines on Employee Selection Procedures issued by the U.S. Departments of Labor and Justice and the EEOC offer generally accepted rules for selection procedures and prevailing standards for validation of selection tests.

Defensible selection protocols are valid and reliable. In the context of HRM, validity refers to the adequacy of the method or instrument to measure accurately and as intended the extent to which candidates demonstrate the KSAs for a particular job. A valid selection method or instrument is proven to be job-related. After researchers are satisfied that a variable is valid, then they direct attention to whether inquiry about that variable or some relationship between variables can produce reliable results. In selection processes, employers focus upon reliability to affirm that some method or instrument is, or can be, applied consistently over time and across a variety of applicants. Reliability is also ensured when the instrument is unambiguous and elicits consistent outcomes.

Three types of validity establish job relatedness: content validity, criterion-related validity, and construct validity. Content validity means that test questions and processes (such as assessment center exercises) are directly related to the KSAs needed to perform the duties and responsibilities of a job. To be valid, the test should cover the whole domain of the job, and not fail to include important KSAs.

Criterion-related validity means the test results or scores have a strong relationship to required job behaviors and future performance. Using archival records, employers may demonstrate criterion-related validity by showing that scores on a selected test or series of tests correlate with indicators of success in the job. Such indicators include performance evaluations, retention rates, subsequent promotion rates, or records of follow-up training required.

Construct validity is the most abstract of the three. At times, the minimum or preferred qualifications are associated with applicant characteristics that cannot be directly observed. In these situations, employers must rely upon surrogate measures presumed to be indicative of the desired trait. For example, law enforcement employers seek officers who are mentally stable and well adjusted, given that these persons are armed with lethal weapons and are legally empowered to use force to enforce the law when necessary. Although these character traits cannot be directly observed, several psychological inventories have sufficient proven predictable power to permit a hiring authority to disqualify a candidate for having failed a psychological screening test.

Selection Methods

As Exhibit 7.2 illustrates, there are several methods commonly used by employers. Using the KSAs, minimum qualifications, and preferred/desired qualifications as a guide, a series of protocols can be used to determine who among the candidates who are qualified best suits the position. As not all jobs are the same, selection methods differ somewhat from job to job.

Application Forms and Resumes

Used to screen out applicants who do not meet the minimum qualifications and to gather information for personnel records, these selection devices can provide information on an applicant's basic qualifications, such as their level of education, employment experience, and job skills. They usually provide personal employment information such as name, address, social security number, and telephone number.

Exhibit 7.2 Common Selection Methods in Sequence

- Application forms and resumes: evaluate candidate training and experience.
- KSA or performance tests: measure and evaluate abilities and skills.
- Interviews/oral examinations: evaluate knowledge, communication skills, and lessons learned from experience.
- Background investigations: evaluate past performance and behavior.
- Probation (on-the-job): measure and evaluate performance on the job.

Source: Authors.

As with all selection protocols, the information requested on applications should be related directly to the job to be done by the prospective employee, and questions should not be asked that directly or indirectly lead to information about age, race, color, sex, religion, national origin, or physical disability. In addition, employers should take care not to request personal information that is unrelated to required employment information or potential job performance. For example, although common questions on application forms include age and marital status, this information is often irrelevant to the eventual performance of the job and could be used to make illegal hiring decisions. Such information may be needed for determining benefits, but should be collected only *after* a hiring decision has been made.

Because most information on job applications is factual (places of employment, degrees earned, certifications, etc.) the information can—and should—be verified prior to any offer being made. Managers must exercise caution owing to the strong evidence that nearly half of all applicants exaggerate their qualifications on application forms and resumes (Becker and Colquit 1992; Wood, Schmidtke, and Decker 2007). Ask for supporting documentation (such as education transcripts, certificates, degrees awarded) and contact former employers to confirm prior work experience.

Eligibility Lists

A list of applicants meeting the minimum qualifications can be further filtered to obtain those individuals considered most promising for further evaluation. The phrase 'rule of three' denotes the widespread practice (whether by tradition or required in policy or statute) of elevating the top three candidates for more rigorous review. In some extreme cases, only one candidate is forwarded through the remaining selection protocol (e.g., interviews or KSA testing), but managers usually find a single eligible candidate too limiting a choice. Eligibility lists may certainly include more, perhaps as many as five to ten certified or eligible candidates for most job openings. Some organizations certify the eligibility list using a percentage of those who meet all minimum qualifications, establish categorical groupings such as satisfactory, good, and excellent, and allow more rigorous selection methods to be applied to all candidates within a category (e.g., all of the those applicants vetted as 'excellent' during the initial review).

Many public organizations, owing to policy or statute, award extra consideration in the selection process to veterans (veterans' preference). For example, during the development of the eligibility list, veterans may be given extra 'points' and ranked higher on the list of eligible candidates.

Testing

KSA tests may be written or real-time demonstrations of skills and abilities. Such tests often have face validity, meaning they appear to measure specific KSAs required on a job, but, under close scrutiny, they may not be essential to job performance. These tests should always be reviewed for validity, and organizations have several options in obtaining validated selection tests. Several public personnel organizations (including the International City and County Management Association (ICMA) and IPMA) offer a range of standardized validated tests for use in local governments. Consultants may be hired who specialize in the construction of valid selection tests. In addition, managers may design their own test validation procedures, if they have the relevant expertise.

Testing fell into disfavor with the courts and public employers in the 1960s and 1970s, because many general tests used at that time (such as intelligence and mechanical comprehension tests) were not clearly tied to performance in a specific job and simultaneously had an adverse impact on minorities.

Tests that have been carefully constructed to measure indicators related to job performance are becoming increasingly used to help managers make informed hiring decisions. Even tests of intelligence and employee character are being used in situations where strong criterion validity evidence is available (Behling 1988). Managers should be aware that the ADA (1990) requires that written and physical tests allow for "reasonable accommodation" of applicants taking these tests.

Demonstration tests may be given to applicants to measure their ability or skill at performing some specific aspects of a job, or to assess their ability to be trained to do the work in question. As these performance tests are taken from an important function of the actual job, there is a strong relationship between the test and the job, and they are consequently considered content–valid. Such tests are expensive to administer on a per person basis, however. These tests frequently simulate a major facet of the job and evaluate skills for manual jobs, for computational ability, or computer skills. These assessments may include physical tests of some type to mimic actual job tasks. Such physical tests must accurately reflect the common physical requirements of the job and cannot eliminate candidates for the inability to perform extreme cases of the physical requirements. Furthermore, the ADA prohibits employers from discriminating against employees who cannot perform "marginal" physical requirements of the job or, in other words, infrequent or nonessential physical tasks.

Interviews

Besides the application form, interviewing is probably the commonest selection method used by employers. The interview also may well be the least valid and reliable method of selecting future employees (Huffcutt and Arthur 1994). Managers tend to use the interview to determine a candidate's ability to communicate and interact effectively, and to ask probing questions about performance and behavior in circumstances similar to potential job situations.

The validity of interviews becomes questionable when the interviews stray into areas of questioning not related to the job. Personal interaction and human nature can combine in the interview to produce error and uncover even subconscious bias. Exhibit 7.3 offers a few of the common errors that may cloud an interviewer's judgment. Other factors that can influence the outcome of an interview include

---

Exhibit 7.3 Common Errors Affecting Interviewer Judgment

- *Similarity error*: a candidate may appear similar to the interviewers and therefore be inappropriately favored by the panel.
- *Comparison error*: in comparison with the applicants as a whole, one candidate may stand out, but still not meet the position requirements.
- *First impression error*: if a candidate becomes a favorite of those interviewing owing to information on the application form or other communication, then she or he might gain an advantage before any interviewing actually occurs.
- *Halo and horns effect*: if a candidate qualifies for one aspect of a job, this may influence the remainder of the interview. Conversely, interviewers may overreact to one unfavorable response. Unfortunately for the job candidate, negative impressions may influence interviewers to a greater degree than positive.

Source: Authors.

nonverbal behaviors such as body language, accented language, friendliness, posture, and enthusiasm. General appearance, including clothing worn by candidates, may influence an interview. Research indicates that nonverbal behavior tends to have a greater influence on a hiring decision in an interview than verbal responses. Unfortunately, interviewer biases due to age, race, and sex may inappropriately influence decisions derived from interviews.

In addition, administrators may lack the necessary training to conduct the interview properly and may have poor listening and communication skills of their own. Much of the important information transmitted during an interview, like that in much of human communication, may never be heard, or it may be misinterpreted because of error and bias.

The reliability of interviews can be poor. In most cases, interviews conducted by more than one person benefit from multiple perspectives and offer the additional advantage of protecting the interviewers from false claims made by disgruntled candidates. Although agreement between interviewers on the facts and overall evaluations of candidates tends to be high, inter-rater reliability on subjective characteristics such as candidate leadership potential or honesty is less so. Another aspect of reliability is consistency, or how the interview is conducted for one candidate compared with others. Although it is common to have an established list of questions that are asked of each candidate, it may be that the line of questioning diverges from the script during the actual interview.

Managers should ask anything they feel is important to understanding how the candidate will perform on the job, but the focus must be job-related. Although it might be helpful to know about an individual's personal life so that 'unit fit' could be assessed, such questions are not appropriate and should be seen as out of bounds in interviews. Many interviews consist of questions that offer little information about how a candidate will perform in the position being considered. Questions leading to yes or no responses, although useful to confirm facts, provide little information about the candidate. Other general questions, such as "What is your greatest weakness," contribute little to a rational hiring decision. The best questions are those that provide the interview panel with information about the candidate's knowledge, skills, abilities, and attitudes necessary to perform successfully in the job. Thoughtful questions might ask what the candidates would do in a hypothetical situation (related to the job to be performed), or, better yet, how they have handled such situations in previous positions, if their application reveals such experience. Having been found valid and reliable with respect to a particular class of job, behavioral and situational questions that have been demonstrated to be good predictors of future performance should constitute the major portion of the job interview.

Interviews are resource-intensive in terms of the time and preparation, for both candidates and the interviewers. It is important to make this commitment of resources matter. Thus, in addition to the importance of a job analysis, successful selection processes include the following steps in preparation for interviews:

1. Assemble a panel of individuals with an interest in who fills the job and train them in proper interviewing techniques and ways to avoid the common interviewing errors.
2. Among panel members, decide on the objectives for the interview. These should include information items not accessible through other selection methods.
3. Plan past-behavior and hypothetical-situation questions in advance of the interviews to direct the meetings into areas that are important to understanding how each candidate will perform in the job.
4. Use a standardized rating scale to evaluate each candidate on the same questions, and then discuss these evaluations with the panel of interviewers following all of the interviews.

Diversity and the Relevance of Candidate Information

The questions outlined in Exhibit 7.4, whether asked in an interview or included on an application form, are usually illegal, because they lead to information that could be used to discriminate against protected classes of applicants. There may, of course, be relevant, performance-related information that would contribute to a hiring decision. In those cases, alternative phrasing offers the means to acquire necessary information without introducing illegal queries. In rare cases, a legitimate job requirement, referred to as a BFOQ, may require questions related to otherwise illegal information. For example, a female guard may be required for a specific position (e.g., conducting body searches) in an all-female jail facility. After the hiring decision is made, it is necessary to gather together all the information collected during the search and selection process for personnel records and for the proper determination of employment benefits.

Assessment Centers

Management positions often require an employee to perform a wide variety of tasks. Testing and interviews alone may only assess a few of the many tasks expected of these employees, and so, in such cases, assessment centers offer a mechanism to appraise the abilities of candidates applying for managerial and other complex jobs (Arthur et al. 2003).

These assessment center processes use a variety of techniques intended to replicate the situations facing managers. For example, a common technique is the in-basket exercise. Candidates receive an in-basket full of letters, memos, and telephone messages and must handle each item by determining the importance and urgency of each, then making decisions about how to act on the information available to them. Another technique involves a leaderless-group problem. The assessment center brings together a small group of candidates to solve a management problem. The solution is not as important as the process for problem solving developed by the group and the behavior of the participants in the process with respect to the demonstration of good listening skills, patience, civility, and other traits related to effective collaborative leadership. Candidates are observed and scored on their leadership traits and ability to work in groups. Interviews may be included during which the candidate is asked questions about their behavior on some of the exercises and is asked to comment upon their experience handling work situations similar to those expected to be performed on the job.

Assessment centers may also include job-specific written tests measuring personal characteristics such as leadership, personality, management style, and intelligence. KSA tests for such activities as writing memos, handling a problem employee, using listening skills, preparing and delivering a speech, and dealing with sexual harassment problems are common challenges featured in assessment center processes. Management exercises or games such as delegation, team building, conflict management, and performance evaluation are common as well. Job simulations might entail an elaborate series of job-related situations, and the candidates must assume roles assigned by the assessors. Such simulations allow for multiple responses and feature preplanned, progressive steps for the candidates to act upon as the simulation unfolds.

Typically, a group of candidates for the same position undergo simultaneous testing in an assessment center. Assessment centers utilize a team of trained evaluators to conduct the tests, and then they collectively discuss the results. The assessment team may include representatives from the employing departments who can contribute to the wide range of perspectives useful for identifying the preferred candidate.

Content validity is one of the most important advantages of assessment centers, as the exercises can focus on very specific aspects of the job. Assessment centers can also reliably test a number of

Exhibit 7.4 Reframing Illegal Questions

Illegal Question	Alternative Wording
Race, creed, and national origin	
What is your race (on some application forms)?	Are you legally able to work in the United States?
What organizations do you belong to?	Who would you like to be notified in the event of an emergency?
What country does your family come from?	
Where are you a citizen?	
What is your previous foreign address?	
What is your birthplace?	
Have you acquired the ability to read, write, or speak a foreign language?	
What is your native language?	
Sex, marital status	
Are you male or female? (often on application forms)	Do you have relevant work experience while using another name?
What is your maiden name?	
Have you changed your name?	
What is your sexual orientation?	
Are you married?	
Are you pregnant?	
How many children do you have?	
Do you have childcare?	
Do you plan on having any more children?	
Age	
What is your age?	Information about age is almost always unnecessary
What is your birthday? (often on application forms)	

Disability

What is your height and weight?

Is there any reason you would not be able to perform the responsibilities and tasks of this position?
Do you have any disabilities?
Have you had certain diseases?

Religion

What is your religion?

Would you be able to perform the required duties of this position?
What religious holidays do you celebrate?
In what groups are you a member?

Military service

Have you been dishonorably discharged from the military?

Do you have relevant work experience?

Criminal record

Have you been arrested?

Have you been convicted of a crime related to the duties and responsibilities of this position?
Have you been convicted of any crime?

Source: Drawn from Balbresky 1993 and Buford 1991, pp. 170–171.

candidates going through very similar testing procedures. The biggest problem with assessment centers is their high cost. These candidate evaluation processes can run for 1–5 days and occupy the time of numerous assessors and candidates. Because of the cost, assessment centers are usually used only for candidates applying for upper-level management or highly technical positions in large agencies or jurisdictions.

There is also a risk of bias in assessment centers related to measurement standards. Socially accepted characteristics of good managers or leaders are sometimes biased against women candidates, who often display management traits that are different from those of men (Huffman and Cohen 2004; Scott and Brown 2006). Successful managers may display certain male-oriented management traits, but female-oriented traits are equally valid predictors of good leaders and managers (Eagly, Johannesen-Schmidt, and van Engen 2003). Well designed assessment center processes developed by experienced assessment teams are increasingly sensitive to such potential gender-based threats to the validity of assessment centers and make explicit provision for the differential assessment of male and female candidates (Bowen, Swim, and Jacobs 2000; Davison and Burke 2000).

Background Investigations and Reference Checks

Reference checks verify information obtained from candidates from the application form, testing, and interviews. Another valuable use of reference checks is to determine a record of past performance, as this is most often a good indicator of future performance. Unfortunately, there is substantial evidence that some candidates are inclined to embellish or even outright falsify their application materials (Kuhn, Johnson, and Miller 2013; Wood, Schmidtke, and Decker 2007). Former employers and others familiar with the job candidate's workplace accomplishments can provide important information about the prospective employee's work habits and abilities. Additionally, the check can be used to confirm interviewer/rater/observer perceptions of candidate performance demonstrated during simulations and exercises.

As part of standard selection protocol, organizations should request applicant approval for verification of their references and application material. Good practice and common courtesy both demand that organizations inform the candidate that, as a function of the selection process, former employers and others who are familiar with the candidate's work will be contacted in the course of the selection process. In some cases, candidates may wish to have reference checks occur only at the point where they are in serious contention for a position. This is a quite common request, especially for management positions where the applicant wishes to keep, at least initially, his or her job search activity confidential. Mechanisms to provide such notice may include a notification and check-off on the application form, or a separate signed release.

The candidate should provide an initial reference list, possibly including former employers and instructors, as well as others who can speak to the candidate's suitability for the position. In the course of speaking with listed references, the common practice of asking the listed references for others who are familiar with the candidate's work history offers organizations possible sources other than those volunteered by the candidate, barring a need for discretion and a previously negotiated expectation of confidentiality during a certain stage of the search. Reference checks conducted by telephone may save time and allow spontaneous responses from those interviewed. Background checks by traditional mail (potentially slow) or email have both advantages and disadvantages associated with their use. Although responses could be carefully crafted and uninformative, such communications could also be more thoughtful than spontaneous answers. Reference checks may occur in person occasionally, but these are typically done only for high-ranking, security-sensitive positions.

Organizations that fail to conduct reference checks risk wasting resources and making poor hiring decisions. If candidates give false information in the selection process, or have past behavioral problems not easily found out, then employers are obligated to determine whether these issues are present. The employer can be liable for negligent hiring if the hired employee causes harm, when a pattern of behavior in past employment indicated the presence of this danger. Conversely, former employers can be liable for negligent referral if they hold back information that could have prevented a person from causing harm to others in a future job situation. Liability questions may also surround former employers who give unjustified or unflattering references to prospective employers that are not merited. Because of this possibility, many organizations have policies limiting the information provided to other organizations to only factual information about the job description and dates of prior employment.

Introduction to the Reading

The following excerpt from a U.S. Merit Systems Protection Board study offers a thorough review of the best practices associated with reference checking. Although this document takes the perspective of federal selection, the recommendations are germane to nonprofit organizations of all sizes and to virtually all tribal, state, and local governments. The general protocols for efficient and effective reference checks include advance preparation of the standard questions, being certain that the questions are demonstrably job–related, and focusing the questions on the reference's observations of work behavior. Consider the following questions as you review this material:

1. What should the hiring organization's strategy be in seeking references?
2. How should reference providers be selected?
3. What legal issues face those who provide references?
4. How should a search committee evaluate the results of references?

Onboarding: Making the Most of a Hire

The decision to hire, while momentous, only begins a new and important stage in the relationship between employers and staff. In addition to considering any contracted arrangements and probationary periods, employers must pay close attention to the entire process by which it brings new employees 'on board'.

Employment Contracts

Individual employment contracts are agreements between the governmental agency or nonprofit organization and an employee that describe job responsibilities, reporting arrangements, the terms of employment, and separation provisions. These contracts are useful to attract key personnel by specifying salary, benefits, and incentives, and they can include protections against arbitrary firings and processes for appealing adverse actions.

Because employment contracts are legally binding on the agency and the employee for the term of the contract, employers should take great care in drafting the document. Employment contracts are useful for managers in politically sensitive positions, such as city and county managers, because their employment can otherwise be terminated for reasons completely unrelated to work performance. Such contracts are not an advantage for a local government when offered to rank–and–file employees, because case law protects these employees against arbitrary dismissal.

Excerpt 7.1 Reference Checking

Reference checking is a common and familiar hiring practice. Minimally, a reference check involves a conversation—usually a phone conversation—between a potential employer and someone who knows the job applicant. . . .

A review of best practices in hiring reveals that reference checking is widely practiced in both public and private sectors. It is used both to verify information obtained from job applicants, such as facts about previous employment, and to assess skills and abilities relevant to the job to be filled. There is marked variation in the degree to which employers structure and standardize reference checking. Training in effective reference checking is often not available to those who must conduct it. Increasing attention to structuring reference checking according to best practices and shifting responsibility from human resources (HR) personnel to hiring supervisors has the potential to raise the perceived and actual value of reference checking. Employers who do not check references give a variety of reasons. Checking references may seem too time intensive when long-term benefits are ignored. Employers may trust the referrals from friends or current employees, while ignoring risks of perceived favoritism. Some employers want to avoid redundant assessments, and mistakenly believe that reference checks are always duplicative of other assessments. And some employers just do not want to risk uncovering disconfirming evidence about a job applicant to whom they have become emotionally committed. Reference checking raises legal concerns as well. It is legal to request information about an applicant's past job performance. Reference checkers in general have a qualified immunity against charges of invasion of privacy so long as they restrict their inquiries to job-related issues. Many organizations require applicants to sign a formal waiver that gives reference checkers permission to discuss on-the-job behavior with former employers. . . .

Conducting reference checks has a number of advantages. Direct benefits include making better and more informed hiring decisions, improving job–person match, improving on self-report assessments of training and experience, demonstrating fairness and equal treatment of all job applicants, and sending a message about the high expectations of the employer. Longer term benefits include avoiding the costs of a bad hire, maintaining employee morale by making quality hires, and gaining the public's trust that civil servants take hiring seriously. . . .

Many reference providers have misconceptions about potential liability associated with providing information about former employees. However, providing reference information need not be avoided—it can be done within the bounds of legality. Reference providers should play their role carefully, but need not fear legal consequences if they follow a few guidelines. They should verify that a reference checker is legitimate. They should avoid providing letters of reference because these are less useful in reference checking. Reference providers can avoid the appearance or actuality of maliciousness by keeping their comments focused on the applicant's job-related behavior. By providing examples and detailed descriptions, reference providers ensure that their evaluative judgments are firmly grounded in reality. Job applicants should support reference checking and play an active role in making connections between reference checkers and reference providers. They should select reference providers who have observed their work and who are available to communicate their observations clearly and accurately. Applicants should be candid about their strengths and weaknesses in the hiring process. Any less-than-flattering information about the applicant is best communicated to the employer by the applicant, rather than discovered during reference checking. . . .

Reference checking has an important role to play in the . . . hiring process. It should be more than a formality conducted by administrative staff. It should be more than a casual, unstructured phone conversation between supervisors. It should certainly not be an illegal and inappropriate exchange of gossip about unsuspecting applicants. Reference checking can improve the quality of the . . . workforce by reducing the number of unqualified, unscrupulous, and otherwise unsuitable applicants whose liabilities escaped detection during the earlier phases of the hiring process. If reference checking is to reach this potential, it will require cooperation among . . . hiring officials, applicants, . . . and reference providers.

Source: U.S. Merit Systems Protection Board 2005.

Probationary Period

The most valid predictor of future performance is actual past performance on the job. Most public organizations make use of a probationary period of 3 months to 1 year. During this period, managers may carefully evaluate the performance of a provisional employee while that individual has fewer employment rights than do permanent employees. The length of the probationary period is determined by the amount of time it takes to learn the responsibilities of the job and to accumulate a performance record that can be evaluated.

The probationary period may be considered as both part of the employee selection process and as a learning time frame for new employees. Whatever the purpose, managers are responsible to train employees in this status and evaluate their performance and responsiveness to the training provided. Regular and frequent evaluations should provide the employee with feedback on performance and guidance as to necessary improvement where indicated. At the end of the probationary period, a manager should schedule a final evaluation with the employee to determine whether, and under what conditions, employment should continue. With proper training and regular guidance, the outcome of the final evaluation should most often come as no surprise to the employee.

Employee Orientation

New employees need to understand the requirements of their new job and the workplace norms of the organization. Newly appointed employees may experience a degree of anxiety in a new job. Generally, they look for signs of acceptance on the part of their new coworkers and seek an understanding of how things are generally done in the organization so that they can 'fit in' to a new social system where they work. According to Bauer (2010, p. 2):

Informal onboarding refers to the process by which an employee learns about his or her new job without an explicit organizational plan. *Formal onboarding* refers to a written set of coordinated policies and procedures that assist an employee in adjusting to his or her new job in terms of both tasks and socialization.

A formal orientation session can prevent misunderstandings and invalidate informal communications that may be inconsistent with official policies and practices. An employee orientation checklist can be very helpful to ensure that nearly all of the topics needed for the successful integration of the new employee are covered. Exhibit 7.5 offers a sample of the categories of activity and information useful to organization entrants. In general, orientation addresses four major categories: socialization, the work environment and resources, employment policy and logistics, and performance (including training and development). Socialization includes the general meet and greet, as well as setting up various mentoring scenarios and giving information about dress code and other conduct protocol. The best ongoing source of information may be from coworkers who explain facts and situations in the context of the organization's way of doing things. Mentoring or arranging for the opportunity to meet with several coworkers informally, such as in a lunch setting or after work, can help the new employee feel comfortable asking questions and provide an opportunity to learn many of the values and professional and ethical norms. The work environment includes the physical area, as well as information about the location of resources needed to complete tasks (e.g., supplies, policy manuals). Employment policy and logistics deal with the technical issues related to compensation, benefits, how to submit leave forms, and the like. Performance relates to the specific and general expectations for performing the job, as well as anticipated training, development, and assessment.

Exhibit 7.5 Onboarding Checklist

Before the New Employee Begins

- Contact the employee to review start date/time, dress code, parking/transportation.
- Set up the work area, including requisite technology/equipment, phones, and data lines.
- Set up system access such as general security, keys, passwords, ID, or prepare paperwork for first-day signature.
- Update organizational communication/org chart.
- Prepare employee signage such as nametags, business cards, keys.
- Prepare/provide welcome packet with mission/vision/HIPAA/FERPA as appropriate, manuals, policy information, job description, compensation/benefit information, organization chart, phone/email lists, maps, parking/transportation, staff list with basic position description and contact information.
- Prepare other employees for new arrival, including announcements, including others in reviewing orientation, notice on new member's role/responsibilities.

First Day

- Personally welcome the new staff member when they arrive.
- If the employee has not completed an I-9, take them to Human Resources to complete.
- Describe the orientation plan for the first few days.
- Give a local tour of work area, including restrooms, kitchen, emergency exits, and emergency assembly points.
- Review building and workplace security procedures, safety/accident procedures, location of first aid supplies, how to report hazards, location of emergency assembly point, fire alarms, extinguishers, etc.

- Have employee sign any forms required.
- Review orientation packet, especially policies and procedures of immediate need in performing simple work assignments on the first day.
- Introduce coworkers, any assigned mentor/guide.
- Show how to use the telephone system, access computer, and use software and other equipment for initial assignments.
- Allow time to set up workspace, including communication systems such as voicemail and email.
- Give a simple initial work assignment.
- Meet with the new employee at the end of the day to answer questions and find out how the day went.

First Week

- Describe or have a list of regular meetings and other regularly scheduled items that the employee should place on their schedule.
- Review overall organizational chart and discuss department's function and interrelationships with other departments and reporting structures.
- Review the job description and performance standards, including dress code, workspace care/neatness, and parameters for personal displays.
- Describe who and how to notify about sick or vacation days; include any departmental policies about requesting vacation.
- Review work schedule: lunch breaks, time sheets, overtime needs/policies, assignments.
- Review how often to check in about assignments and when and how to ask for help.
- Review types of assistance available: mentor/guide, desk or procedure manuals, Websites, etc.
- Review policies regarding visitors, personal phone calls, copies, faxes, etc.
- Provide copies of, or Web link to, policy manuals, office procedures, and policies.
- Review how to handle confidential information based on employee's position.
- Show how to send and where to receive U.S. and campus mail and provide location of the closest USPS mailbox for personal mail.
- Explain support groups and other resources for training.
- Provide job assignments and meet as needed to answer questions.
- Begin the performance planning process and schedule any additional training required.
- Meet with the new employee at the end of the week to answer questions and find out how the week went.

First Month

- Schedule regular meetings with the new employee to answer questions.
- Confirm that benefits/compensation are being handled smoothly.
- Ensure adequate access to technology and organizational systems.
- Discuss review process.
- Review performance standards and job description.
- Check in on new employee's understanding of policies and processes.

First 3 Months

- Confirm short- and long-term performance goals.
- Review performance with the degree of formality outlined in probationary agreements.
- Check in with questions.

First 6 Months

- Confirm short- and long-term performance goals.
- Review performance with the degree of formality outlined in probationary agreements.
- Check in with questions.

Source: This compilation is drawn from Boise State University n.d. and the University of Minnesota n.d.

An orientation session should also be scheduled with personnel specialists to explain employee benefits and the method of pay distribution. Employees should understand the culture of the organization, including its history, the important people involved in the clientele community, the structure of government within which their agency is situated, and the way each department integrates into the overall mission of the jurisdiction in question.

Summary

Recruitment and selection describe methods employed by HR officials to attract and hire qualified candidates for service in the organization. Finding people with the appropriate qualifications and matching them with vacancies in the organization are fundamental to an organization's success. Failure to find the right matches of people to positions can result in performance and behavior problems that can plague an organization for many years to come. Owing to the ongoing professionalization of public service, public personnel systems virtually everywhere in the country have developed rules and regulations to open their employment systems to all qualified applicants. Theoretically, these systems eliminated the ability of public officials to hire or fire employees with either favoritism or malice. Many public and nonprofit organizations continue to experiment with innovations in recruitment and selection, while maintaining the objectives of merit selection and equity in the treatment of applicants and employees. This is a difficult balance, resembling more the swinging of a pendulum than the scales of justice.

A Manager's Vocabulary

- Content validity
- Criterion validity
- Construct validity
- Reliability
- Internal recruitment
- External recruitment

- Bona fide occupational qualifications (BFOQs)
- Application forms
- Written tests
- Interview (oral examination)
- Background investigations
- Probationary period
- Assessment center
- Interview error

Study Questions

1. What advantages of government employment would you emphasize when advertising for new employees?
2. What places or publications would be the most effective for finding qualified minorities and women candidates for government employment?
3. What types of job are best recruited internally? Externally?
4. In what cases would it be appropriate to hire a recruiting firm to help find candidates for job openings?
5. Why might validity be a concern during an interview process?
6. What set of selection methods is best for an entry-level professional position? And for middle management?

Exercises

Exercise 7.1 *Preparing a Recruitment Plan*

Select a job in a public agency near you and interview the incumbent of that job to determine the knowledge, skills, and abilities needed to perform that job, and then prepare a recruitment plan for someone to fill that job.

Exercise 7.2 *Developing a Position Advertisement*

Prepare an advertisement for the newspaper of the largest city near you for a *policy analyst* in your department of transportation. In addition to this advertisement, in what other forums would you distribute information about this position?

References

Americans with Disabilities Act of 1990, 42 U.S.C., ch. 126.

Arthur, Winifred, Eric A. Day, Theresa L. McNelly, and Pamela S. Edens. 2003. "A Meta-analysis of Criterion-related Validity of Assessment Center Dimensions." *Personnel Psychology* 56 (1): 125–154.

Balbresky, Paul. 1993. "An Employment Related Lawsuit May Put Your Local Government at Risk." *Public Management* 75 (11): 13–15.

Ban, Carolyn. 1997. "Hiring in the Public Sector: Expediency Management or Structural Reform." In *Public Personnel Management: Current Concerns, Future Challenges*, 2nd ed., Eds. Carolyn Ban and Norma Riccucci, 189–203. New York: Longman.

Bauer, Talya. 2010. *Onboarding New Employees: Maximizing Success*. Society for Human Resource Management. www.shrm.org/about/foundation/products/documents/onboarding%20epg-%20final.pdf (accessed June 23, 2015).

Becker, Thomas E., and Alan L. Colquit. 1992. "Potential Versus Actual Faking of a Biodata Form: An Analysis Along Several Dimensions of Item Type." *Personnel Psychology* 45 (2): 389–408.

Behling, Orlando. 1988. "Employee Selection: Will Intelligence and Conscientiousness Do the Job?" *Academy of Management Executive* 12 (1): 77–86.

Boise State University. n.d. "Boise State University Supervisor's Checklist for New Employees." http://vpfa.boisestate.edu/process/uformsdocs/hrs/empserv/supervisorhiringchecklist.pdf (accessed June 23, 2015).

Bowen, Chieh-Chen, Janet K. Swim, and Rick R. Jacobs. 2000. "Evaluating Gender Bias on Actual Job Performance of Real People: A Meta-analysis." *Journal of Applied Social Psychology* 30 (10): 2194–2215.

Buford, James A., Jr. 1991. *Personnel Management and Human Resources in Local Government*. Auburn, AL: Auburn University Press.

Choudhury, Enamul H. 2007. "Workforce Planning in Small Local Governments." *Review of Public Personnel Administration* 27 (3): 264–280.

Davison, H. Kristi, and Michael J. Burke. 2000. "A Meta-analysis of Sex Discrimination in Simulated Selection Contexts." *Journal of Vocation Behavior* 56 (2): 225–325.

Eagly, Alice H., Mary C. Johannesen-Schmidt, and Marloes L. van Engen. 2003. "Transformational, Transactional, and Laissez-faire Leadership Styles: A Meta-Analysis Comparing Women and Men." *Psychological Bulletin* 129 (4): 569–591.

Fisher, Cynthia D., Lyle F. Schoenfeldt, and James B. Shaw. 1996. *Human Resource Management*, 2nd ed. Boston, MA: Houghton Mifflin.

Hays, Steven W., and Jessica E. Sowa. 2010. "Staffing the Bureaucracy: Employee Recruitment and Selection." In *Handbook of Human Resource Management*, 3rd ed., Ed. Stephen E. Condrey, 97–124. San Francisco, CA: Jossey-Bass.

Huffcutt, Allen I., and Winfred Arthur Jr. 1994. "Hunter and Hunter (1984) Revisited: Interview Validity for Entry-Level Jobs." *Journal of Applied Psychology* 79 (2): 184–190.

Huffman, Matt L., and Philip N. Cohen. 2004. "Occupational Segregation and the Gender Gap in Workplace Authority: National Versus Local Labor Markets." *Sociological Forum* 19 (1): 121–147.

International Public Management Association for Human Resources. 2014. "HR Resources." ipma-hr.org (accessed May 15, 2014).

Jorgensen, Lorna, Kelli Fairless, and W. David Patton. 1996. "The Underground Merit System: A Look at Merit in the State System." *Review of Public Personnel Administration* 16 (2): 5–21.

Kuhn, Kristine M., Timothy R. Johnson, and Douglas Miller. 2013. "Applicant Desirability Influences Reactions to Discovered Resume Embellishments." *International Journal of Selection and Assessment* 21 (1): 111–120.

Llorens, Jared J. 2011. "A Model of Public Sector E-Recruitment Adoption in a Time of Hyper Technological Change." *Review of Public Personnel Administration* 31 (4): 410–423.

Llorens, Jared J., and J. Edward Kellough. 2007. "A Revolution in Public Personnel Administration: The Growth of Web-Based Recruitment and Selection Processes in the Federal Service." *Public Personnel Management* 36 (3): 207–222.

Minnesota, University of. n.d. "Onboarding Toolkit for Managers." www1.umn.edu/ohr/prod/groups/ohr/@pub/@ohr/@toolkit/documents/asset/ohr_asset_175052.pdf (accessed June 23, 2015).

Mosher, Frederick C. 1991. "Merit, Morality and Democracy." In *Classics of Public Personnel Policy*, 2nd ed., Ed. Frank J. Thompson, 34–46. Pacific Grove, CA: Brooks/Cole.

Ritz, Adrian, and Christian Waldner. 2011. "Competing for Future Leaders: A Study of Attractiveness of Public Sector Organizations to Potential Job Applicants." *Review of Public Personnel Administration* 31 (3): 291–316.

Rush, Catherine, and Lizbeth Barclay. 1995. "Executive Search: Recruiting a Recruiter." *Public Management* 77 (7): 20–22.

Savas, E. S., and Sigmund G. Ginsburg. 1973. "The Civil Service: A Meritless System?" *Public Interest* 32 (summer): 70–85.

Schweyer, Allan. 2004. *Talent Management Systems: Best Practices in Technology Solutions for Recruitment, Retention and Workforce Planning*. Canada: John S. Wiley.

Scott, Kristyn A., and Douglas J. Brown. 2006. "Female First, Leader Second? Gender Bias in the Encoding of Leadership Behavior." *Organizational Behavior and Human Decision Processes* 101 (2): 230–242.

Shafritz, Jay. 1974. "The Cancer Eroding Public Personnel Professionalism." *Public Personnel Management* 3 (6): 486–492.

Society for Human Resource Management. 2014. "Templates and Samples." www.shrm.org (accessed May 15, 2014).

Trahant, Bill, and Steve Yearout. 2006. "Competing for Talent in the Federal Government: Part I." *The Public Manager* 35 (1): 57–61.

U.S. Merit Systems Protection Board. 2005. "Reference Checking in Federal Hiring: Making the Call." www.mspb.gov/studies/browsestudies.htm (accessed April 17, 2014).

U.S. Office of Personnel Management. 2014. "Assessment & Evaluation." www.opm.gov/services-for-agencies/assessment-evaluation/online-assessment/ (accessed May 15, 2015).

Wood, Jennifer L., James M. Schmidtke, and Diane L. Decker. 2007. "Lying on Job Applications: The Effects of Job Relevance, Commission, and Human Resource Management Experience." *Journal of Business & Psychology* 22 (1): 1–9.

8 Salary and Wages

Learning Objectives

- Introduce the rationales for compensation policy in organizations.
- Outline intrinsic and extrinsic sources of employee motivation.
- Explore traditional approaches to compensation, along with innovations in compensation, including broadbanding, merit pay, and skill-based pay.
- Review compensation issues related to equity and recruitment.

Compensation, the principal means by which organizations attach value to the jobs established in their workforce, refers to the total package of salary and benefits paid to an employee (see Exhibit 8.1). Compensation mechanisms include hourly wages, pay by unit of work (piecework), or salary (without or without the option of overtime). Additionally, the total sum of remuneration includes these base wages plus both short-term incentives, such as bonuses and awards, and long-term incentives, such as 'comp time' (banked compensated time off) and extra compensation for productivity improvements or cost reductions, as well as various monetary and nonmonetary benefits or privileges (Roy 1991). This chapter discusses salary, and we explore the details of monetary and nonmonetary benefits in Chapter 9.

Ideally, compensation policies and practices are integrated with the larger HR efforts of the organization, and they should help the organization achieve its mission and follow through on its strategic plans. For example, compensation policy is critical to an organization's ability to recruit and retain the best employees, and it has an important impact on employee morale and workforce productivity. An understanding of how public sector compensation programs work in practice and a clear comprehension of why a compensation system is structured the way it is, especially its role in recruitment, retention, and sustaining productivity, represent a critical part of public sector management generally, and HRM in particular.

Salaries in the Public Policy Process

The use of complicated classification tables and salary ranges might suggest that the determination of salaries in the public sector is a precise scientific process. The reality is that salaries and wages are very much a key part of the political process within which public agencies operate. Public employee pay levels are determined as part of the budget-making process, involving elected officials in both the executive and legislative branches. Budget makers must weigh the cost derived from the maintenance of competitive employee salaries and wages against other public needs. This political reality often means that public sector salaries do not share the market competitive emphasis that

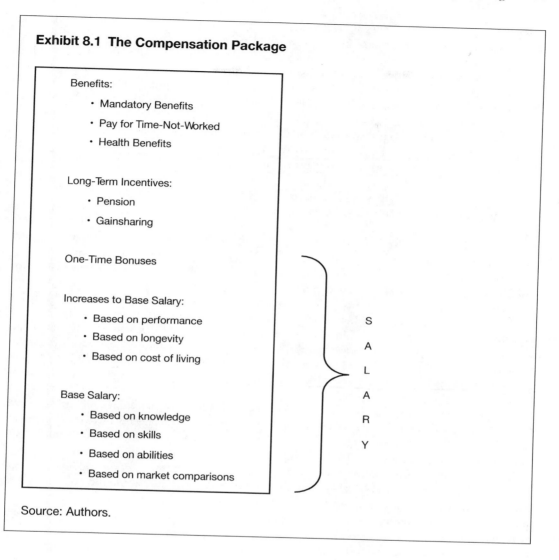

Exhibit 8.1 The Compensation Package

Benefits:

- Mandatory Benefits
- Pay for Time-Not-Worked
- Health Benefits

Long-Term Incentives:

- Pension
- Gainsharing

One-Time Bonuses

Increases to Base Salary:

- Based on performance
- Based on longevity
- Based on cost of living

Base Salary:

- Based on knowledge
- Based on skills
- Based on abilities
- Based on market comparisons

S
A
L
A
R
Y

Source: Authors.

private sector organizations' salaries and wages do (Risher and Fay 1997). In fact, as Risher (1994, p. 650) notes, "the need to pay competitively is almost never the controlling factor in public wage decisions."

Comparisons between public compensation rates and private sector rates are complicated and politically charged. Scholars argue that *what* counts as compensation and *for whom* it counts both have enormous implications for our conclusions about differences between the public and for-profit sectors (Belman and Heywood 2004). To consider such comparisons properly, we must keep in mind that the difference between compensation rates in the form of salary is only part of an overall compensation package. As Reilly (2012) argues, the level of government, the existence and relevance of unions and civil service protocols, the type of job, a variety of demographic factors, and the type and typing of salaries, incentives, and benefits combine to influence comparisons between the public, nonprofit, and private sectors. Thus, intelligent, well-meaning individuals may look at the same set of data and draw entirely different conclusions.

Taylor and Taylor (2011) found that, in aggregate, most of the fifteen countries they studied (Canada, Great Britain, Germany, Slovenia, Israel, Japan, Taiwan, Australia, and New Zealand) paid public employees above market rates. However, the United States, Denmark, France, Bulgaria, and Russia did not; they were either at par or below. This result is more nuanced than might appear in the United States, where higher-ranking public sector employees were paid lower in general than the private sector for comparable positions, and lower-level positions received higher than market pay. In the United States, average salaries for lower-level jobs, especially at the federal level, tend to be higher for public sector workers than they are for private sector workers (Belman and Heywood 1996, 2004; Bender and Heywood 2010; Risher and Fay 1997). Management and professional workers consistently enjoy higher salaries in the private sector (Risher and Fay 1997; Witt 1988).

This pattern of compensation may be due to the influence of public sector unions in negotiating on behalf of workers who tend to be concentrated at the low end of the organization's hierarchy, or it may be the result of some classification systems pulling lower salaries higher than the market owing to value comparisons. State and local workers, however, may not have the salary advantage for either high- or low-level positions, as research indicates that compensation is below market for many employees in state and local government service (Bender 2003; Bender and Heywood 2010). Although Kearney (1992, p. 22) notes that, "unions are associated with higher wages and benefits in state and local government," their monetary impact on compensation is estimated to be lower than that of private sector unions. In general, researchers have found that educational attainment, gender, race/ethnicity, and work experience are influential variables in terms of comparing particular categories of workers (Keefe 2010; Llorens 2008). Formal educational attainment, it seems, commands a higher premium in the private sector compared with the public sector (Bender and Heywood 2010; Keefe 2010).

Compensation in the nonprofit sector is very much a function of organization size. Little research has focused upon nonprofit organizations in terms of compensation, probably owing to the widespread assumption that heavy reliance is placed on volunteers in nonprofit organizations, with a small cadre of professional staff being salaried. However, Oster (1988) found that executive compensation varies widely within the nonprofit sector, depending upon the fiscal size of the nonprofit and the scope of activities (e.g., the arts or social services). However, perceptions about the philanthropic and voluntary nature of nonprofit activities also serve to limit the salary ranges, as directing boards are concerned about the public perception that the nonprofit may be spending too much on overhead costs such as salaries as opposed to direct services to clients (Oster 1988, p. 219).

Clearly, recruiting and retaining employees when public sector wages are lagging behind private sector rates can be challenging, especially in key job categories such as computer network specialists and operations engineers. Many public sector organizations have established separate salary structures for the most highly competitive job categories, to avoid the legendary inflexibility of the traditional General Schedule (GS) system. Governmental reluctance to implement recommended salary increases may be due to the combination of an inability to pay competitive salaries and political reluctance *to tax* the public at a level adequate for maintaining competitive salaries (Belman and Heywood 1996; Davis and Gabris 2008; Leavitt and Morris 2008).

Employee Motivation: Money, Service, or Something Else?

Many assumptions about the utility of compensation patterns are derived from organization theory and the goals for compensation. A basic premise of the contemporary political ideology founding the notion of democracy is the autonomy of citizens. Furthering this, the ideology of market paradigms purports that, as we have the autonomy to contract our services/labor with other individuals and organizations for compensation, we are, therefore, motivated to do so. Theories of human motivation generally include need, expectancy, and equity as primary drivers of human actions in social life. Maslow (2011) and McClelland (1970, 1976) argued that the driving force of human behavior lay in unsatisfied needs, though they differed sharply on whether those needs were socially constructed or inherent (Gortner, Nichols, and Ball 2007). Conversely, Vroom (1995) defined behavior as voluntary and self-initiated, but based upon an individual's expectations about likely outcomes in response to certain cues given to superiors with command over rewards and punishments. In yet another approach to human motivation, Adams (1965) noted that people engage in an ongoing comparison of themselves with others and assess relative expenditures of time, talent, and effort to assess how equitable their treatment/reward is relative to that of relevant others.

Perry and Wise (1990, p. 368) articulated the concept of public service motivation as "an individual's predisposition to respond to motives grounded primarily or uniquely in public institutions and organizations." Since their seminal article, a great deal of scholarship has considered what this idea means for public employees and the relationship between this concept and job satisfaction for employees in public sector and nonprofit sector work. In considering whether such a motivational frame is solely a function of individual characteristics, or whether external factors (such as management or organizational goals) may play a role, Jung and Rainey (2011, p. 29) offer the notion of "public duty motivation" to reflect the nuances of a number of questionnaire items used in their analysis (e.g., "I am motivated to do a good job by my duty as a public employee"). In a recent cross-national study conducted by Taylor and Taylor (2011, p. 81), they conclude that public service motivation, especially in the United States, has enormous implications for management:

> The effort levels of the American public sector workforce appear to be most profoundly shaped by public service motivation . . . results suggest that wages account for a relatively small proportion of the American group's output in the form of effort put forth.

We will consider the implications of compensation and its utility in attracting, motivating, or retaining employees as we consider traditional compensation systems, as well as a few of the more common innovations in place in some public service settings across the country.

Compensation Systems

Several different approaches to compensation systems are described in this chapter. We begin with the traditional compensation systems based upon the job classification and job evaluation systems discussed in Chapter 7. Frustrations with the traditional system prompted several innovations to modify the traditional systems to fit the swiftly changing nature of today's knowledge-based private sector firms and public sector agencies and nonprofit organizations. As Exhibit 8.2 demonstrates, each system type links to a different set of criteria to determine the level of pay awarded to employees.

Traditional Systems

The heart of the traditional compensation process is the assignation of a salary level for each category of job. Job classification tables are used to establish pay grades and pay ranges within each grade. To illustrate this point, Exhibit 8.3 depicts the compensation schedule for the State of Idaho (FY 2015). The grades for classified jobs in the state system are analogous to the long-established federal

Exhibit 8.2 Types of Compensation System

Compensation Systems	Linkages to Pay Levels
Traditional compensation system	Pay linked to seniority and rank
Broadbanding	Pay linked to broad occupational categories
Merit pay	Pay linked to job performance
Skill-based/competency pay	Pay linked to employee knowledge
Gainsharing	Pay linked to group performance

Source: Authors.

Exhibit 8.3 State of Idaho Compensation Schedule, FY 2015, effective 6/8/14

Pay Grade	Minimum Points	Mid-Grade Points	Maximum Points	Minimum Annual Salary, $	Policy Level, $	Maximum Annual Salary, $
D	below 110 points			15,080	21,133	26,416
E	110	119	130	16,058	23,608	29,515
F	131	142	154	18,075	26,582	33,238
G	155	169	184	20,530	30,181	37,731
H	185	201	219	23,629	34,757	43,451
I	220	240	262	27,602	40,602	50,752
J	263	286	312	31,138	45,781	57,221
K	313	341	372	34,861	51,272	64,085
L	373	406	443	39,354	57,886	72,363
M	444	485	528	44,491	65,437	81,806
N	529	578	630	49,171	72,301	90,376
O	631	688	750	53,290	78,354	97,947
P	751	828	904	58,261	85,675	107,099
Q	905	998	1,090	64,126	94,307	117,894
R	1,091	1,176	1,292	71,136	104,624	130,790
S	1,293	1,399	1,531	79,810	117,354	146,702
T	1,532	1,665	1,822	90,126	132,538	165,672
U	1,823	1,980	2,166	102,419	150,613	188,261
V	2,167	2,354	2,575	117,062	172,162	215,197

Source: Idaho Division of Human Resources. 2014. "FY 2015 Pay Schedule." http://dhr.idaho.gov/compensation.html (accessed May 20, 2014).

government's GS schedule. The exhibit also displays the point value for each job derived from the Hay factor plan, as well as the corresponding minimum, midpoint (often called the policy line), and maximum annual salary in dollars.

The information in Exhibit 8.3 is used in Exhibit 8.4 to illustrate the structure of pay grades and ranges graphically. Pay grades are "groupings of a variety of positions of similar internal job ranking" (Roy 1991, p. 108). Each pay grade features a minimum (see point *a* in Exhibit 8.4), midpoint (see point *b*), and maximum (see point *c*) salary range. The midpoint is used as a control point for the administration of pay, and the policy line for this pay schedule is the slope at each midpoint (*bde*).

Pay grades and ranges can be developed in two primary ways. First, grades can be assembled based upon the internal ranking of the value of the job; for example, point values assigned by the Hay factor method can be used to align pay grades and ranges. Or, second, grades can be separated by equal numbers of points, or by a predetermined percentage of points between grades. Pay grades and ranges can also be developed using the salary midpoints to distinguish one grade from another: for example, having a 10 percent difference between one grade's salary midpoint and the next. The job evaluation and classification process assigns value to each job, and salary ranges should reflect that process of prioritizing.

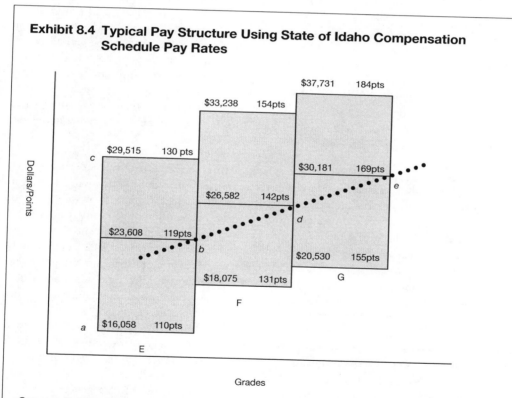

Exhibit 8.4 Typical Pay Structure Using State of Idaho Compensation Schedule Pay Rates

Source: Point values and dollar figures taken from Exhibit 8.3, State of Idaho Compensation Schedule, and adapted by the authors.

The concept of equity in the context of compensation practices has to do with the employee's perception that the organization's compensation schedule and policies are *fair*. Fairness in pay is often assessed in terms of its proportionality in the internal ranking of jobs (internal equity), and in the comparability of the compensation schedule and policies relative to those of competing organizations (external equity). Research has demonstrated that employee reactions to perceived inequities (internal and external) in the compensation structure can have a major influence on decisions about accepting or rejecting job offers, whether to stay with an organization, and/or how hard to work at the job (Wallace and Fay 1983). Analyzing jobs and ordering them within the classification system form a systematic way of assigning more value, and hence more pay, to the jobs that are more highly prioritized in the organization. This alignment of jobs according to intrinsic value ensures the internal equity of the organization's salary structure (Risher and Fay 1997). This, according to Adams (1965), may be a source of motivation to employees (if they feel they are treated justly relative to others) or demotivation (if relative effort does not cue reward). Shore, Tashchian, and Jourdan (2006) found a relationship between external equity and turnover, but noted that motivation was more closely linked to internal equity.

In theory, minimally qualified new employees would start at the bottom of the range for their particular grade, whereas new employees with more experience and greater skills would begin at a higher point in the range (Risher 1997, p. 40). Ideally, the midpoint of each salary range should be tied to a competitive pay level in the relevant job market. Federal salaries have used private sector wage comparisons to ensure comparability between public and private civilian wages since the adoption of the Federal Pay Comparability Act of 1970. Local governments in many states use periodic salary surveys of other comparable jurisdictions in their metropolitan area, state, or geographic region, when setting salary ranges (Leavitt and Morris 2008). This process of assessing comparability in salaries is intended to ensure the approximation of external equity of the salary structure. Though many state and local governments use some type of systematic comparability study when setting their salary rates, often focusing upon average earning differentials, these surveys are quite often rather imprecise, as Belman and Heywood (2004, p. 568) observe:

> The average earnings differential measures whether characteristics typical of one sector will be rewarded differently in the other. Thus, if the characteristics of a public-sector worker result in an estimated private-sector wage different from his or her actual earnings, that worker is not being paid comparably. Yet the average of such comparisons should not be taken as an estimate of comparability. If half of public sector workers are 'overpaid' by 20 percent and half are 'underpaid' by 20 percent, the average differential will be close to zero, suggesting comparability when, in truth, no workers are being paid comparably. This is more than just the point that averages may not apply to each worker. Instead, it is a contention that the dispersion in individual earnings comparability must be as important as (and in many cases more important) the average.

Salary surveys can be useful for helping an organization maintain its salary structure's external equity by comparing the organization's pay structure with that of a relevant competitive market (Davis 2011; Wallace and Fay 1983). Put more directly, a salary survey can help the organization avoid paying too much or too little for the labor provided by its workforce (Lichty 1991). Salary surveys can be done internally by the organization, or it can make use of data generated by the federal or state government, by governmental associations (e.g., the ICMA), private consulting firms, or trade associations. Whatever the source, the classic pattern observed by Wallace and Fay (1983, p. 112) still tends to hold true:

1. Select the jobs to be surveyed.
2. Define the relevant labor markets.
3. Identify comparison organizations.
4. Decide what information to request from the comparison organizations (base salaries versus bonuses or benefits).
5. Decide on a data collection technique (e.g., telephone versus mail versus online surveys).
6. Administer the survey.

Many external sources of data can be used for salary survey purposes. The BLS produces periodic area wage surveys and industry wage surveys. Other sources of external salary data may include professional associations and private consulting firms specializing in compensation analysis. Compensation analysis is technical and complex work, always requiring a nuanced application of standard statistical techniques (Davis 2011). An accurately done and timely salary survey can help management make informed pay decisions. This is important, not only in individual pay considerations, but also in setting a larger workforce compensation policy for the organization.

Tensions in Traditional Systems: Inflexibility

In a review of the federal government's compensation system, Wamsley (1997) identifies several noteworthy concerns. First, she describes the classification system concept as too often inefficient in implementation, owing to the complexity of precisely classifying positions in a mechanical way (p. 27). Moreover, rapid changes in technology and job content can make even the most carefully crafted job classifications obsolete in a rather short time (p. 28). The inherent inflexibility of classification systems makes it difficult to respond to these changes, leading managers to seek various workarounds (p. 31) to reward valued employees. Similarly, in tight budget times, training and development programs are frequently among the first cuts made, leading to a widening gap between the skills needed and those held by job incumbents. Wamsley also decries problems with automatic, longevity-based wage increases. Over time, this practice may erode the principle of equal pay for equal work and disrupt the internal equity of the salary structure (p. 29).

Tensions in Traditional Systems: Ethics in Compensation Equity

Managing internal and external equity can be challenging for an organization, because the goals of each can come into direct conflict. For example, keeping up with rapidly rising salary rates to maintain external equity may distort the internal equity of the compensation schedule by bringing in new employees at higher salaries than those who have been with the organization a longer time (Wallace and Fay 1983). Problems with either kind of equity can affect employee behavior adversely. Failure to maintain external equity hinders the organization's ability to recruit and retain high-quality employees. Conversely, failure to maintain internal equity can poison employee morale and undermine the perceived legitimacy and fairness of management among longtime employees whose loyalty to the organization is not rewarded.

Tensions in Traditional Systems: Premiums for Technology Staff

Key challenges facing public sector organizations lie in the recruitment and retention of staff competent in all fields related to technology. For example, staff expertise with IT has been increasingly valued, as various forms of e-government have become widely adopted in government at all levels (Belanger and Carter 2008). Generally, technology solutions have become more common in government operations and policy-making. Compensation is a critical part of this process. The scarcity of qualified IT applicants results in relatively high salaries compared with other knowledge workers of equivalent age and experience. A recent study commissioned jointly by the Ford Foundation and the John D. and Catherine T. MacArthur Foundation (Freedman Consulting 2014, p. 5) noted:

> A major gap between the public interest and for-profit sectors persists . . . [due to] superior for-profit recruitment and retention models. Specifically, the for-profit sector was perceived as providing both more attractive compensation (especially to young talent) and fostering a culture of innovation, openness, and creativity that was seen as more appealing to technologists and innovators.

Traditional compensation systems can make it difficult for public managers to offer competitive salaries, as changing salaries and/or benefits may require legislative approval. Some public jurisdictions have established differential salary schedules for professions whose market salaries are much too high for the rest of the classification system, for example, engineers or physicians. Other jurisdictions focus on the flexibility in benefits packages possible in the public sector; for example, some jurisdictions allow off hours consulting, comp time banking, telecommuting, and flexible work scheduling as nonmonetary inducements to IT employees and others in specialized jobs of high strategic value to the organization.

Tensions in Traditional Systems: Diversity and Salary Gaps

Despite civil rights laws to prevent discrimination and the equal pay laws described in Chapter 4, a substantial gap persists between the earnings of men and women generally, and the differential is especially striking for women of color. Both ethnicity and gender appear to have implications for median earnings. According to the U.S. Census Bureau, median earnings for men overall was estimated at $47,473, compared with $37,412 for women; in effect, women earn 78.8 percent of men's median earnings. When this type of compensation data is disaggregated by ethnicity, then, as Exhibit 8.5 demonstrates, Asian men, as a group, earned a median income of $56,817 as the high-earning group, compared with Hispanic/Latino women at $27,892.

Some of the difference in earnings noted may be attributed to the process of occupational segregation. White men tend to be concentrated in certain occupational categories with higher salaries than those occupied generally by white women or nonwhite workers. The higher salaries for some occupations versus others are a reflection of classification and compensation systems that place a higher valuation on those particular occupations and the attendant KSAs. Goldberg Day and Hill (2007, p. 41) found:

> Autonomy and authority at work are associated with higher pay for both women and men. Occupations associated with higher pay for women include business and management; engineering/architecture; computer science; and research, science, technology. For men, working in engineering/architecture, computer science, and medical professions increases pay.

As Keefe (2010) observed, education matters in terms of any pay differentials between public and private sector workers generally. However, Goldberg Day and Hill (2007, p. 3) note:

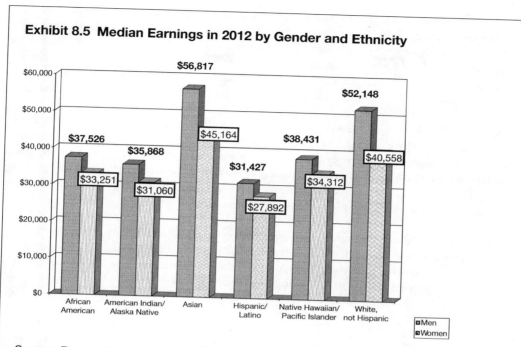

Exhibit 8.5 Median Earnings in 2012 by Gender and Ethnicity

Source: From U.S. Census Bureau. 2012. "American Community Survey 1-Year Estimates, S2002. Median Earnings in the Past 12 Months by Workers by Sex and Women's Earnings as a Percentage of Men's Earnings by Selected Characteristics." factfinder2.census.gov/faces/nav/jsf/pages/index.xhtml (accessed June 9, 2014).

The pay gap between female and male college graduates cannot be fully accounted for by factors known to affect wages, such as experience (including work hours), training, education, and personal characteristics . . . to discover discrimination is to eliminate the other possible explanations. In this analysis the portion of the pay gap that remains unexplained after all other factors are taken into account is 5 percent one year after graduation and 12 percent 10 years after graduation. These unexplained gaps are evidence of discrimination, which remains a serious problem for women in the work force.

Llorens (2008) found gender differences among state employees, with women earning an average pay premium and male employees registering an average pay penalty in comparison with the private sector. Goldberg Day and Hill (2007) observe that sector matters, in that men who work in nonprofits tend to earn less than those who are either self-employed or working in the private, for-profit realm. Although Llorens and Stazyk (2011) did not find a statistically significant association between external equity and turnover, they speculated this may be owing to possible effects of gender and ethnicity (e.g., equity expectations might attract those who believe that the private sector would hold disparity), preferences for benefit packaging, and public service motivation as incentives that compete with comparatively lower wages.

In the 1980s, scholars and practitioners alike questioned the relative importance placed on certain KSAs as opposed to others whose relative appraisals underlie the classification systems, resulting in imbalanced pay structures. This questioning led to what is referred to as the "comparable worth debate." Although there have been challenges to gendered discrepancies in compensation systems, the implementation of remedies has usually met with resistance from legislatures unwilling to fund such systemic raises in public salaries as would be required to implement comparable worth. At times, the courts seemed to hold a strict line on the types of remedy that might be available through the judicial system. Thus, Riccucci (2008) argued that *Ledbetter v. Goodyear Tire and Rubber Company* (2007)—which would have enforced a strict statute of limitations and a narrow window during which a plaintiff could challenge compensation disparities—would have a chilling effect on pay discrimination complaints, resulting in worsening of pay inequality in the workplace. Soon after, the Lilly Ledbetter Fair Pay Act of 2009 amended the Civil Rights Act of 1964 to require that the 180-day statute of limitations for filing a pay discrimination lawsuit be reset with each new paycheck received by a would-be plaintiff.

General concerns about the complexity, inflexibility, and lack of focus on or connection to performance have damaged the credibility of traditional compensation systems. Thus, a variety of changes to compensation systems have been proposed, and some have been implemented, with varying degrees of success being reported in the research literature.

Broadbanding

In broadbanding, a complicated system of salary grades that might encompass a variety of jobs is consolidated into a few layers with far more expansive ranges, to allow managers greater flexibility in setting pay levels for their employees within these bands. In their classic text on compensation, Milkovich, Newman, and Gerhart (2011, pp. 269–270) attribute several distinct advantages to broadbanding:

- [offering managers the] flexibility to define job responsibilities;
- support[ing] redesigned, downsized, or boundaryless organizations;
- foster[ing] cross-functional growth and development [for employees].

Exhibit 8.6 Traditional versus Banded Compensation Structure

Traditional Compensation		Banded Structure	
Grade	Title	Band	Title
14	Sr. budget analyst	6	Sr. budget analyst
12	Budget analyst III		
10	Budget analyst II		
8	Budget analyst I	5	Budget analyst

Source: Authors.

Exhibit 8.6 compares a traditional narrow grade system with a broadbanded alternative. The number of appropriate pay bands may vary between organizations, but usually includes one band for each layer of management. The salary ranges within each band are unhooked from midpoints, and they are wider than pay grades and ranges found in traditional compensation systems. Risher (1994, p. 655) described broadbanding as an increasingly popular type of reform of compensations systems because it:

- reduces the administrative costs of the salary program;
- deemphasizes hierarchy and fine distinctions between similar jobs;
- facilitates the creation of effective teams;
- provides more flexibility to reward individual contributions;
- makes it easier to reorganize and redefine job responsibilities;
- facilitates lateral career moves;
- eliminates some difficulties with RIFs;
- reduces tension between HR and the rest of the organization over job evaluation decisions.

Whalen and Guy (2008) reported a modest level of implementation of broadbanding (sixteen of fifty states at the time of their study, and only twelve with full systems). Their basic conclusion was that the usual rationales for implementation (greater flexibility for management and a more streamlined compensation system) were not realized in the compensation systems they investigated in some detail. In particular, they observed that (2008, pp. 362–363):

> the most significant lesson learned by states that have implemented broadbanding is that success is highly dependent on changes to all consequential components. Broadband reforms must include more than simply a change in job class structure . . . neglect for secondary although significant elements is a recipe for failure.

Paying for Performance

The commonest reform to traditional compensation systems advocated in the HRM literature is merit pay, or pay for performance. Merit increases can be given either as a percentage increase to one's base salary or as a one-time bonus. Adding to the base salary is more costly to the organization in the end; however, fearing to appear too generous in the eyes of their constituents, policymakers often resist providing bonuses.

In traditional compensation systems, employees are rewarded for seniority. As their tenure with the organization increases, so does their progression through the organization's salary ranges. In theory, merit pay provides that direct link to performance, without regard to longevity. Successful merit pay approaches logically demand that organizations can measure performance and accurately assess it. In addition, an organization's coffers should be able to pay as promised. Finally, merit pay should be an incentive, not a deterrent, to enhanced performance. The concept of merit pay is popular and appears to be experiencing renewed interest, according to Perry, Engbers, and Jun (2009). However, longstanding empirical studies assessing its effectiveness point to several problems with implementation and sustainability.

Challenges with Merit Pay: Measurement, Resources, and Motivation

Fundamentally, effective merit pay systems require a performance appraisal process capable of correctly distinguishing the truly meritorious from those less so (Kellough and Lu 1993; Schay 1997). Two problems relevant to merit pay occur: performance appraisal instruments may be inadequate and/or the raters employing them may be inaccurate.

The performance appraisal instrument may not be sufficiently valid (measuring what is intended) or reliable (consistently replicating a finding), making it impossible to discriminate accurately between highly meritorious and less meritorious employees. Second, managers may be unwilling or unable to make meaningful distinctions among their own employees using the organization's performance appraisal system. Dividing the amount of money allocated for merit among large numbers of employees makes each employee's share very small. Naturally, this near universal distribution of small pay increments decreases the ability of managers to motivate effectively with salary.

The inability or unwillingness of managers to determine which employees are worthy of merit pay and which are not may be related to commonplace challenges with performance appraisal systems generally. Chapter 10 will consider these issues in greater detail. In general, with limitations in standardized criteria for evaluating employees and assigning merit pay awards, overt bias (for example, against women) or incidental bias (for example, the 'halo effect') can enter the evaluation process in pernicious ways (Kellough and Lu 1993).

The problems associated with merit pay and the performance evaluation process can present public managers with an ethical dilemma about the most equitable way to distribute merit increases. Is it ethical for managers to rely on performance evaluations they believe to be somewhat inaccurate? Is there an ethical responsibility to be honest in the performance evaluation process? Is it an ethical problem that a large number of employees (perhaps undeservingly) were rated above average, or is it more ethical for a manager to advocate for higher salaries for employees they feel are already falling behind market salary rates? Perhaps managers should divide the merit increases equally, but would this be fair to the best employees to reward them equally with poor performers? The issue of ethics and compensation presents public managers with many vexing questions relating to fundamental fairness.

The amount of money provided as 'merit' money is often not large enough to motivate employees adequately (Kellough and Lu 1993; Risher and Fay 1997; Schay 1997). Most organizations endeavor to combine cost-of-living increases with merit pay, thereby decreasing the amount of money tied to performance (Witt 1988). Ingraham's study of state implementation of pay for performance found that, "a large majority of the states reported problems with inadequate, inconsistent, and in some cases *no* funding. Of the 21 states responding, only 4 reported funding every year of the program's life" (1993, p. 353). Most recently, the Center for State and Local Government Excellence (2014, p. 2) found, in a survey of state and local personnelists, that only 36.7 percent of respondents were reporting pay increases, and more than half were making changes to reduce the 'cost' of compensation, including 61 percent reporting shifts to health benefits and 53 percent indicating that costs were being shifted to employees. Kellough and Selden (1997) suggest that inadequate funding makes merit pay implementation very difficult, especially in combination with pressure to maintain the internal and external equity of the salary system. These pressures also lead to reductions in the pool of money allocated to merit pay in the past.

Finally, let us return to a consideration of compensation as a motivating device. Pay for performance is based on expectancy theory—that is, the individual believes his or her personal effort leads to desired levels of performance, resulting in desired outcomes such as a higher salary (Perry 1986, pp. 57–69). Studies of what actually motivates employees, however, indicate that intrinsic factors such as feeling valued or serving the public interest may be as important in motivation as distinctly extrinsic factors, such as salary or wages (Kellough and Lu 1993, p. 54; Meyer 1975, p. 40).

Per Taylor and Taylor (2011, p. 81):

> The effort levels of the American public sector workforce appear to be most profoundly shaped by Public service motivation . . . results suggest that wages account for a relatively small proportion of the American group's output in the form of effort put forth.

Kellough and Selden found that only 39 percent of personnel managers in U.S. states believed that merit pay increased motivation among their employees (1997, p. 11). Merit pay programs seem to have been most effective at increasing productivity in routine, nonmanagerial jobs (Perry 1986, p. 60). Stazyk (2013) found, in a study of local managers in more than 500 jurisdictions, that merit pay, public service motivation, and job satisfaction tend to associate positively with one another, and that performance pay may enhance job satisfaction where employees are not as intrinsically motivated (e.g., have a reduced level of public service motivation). In various literature reviews and meta-analyses, scholars tend to reach the conclusion that merit pay does not seem to be associated with enhanced future performance (Perry, Engbers, and Jun 2009; Perry, Mesch, and Paarlberg 2006).

Merit Pay Persists Despite Problems

Given all the problems with merit pay and the difficulties associated with its implementation and sustainability in difficult fiscal times, it is fair to question why the concept remains so popular. One reason is that pay for performance is a private sector innovation, and it is rather commonly assumed that private sector techniques will improve public sector performance (Ingraham 1993, p. 348). This stereotype persists in spite of numerous studies indicating that pay for performance has been less than fully successful in most cases (Perry, Engbers, and Jun 2009). Another reason for merit pay's popularity is its role in the "symbolic politics" of keeping the public bureaucracy accountable, coupled with a certain reluctance to admit such a large investment of public funds has been pretty much a failure (Kellough and Lu 1993, pp. 55–56).

Weibel, Rost, and Osterloh considered the relationships of pay to performance in a large-scale meta-analysis encompassing studies conducted between 1971 and 2006 (2010). Although their data are not specific to the public sector, they observe that, "pay for performance causes a cognitive shift . . . [strengthening] extrinsic motivation for behavior (causes a price effect) . . . [while weakening] intrinsic motivation for behavior (causes a crowding-out effect)" (p. 404). They caution policymakers considering these systems for the public sector that (pp. 404–405):

1) Pay for performance can potentially create a strong crowding-out effect [with implications for public service motivation] . . .
2) Public funding is clearly more limited than private sector funding . . . [thus] the price effect of pay for performance in public management tends to be rather small . . .
3) Pay for performance might reduce investments in policy expertise . . .
4) Pay for performance requires the precise measuring of performance and the attribution of this performance to individual efforts to be effective . . .
5) The application of performance-contingent rewards also carries the danger of political manipulation . . . pay for performance for politicians and high-level public service agents . . . [may] not make sense because these individuals are the ones who decide the very standards by which they are compensated.

Skills and Competencies: Linking Pay to Knowledge

Another reform of traditional compensation programs that many public sector organizations are considering is skill-based pay (SBP, or sometimes called competency-based pay). In traditional programs, employees are rewarded based on the job that they occupy, along with the length of time they have held the position. Jobs are ranked in classification systems according to the value and level of KSAs required for a particular job. The salary structure reflects that prioritizing, giving higher salaries to those with more demanding jobs according to the classification schedule. According to Shareef (1994), in SBP, the unit of analysis is not the job that the incumbent holds, but rather what skills the employee possesses and acquires. In other words, "they are paid for skills they are capable of using and not for the jobs they are performing at a particular point in time" (Shareef 1994, p. 61). Consequently, it is possible that, although an employee's job does not change, evidence that he or she has mastered a set of skills valued by the organization might result in a pay increase.

Implementation of skill-based pay can take several distinct forms. Employees can be rewarded for knowing more about a specialized area or their *depth of skill*; they can be rewarded for learning skills that are "upstream, downstream or parallel" to their position in the production or service delivery phase (the *breadth of skill*); or they can be rewarded for self-management skills such as scheduling of work, problem solving, or training, which are *vertical skills* (Shareef 1994, p. 61). Ledford and Heneman differentiate SBP from the traditional systems because the focus is upon employees, not on the positions they hold in the organization (2011, p. 2):

> In SBP systems, employees receive additional pay only after they demonstrate the skills, knowledge, and/or competencies that the system rewards. Thus, SBP is a person–based system, because it is based on the characteristics of the person rather than the job. In more common job-based pay systems, pay is based on the job, which employees are entitled to receive even if they are not proficient in their position.

The advantages believed to be associated with SBP include increased flexibility to move employees with necessary skills to new positions within the organization as needed, with this flexibility being especially helpful in periods of cutback management or downsizing (Shareef 1994, p. 66). SBP systems

---

Exhibit 8.7 Comparison of Different SBP Types

Skill Emphasis	Depth	Breadth of Self-Management
Examples	Skilled trades systems, dual career ladder, academic career	SBP supporting high involvement and lean systems Competency pay for professionals
Organization's goals	Deeper employee expertise	Greater employee capability Flexibility Broader perspective Increased self-direction New and/or deeper skills
Conditions germane to type	Competitive demand for specialized expertise; multiyear training cycles for key skills, making employee retention highly desirable	High involvement and lean organizations High employee versatility and capability Organizations requiring new or deeper skills of managers and professionals

Source: Adapted from Figure 2: Comparison of Different SBP Types, in Ledford and Heneman 2011, p. 11.

might also prove important in improving employee satisfaction and promoting personal development (Gupta 1997, p. 135) in periods when new managers come on board to 'fix' organizations that exhibit poor performance and/or display dysfunctional interpersonal relationships harmful to the accomplishment of their mission.

However, fundamental to successful implementation is the organization's ongoing ability to monitor and assess the quantity and quality of skills learned by employees accurately. Although this assessment may be handled through certification testing or by some alternative reliable means (Gupta 1997; Shareef 1994), these pay systems require a significant investment in training and assessment. In the short run, SPB may cost the organization more in total salary, as employees accumulate more skills (Gupta 1997, p. 134). Like broadbanded systems, skill-based pay is better suited administratively to flatter organizations employing a strong workplace team orientation (Gupta 1997, p. 133). Echoing the conclusions offered by Whalen and Guy (2008), Shareef (2002) observed that, in one state, SBP's potential was not realized because other necessary personnel system designs and implementation mechanisms (e.g., job design, performance appraisal, and employee development), management culture, and internal/external political environments were demonstrably "incongruent" with SBP. He argued in this regard:

> public agencies using SBP as a catalyst for institutional transformation must (a) be prepared for simultaneous systems redesign to support the SBP intervention, (b) address the job security needs of managers, and (c) produce successful outcomes to maintain political support throughout implementation and diffusion.
>
> (p. 233)

Team-Based Performance Pay Programs

Incentive plans borrowed from the for-profit sector for application to the public or to the nonprofit sector are not always compatible with the public interest values. Clearly, incentives based on profit gains are not compatible in an environment where organizational success is not based upon profit margins and market share. However, concepts such as gainsharing describe various pay incentives designed to reward group performance, in contrast to individual pay-for-performance programs. Similar to the logic of profit sharing, this particular incentive system was developed for use primarily in the manufacturing sector. According to researcher Gardner (2011), gainsharing plans are distinguishable from other goal–reward structures because, in this type of program, employees are consulted on productivity improvements after a performance baseline has been established, and productivity 'gains' are then distributed across the entire participating group, rather than to individual employees. Gainsharing programs encourage changes in employee behavior by financially rewarding improvements in productivity and/or cost savings (Milkovich, Newman, and Gerhart 2011). The positive impact of group incentives on employee attitudes and morale is also important. Gainsharing may increase the long-term identity of the employee with the organization, and improve employee morale generally (Ross and Ross 1991).

There are many ways to calculate the financial rewards used in the various gainsharing plans that have been implemented. According to Ross and Ross (1991, p. 181), whether based upon physical measures such as the number of units produced or more broadly construed as sharing a percentage of cost savings, measures used to calculate rewards should:

- be perceived as fair by employees, management, and customers;
- meet management's objectives for performance improvement;

- be understandable;
- be easy to administer.

Introduction to the Reading

The following reading touches upon several themes in this chapter, notably the implications of compensation for employee motivation and the political nature of the discussion of public sector compensation. Not surprisingly, it is difficult to consider compensation without its correlate of benefit packaging, a topic addressed in greater detail in the next chapter. Thus, Reilly bridges compensation with benefit packaging in the particular context of public sector personnel policy. Please consider the following questions in this reading:

1. What are some of the challenges in accurately measuring pay differences between public and private workers?
2. What is the rationale for political support of increasing benefits rather than salary?
3. What worker characteristics matter in considering pay levels and compensation between the public and nonprofit sectors?
4. What are the implications of Reilly's argument that the proportion of teachers in state/local government employment rosters may explain compensation differences between the public and private sectors?
5. Why does Reilly argue we should consider the role of deferred benefits in comparing differences between the public and private sectors?
6. What has been the track record for attempts to reform public sector compensation systems with the use of broadbanding, merit pay, and skills- or competencies-based pay?

Excerpt 8.1 Rethinking Public Sector Compensation

Organizational management in the state and local public sector has witnessed personnel professionals who are more active in developing flexibility and efficiency in their personnel systems, which also align with the organization's goals. Some modern state and local personnel systems consist of elaborate structures of merit system rules and regulations. Improving government performance is a significant factor and force in attempts to reform state personnel systems. As the federal government has been pushing the implementation of merit systems in the state and local systems, the centralized personnel system has begun to decentralize its power (Shafritz, Russell, and Borick 2011). The current basis for this decentralization is that the fundamental aspects of the merit system have been established in the public sector and that decentralization will increase efficiency and effectiveness (Klinger 2006). . . .

Merit pay was introduced to address some of the hindrances to effective management, and is a system for motivating employees that usually involves performance-based rewards given to individuals that compensate different performance with varying levels of raises in base pay or salary (Risher, Fay, and Perry 1997). Merit pay is easy to understand from a theoretical perspective but often very difficult to implement effectively in the public sector. As with any other policy, the utilization of merit pay can be analyzed and understood by looking at the internal and external environment in which the organization operates. Performance-based and merit pay systems are often opposed by unions and employee groups, who favor more compressed wage systems and are often concerned that raises would be used by managers as blatant displays of power or administered in an unequal and/or inconsistent manner. Often, management and unions have worked together to avoid implementing a performance-based reward system because of the work needed to do so effectively.

In 2001, after returning to county government in Clark County, Nevada (the Las Vegas Valley), to be chief executive after a few years at the University of Nevada, Las Vegas, I was disappointed to learn that the county's performance-based reward system had been dismantled. After years of tense discussions and debate, management and the union had jointly adopted the merit system in place at the time. The system included an annual evaluation of all employees that featured a performance-based evaluation, resulting in a 0 to 6 percent increase in base pay. That system was eliminated and replaced by a 0 or 4 percent increase so that, in essence, nearly everyone received a 4 percent increase yearly on top of their step increase (for those who had not topped out of their salary range), as well as negotiated cost-of-living increases. In essence, the organization had moved from an agency that valued high performance and rewarded high performers to one that treated everyone in the organization in the same manner. County management and the head of the local union had adopted the change as a "side bar" agreement, meaning that it did not have to come back to the vote of members. Both sides had decided that the performance-based evaluation was more of a headache to administer. Instead of implementing the necessary training needed to conduct evaluations in a fair and consistent manner, they had chosen to take the easy way out, as well as one that minimized grievances. . . .

Upon my return, I was successful in implementing a management plan that was focused 100 percent on performance (no annual cost-of-living raise, no longevity pay, and the ability to award sizable bonuses), but was only partially successful in getting the union to agree to a return to the same type of performance-based pay.

With the significant restraints involved in managing public organizations, including limited resources and diminishing budgets, the merit increase system needs to innovate or develop alternatives in order to be effective. One-time bonuses, with little or no raise in base pay, is one feasible alternative. Other alternatives include creating a distinct budget line that provides funds for exceptional employee performance, setting a cap on merit pay at pay range midpoint, and lump sum increases (Risher, Fay, and Perry 1997). A good part of the blame for the failure to properly enforce the principles of the merit system rests not only with executive management but with departmental management, who fail to recognize their responsibility to the public trust and avoid conflict by giving out undeserved merit increases—with zero accountability. . . .

Traditional public compensation systems operate under the assumption that organizations and jobs change gradually, the traditional system has operated with centralized control and very detailed job descriptions, and was based originally on the principles of scientific management and the work of early industrial engineers. The goals of many of these traditional models do not align well with the needs of the current public personnel environment, which is constantly changing, and where organizational problem solving occurs across jurisdictional boundaries (Goldsmith and Eggers 2004; Reilly 2007; Risher 1997). Risher and Fay (1997) offer a new system for wage management that focuses on broadbanding, making pay levels consistent with the current trends in the labor market, pay-for-performance, relegating personnel accountability to line managers, and the elimination of entitlement.

Many of these concepts for new public wage management systems have previously been used in the private sector (Lawler 2000). The employment needs in both the public and private sector have shifted toward employees who possess complex knowledge and skills. These employees do not have traditional concrete job activities; instead they have roles with general duties that they carry out in a flexible manner. The challenge to organizations in general, which can be translated to the public sector, is to create compensation systems that are able to adapt to the changing environment (Lawler 2000).

Lawler argues that to implement a successful pay system in the modern personnel arena, organizations should compensate individuals according to their individual worth in the job market, including the skills and knowledge that they possess, and not the worth of their job. To create a pay system that compensates individuals in line with their market value, organizations must develop a system to measure an employee's knowledge and skills that can be translated and compared in the external market. A successful pay system must reward excellence, through policies such as pay-for-performance so as to attract and retain superior performance. No single pay-for-performance plan fits every organization, so an organization's mission, framework, and management style must be considered when creating pay-for-performance plans to reward employees. Offering multiple performance plans could provide the opportunity for employees to choose the way in which they wish to be compensated, which may have an effect on future motivation and performance (Lawler 2000).

Excerpt References

Goldsmith, S., and W. D. Eggers. (2004). *Governing by Network: The New Shape of the Public Sector*. Washington, DC: Brookings Institution Press.

Klinger, D. E. (2006). Societal values and civil service systems in the United States. In *Civil Service Reform in the States: Personnel Policy and Politics at the Subnational level*, Eds. J. E. Kellough and L. G. Nigro, 11–32. Albany: State University of New York Press.

Lawler III, E. E. (2000). Pay strategy: New thinking for the new millennium. *Compensation and Benefits Review*, 32, 7–12.

Reilly, T. (2007). Management in local governments. *Administration in Social Work*, 31(2), 49–66.

Risher, H. (1997). The search for a new model for salary management: Is there support for private sector practices? *Public Personnel Management*, 26(4), 431–439.

Risher, H., and C. H. Fay. (1997). *New Strategies for Public Pay: Rethinking Government Compensation Programs*. San Francisco, CA: Jossey-Bass.

Risher, H., C. H. Fay, and J. L. Perry (1997). Merit pay: Motivating and rewarding individual performance. In *New Strategies for Public Pay: Rethinking Government Compensation Programs*, Eds. H. Risher and C. Fay, 207–230. San Francisco, CA: Jossey-Bass.

Shafritz, J. M., E. W. Russell, and C. P. Borick. (2011). *Introducing Public Administration* (7th ed.). Boston, MA: Pearson Longman.

Source: Excerpt from Reilly 2012, pp. 26–32.

Summary

Compensation is critical to the success of HRM generally. Connected to the motivation, morale, and retention of valuable employees, compensation systems that are not competitive between organizations, levels of government, and sectors can hinder public and nonprofit sector performance. The compensation system chosen by an organization must fit the overall mission and culture of the organization and it must link up with the structure and management practices in place.

A Manager's Vocabulary

- Pay grades
- Pay range
- Salary midpoint
- Policy line
- Internal equity
- External equity
- Salary survey
- Comparable worth
- Merit pay
- Expectancy theory
- Gainsharing
- Broadbanding
- Skill-based pay
- Public service motivation

Study Questions

1. What are the types of compensation system and how is each one linked to pay levels?
2. What are some of the major problems with traditional compensation systems?
3. Is pay for performance effective? Why or why not?
4. Explain the benefits of broadbanded pay systems.

Exercises

Exercise 9.1 Surveying for External Equity

Safeville City is about to renegotiate its contract with the collective bargaining unit representing its local police force. The major issue up for negotiation is salary levels. The union is using a survey of cities of comparable size in Safeville's three-state region. The city council has decided to use comparison salaries only from organizations and corporations within a 100-mile radius, as nearly 100 percent of Safeville's existing police force resides within that area.

1. Design a salary survey process that Safeville City should follow to determine equitable salary levels for its police department.
2. What are the pros and cons of the approaches taken by the city council and police union?

Exercise 9.2 Renovating the State's Compensation System

The governor has asked you to investigate the advisability of moving your state's compensation system from a traditional system that increased salaries based on time in rank to either a pay-for-performance or broadbanded system.

1.   What do you recommend to the governor?
2.   What are the advantages and disadvantages of each type of system?

References

Adams, J. Stacy. 1965. "Inequity in Social Exchanges." In *Advances in Experimental Social Psychology*, Ed. L. Berkowitz, 267–300. New York: Academic Press.

Belanger, France, and Lemuria Carter. 2008. "Trust and Risk in e-Government Adoption." *The Journal of Strategic Information Systems* 17 (2): 166–176.

Belman, Dale, and John S. Heywood. 1996. "The Structure of Compensation in the Public Sector." In *Public Sector Employment in a Time of Transition*, Eds. Dale Belman, Morley Gunderson, and Douglas Hyatt, 127–162. Madison, WI: Industrial Relations Research Association.

———. 2004. "Public Sector Wage Comparability: The Role of Earnings Dispersion." *Public Finance Review* 32 (6): 567–587.

Bender, Keith A. 2003. "Examining Equality Between Public- and Private-Sector Wage Distribution." *Economic Inquiry* 41 (1): 62–79.

Bender, Keith A., and John S. Heywood. 2010. Out of Balance? Comparing Public and Private Sector Compensation Over 20 Years. Report, Center for State and Local Government Excellence, April. http://slge.org/publications/out-of-balance-comparing-public-and-private-sector-compensation-over-20-years (accessed May 23, 2014).

Center for State and Local Government Excellence. 2014. State and Local Government Workforce: 2014 Trends. ipma-hr.org (accessed June 2, 2014).

Davis, John H. 2011. *Statistics for Compensation: A Practical Guide to Compensation Analysis*. Hoboken, NJ: John Wiley.

Davis, Trenton J., and Gerald T. Gabris. 2008. "Strategic Compensation: Utilizing Efficiency Wages in the Public Sector to Achieve Desirable Organizational Outcomes." *Review of Public Personnel Administration* 28 (4): 327–348.

Freedman Consulting. 2014. *A Future of Failure? The Flow of Technology Talent into Government and Civil Society*, Washington, DC. fiercegovernmentit.com/story/severe=shortage-tech-talent-government-says-report/2014-04-23 (accessed June 2, 2014).

Gardner, Alexander C. 2011. "Goal Setting and Gainsharing: The Evidence on Effectiveness." *Compensation & Benefits Review* 43 (4): 236–244.

Goldberg Day, Judy, and Catherine Hill. 2007. "Behind the Pay Gap." American Association of University Women Educational Foundation. www.aauw.org/files/2013/02/Behind-the-Pay-Gap.pdf (accessed June 23, 2015).

Gortner, Harold F., Kenneth L. Nichols, and Carolyn Ball. 2007. *Organization Theory: A Public and Nonprofit Perspective*, 3rd ed. Belmont, CA: Thomson.

Gupta, Nina. 1997. "Rewarding Skills in the Public Sector." In *New Strategies for Public Pay*, Eds. Howard Risher and Charles H. Fay, 125–144. San Francisco, CA: Jossey Bass.

Ingraham, Patricia W. 1993. "Of Pigs in Pokes and Policy Diffusion: Another Look at Pay-for-Performance." *Public Administration Review* 53 (4): 348–356.

Jung, Chan Su, and Hal G. Rainey. 2011. "Organizational Goal Characteristics and Public Duty Motivation in U.S. Federal Agencies." *Review of Public Personnel Administration* 31 (1): 28–47.

Kearney, Richard C. 1992. *Labor Relations in the Public Sector*, 2nd ed. New York: Marcel Dekker.

Keefe, Jeffrey H. 2010. "Debunking the Myth of the Overcompensated Public Employee." Economic Policy Institute Briefing Paper #276, September 15, Washington, DC: Economic Policy Institute. www.epi.org/publication/debunking_the_myth_of_the_overcompensated_public_employee/ (accessed May 22, 2014).

Kellough, Edward J., and Haoran Lu. 1993. "The Paradox of Merit Pay in the Public Sector: Persistence of a Problematic Procedure." *Review of Public Personnel Administration* 13 (2): 45–64.

Kellough, Edward J., and Sally Coleman Selden. 1997. "Pay for Performance Systems in State Government." *Review of Public Personnel Administration* 17 (1): 5–21.

Leavitt, William M., and John C. Morris. 2008. "Market-Based Pay in Action: Municipal Strategies and Concerns in the Cities of Hampton Roads." *Review of Public Personnel Administration* 28 (2): 178–189.

Ledbetter v. Goodyear Tire and Rubber Company, 550 U.S. ____, 127. S. Ct. 2162 (2007).

Ledford, Gerald E., Jr., and Herbert G. Heneman III. 2011. Skill-Based Pay. Prepared for the Society for Industrial & Organizational Psychology, Inc. "SIOP Science" Series, Published by the Society for Human Resource Management (SHRM). siop.org/SIOP-SHRM/ (accessed May 29, 2014).

Lichty, D. Terence. 1991. "Compensation Surveys." In *The Compensation Handbook*, 3rd ed., Eds. Milton L. Rock and Lance A. Berger, 87–103. New York: McGraw Hill.

Lilly Ledbetter Fair Pay Act. 2009. Pub. L. 111–2, S181.

Llorens, Jared J. 2008. "Uncovering the Determinants of Competitive State Government Wages." *Review of Public Personnel Administration* 28 (4): 308–326.

Llorens, Jared J., and Edmund C. Stazyk. 2011. "How Important Are Competitive Wages? Exploring the Impact of Relative Wage Rates on Employee Turnover in State Government." *Review of Public Personnel Administration* 31 (2): 111–127.

McClelland, David C. 1970. "The Two Faces of Power." *Journal of International Affairs* 24 (1): 29–47.

———. 1976. *The Achieving Society*. New York: Irvington.

Maslow, Abraham H. 2011. "A Theory of Human Motivation." In *Classics of Organization Theory*, 7th ed., Eds. Jay M. Shafritz, J. Steven Ott, and Yong Suk Jang, 171–182. Boston, MA: Wadsworth.

Meyer, Herbert H. 1975. "The Pay for Performance Dilemma." *Organization Dynamics* 3 (3): 39–50.

Milkovich, George T., Jerry M. Newman, and Barry Gerhart. 2011. *Compensation*, 10th ed. New York: McGraw-Hill.

Oster, Sharon M. 1988. "Executive Compensation in the Nonprofit Sector." *Nonprofit Management & Leadership* 8 (3): 207–219.

Perry, James L. 1986. "Merit Pay in the Public Sector: The Case for a Failure of Theory." *Review of Public Personnel Administration* 7 (1): 57–69.

Perry, James L. and Lois Recascino Wise. 1990. "The Motivational Bases of Public Service." *Public Administration Review* 50 (3): 367–373.

Perry, James L., Trent A. Engbers, and So Yun Jun. 2009. "Back to the Future? Performance-Related Pay, Empirical Research and Perils of Persistence." *Public Administration Review* 69 (1): 39–51.

Perry, James L., Debra Mesch, and Laurie Paarlberg. 2006. "Motivating Employees in a New Governance Era: The Performance Paradigm Revisited." *Public Administration Review* 66 (4): 505–514.

Reilly, Thom. 2012. *Rethinking Public Sector Compensation: What Ever Happened to the Public Interest?* Armonk, NY: M. E. Sharpe, pp. 26–32.

Riccucci, Norma M. 2008. "A Major Setback for Pay Equality: The Supreme Court's Decision in *Ledbetter v. Goodyear Tire & Rubber Company*." *Review of Public Personnel Administration* 28 (1): 91–96.

Risher, Howard. 1994. "The Emerging Model for Salary Management in the Private Sector: Is it Relevant to Government?" *Public Personnel Management* 23 (4): 649–665.

———. 1997. "Salary Structures: The Framework for Salary Management." In *New Strategies for Public Pay*, Eds. Howard Risher and Charles H. Fay, 40–56. San Francisco, CA: Jossey Bass.

Risher, Howard, and Charles H. Fay. 1997. "Rethinking Government Compensation Programs." In *New Strategies for Public Pay*, Eds. Howard Risher and Charles H. Fay, 1–17. San Francisco, CA: Jossey Bass.

Ross, Timothy L., and Ruth Ann Ross. 1991. "Gain sharing: Sharing Improved Performance." In *The Compensation Handbook*, 3rd ed., Eds. Milton L. Rock and Lance A. Berger, 176–189. New York: McGraw-Hill.

Roy, Thomas S. 1991. "Pricing and the Development of Salary Structures." In *The Compensation Handbook*, 3rd ed., Eds. Milton L. Rock and Lance A. Berger, 104–112. New York: McGraw Hill.

Schay, Brigitte W. 1997. "Paying for Performance: Lessons Learned in Fifteen Years of Federal Demonstration Projects." In *New Strategies for Public Pay*, Eds. Howard Risher and Charles H. Fay, 253–271. San Francisco, CA: Jossey Bass.

Shareef, Reginald A. 1994. "Skill Based Pay in the Public Sector: An Innovative Idea." *Review of Public Personnel Administration* 14 (3): 60–74.

———. 2002. "The Sad Demise of Skill-Based Pay in the Virginia Department of Transportation." *Review of Public Personnel Administration* 22 (3): 233–240.

Shore, Ted H., Armen Tashchian, and Louis Jourdan. 2006. "Effects of Internal and External Pay Comparisons on Work Attitudes." *Journal of Applied Social Psychology* 36 (10): 2578–2598.

Stazyk, Edmund C. 2013. "Crowding Out Public Service Motivation? Comparing Theoretical Expectations with Empirical Findings on the Influence of Performance-Related Pay." *Review of Public Personnel Administration* 33 (3): 252–274.

Taylor, Jeannette, and Ranald Taylor. 2011. "Working Hard for More Money or Working Hard to Make a Difference? Efficiency Wages, Public Service Motivation, and Effort." *Review of Public Personnel Administration* 31 (1): 67–86.

U.S. Census Bureau. 2012. "American Community Survey 1-Year Estimates, S2002. Median Earnings in the Past 12 Months by Workers by Sex and Women's Earnings as a Percentage of Men's Earnings by Selected Characteristics." factfinder2.census/gov/faces/nav/jsf/pages/index.xhtml (accessed June 9, 2014).

Vroom, Victor H. 1995. *Work and Motivation*. San Francisco, CA: Jossey-Bass.

Wallace, Mark J., and Charles H. Fay. 1983. *Compensation Theory and Practice*. Boston, MA: Kent.

Wamsley, Barbara S. 1997. "Are Current Programs Working? Views from the Trenches." In *New Strategies for Public Pay*, Eds. Howard Risher and Charles H. Fay, 25–39. San Francisco, CA: Jossey Bass.

Weibel, Antoinette, Katja Rost, and Margit Osterloh. 2010. "Pay for Performance in the Public Sector—Benefits and (Hidden) Costs." *Journal of Public Administration Research and Theory* 20 (2): 387–412.

Whalen, Cortney, and Mary E. Guy. 2008. "Broadbanding Trends in the States." *Review of Public Personnel Administration* 28 (4): 349–366.

Witt, Elder. 1988. "Are our Governments Paying What it Takes to Keep the Best and the Brightest?" *Governing* 2 (3): 30–39.

9 Benefits

Learning Objectives

- Understand the key differences between public and private sector organizations and the packaging of benefits.
- Understand the implications of workforce demographics for benefit packaging.
- Understand how voluntary and nonvoluntary benefits each affect organizations and employees differently.
- Understand the implications of the Affordable Care Act for public and nonprofit workers and the organizations in which they work.
- Understand emerging issues in retirement programs that warrant the ongoing attention of policymakers, managers, and workers.

Once considered a relatively minor aspect of HRM, employment benefits today are a major dimension of workforce management. As the diversity of jobs, skills, services, and persons employed in nonprofit agencies and the public service has grown to a great extent, so too has the range of benefits developed to attract, motivate, and retain the workforce needed to address the challenges of contemporary public life. This chapter explores some of the major perennial concerns and a number of the newer developments in the benefits administration area and sets forth how benefit management plays a large role in contemporary HRM practice.

Introduction to the Reading

The excerpt for this chapter, authored by Dennis Daley, is subtitled, "Not on the Fringes Anymore." This play on words points to the increasingly important role that benefits play in an organization's total compensation package. As Daley notes, benefits generally have fallen in the range of 20–40 percent of the overall cost of an employee's compensation package, and this general range continues to hold true today. This cost is likely to increase, however, as the price of health care, a critical part of most benefits packages, continues to increase at a rate higher than other consumer items—though at a lower rate of increase than was the case prior to the enactment of the Affordable Care Act. Thompson (2013, p. s3) notes that, "with medical science persistently yielding new and often expensive treatments, and with the elderly growing as a proportion of the population, pressures to spend more on health care intensify." The once rapidly increasing cost of health care and the substantial proportion of Americans who were without health insurance coverage were the primary catalysts for the passage of the Patient Protection and Affordable Care Act (ACA) of 2010.

Furthermore, the presence or absence of certain benefits may be a deciding factor in recruiting and retaining needed employees in job classifications where a competitive employment market exists.

Benefits are indeed no longer to be considered 'fringe': although a significant cost to the organization, these benefits represent an important management tool for public administration and a significant element in considerations of remaining in public service or nonprofit employment versus moving to private sector employment.

Many benefit programs, chief among them being Social Security and Workers' Compensation, were established by government mandate. Social Security is a federal program, generally administered and available across all states. Other benefit programs have been added as public sector and nonprofit employers have come to appreciate the importance of supporting healthy, motivated employees and have recognized the substantial role that benefits packages play in keeping them that way.

The changing nature—and criticality—of benefits packages is also a reflection of workforce demographics. The increased entry of women with children and the rapidly growing number of employees who care for aging parents have led to the development of work–life programs. These types of benefit include childcare options, family-friendly scheduling of leaves, and flexible workdays designed to permit effective parenting while contributing to the agency's ongoing work and responsibilities.

Finally, Daley points to the importance of educating a public sector workforce about the benefits package options available to them. Finding an effective way to communicate about the choices offered in a complicated benefits options setting is a continuing challenge for HRM professionals. As you read the following selection, keep the following questions in mind:

1. Why does Daley say that benefits are not "on the fringes" anymore?
2. How do changes in the demographic makeup of the workforce affect employee interest in benefits and their administration?

Overview

One way to describe benefits is by their function—that is, those related to health care, pensions, special pay options, and employee development. Another way to examine the myriad of benefits available to employees, and the role of those benefits in the compensation package, is to consider what benefits might be voluntarily offered by organizations, what benefits are mandated by federal or state laws or local ordinances, and whether benefits might be encouraged, but not necessarily required, by government. Benefits that might have been voluntary in the past have, in some cases, become codified over time through the political process. Voluntary benefits are offered in response to competitive practices in a region or a particular industry, tax-based inducements, or even an organization's management philosophy concerning incentives and work–life balance.

As we discussed in Chapter 8, compensation policies will differ between public, for-profit and nonprofit organizations for a variety of reasons. Smaller organizations may not have the resources (or the legal requirements) to offer some benefits. Organizations may also be exempted by otherwise universal government requirements to offer certain benefits. Small for-profit or nonprofit organizations may not offer formal benefits packages beyond those mandated, although a variety of nonmonetary, informal benefits (e.g., flexible working hours, comp time) may be available (Fredericksen 1999). Nevertheless, despite the cost, an organization sees advantages to providing a wide array of employee benefits when recruiting in a competitive marketplace. Many demographic factors combine in their respective impacts to offer opportunities to savvy managers and organizations who seek to attract, hire, and retain well-qualified employees whose knowledge is important for the attainment of their agency mission. Crumpacker and Crumpacker (2007) argue persuasively that organizations should pay attention to the values and attitudes associated with different generations in defining HRM policies.

Excerpt 9.1 Not on the Fringes

Benefits are a major component in compensation. They can compose from 20 to 40 percent of the total compensation package. Yet, benefits are still a hodgepodge. Mainly composed of health care and retirement pension programs, benefits also include a vast array of miscellaneous services. Further complicating matters is the fact that not all benefits are tangible; many offer intrinsic incentives upon which it is difficult to place a dollar value. Furthermore, the value of benefits, even those with clear price tags, actually will vary from individual to individual. However, benefits still serve the same set of purposes that pay does—to attract, retain, and motivate employees. . . .

Because benefits compose a growing proportion of the total compensation package, it is necessary to treat benefits with the same strategic pay considerations to which wage and salary decisions are subjected. While benefits are more likely to satisfy attraction and retention needs than to be motivational, this latter role should not be over looked. Hence, organizationally specific information on benefits desired by employees, whether public or private, is important (Moore, 1991; Bergmann, Bergmann, & Grahn, 1994; Davis & Ward, 1995; Streib, 1996). . . .

Since the major benefits that organizations provide deal with health and retirement, employees are forced to take care of these long-term requirements . . . [and] if individuals are allowed to make their own choices in these matters, they are likely to prefer present pressing needs and discount future uncertainties. [In some ways] . . . forcing employees to make decisions that adequately take into account the long-term may be authoritarian or paternalistic, but it is also insurance for the organization's future well-being. . . .

Organizations may use a wide array of other benefits—special pay, employee development, business expenses, living expenses, and social activities—to induce employees to affiliate, remain, and stay motivated. . . .

Motivation can be further enhanced through cafeteria benefit plans. These attempt to fine-tune the benefits offered by allowing the individual to allocate their benefit dollars among those options that they themselves deem most useful. . . .

Benefits are part of the total compensation package. Their worth needs to be communicated to the employee. Benefits compose a large portion of the compensation package . . . [and thus,] the inclusion of benefits information states the true wage and effort bargain.

Excerpt References

Bergmann, T. J., Bergmann, M. A. & Grahn, J. L. (1994). How important are employee benefits to public sector employees? *Public Personnel Management*, 23 (3), 397–406.

Davis, E. & Ward, E. (1995). Health benefit satisfaction in the public and private sectors: The role of distributive and procedural justice. *Public Personnel Management*, 24 (3), 255–270.

Moore, P. (1991). Comparison of state and local employee benefits and private employee benefits. *Public Personnel Management*, 20 (4), 429–440.

Streib, G. (1996). Specialty health care services in municipal government. *Review of Public Personnel Administration*, 16 (2), 57–72.

Source: Excerpt drawn from Daley 1998, pp. 5–20.

The artful mixing of benefit inducements can often make the difference between success and failure in critical job searches.

This chapter looks first at the key usual differences between public and private benefits and considers the commonest benefit programs. Next, we explore benefits as a management tool and, in the process, consider the principal challenges inherent in benefit administration.

Differences and Similarities Between Public and Private Benefits

The Employee Benefit Research Institute (EBRI 2009, pp. 411–415) points to several noteworthy differences between public and private sector benefit programs. First, public employee benefit plans are products of the political process. Plan features, including eligibility, level of contributions required, and types of benefit, are delineated in statutes and ordinances. Major changes to public sector benefits packages often must occur within the political decision-making process. Many interest groups attend to these changes, including both taxpayer groups interested in limiting public spending and collective bargaining units that represent public employees. Because tax monies largely pay for public employee benefits, spending on benefits is a public, political issue.

A second key difference between the public and private sectors is the role federalism plays. State and local governments do not pay taxes. Thus, tax incentives to offer certain benefits are not equally persuasive to them as they would be to private corporations. Also, federalism allows states some flexibility in the types and levels of benefit provided in some benefit programs. For example, the EBRI (2009, p. 415) explains that:

> While private-sector employees are universally covered by Social Security, public-sector employee participation is dependent on whether or not the state in which they work has an agreement with the federal government for state and/or local government employee coverage. In a few states, no public-sector employees participate in Social Security, and in many states certain segments of the public-sector work force (such as teachers, police, and fire employees) are excluded, while the balance of the public employee work force participates.

Another difference between public and private sector benefit systems is that the administrator of the benefit plan may not be the direct employer of the covered individual. For example, state-run retirement systems might oversee the benefit programs of multiple local governments. Local government jurisdictions often handle certain components of a benefit plan themselves, or contract with an external provider. Some states might offer system-wide plans in which local government employees could opt to participate. In some states, local government associations establish a 'risk pool' for insurance programs for smaller jurisdictions, some where even relatively small cities and counties can derive the benefit of expanded scope of participants and thereby derive the benefits of lower costs and expanded benefits for their employees.

A fourth key difference between benefits in the public and private sector is that the public sector often provides different benefits packages to different occupational groups. The commonest examples are law enforcement and fire fighting employees who generally have their own retirement systems that are frequently supplemented by contributions from the state. Benefits plans designed specifically for public school teachers are another example of benefits packages that are frequently self-standing in many states. Additionally, whereas private sector companies often provide separate benefits for executives, this practice is much rarer in the public sector. Equity in benefit access across an organization's hierarchy is a more common practice in government employment.

Finally, according to the U.S. Department of Labor's National Compensation Survey (U.S. Department of Labor, Bureau of Labor Statistics 2009, p. 165), most private sector employees with retirement plan options have access to defined contribution (61 percent) rather than defined benefit (21 percent) plans. Although defined contribution plans are becoming more common in the public sector (30 percent), most public employees (84 percent) have access to defined benefit plans (2009, p. 326). More discussion of these different approaches to retirement benefits is offered later in this chapter.

Despite these common differences, the EBRI notes both the public/nonprofit sector and private sector share a strong common interest in recruiting, motivating, and retaining good employees. Benefits are an increasingly important part of the overall compensation package developed by organizations in whichever sector, and managers use benefits strategically as important targeted incentives to recruit and retain key personnel.

Common Benefit Programs

As Exhibit 9.1 illustrates, government mandates certain benefits. Government revenues and some combination of required proportional contributions/tax from either employees, employers, or both, fund these benefits. Eligibility for benefits may derive from financial need or some other criterion articulated in law or administrative regulations. Mandatory benefits often reflect political preferences on minimum safety nets that should be extended in society. These public policies are then implemented through a combination of direct requirements of employers and employees, or through fiscal penalties for a failure to offer particular benefits. These policies may change in response to political preferences. For example, in the first edition of this text and in the most recent EBRI Fundamentals report, neither health insurance nor Family Medical Leave Act (FMLA) benefits were listed as 'mandatory'. However, given more recent statutory provisions, FMLA leave benefits and health insurance (along with vision and dental coverage for children) are included in the 'mandatory' category for the purpose of this chapter discussion.

In the following sections, more information about each of the benefits listed in Exhibit 9.1 is offered. In addition, we explore a selection of voluntary benefits. That information is presented and

---

Exhibit 9.1 Benefits Generally Mandated by Government

Social Security Retirement (OASI)*
Workers' Compensation*
Supplemental Security Income (SSI)*
Health Insurance**

Social Security Disability Insurance (DI)*
Unemployment Insurance*
Family Medical Leave Act*
Dependent Dental and Vision Insurance**

Excerpt Notes

* Eligibility based on state/federal statutory criteria and agency regulation. Financed from general government revenues and mandated contributions.
** Per the Affordable Care Act.

Source: Derived from Employee Benefit Research Institute 2009, p. 6; U.S. Treasury Department 2014; and healthcare.gov.

categorized in terms of the tax treatment accorded the benefit value. To simplify the following discussion, general social safety net programming for health care such as *Medicare* and *Medicaid* are not included in the context of benefits within compensation packages.

Mandatory

Social Security Retirement, also known as *Old Age and Survivors Insurance* (or OASI) provides retirement income for workers 62 and older, their spouses, surviving spouses, and dependents. Established in 1935, this program is funded principally with payroll taxes. Although nearly universal for private industry, interestingly, not all public employees participate in social security (Employee Benefit Research Institute 2009, p. 415). Participation in social security depends upon whether a state has opted in for coverage of its state and local workers. Also, certain occupations have been included or excluded from social security, some being excluded as a function of alternative retirement plans or collective bargaining agreements featuring retirement system benefits. In comparison, Supplemental Security Income (SSI) provides assistance to the aged, blind, and disabled on a means-tested basis. The federal treasury funds this program. Each state may add to benefits if it chooses, hence the substantial differences that arise between states with respect to benefits arising to Medicaid recipients.

Social Security Disability Insurance, or DI, provides payments to workers meeting the statutory definition of disability. For SSI, the definition specifically excludes partial or short-term disabilities; SSI benefits are distributed only for total permanent disability. According to the U.S. Social Security Administration (2014), the definition of disability for SSI is different from that of other programs, in that an individual is disabled if he or she can neither do the work done before, nor adjust to other work because of his/her medical condition, and this disability either is expected to last, or has lasted, for at least 12 months, or is expected to result in death. This program was established in 1956. A recipient's monthly DI benefits depend on prior annual earnings.

Another mandatory safety net program associated with employment is unemployment insurance. This policy is actually operated through an intricate network of state and federal laws. Funded as a payroll tax, it provides payments based on a percentage of prior pay, as long as an individual is actually looking for work in the same or related area of employment. Benefit levels vary from state to state.

As with unemployment insurance systems, workers' compensation is operated as a combination of state and federal programming. The National Academy of Social Insurance (2008) explains that the scope of workers' compensation insurance, for employees who are injured while on the job or who contract work-related illnesses, is intended to cover medical care and rehabilitation and provide cash benefits sufficient to help maintain a household. In some cases, workers' compensation may pay benefits to the families of workers who die from work-related causes. Although the federal government offers some programs specific to federal employees or employees in certain industries (such as coal mining and railroads), most coverage occurs at the state level. Because each state establishes and administers distinct workers' compensation programs, there is great variability in terms of eligibility and processes for compensation and recovery. Not all states cover public sector employees.

The FMLA permits employees to take up to 12 weeks of unpaid leave during any 12-month period to tend to family needs. The employee is entitled to either retain the position held before taking leave, or be relocated to an equivalent position. Employees must give employers 30 days' notice whenever possible. Employees may take FMLA leave for any of the following purposes:

- the birth and care of a child;
- adoption or foster care placement of a child with the employee;

- caring for family members (spouse, child, or parents) with serious health problems; or
- taking care of the employee's own serious health problems.

FMLA leave is unpaid. More information about paid family leave is detailed in the following section on voluntary leave.

Health insurance can now be considered a nonvoluntary or mandatory benefit to be offered by most employers. With the advent of the ACA of 2010, larger employers (those with more than fifty employees, beginning in 2016, and more than 100 employees in 2014) will pay a penalty for failing to offer health care insurance to a statutorily prescribed percentage of full-time employees, along with the required level of insurance for dependents of eligible employees. Neither vision nor dental insurance are mandatory inclusions for most employers, except that these benefits should be accessible to eligible employee dependents under 18 years of age. Under the ACA, health benefits are termed either minimum essential coverage or essential health benefits. This designation shifts the extent to which employers are mandated to offer the benefit. Though federal subsidies were affirmed in *King v. Burwell* (2015), court cases continue to establish the nuances of what may or may not be required of employers. For example, in *Burwell, Secretary of Health and Human Services v. Hobby Lobby Stores, Inc.* (2014), the court held, in a divided opinion, that closely held private, for-profit corporations may elect not to offer certain medical insurance benefits (e.g., contraception), if they argue and establish to the satisfaction of the court that such benefits violate their free exercise of religion.

Within the baseline requirements established by ACA, health care plans differ in terms of the degree of latitude that individuals have in selecting their medical provider and the facility in which they receive treatment. Plans (and providers) also differ in terms of whether costs are reimbursed (and how much), and whether the reimbursement is sent directly to the provider or to the individual. Some plans designate a preferred provider/facility wherein the covered employee has a larger proportion of their expenses covered by virtue of contracted rates negotiated between the provider and the health care plan administrating entity. Health maintenance organizations (HMOs) offer some array (usually prepaid or reduced in cost) of services from contracted doctors or facilities. Individuals are required to have health coverage, whether through government support programs (such as Medicare or Medicaid), individual, private insurance, or through an employer. Without such coverage, they may seek insurance through state-level insurance exchanges. Employers may seek coverage for their employees (and receive commensurate tax benefits) or be subject, according to the size of the organization, to penalties.

Voluntary

Some voluntary benefits offered by organizations may be fully taxable, such as paid lunches, rest periods, severance pay, or various cash bonuses and awards (Employee Benefit Research Institute 2009, p. 6). However, many voluntary benefits are either tax-exempt to the employee, offer tax benefits either to the employer or employee, or grant tax advantages (e.g., are tax-preferred) to either the employee or employer, or both.

Certain benefits are exempted from taxation as they are not formally 'valued' as part of an employee benefits package. Examples of these benefits include the availability of parking or certain retail discounts, such as when cell phone providers offer a percentage discount to employees of particular organizations. Educational assistance programs might be exempted in terms of taxes. So, too, might the convenience of having a cafeteria or exercise facility available to employees be an attractive benefit, without any tangible value assigned to a particular employee's compensation package. Childcare might be available for a reduced rate, or perhaps organizations allow employees to bring children to the

---

Exhibit 9.2 Sample Voluntary Benefits—Tax-Advantaged (Exempt, Deferred, or Preferred, Subject to Conditions and Limitations)

Employee and dependent health insurance
Dental insurance
Educational assistance
Discounts
Parking
Life insurance
Various sick and personal leave programs
Keogh plans

Retiree health insurance
Vision insurance
Childcare
Flexible spending accounts
Cafeteria facility or meals
Long-term disability insurance
Sickness/accident insurance
Defined benefit pension plans

In addition there are defined contribution retirement plans, including money purchase pension plans, deferred profit-sharing plans, savings and thrift plans, simplified employee pension plans, individual retirement account plans, and cash or deferred arrangements (Sec. 401(k), Sec. 403(b) & Sec. 457).

Source: Derived from American Dental Association 2013; Anspach 2014; Employee Benefit Research Institute 2009, p. 6.

---

workplace under particular circumstances. A certain proportion of the costs of childcare may also be tax deductible. Flexible spending accounts (FSAs) can be dedicated to medical expenses or to dependent care. Although provisions and exclusions may differ between jurisdictions, funds for an employee's FSA may be automatically deducted from wages/salaries and may be exempt from payroll taxes.

Tax-deferred benefits include leave, insurance, and retirement benefits. Two of the commonest and readily recognizable forms of paid leave are for vacation or illness. Other forms of leave may include parental leave (maternity or paternity), funeral or bereavement leave, military leave in the case of employees who are called into service or have regular National Guard rotations, or even public service leave for jury duty or voting. Organizations may make pooled life or disability insurance available for some multiplier of the employee's salary (at a reduced cost compared with acquiring insurance through a private provider). For these benefits, generally, the taxable value of the benefits is often deferred until earned benefits are distributed. The value of available insurance and leave is not taxed, but such insurance benefits and leave pay are generally taxed upon distribution to the beneficiary.

Retirement plans are usually tax-deferred. Defined benefit pension plans are those that distribute a designated amount to an employee upon retirement. The amount paid is often driven by a formula (e.g., some combination of highest salary, years of service, and/or years of service at a given salary level). These plans "promise employees future benefits at retirement in relation to the work they performed during their service with the organization. The employing organization accumulates designated assets held in trust as it becomes obligated to pay the future liability" (Eaton and Nofsinger 2008, p. 108). As Exhibit 9.3 illustrates, the employer (or the pension administrator) primarily assumes liability and the administrative burden. Public sector defined benefit pensions are exempt from the extensive reporting requirements and administrative oversight required by the Employee Retirement Income Security Act of 1974, also known as ERISA (Employee Benefit Research Institute 2009,

Exhibit 9.3 Responsibilities for Retirement Planning

Defined Benefit Plans	*Defined Contribution Plans*
Employer	
Provide significant reporting to DoL Submit a GASB #25 statement Manage pension assets Project benefits for all eligible employees Invest assets appropriately Develop benefit formula for eligible employees	Provide significant reporting to DoL Set up relationship with third-party administrator to manage employees' accounts Match employee contributions, if applicable Provide investment fund options for employees
Employee	
Maintain service until vested Contribute to pension, if applicable	Understand risk tolerance Understand asset allocation Choose funds that are favorable for achieving their projected goal Project income needed for retirement

Source: This exhibit is denoted as Table 2, Responsibilities for Retirement Planning, p. 374, in Holland, Goodman, and Stich 2008.

p. 428). Unfortunately, Eaton and Nofsinger (2008, p. 127) note a disturbing trend of underfunding defined benefit pensions, even during growth periods in the economy and tax revenues, arguing that:

> This problem of underfunding will likely continue and is particularly challenging because pension plans are now paying out more in benefits annually than they are receiving in contributions. With the Baby Boom generation just beginning to enter retirement, the underfunded public pension plans will be financially pressed. The underfunding is likely to get worse and become more problematic as the population ages.

A Pew Center study (Pew Center on the States 2010) estimates that the unfunded liability of retirement benefits promised to public state employees, nearly a trillion dollars, is not solely attributable to recent economic downturns, but is rather a function of decisions made by elected officials even during periods of economic growth and robust tax revenues. State reforms proposed in response to the looming crisis include one or more of the following: submitting actuarially cued contributions, lowering benefits and increasing the retirement age, sharing the investment risk with employees, increasing employee contributions, and improving investment oversight (Pew Center on the States 2010, pp. 33–39).

Defined contribution plans are usually administered through a contract arrangement by a third party. For example, VALIC and TIAA-CREF are common among public universities. The employer does not have to administer the pension, and the employee handles much of the responsibility for retirement planning. Consider again the distribution of responsibilities described by Holland, Goodman, and Stich (2008) in Exhibit 9.3. In defined contribution plans, individual employees, rather than fund managers, make decisions about asset allocation and either tolerance or avoidance of risk. An employee must make retirement decisions based on the income that she or he projects they will require, not upon an anticipated amount derived from a distribution formula comprised of variables such as his or her salary history and service time.

The Rationale for Monetary and Nonmonetary benefits

Although substantial scholarship contends that public service motivation plays a substantial role in the decision of individuals to join and stay with a public or nonprofit organization (Perry and Wise 1990; Taylor and Taylor 2011), the monetary and nonmonetary benefits available to employees clearly matter as well. Safety net programming (e.g., retirement, health insurance, or disability protection) is important enough that the federal government has mandated various components. Organizations have gone beyond those mandates to offer supplemental benefits and to develop new, creative means to attract, retain, and reward productive employees. Nugent (2009, p. 8) reports on a MetLife benefit trends survey suggesting that:

> more than half of U.S. workers (52 percent) now obtain the majority of their financial and retirement products through the workplace. As the workplace has become the dominant starting point for building a strong financial safety net for many people, employers have a timely opportunity to help employees plan and protect their personal safety nets and potentially enhance employee loyalty in the process.

Exhibit 9.4 sorts benefits by motivation and goals. Benefits may respond to employee priorities about health, retirement, disability, and other safety net concerns, quality of life issues in terms of convenience and overall well-being, or various incentives linked to productivity and retention. A number of benefits might also serve multiple needs. For example, although wellness benefits might advantage an employee directly in terms of reducing stress or easing the challenge of balancing work and personal responsibilities, these benefits might also contribute to reducing demand on health care services. Improving an employee's health (and that of his/her family) can reduce the costs of health insurance due to stress-related illnesses and other preventable costs related to the fitness of the pool of insured individuals. Providing child- or eldercare might ease the demands upon an employee, enhancing that employee's productivity or improving their interest in continuing employment.

As Exhibit 9.5 illustrates, in 2009, prior to the enactment of the ACA, the preponderance of public sector workers had access to medical care, although there was some difference between categories of workers (e.g., natural resource/construction versus service workers, for example). The 'why' of this could be due to a number of factors, including bargaining agreements and whether workers were full-time, part-time, or seasonal employees. With ACA, according to the U.S. Treasury Department (2014), access should not fall below 95 percent for full time (e.g., 30 hours or more) by 2016, or employers will face penalties. Critics of ACA suggest that this requirement may cause employers to restructure their workforce from full-time to part-time workers to avoid the mandate to provide health care benefits. According to Van de Water (2013, p. 2), although "some employers have announced they are cutting certain employees' hours to avoid the requirement to provide health coverage to full-time workers, . . . they are the exception." In fact, Van de Water points to BLS statistics in arguing (2013, p. 2): "if health reform's employer mandate were distorting hiring practices in the way critics claim, we'd expect the share of involuntary part-timers to be growing. Instead . . . it is down about one percentage point from its peak."

Exhibit 9.4 Select Types of Benefit by Function

Health Care

Employee and dependent health insurance	Retiree health insurance
Dental insurance	Vision insurance
Medicare (Social Security HI, SMI)	Medicaid

Retirement Income Benefits

Social Security Retirement (OASI)	Supplemental Security Income (SSI)
Keogh plans	Defined benefit pension plans
Defined contribution pension plans (see Exhibit 9.2 for examples)	

Other Disability & Safety Net Benefits

Social Security Disability Insurance (DI)	Supplemental Disability (short-/long-term)
Life insurance	Workers' compensation
Unemployment insurance	Severance pay
Legal assistance	

Quality of Life—Well-being and Convenience

Childcare or eldercare	Paid lunch, cafeteria facility, or meals
Employee assistance programs	Discounts
Flexible spending accounts	Parking
Leave options including: vacation, parental, illness, bereavement, civic (e.g., voting, jury duty, military)	

Incentives and Rewards—Productivity and Retention

Bonuses	Awards (monetary and nonmonetary)
Education	Office Space/location/equipment/tech
Conference or travel funds	Celebrations and festivities
Gifts/organizational paraphernalia	

Source: Adapted from p. 7 of Employee Benefit Research Institute 2009.

Exhibit 9.6 draws upon the National Compensation Survey conducted by the U.S. Department of Labor. It confirms the propensity of public sector employers to offer defined benefit rather than defined contribution retirement systems. Life insurance appears to be a common benefit at the state and local government level. On average, more than one third of state/local workers have access to long-term disability insurance, while short-term disability insurance appears available to between one quarter and one third of employees.

Paid leave benefits are detailed in Exhibit 9.7 for state and local government employees. Leave benefits can arguably be included with safety net benefits, as well as general quality of life benefits dealing with employee wellness and convenience. Certainly, paid leave can be used as a reward for performance, and the lack of leave might generate retention issues. In general, across all worker

Exhibit 9.5 State and Local Government Employee—Health Care Benefits, Percentage of Access Levels

Category and Characteristics of Workers	Medical, %	Dental, %	Vision, %	Outpatient, Prescription Drug, %
Management or professional	90	55	38	89
Service	81	49	35	79
Office & administrative support	88	57	40	87
Natural resource, construction & maintenance	95	62	41	93
Production, transportation & material moving	83	58	35	83
Local government	86	53	34	84
State government	94	59	49	93
All workers	88	54	38	86

Source: U.S. Department of Labor, Bureau of Labor Statistics 2009, pp. 354–357.

Exhibit 9.6 State and Local Government Employee—Retirement and Insurance Benefits, Percentage of Access Levels

Category and Characteristics of Workers	Retirement		Insurance		
	Defined Benefit, %	Defined Contrib., %	Disability Short-term, %	Disability Long-term, %	Life, %
Management or professional	87	30	22	38	80
Service	77	28	23	28	75
Office & administrative support	82	33	26	35	81
Natural resource, construction & maintenance	87	34	30	41	90
Production, transportation & material moving	80	89	22	29	77
Local government	82	25	22	35	78
State government	87	45	28	35	86
All workers	84	30	23	35	80

Source: U.S. Department of Labor, Bureau of Labor Statistics 2009, pp. 326–327, 386–387.

categories, employees appear to have access to paid leave benefits at a far higher aggregate level than they have access to safety net benefits such as disability and life insurance. More than half of all state and local workers, regardless of work category, appear to have access to paid leave. Although sick leave is commonest among employees in general, jury duty is also widely available.

FMLA established that any employee may take leave under certain conditions, and that adverse action would not result because of this allowable leave-taking. However, employers are not required to offer paid leave for FMLA beyond that already provided in the benefits package. Some combination of sick and vacation leave can be used to respond to time away from work in these scenarios. Some organizations also allow employees to 'donate' sick leave to one another as well.

Employee assistance programs provide support for workers dealing with significant personal demands and may include support for addictions (alcohol or drug), as well as assistance in negotiating

Exhibit 9.7 State and Local Government Employee—Paid Leave Benefits, Percentage of Access Levels

Category and Characteristics of Workers	Holiday, %	Sick, %	Vacation, %	Jury Duty, %
Management or professional	56	90	44	92
Service	77	85	75	88
Office & administrative support	87	90	85	91
Natural resource, construction & maintenance	95	94	95	91
Production, transportation & material moving	76	88	64	87
Local government	60	88	51	90
State government	91	94	86	94
All workers	68	89	60	91

Source: U.S. Department of Labor, Bureau of Labor Statistics 2009, pp. 442–443.

Exhibit 9.8 State and Local Government Employee—Quality of Life Benefits, Percentage of Access Levels

Category and Characteristics of Workers	Childcare, %	Flexible Workplace, %	Commuting Subsidy, %	Wellness Programs, %	Employee Assistance Programs, %
Management or professional	14	5	9	53	74
Service	12	4	10	50	72
Office & administrative support	15	5	15	52	73
Natural resource, construction & maintenance	12	2	13	55	75
Production, transportation & material moving	6	—	13	42	66
Local government	9	2	7	46	69
State government	27	—	21	70	86
All workers	13	4	11	52	73

Note: Dash indicates no workers in this category, or data did not meet publication criteria

Source: U.S. Department of Labor, Bureau of Labor Statistics 2009, pp. 462–463.

life crises and events (e.g., divorce, family relationships, bereavement, etc.) and support in dealing with conditions, such as depression, that have ramifications for medical health as well as productivity and relationships. These employee assistance programs and the benefits offered therein may work in concert with provisions in an employer's health insurance package. According to Exhibit 9.8, these programs appear to be commonest at the state level, but more than two-thirds of local government workers, per the National Compensation Survey, have access to employee assistance programs. In addition, state government workers (70 percent) also appear to be substantially more likely to have access to wellness programs compared with local employees (46 percent). Other 'quality of life' benefits depicted in Exhibit 9.8 are far less common (e.g., childcare, flexible workplace arrangements, or commuting support). However, the childcare and commuting subsidies are three times more likely in state government than among local government employees. In the next section, we will consider various quality of life benefits, also known as work–life benefits, in detail, with particular attention to the attendant management implications.

Managing the Workforce through Work–Life

Many work–life programs began in response to the rapidly increasing number of women in the workforce. Employers recognized that increased flexibility in hours and opportunities to access and pay for childcare were critical to attracting, motivating, and retaining workers with responsibility for children, prompting the programs to be termed 'family friendly'. Eventually, however, employers saw that all employees, not just those with immediate childcare responsibilities, appreciated the benefits labeled as 'family friendly'.

According to Lockwood (2009), four generations populate the contemporary workforce for public, private, and nonprofit organizations: Matures (Traditionalists or Depression babies), Baby Boomers, Gen X, and Millennials (Gen Y or Nexters). Not surprisingly, employees at these various life stages value access to the same workplace flexibility developed for those employees with pre-school and school-aged children. Mills (2001) comments upon tensions that may erupt in the workplace between those who receive supportive arrangements by virtue of their status as parent and those who do not have those obligations. Readers of this text may be familiar with these tensions, as one individual in the workplace spends time on the telephone to monitor kids, or might leave early to watch a child's soccer game or take a toddler to a pediatric appointment. Often, others are asked to pick up the slack on these occasions, and it might be awkward to challenge such diffusion of the workload on the grounds of 'fairness'. However, perhaps less flexibility is granted to the worker who is concerned about the well-being of an ailing parent or friend. Employees may even face judgment by others in their workplace about whether their health, grief, or worry is a legitimate basis for leave. One of the text authors recalls the anguish of a coworker who sought to take her pet to a veterinarian and manage the aftercare of an emergency surgery. This person was denied leave by her supervisor because it was "just a dog." These scenarios prompt Mills (2001, p. 19) to argue as follows:

> company policies [should] . . ., as far as possible, treat parents and non-parents alike, by extending to all the benefits needed primarily by parents. This would mean offering a mix-and-match menu of benefits from which all workers could choose: health insurance for dependents, additional vacation time, flextime, and so forth. The case for uniform (but more generous) benefits goes like this. Employees have many needs, beyond the need to care for small children. As we move through the cycle of life, the need to care for growing children is replaced by the need to care for aging parents (though some, in the so-called "sandwich generation," may face both needs simultaneously). Employees who struggle with poor health would welcome a less strenuous

schedule. Benefits such as flextime and enhanced personal leave (e.g., the typical European worker receives six weeks of annual leave, to our two weeks) would greatly enrich the lives of all workers, parents and non-parents alike.

Employers generally have increasingly turned to work–life programs as they have come to appreciate the improved productivity that has often resulted from the adoption of these policies. There is also some evidence that flexibility in hours and workplace benefits can be critical in the retention of valuable employees. Drawing upon data collected in 2010 by the Office of Performance Management, researchers Ko, Hur and Smith-Walter (2013) found that flexible work scheduling and dependent care programs positively influenced job satisfaction and perceived organizational performance in many different organizational settings.

Clearly, life stage matters in terms of the priorities that employees have about their nonwork life relative to work life. However, broad generalizations about workers' motivation and priorities based solely upon age, though tidy, may not be particularly accurate. Although a cohort may share existence during a set of historical events, each individual's demographic characteristics, family circumstances, or geographic location may influence their perception.

In general, however, Beutell and Wittig-German (2008, p. 520) argue that there are fairly common perspectives held by clusters of employees based upon their generation, especially in regard to work–life balance:

> Xers also value flexibility and expect employers to accommodate their work–family–life issues. Boomers who tend to view work as an anchor in their lives may see Xers (who might report to them) as less involved in work because of this work–life orientation. Work–family programs and organizational support for managing the life space may be perceived very differently by these groups: boomers may see such programs as desirable while Xers view them as indispensable and want to have a say in shaping and evaluating these programs. HR managers need to be aware of such generational issues without reifying the characteristics ascribed to each group, realizing that these are but generalizations. However, it must be acknowledged that generational diversity is important in the workplace and that the shift towards flexibility will increase as generation X and generation Y, who strongly value family, assume leadership roles.

Diversity in Families and Benefit Packaging

At issue in benefits administration has been a debate over whether or not to extend various benefits, such as health and life insurance, to the partners of unmarried employees. Although this was often framed as a gay and lesbian rights issue prior to the U.S. Supreme Court ruling establishing marriage equity nationwide (*Obergefell v. Hodges* 2015), many corporations and jurisdictions allow "domestic partners" to include unmarried heterosexual couples.

In the first edition of this text, we reported that several states and as many as 165 cities and counties have passed laws or established policies providing for domestic partner benefits (Witt and Patton 1998). Most jurisdictions have requirements to qualify for domestic partner benefits, typically including requirements that domestic partners not be related, that neither person be married to anyone else, and that the couples attest that they are living in a committed relationship. Some ordinances and policies require documentary evidence of financial interdependence as well (Gossett 1994).

Health care benefits are increasingly extended to unmarried domestic partners (both same sex and opposite sex) in both the public and private sectors. State and local governments appear to demonstrate a slightly greater propensity to offer such benefits in health care. However, health care is not the

---

Exhibit 9.9 Health Care Benefits for Employees and Unmarried Domestic Partners

Per the "National Compensation Survey: Employee Benefits in the United States, Fact Sheet, March 2013":

In aggregate, among civilian workers, health care benefits are available to:

- 32 percent of unmarried, same sex domestic partners;
- 26 percent of unmarried, opposite sex partners.

By economic sector, health care benefits for domestic partners are available as follows:

- Private, for-profit:

  - 31 percent for same sex;
  - 26 percent for opposite sex partners.

- State/local government:

  - 33 percent for same sex partners;
  - 28 percent for opposite sex partners.

Source: U.S. Department of Labor, Bureau of Labor Statistics 2013.

---

only important benefit for employees and their families. Retirement benefits offer another significant safety net benefit, and Exhibit 9.10 draws upon BLS data to report that state and local governments extend survivor benefits to nearly half of public sector workers with defined benefit coverage even before the recent U.S. Supreme Court ruling on marriage equity.

Focus on Flexibility

One type of work–life program that has gained considerable popularity is the use of alternative work schedules. Two broad categories of such alternative arrangements are *flexible work schedules* (FWSs) and *compressed work schedules* (CWSs). Usually, FWSs include hours that are 'core' and required of all employees and hours that are 'flexible', so that employees may modify arrival and departure times. CWSs refer to scenarios wherein employees work a regular 40-hour week over fewer days (for example, four 10-hour days). Several practical considerations warrant management attention in the design, implementation, and evaluation of flexible workplace policies, such as state/federal law, core versus flexible times in terms of service delivery, workflow, lunch and break hours, vacation, and personal time.

Employers are utilizing flexible work schedules as they realize that they can help retain and recruit valuable employees who need or wish to have flexibility. Studies conducted in this area have generally indicated that flexible work schedules can increase productivity, decrease turnover, and reduce employee stress in a wide range of settings (Solomon 1996, p. 35). In many cases, varying the hours that employees are in the office may allow the organization to offer more expansive access to customers without paying overtime (Smith 1999a, p. 16). McMenamin notes (2007, p. 3) that, "nearly one-third of wage and salary workers have flexible schedules." To put this in context, he (2007, p. 11) observes:

Exhibit 9.10 Defined Benefit Retirement for Employees and Survivors

Per the "National Compensation Survey: Employee Benefits in the United States, Fact Sheet, March 2013":

In aggregate, defined benefit retirement coverage is as follows:

- Private, for-profit: 19 percent of employees have access;
- State/local government: 83 percent of state and local government employees have access.

Of those who have access, in aggregate, defined benefit retirement unmarried partner *survivor* benefits are available as follows:

- 15 percent of all civilian workers may also access survivor benefits for unmarried, same sex domestic partners;
- 14 percent of civilian workers have access to such a provision for opposite sex partners.

By economic sector, defined benefit retirement unmarried partner survivor benefits are as follows:

- Private, for-profit:

    - 9 percent for same sex;
    - 8 percent for opposite sex partners.

- State/local government:

    - 50 percent for same sex partners;
    - 48 percent for opposite sex partners.

Source: U.S. Department of Labor, Bureau of Labor Statistics 2013.

The timing of work is continually evolving. Despite a recent decline in the percentage of people who say that they can vary their hours of work, the proportion of workers with this option is more than double that of 20 years ago. Over the same period, the proportion of workers with alternate shifts has remained fairly steady.

Not every job or employee, however, is well suited to flexible work scheduling. Some jobs, for example, require in-person contact and, as a consequence, might be less suitable for a compressed workweek schedule wherein an employee is in-house for only 4 days a week. There are also limits to flexibility, as every organization will have 'core hours' during which all or nearly all employees need to be present. Some employees—for example, those with small children in day care, or those who become too exhausted from an extended workday—are also not good candidates for a compressed workweek with 10-hour days (Smith 1999a, p. 16). Conversely, perhaps the employer has no business making these judgments for employees. Rather, the productivity of a particular employee should be the sole consideration. A further concern for the organization in regard to compressed workweeks is to pay attention to how weeks with holidays will be handled so that workers with compressed schedules will continue to get the same amount of vacation/holiday time as those not working on compressed schedules (Smith 1999a, p. 16).

Benefiting from Technology: Telecommuting

One of the greatest advantages to come from the development of the personal computer and the Internet is the ability to allow workers to work from home or some other location away from the workplace. This flexibility can be invaluable to workers who, for a personal reason such as childcare or injury, need to work from home. Advantages to reducing commutes for employees include reducing traffic congestion, improving air quality, and shifting time spent on the commute to personal and/or work-related activities.

The use of telecommuting has increased rapidly across the country. The number of U.S. workers using technology to work from home rose from an estimated 1.8 million workers in 2005 to 3.3 million workers in 2012 (Global Workplace Analytics 2013). This figure represents 2.6 percent of the overall U.S. work population. Interestingly, when it is deconstructed by type of employer, 3.3 percent of federal government workers, 1.2 percent of the local government workforce, 2.4 percent of state government employees, and 2.9 percent of nonprofit personnel telecommute (Global Workplace Analytics 2013).

Although employees may enjoy the added flexibility provided by telecommuting options, successful implementation will require that organizations develop thoughtful policies regarding telecommuting. In particular, because the employee's home becomes a remote work site, and therefore subject to many of the same laws that govern safety in the main work area, policies and clear expectations are important. According to the Telework Coalition, jobs that are most suitable for teleworking have the following characteristics (2014):

- Work activities are portable and can be performed as effectively outside the office.
- Job tasks are easily quantifiable or primarily project oriented.
- An essential component of job responsibility consists of reading and/or processing tasks.
- Contact with other employees and customers is predictable.
- The technology needed to perform the job off-site is currently available.
- Cyclical work does not present a problem.
- Security and confidentiality of data can be adequately assured.
- Most work handled is not classified.

As with other flexible benefits options, expectations must be clear. In particular, it is important to emphasize that telecommuting is a benefit, not an entitlement. Thus, telecommuting should be offered to employees when it helps the organization achieve its performance goals. Not all employees may be good candidates for telecommuting. However, the Telework Coalition does offer suggestions in terms of screening characteristics to help managers make wise decisions regarding telecommuting:

- The employee has demonstrated motivation, independence, and dependability in accomplishing work assignments.
- The employee can deal with less-frequent face-to-face contact with others.
- The employee has good time-management skills.
- The employee's overall performance evaluations are fully successful or higher.

- The employee has clearly defined performance standards.
- The employee has received supervisory approval for participation.
- The employee is willing to sign and abide by a written agreement that requires participation in training and evaluation sessions.
- The employee has satisfied adequate home workstation requirements, including the availability of equipment.
- The employee is careful to protect the confidentiality, and ensure security, of data.

Administering Benefits Ethically and Cost-Effectively

Whether an organization handles administration of benefits in-house, contracts with a different level of government, or offers benefits through a third-party provider, administrators must pay attention to costs, the efficiency and effectiveness of provision, and the quality and accuracy of the information provided to employees about their coverage. Employee benefits are among the fastest growing portions of the cost of compensation. In 1996, benefits constituted approximately 28 percent of compensation costs (Fredericksen and Soden 1998, p. 24). To compare, in 1929, fringe benefits constituted only 3 percent of the cost of compensation (Levine 1993, p. 38). Most recently, average benefits were 31.2 percent of compensation costs (U.S. Department of Labor, Bureau of Labor Statistics 2014).

Benefits packages are, in general, more costly in the public sector than in the private sector compared with salary. For example, although many public sector employees have tried to compensate for less than competitive salaries by increasing benefits packages, the reluctance of Congress, state legislatures, and county and city councils to increase taxes may be a limitation to keeping pace with private sector benefits packages (Fredericksen and Soden 1998, p. 24). Health care costs as a percentage of the cost of compensation have risen from 2.0 percent in 1970 to 8.6 percent in 2014 (Employee Benefit Research Institute 1997, p. 251; U.S. Department of Labor, Bureau of Labor Statistics 2014, Table 1). The rising cost of health care benefits presents a challenge to employers who want to provide competitive benefits packages. This is especially important given that many applicants decide between accepting or declining a job offer depending upon the elements of the benefits package offered (Levine 1993). How can an organization continue to offer an attractive benefits package while at the same time controlling costs?

Many organizations focus on health care, as it represents a fast-growing portion of benefits costs. Clark et al. (2012) point out two areas that warrant particular attention (p. 11):

> Health care associated with chronic diseases and an aging workforce requires a rethinking of certain policies. Similarly, health problems associated with obesity threaten to push costs up faster in the future. These issues highlight the importance of developing effective wellness programs . . . Managing prescription drug costs is a key element of controlling the rising cost of providing health insurance . . . [effective responses include] drug purchasing coalition[s] to reduce costs and implement[ing] measures to reduce the use of specialty drugs.

Jurisdictions are also increasing out-of-pocket contributions and deductibles to control health care costs. According to the U.S. Bureau of Labor Statistics, median annual individual and family deductibles in 1998 were $200 and $400, respectively, but had more than doubled to $500 for individuals and $1,000 for families by 2011 (U.S. Department of Labor, Bureau of Labor Statistics 2012, p. 3). The out-of-pocket maximum contribution likewise nearly doubled during this same period.

The overall distribution of participation by health plan type is shifting to fee-for-service plans with either preferred or exclusive providers or to HMOs, as these were developed to manage costs more effectively. In 1998, 35 percent of full-time state and local government employees were covered by fee-for-service, preferred provider health plans, which rose to 62 percent in 2011 (U.S. Department of Labor, Bureau of Labor Statistics 2012, p. 2). Traditional fee-for-service plans for state and local government employees are now nearly nonexistent, dropping from 25 percent in 1998 to 2 percent in 2011 (U.S. Department of Labor, Bureau of Labor Statistics 2012, p. 2). HMOs appear to be on the decline, dropping from 39 percent in 1998 to 27 percent in 2011 (U.S. Department of Labor, Bureau of Labor Statistics 2012, p. 2).

Another way that organizations attempt to control the cost of benefits while continuing to offer the competitive levels and variety of benefits that employees have come to expect is through offering flexible benefit plans. 'Cafeteria plans' are flexible benefit plans that allow employees to select certain benefits while opting out of others. According to the U.S. Internal Revenue Service (2014), employees must be able to choose among both taxable benefits and qualified benefits. Benefits qualify for inclusion in the pretax category if they do not defer compensation and often include benefits such as accident insurance, adoption assistance, dependent care assistance, or group life insurance. A cafeteria plan entails approval of a Section 125 plan by the employer. Simply offering employees a choice of benefits is not a 'cafeteria plan' in the eyes of the IRS. Organizations control costs by establishing a dollar limit on how much an employee may earn in benefits, but the choice among benefits allows employees to design a benefits package that best suits their personal situation, whether childcare for those with families, or deferred tax annuities for those nearing retirement.

Educating Employees and Managers about Benefits

It is important to communicate with employees about the worth of their benefits packages. Employees need to understand the value of their benefits package, and it is recommended that organizations supply individualized reports outlining each employee's benefits package (Daley 1998, p. 20). The importance of this is noted by one study of employees' perceptions of their benefits packages that found that many thought they had benefits to which they did not actually have access (Fredericksen and Soden 1998, p. 37).

In addition to the more traditional review sessions and brochures, Nugent (2009, p. 10) recommends several approaches to the education of employees regarding their benefit options:

> Delivering the education necessary to help employees make informed benefits decisions is important for increasing the perceived value of the benefits plan. Simply put, communications should be clear and concise. Employers seeking to improve communications can take advantage of multiple media platforms and use techniques that cater to both visual and verbal learning styles. DVDs, streaming video and podcasts can all be considered viable methods for sharing benefits information.

Employees are not the only workers who need to be educated about the organization's benefits package. Managers who must implement scheduling with alternative work schedules or determine whether an employee's absence qualifies under the FMLA need training and education about the organization's benefits also, particularly in regard to new benefits and options as they arise. Given the importance the benefits can have in recruitment, it is furthermore important that managers have a working understanding of the benefits packages to which new employees will have access.

Ethical Considerations and Paid Leave

As Exhibits 9.4 and 9.7 illustrate, there are many forms of paid leave—holidays, vacation, personal leave, funeral leave, jury duty leave, military leave, and family leave. Some forms of leave are quite common: for example, 94 percent of state and 90 percent of local government employees receive jury duty leave. Sick leave is also relatively common, whereas vacation leave was the least common in local governments, at 51 percent, compared with 86 percent for state workers.

One form of paid leave that can be the cause of controversy in an organization is paid sick leave. Although nearly all public sector employees have access to sick leave, potential problems arise when sick leave is the only form of paid leave available. Unscheduled needs to be absent from work, for example, for a medical appointment or to care for a sick child must then be taken as sick leave, even though the employee is not actually ill. This not only results in the encouragement of dishonesty in reporting, but more time may be taken off than is necessary.

The addition of a category of personal leave, which can be used for any purposes, or the combination of personal leave and sick leave gives the employee more flexibility over the use of unscheduled paid leave and has a positive impact on employee morale (Anfuso 1995). Incentives to encourage employees not to use more personal or sick leave than they need can also help hold down the costs of benefits. These incentives may include cash payments for unused sick leave or cash for unused sick leave available at retirement or paid time off given in another form (Rogers and Herting 1993, p. 223). These incentive programs should be checked to make sure they do not violate the ADA's provisions for the protection of workplace rights of the disabled. In addition, the organization should be mindful that these types of incentive program may unintentionally punish parents with small children who must make greater use of sick leave for family issues than employees without children (Smith 1999b, p. 17).

Summary

Benefits will continue to be an important and costly part of the total compensation package of public sector and nonprofit sector organizations. As health care costs continue to escalate, organizations will look to ways to provide access to health care, yet control their proportion of the cost of benefits. An increasing proportion of workers will need to care for aging parents. The 'sandwich generation' may also still have obligations to children. All demographic trends point to the importance of giving employees a variety of benefits from which to choose those that will best fit their life situation. Benefits have positive impacts on productivity, motivation, retention, and morale. As a critical part of the compensation package, benefits are not just on the 'fringes' anymore.

A Manager's Vocabulary

- Social Security Retirement—Old Age and Survivors Insurance
- Social Security Disability Insurance
- Supplemental Security Income (SSI)
- Unemployment insurance
- Worker's compensation
- Defined benefit plans
- Defined contribution plans
- Family and Medical Leave Act of 1993
- Flextime

- Employee assistance programs
- Wellness programs
- Flexible spending accounts
- Domestic partner benefits
- Cafeteria plans

Study Questions

1. What proportion of the total compensation package is devoted to benefits on average?
2. Why might benefits packages differ between the public and private, for-profit sectors?
3. Why might benefits packages vary between the public and nonprofit sectors?
4. How can benefits aid in the recruitment and retention efforts of an organization?
5. How might managers address any abuse of sick leave?
6. What should managers consider as they develop work–life benefit policies such as flexible scheduling?

Exercise 9.1 Fridays Are Sick Days

As the director of the licensing division of the county Department of Motor Vehicles, you supervise fifteen clerks and a shift supervisor. The work is highly stressful, with constant direct contact with the public; often clients are unhappy about some aspect of licensing. In general, your crew is highly efficient and handles customer relations well. You have found that it takes considerable time to train a new employee. When compiling time sheets for a monthly report, you notice that one of your most valuable employees has been submitting sick leave reports every Friday for the last several months. When you inquire about this, she admits that she has not actually been ill, but has had to miss work every Friday to attend a series of meetings with her attorney concerning a custody battle over her young child. She reports that sick leave was her only option under county personnel rules, and that her supervisor, who is a stickler for procedure, will not allow her to leave early because "it would not be fair to the others." Several aspects of this practice warrant your attention:

1. Is using sick leave when not actually ill unethical?
2. What are the implications of a more flexible leave policy for retaining a valuable employee?
3. What staffing challenges arise from this situation?
4. Does leave taking in this way create a hardship for other employees?
5. If change is needed, what should you propose to the county commissioners?

References

American Dental Association. 2013. "Affordability Care Act Dental Benefits Examined." www.ada.org/en/publications/ada-news/2013-archive/august/affordable-care-act-dental-benefits-examined (accessed June 16, 2014).

Anfuso, Dawn. 1995. "Offering Personal Time Rather than Sick Leave Raises Morale." *Personnel Journal* 74 (5): 126.

Anspach, William N., Jr. 2014. "Dental and Vision Coverage under the ACA." www.lexology.com (accessed June 14, 2014).

Beutell, Nicholas J., and Ursula Wittig-German. 2008. "Work–family conflict and Work–family Synergy for Generation X, Baby Boomers, and Matures: Generational Differences, Predictors and Satisfaction Outcomes." *Journal of Managerial Psychology* 23 (5): 507–523.

Burwell, Secretary of Health and Human Services v. Hobby Lobby Stores, Inc., 573 U.S. (2014).

Clark, Robert L., Melinda Sandler Morrill, Emma Hanson, and Jennifer Maki. 2012. State Health Plans During Times of Fiscal Austerity: The Challenge of Improving Benefits While Moderating Costs. Center for State & Local Government Excellence. slge.org/publications (accessed July 3, 2014).

Crumpacker, Martha, and Jill M. Crumpacker. 2007. "Succession Planning and Generational Stereotypes: Should HR Consider Age-Based Values and Attitudes a Relevant Factor or a Passing Fad?" *Public Personnel Management* 36 (4): 349–369.

Daley, Dennis M. 1998. "An Overview of Benefits for the Public Sector: Not on the Fringes Anymore." *Review of Public Personnel Administration* 18 (3): 5–22.

Eaton, Tim V., and John R. Nofsinger. 2008. "Funding Levels and Gender in Public Pension Plans." *Public Budgeting & Finance* 28 (3): 108–128.

Employee Benefit Research Institute. 1997. *Fundamentals of Employee Benefit Programs*, 5th ed. Washington, DC: EBRI.

———. 2009. *Fundamentals of Employee Benefit Programs*, 6th ed. Washington, DC: EBRI. www.ebri.org/publications/books/ (accessed June 12, 2014).

Employee Retirement Income Security Act of 1974 (ERISA).

Fredericksen, Patricia J. 1999. "Benefit Packaging and Employee Retention: The Constraints of Job Sector." Unpublished paper presented at the annual meeting of the Western Political Science Association, Seattle, Washington, March 25–27.

Fredericksen, Patricia J., and Dennis L. Soden. 1998. "Employee Attitudes Toward Benefit Packaging." *Review of Public Personnel Administration* 18 (3): 23–41.

Global Workplace Analytics. 2013. "How Many People Telecommute? What are the Growth Trends?" www.globalworkplaceanalytics.com/telecommuting-statistics (accessed July 2, 2014).

Gossett, Charles W. 1994. "Domestic Partnership Benefits." *Review of Public Personnel Administration* 14 (1): 64–84.

Holland, Joseph H., Doug Goodman, and Bethany Stich. 2008. "Defined Contribution Plans Emerging in the Public Sector: The Manifestation of Defined Contributions and the Effects of Workplace Financial Literacy Education." *Review of Public Personnel Administration* 28 (4): 367–384.

King v. Burwell, 576 U.S. (2015).

Ko, Jaekwon, SeungUk Hur, and Aaron Smith-Walter. 2013. "Family-Friendly Work Practices and Job Satisfaction and Organizational Performance: Moderating Effects of Managerial Support and Performance-Oriented Management." *Public Personnel Management* 42 (4): 454–565.

Levine, Chester. 1993. "Employee Benefits: Growing in Diversity and Cost." *Occupational Outlook Quarterly* 37 (4): 38–42.

Lockwood, Nancy R. 2009. *The Multigenerational Workforce: Opportunity for Competitive Success.* Alexandria, VA: Society for Human Resource Management. www.shrm.org (accessed June 19, 2014).

McMenamin, Terence M. 2007. "A Time to Work: Recent Trends in Shift Work and Flexible Schedules." *Monthly Labor Review* 130 (12): 3–15. www.bls.gov/opub/mlr/2007/12/art1full.pdf (accessed July 2, 2014).

Mills, Claudia. 2001. "Workplace Wars: How Much Should *I* Be Required to Meet the Needs of *Your* Children." *Philosophy & Public Policy Quarterly* 21 (1): 15–20.

National Academy of Social Insurance. 2008. "Workers' Compensation: Benefits, Coverage, and Costs, 2006." Washington, DC: NASI. www.nasi.org/research/2008/report-workers-compensation-benefits-coverage-costs-2006 (accessed June 17, 2014).

Nugent, Anthony J. 2009. "Using Voluntary Benefits Strategically Can Help Employers Address Goals of Retaining Employees and Controlling Costs." *Benefits Quarterly* 25 (2): 7–10.

Obergefell v. Hodges, 576 U.S. (2015).

Patient Protection and Affordable Care Act 2010. 42 U.S.C. §18001.

Perry, James L., and Lois Recascino Wise. 1990. "The Motivational Bases of Public Service." *Public Administration Review* 50 (3): 367–373.

Pew Center on the States. 2010. *The Trillion Dollar Gap: Underfunded State Retirement Systems and the Roads to Reform.* Washington, DC: Pew Charitable Trusts. www.pewcenteronthestates.org (accessed May 31, 2014).

Rogers, Rolf E., and Stephen R. Herting. 1993. "Patterns of Absenteeism Among Government Employees." *Public Personnel Management* 22 (2): 215–236.

Smith, Maureen. 1999a. "Compressed Workweeks: A Working Solution?" *IPMA News*, June: 16.

———. 1999b. "Sick Leave Policies: When Does Use Become Abuse?" *IPMA News*, June: 17–18.

Solomon, Charles Marner. 1996. "Flexibility Comes out of Flux." *Personnel Journal* 75 (6): 34–43.

Taylor, Jeannette, and Ranald Taylor. 2011. "Working Hard for More Money or Working Hard to Make a Difference? Efficiency Wages, Public Service Motivation, and Effort." *Review of Public Personnel Administration* 31 (1): 67–86.

Telework Coalition, The. 2014. "Telework Guidelines." www.telcoa.org/resources/references/telework-tools/telework-guidelines/ (accessed July 2, 2014).

Thompson, Frank J. 2013. "Health Reform, Polarization, and Public Administration." *Public Administration Review* 73 (special): S3–S12.

U.S. Department of Labor, Bureau of Labor Statistics. 2009. "National Compensation Survey: Employee Benefits in the United States." www.dol.gov/dol/topic/health-plans/index.htm (accessed June 12, 2014).

———. 2012. "How Have Health Benefits Changed in State and Local Governments from 1998 to 2011?" *Beyond the Numbers* 1 (5): 1–6. bls.gov (accessed July 3, 2014).

———. 2013. "Healthcare Benefits." bls.gov/ncs/ebs/benefits/2013/benefits_tab.htm (accessed April 22, 2014).

———. 2014. "Employer Costs for Employee Compensation." bls.gov/news.release/ecec.nr0.htm (accessed June 11, 2014).

U.S. Internal Revenue Service. 2014. "FAQs for Government Entities Regarding Cafeteria Plans." www.irs.gov/Government-Entities/Federal,-State-&-Local-Governments/FAQs-for-government-entities-regarding-Cafeteria-Plans (accessed June 24, 2015).

U.S. Social Security Administration. 2014. "Disability Planner: What We Mean by Disability." www.ssa.gov/dibplan/dqualify4.htm (accessed June 17, 2014).

U.S. Treasury Department. 2014. "Fact Sheet, Final Regulations Implementing Employer Shared Responsibility Under the Affordable Care Act (ACA) for 2015." www.treasury.gov/press-center/press-releases/Documents/Fact%20Sheet%2021014.pdf (accessed June 15, 2014).

Van de Water, Paul N. 2013. "Health Reform Not Causing Significant Shift to Part-time Work." Washington, DC: Center on Budget and Policy Priorities. www.cbpp.org (accessed June 19, 2014).

Witt, Stephanie L., and W. David Patton. 1998. "Gay Rights and the City: Initiatives, Ordinances and Personnel Policies." Paper presented at the Annual Meeting of the Western Political Science Association, Los Angeles, March.

10 Performance Management

Learning Objectives

- Develop familiarity with performance appraisal techniques.
- Understand the importance of communication in accurate performance appraisal.
- Understand the implications of performance management for other functional areas.
- Develop familiarity with metrics and the units and levels of analysis for performance information.

A principal theme running through this entire book is the need to integrate HRM and line management activities in organizations as much as possible, and the task of assessing performance is one area where this need stands out particularly clearly. Continuing calls for public sector reform typically highlight private sector approaches to managing productivity. Monitoring performance within organizations through the appraisal process represents "a conscientious effort at formally, rationally and objectively organizing our assessment of others" (Daley 1992, p. 14). The traditional supervisor–subordinate performance appraisal activity is more routinely scrutinized in terms of its utility for contemporary public administration. A more comprehensive, systemic approach to performance is the best way to leverage individual and group achievement toward organizational purposes. Although there is general agreement on the value of a systemic approach, there is no clear consensus as to what particular appraisal techniques are the most effective, or what might be the appropriate protocol for merging performance assessment with other HR activities.

Consideration of performance appraisal raises several questions. Should we consider performance appraisal as a special set of activities managed by an HR department to maintain a uniform appraisal system for the whole organization? Should performance assessment instead be limited to a dyadic process occurring between employees and their supervisors? Should performance assessment retain a focus upon documenting past efforts to reward or punish, or should it be viewed as a means of enhancing future productivity? Should performance assessment be limited to what is accomplished by individuals, or should we consider work groups, departments, or the organization as the proper unit of analysis for assessing performance? Should performance assessment be a distinct activity, or should it occur as a component of an entire system of assessing, managing, and improving individual and group performance to enhance organizational productivity? Should we even assess performance, or should we only focus on dealing with those employees who have recognized deficiencies or have experienced failure in their work? Can we assume that it is possible to agree on what is commendable performance?

In this chapter, we review the techniques in commonest use for carrying out the traditional supervisor–subordinate performance appraisals. This review describes the different instruments and discusses the methods and logic employed in these dyadic appraisals. The importance of the appraiser

dyadic: of or consisting of a dyad; being a group of two

in this process is a necessary part of this discussion, and many of the problems that can ensue are addressed here, along with recommendations for reducing error in the appraisal process. We move beyond traditional dyadic appraisals and consider less-traditional approaches, such as 360-degree evaluation. In addition, we discuss performance from a broad perspective and consider productivity paradigms, reform efforts, and organization-wide performance issues.

Performance Appraisal Techniques and Approaches

The methods used to assess the character and contributions of an employee vary greatly, and so identifying a 'typical' performance appraisal process is impossible. These many approaches to performance appraisal can best be discussed in the context of what is being assessed about the employee: his or her traits, achievements, or bank of competencies. The assessment of traits, achievements, and competencies presumes that these factors are indicative of the execution of workplace tasks, activities, and responsibilities. Performance levels are usually differentiated according to whether performance in a position is proficient, sufficient, or insufficient when compared with a set standard. Unfortunately, in many settings, performance assessment may be neither constructive in outcome nor reliable in its content. The particular standard against which employees are judged may be ambiguous. The rationale for assessment may be inconsistent vis-à-vis the mission, goals, and objectives of the organization. The commitment of appraisers to do a good job of appraisal may vary in strength.

Trait-Based Appraisal

Although the phrases 'employee evaluation' and 'performance appraisal' are often used interchangeably, traditional employee evaluation often entailed an assessment of an employee's personal traits and characteristics, rather than the amount of effort expended on, or quality of execution of, job responsibilities. Although this type of appraisal is often criticized in the professional literature, trait-based appraisal remains all too common in all job sectors. Indeed, trait-based employee assessments are often rooted in trait-based predictors used in the recruitment and selection process (Quinones, Ford, and Teachout 1995; Tett et al., 1994). Assessment of personal characteristics is often used to decide between applicants for positions, and so periodic employee assessment based upon personal traits is a somewhat logical progression.

Trait-based assessment suggests that we can identify general traits that are associated with proficient performance in a particular position and can likewise identify those traits associated with insufficient performance. The sample trait assessment format set forth in Exhibit 10.1 features a list of traits commonly used to assess patrol officer performance in police agencies. These traits are then assessed in terms of a range of descriptors.

Heslin and VandeWalle (2008) argue that managers may become unduly absorbed in the nature of personal traits and assume such characteristics to be static. To the extent managers view traits as either fixed or very difficult to influence, they may potentially disregard the need for training or fail to identify the potential of employees to improve performance when given the proper encouragement and reinforcement from a capable supervisor.

Achievement-Based Appraisal

Performance may be considered as the level of achievement of duties attained, with position-based criteria being used to differentiate among several levels of achievement. The employee's position description serves as a foundational document for these types of assessment. The activities necessary

Exhibit 10.1 Sample Trait-Based Appraisal Instrument for a Patrol Officer

For each officer, the supervisor must indicate the appropriate assessment using the scale below.

Trait	Always Outstanding	Good/ Excellent	Acceptable	Not Acceptable	Fails to Demonstrate
Dependability					
Attendance					
Cooperation					
Initiative					
Health					
Appearance					
Courage					

Supervisor comments:

Employee comments:

Source: Authors.

to discharge the obligations of a particular position (or class of positions) are typically quite detailed. The appraisal of performance hinges upon the responsibilities of the position and a scale of achievement expressed in terms of levels of proficiency, sufficiency, and insufficiency.

In Exhibit 10.2, the sample appraisal instrument for a patrol officer still identifies personal traits or characteristics, such as initiative and appearance, but these are now linked to certain behaviors that serve to demonstrate the expected performance. Many achievement-based performance assessments offer the advantage of shifting evaluation from a person to their performance. The intent remains to examine (and either reward or punish) past behavior.

In recent years, performance appraisal techniques have shifted in their primary focus to the management of performance. Although prior accomplishments are still examined, these efforts are considered in the context of performance goals established at the beginning of the performance appraisal period. Ideally, the employee and their supervisors (or other appropriate parties) would develop these performance goals in consideration of the organization's mission and goals and the activities of others. The instrument displayed in Exhibit 10.3 extends the assessment to specific goals for performance.

Competency-Based Appraisal

The attention of many personnelists and managers has moved to the demonstration of skill or competence as a means to assess the contributions being made by their employees. The guiding presumption is that the more varied and sophisticated the employee's skill set, the greater his or her

Exhibit 10.2 Sample Achievement-Based Appraisal Instrument for a Patrol Officer

For each officer, the supervisor must indicate the appropriate assessment using the scale below.

	Outstanding	*Acceptable*	*Needs Improvement*	*Unsatisfactory*
Initiative	Seeks and sets additional tasks; shows ingenuity; excellent at problem-solving	Resourceful; completes suggested and supplemental work	Routine response; waits for calls; may not follow up	Needs direction and prodding to complete assigned tasks
Attitude toward citizens	Courteous and respectful; takes direction; considerate; demonstrates collaborative approach to problem-solving	Respectful and courteous	Shows little respect; addresses community concerns grudgingly	Poor attitude; impatient with citizen concerns
Appearance	Takes pride in shoeshine; equipment is maintained and properly worn; uniform is pressed	Favorable appearance; generally tidy with appropriate equipment and uniform	Neglectful of appearance; uniform may be unpressed; improper uniform for tasks	Unkempt; slovenly; stained uniform; equipment missing
Ability to take direction	Readily completes assignments; questions are appropriate to address clarity and comprehension	Requires additional information only to complete orders	Can carry out simple orders but needs direction for complex tasks	Clueless
Written communication skills	Excellent, well-worded reports; completed on time and understandable; demonstrates mastery of grammar, spelling, and structure; no errors	Satisfactory; few errors; generally literate	Incomplete reports; demonstrates a lack of basic writing skills	Fundamentally illiterate; cannot communicate in a written form

Source: Authors.

Exhibit 10.3 Sample Achievement-Based Appraisal Instrument for a Patrol Officer Extended to Specific Goals for Performance

For each officer, the supervisor must indicate the appropriate assessment using the previously established goals listed below.

Performance Goal	Goal Weight	Achieved Goal	Exceeded Goal	Didn't Achieve Goal	Comments
Achieve a 20% reduction in calls for service response time for Area I					
Reduce reported incidents of school-related vandalism by 10%					
Attend 12 public meetings to address citizen concerns and suggest problem-solving strategies					

Source: Authors.

capacity for leveraging those skills toward achieving organizational goals. An employee's competency-based appraisal could vary according to the amount of knowledge a person holds about a particular function (depth of skill), or the expanse of knowledge he or she holds about related responsibilities and activities (breadth of skill) (Shareef 1994, p. 61). In addition, employees could be assessed in terms of the potential managerial applications of their skills (vertical skills) (p. 62). Skill sets and competencies offer a useful base for allocating resources and rewards in organizations, but require reliable instruments and processes for assessing the relative competency levels of employees (p. 67).

Performance Appraisal Instruments

Appraisal instruments may employ a combination of trait, achievement, and competency assessments and a variety of methods to identify, measure, and assess employees relative to some standard. Here we look at the commonest methods.

Graphic Rating

A graphic rating instrument employs a scale of assessment responses, similar to the formats used in survey research dealing with attitudes. This is a fairly simple and speedy method. The appraiser completes a scale that represents the qualitative or quantitative degree to which the employee displays a particular trait, masters a specific skill, or discharges a given duty. These rating methods are often used with trait-based assessments as depicted in Exhibit 10.1. They are the most useful when the points along the scale are defined in terms of what each scale score means.

Ranking

In the ranking performance assessment instrument, employees are assessed in terms of their merits relative to those of other employees. Is an employee in the top quartile of all employees with regard to a particular trait, achievement, or competency, or does he or she belong in the bottom quartile? An appraiser who is ranking a group of employees would look at all individuals in the work unit using, for example, the form displayed in Exhibit 10.1. They would rank each worker in comparison with the others according to how well they rate on each trait. Often the constraint exists that only 10 percent of the unit workers can receive 'outstanding', and 10 percent must receive 'failure'. This exercise is analogous to the normal curve discussion that may occur in grading models for some college and university courses. One rationale for ranking is that this method forces the appraiser to differentiate among employees, rather than give all subordinates very similar (and usually high) ratings.

Forced Choice

As with the ranking instrument, the forced choice performance assessment instrument requires the appraiser to choose between employee pairings, selecting the employee in the pairings whose traits, competencies, or performance of duties are superior. Forced choice methods are intended to avoid generic descriptions of employees by requiring raters to make some relative assessment of what each employee does in comparison with others. Potentially, one could then assess areas in which the employee may, on the one hand, need counseling or require additional training, or, on the other hand, deserve to be rewarded or publicly recognized.

In the forced choice model in Exhibit 10.4, the appraiser is asked to designate the commonest actions and least common actions evidenced by a particular teacher relative to other teachers. This method of performance appraisal can be used with trait, achievement, or competency-based appraisals.

Behaviorally Anchored Rating Scales

Similar to the graphic rating scales, behaviorally anchored rating scales (BARSs) aid the appraiser by offering degrees of achievement that can be used to assess an employee. However, instead of placing a focus on personal traits, BARS processes direct attention to overt indicators of performance derived from a particular position description. The appraisal sample in Exhibit 10.2 provides some guidance as to the range of behaviors that may be associated with a particular trait or skill. BARS instruments are very complex and time-consuming to develop for each type of position in an organization. They are so closely linked to an employee's position description that, if a description changes, so must the appraisal instrument. For example, as police organizations shifted policing philosophies from traditional

Exhibit 10.4 Forced Choice Performance Assessment Instrument for a Teacher

Performance Categories	*Select the strategy most commonly used by the educator for each performance category*	*Select the strategy least commonly used by the educator for each performance category*
Instructional Strategies	Provides opportunities for students to participate actively and successfully – Varies activities appropriately – Interacts with groups appropriately – Solicits student participation – Extends responses and contributions – Provides time for response and consideration – Implements at appropriate level	Provides opportunities for students to participate actively and successfully – Varies activities appropriately – Interacts with groups appropriately – Solicits student participation – Extends responses and contributions – Provides time for response and consideration – Implements at appropriate level
	Evaluates and provides feedback on student progress during instruction – Communicates learning expectations – Monitors student performance – Solicits responses and demonstrations for assessment – Reinforces correct response or performances – Provides corrective feedback and clarifies – Repetitive review/none needed	Evaluates and provides feedback on student progress during instruction – Communicates learning expectations – Monitors student performance – Solicits responses and demonstrations for assessment – Reinforces correct response or performances – Provides corrective feedback and clarifies – Repetitive review/none needed

Source: Authors.

to community-oriented to problem-oriented policing, an officer's responsibilities might have broadened from strict crime control to encompass crime prevention and, later, problem analysis and prevention. The different police service philosophies would result in a fairly dramatic change in an officer's position description (or would if it were updated), and the BARS performance appraisal instrument would change accordingly.

Essay

Attempts to address the limitations of graphic scales and overcome some of the rigidity of the ranking method have led to either the inclusion of essay sections in many appraisal instruments or the complete replacement of graphic scales with a detailed narrative essay. Thus, in essay performance instruments, appraisers have the opportunity to outline achievements, point out extraordinary conditions or events affecting the person being rated, and suggest the importance of particular skills or traits that an employee can leverage to accomplish organizational goals. If the appraiser is skilled in written communication, essay instruments serve to individualize an appraisal, reflecting considerations about an employee that might not be conveyed in uniform formats such as a rating scale or forced choice instrument. Appraisal instruments often include narrative sections as a direct reflection of the need for context and situational factors affecting quantitative ratings. Examples include sections to justify a rating, provide an overall assessment of the employee, or include employee comments regarding the assessment made of his or her performance.

Objective/Goal

In the case of the objective/goal performance assessment instrument, the appraiser focuses on some previously established goals or objectives for which the employee is responsible. The appraisal examines the extent to which the employee was able to meet these goals. Although these appraisals are often achievement-based, the goals may be directly related to the acquisition of a skill or development of a trait. For example, an employee might have developed a set of performance goals for the coming year. Some of these goals could relate to a particular set of achievements (e.g., developing a Web page to communicate crime statistics to a community or presenting relevant research to a fixed number of civic groups). Goals may be linked to the acquisition or enhancement of certain skills (e.g., training in computer software). Other goals may be linked to traits (e.g., improved clarity in verbal communication or an improved physical fitness rating). The method assumes a benchmark for an employee and presupposes that successful employees will tend to improve their personal characteristics, exceed previous accomplishments, or enhance their skills. Ayers (2013) suggests, based on her research and experience, that this approach is ideal for linking individuals to overall organizational mission per the logic of a strategic planning process.

Critical Incident

In the case of critical incident, the appraiser develops a sample of activities, events, or incidents from a certain time span for an employee. Using this sample, the appraiser considers these vignettes as evidence of whether the employee meets some identified performance standard. The BARS approach may be based upon a critical incident study for various groups of employees doing similar work. The performance standards used to assess employee performance may be derived either from focus group sessions or employee surveys conducted among employees doing substantially equivalent work.

Appraising the Performance of Appraisers

All performance appraisal methods depend on the skills and training of the appraiser. In general, the appraiser's written and verbal communication skills are critical to the utility of the appraisal. In addition, the knowledge that the appraiser has of the employee's position, responsibilities, background, and abilities contributes to whether the appraisal is general and vague or specific and directly relevant to the demands of a particular job. Certainly, the mode of the appraisal—traits, competencies, or achievements—will drive the composition of the instrument and ultimately determine how closely it might be linked to some organizational definition of higher versus lower performance. Finally, in the ideal situation, appraisers objectively consider the contributions that different employees make to the organization. Unfortunately, appraisers are seldom perfectly objective or innately skilled and may not be able to assess performance accurately. Personal bias, selective memory, and unreliable assessment variables can limit the utility of many assessment programs. Here we look at the commonest problems encountered in appraisals.

Personal Bias

Personal bias may occur when an appraiser holds a negative view of the employee that is not related to job performance. The source of disdain (e.g., racism, sexism, or a personality conflict) can vary, but in these situations employees are assessed in an unfavorable light regardless of their actual achievements, personal characteristics, or skills. The reverse may be true as well. Some appraisers may try to compensate for their feelings toward an employee by offering an unrealistically positive assessment of the employee's contributions. Although we often use the term bias to suggest malicious differentiation, the appraiser may in fact be unaware that he or she is assigning more positive assessments of employee performance than might be warranted.

Halos and Horns

The "halo effect" occurs when the employee can do no wrong in the eyes of the appraiser (Murphy and Cleveland 1991). In this case, the appraiser assesses all that an employee does positively. This may be owing to the kindness and compassion of the rater, but could also be linked to whether the appraiser likes the employee, or seeks to address past inequities. This bias is quite common, because appraisers are generally rather reluctant to record a negative assessment of performance (Dorfman, Stephan, and Loveland 1986). Conversely, the "horns effect" occurs when an employee is always assessed more stringently, either out of dislike or from a desire to appear tough or demanding to employees and/or the appraiser's supervisors.

Constant Error

In some cases, appraisals conducted by a particular individual are *generally* considered to be either too harsh or too lenient; this is referred to as a constant error. The accuracy of an employee's appraisal is evaluated in terms of the appraiser rather than the employee. We may see this in academic settings when one instructor is considered to be especially demanding and critical and another is considered to be an 'easy A'. Either way, there is an assumption that the employee (or the student) did not merit the appraisal (or grade) received.

Recency Effect

The recency effect could occur using most methods, but may be especially problematic on instruments using the more open formats found in the essay and critical incident methods. With the recency effect, the appraiser may be biased by actions or events (positive or negative) occurring closer to the appraisal point, whereas other relevant events would have receded from consideration.

Central Tendency

Rating employees to the average, often called central tendency, is a response to several factors. Appraisers may have difficulty in ranking employees according to the assessment criteria, may be pressed for time, or may have a predilection for equity in all such interpersonal judgment situations. Regardless of the underlying rationale, central tendency occurs when employees are all rated the same (or close to it) according to some achievement, competency, or trait norm prevailing in that unit or organization.

Reducing Appraiser Error

Several mechanisms may help reduce rating error. The design of the appraisal instrument can help reduce rater error. If the traits, competencies, and achievement categories are well defined, and instructions are clearly outlined, error can be minimized to a considerable extent. The more closely measures can be linked with performance goals derived from the agency's mission, the less margin for error may be present. Appraisal systems that rely upon easily identified and documented indicators for which objective standards can be ascertained will certainly be less suspect than systems with a great deal of subjectivity and appraiser latitude in defining objectives and deriving obscure measures. Alternatives to the traditional dyadic appraisal models, such as the 360-degree evaluation process discussed later in this chapter, could offer the advantage of multiple appraisers to control for rater bias.

Ideally, the timing of the appraisal should be linked to the purpose of the performance assessment. Poor timing can contribute to appraiser bias. If all appraisals are due during the busiest time of the year, or are required before an employee has really had an opportunity to perform (e.g., immediately after hire, or soon after taking on a new project), then a legitimate assessment is unlikely.

Often, appraisal is left to supervisors who, while knowledgeable about the work, may be inexperienced in performance appraisal or may lack interest in its repeated use. Appraiser training is an important measure for reducing assessment error. To address problems with rater bias, many researchers recommend a classic approach of training coupled with the use of performance diaries in which the appraiser documents employee performance with entries in the diary over the course of the appraisal period (Bernardin and Beatty 1986; Maroney and Buckeley 1992). In addition to the rather obvious need to train appraisers in how to use a particular performance appraisal instrument, organizations can require appraisers to articulate a clear understanding of the purpose of the appraisal process and its applications in HRM (Brown and Benson 2003; Oh and Lewis 2009; Reinke 2003). Furthermore, appraisers may need training in how to work collaboratively with employees to assess performance. Appraisers may even require basic interpersonal education in how to discuss uncomfortable topics. Some sensitivity training may be necessary to address the demands of an increasingly diverse workforce in terms of communication styles, value differences, or cultural norms regarding such matters as time urgency, physical space between people in conversation, or social roles (Islam 2013).

Performance Management and Implications for Diversity

Assessing the performance of individual employees according to some common yardstick is a task fraught with problems. Several commonly experienced problems come immediately to mind. First, concerns arise from cultural differences that may exist in the assessment of concepts such as time, quality, and effectiveness—critical components of performance. People from different cultures or geographical locations do not necessarily have the same vision of what a deadline may mean, or what appropriate customer service requires. Diversity is not limited to issues of ethnicity or gender. Differences in professions and disciplinary socialization can have significant effects upon performance assessment for a work group. If a work group transcends functional lines (e.g., a group encompassing marketing specialists, financial managers, and engineers as members), then the differences in professional focus have noteworthy implications for how these different disciplines view what it is they are supposed to accomplish.

Assume a group was assembled from across departments in a local government to develop a new transit system. For the marketing people, a job well done might have a great deal to do with the saturation of the community with educational materials and much less to do with the cost of the project. However, for the financial person, project cost could signal success or failure, regardless of how well the project is received by the community. For the engineers, neither cost nor popular approval may be as important as the engineering integrity of the design itself. These forms of bias are unintentional, but nonetheless pose problems for performance management. One important aspect of 'leadership' is the use of superior position to build mutual respect and appreciation for the diverse perspectives and skills required to achieve excellence in an organization.

Sadly, there may be instances of bias drawn from personal prejudice. It is entirely possible (albeit both dysfunctional and ethically offensive) that individuals in organizations employ negative stereotypes to weigh the relative contributions of others. This potential for bias is of particular concern when activities related to the achievement of performance goals are not easily measured, as in the case of work-related communication and relationship building. Certainly, the potential for appraiser bias is of grave concern when organizations use performance assessment as a means to distribute rewards and punishment within the organization. Most distressing, from the perspective of this text's authors, is any potential for an organization serving the public interest to harbor this type of systematic disparagement or exclusion. Thus, efforts to encourage transparency and ensure due process in the distribution of resources are especially important.

Technology and Performance Management

According to Biro (2013), organizations are becoming more discerning about the technology adopted in the workplace. In particular, however, organizations seek technologies that allow them to acquire and analyze performance-based data. Also, as Biro (2013, paragraph 7) notes, "real time talent management matters . . . a formal employee review every six months is fast becoming obsolete. What is far more important is software that enables us to stay on top of things in real time." Performance evaluation and measurement used to operate on defined periods—a workweek, a quarter, or a year. However, technology mobility has enhanced access and increased the speed of action and reporting. As Kalman (2011, paragraph 4) noted in summarizing the situation, "by relying on providing employee feedback annually—or semi-annually—after the fact, organizations are relinquishing an opportunity to increase productivity and performance now."

Ethical Issues in Performance Management

In seeking the best approach to performance management, we may too easily forget that performance management is about people and their relationship to each other in the context of work. In addition to the danger of excessively objectifying employees in this process, other potential problems come to the forefront.

Can employees simply become objects to be manipulated through performance management systems? The premise behind the management by objectives (MBO) performance model is that managers, in collaboration with their employees, can establish objectives for employees that will serve as a baseline for assessing performance at the end of a fixed time frame (usually 6 months or a year). This model assumes that the objectives decided upon are both achievable and challenging. Would the same concerns about rater bias be applicable to the establishment of the performance objectives? Is there anything wrong with methodically establishing high performance standards to weed out 'low performers'? Daley (2008, p. 45) would argue that these individuals "may represent an underutilized resource . . . [and] overall employee loyalty can be enhanced when others witness . . . [supervisor efforts to] . . . rehabilitat[e] or salvag[e] these employees." Are long-term organizational goals necessarily enhanced by constantly raising the bar for employees?

Additionally, software applications have been developed to streamline the appraisal process, particularly for large organizations. Computerization of performance management can offer some advantages in terms of the elaborate data collection possible, but may sacrifice the critical interpersonal dynamic of an effective performance system. Reliance upon performance assessments through computers may limit the communication and careful individualized assessment of a person's work effort. Sayre's caution that HRM could result in a "triumph of technique over purpose" could easily have been written in response to the boom in computer-based HRM and asynchronous communication (e.g., email, blogs, and memoranda).

While other ethical issues might derive from scenarios where we assess employee contributions and distribute rewards, a trend in private sector-specific scholarship raises the notion of a care-based paradigm (a corollary to the corporate social responsibility scholarship) where HR might focus on employee well-being. In the context of a performance management chapter, this suggests paying attention to whether performance appraisal approaches consider employee well-being. Scholars in this domain often ascribe to a 'stakeholder view' of organizations, wherein employees are among the stakeholders and are valued accordingly. Although this perspective is derived from the private sector, the public service mission, common to nonprofit and public sector organizations, suggests that this model might be readily transferable to government and the nonprofit sector from the business community (Crilly and Sloan 2012).

For example, Boyd and Gessner (2013) caution organizations to consider that common metrics may do little to create fairness or engage employees in the systematic creation and application of performance standards. Islam (2013) echoes this caution in assessing the means by which many organizations recognize high-performing employees, arguing that these programs may harm the necessary social bonds that must develop when so much of the most important work happens in a team-based setting. Perhaps, the logic of this movement explains, we should not laud individuals when we wish to reward teams, nor should we bury individual achievement within a team setting if we, conversely, need strong, individual leadership. Do we reward what we wish to encourage?

Influences on Individual Performance

There are many things that impact an individual's performance. Factors outside the direct control of the individual could include a range of technical and policy constraints upon performance. For example, vague organizational goals, an inappropriately heavy workload, and responsibility incommensurate with authority would most certainly hamper the most competent of employees. Clearly, employees need to have sufficient resources and tools to do their jobs. An employee who is responsible for a Website, but does not have access to the necessary technology, certainly cannot attain high (or even expected) performance. If a staff member must complete detailed complex tasks, but also handle department reception, then the physical environment could detract from the employee's ability to perform.

There are internal factors as well. Does the employee have sufficient training and skills to perform a particular task? Are there other abilities or personal characteristics that may limit or impede performance? Suppose a graduate student is charged with a heavy load of data entry and is locked in a small room, with no window and only a computer for company. This scenario may be appealing to a person who prefers quiet, autonomy, and limited social interaction; for such persons, this arrangement may contribute to performance. A different employee who tolerates noise and craves social interaction may achieve only poor performance in the same physical environment.

Beyond the Boss–Employee Assessment: Groups, Directions, and Practice

Hays and Kearney (2001) suggest that performance management systems of the future will likely reflect increased sensitivity to the structure of the organization, and they will be more closely linked to planning and an assessment of the formal and informal environment of the organization. In addition, variations on the traditional supervisor–subordinate model of performance appraisal will become increasingly common, with the use of peer and client evaluations and team-based approaches to performance management progressively coming to the fore.

A model of performance assessment that incorporates multiple raters—commonly peers, supervisors, clients, and even subordinates—is called the 360-degree evaluation. The premise behind 360-degree models is that multiple raters, each familiar with different views of their colleague's work, assess performance using some standard instrument. In application, 360-degree evaluation is supposed to help an employee improve their overall performance by developing skills or addressing communication problems highlighted in the all-inclusive process of assessment.

Tornow (1993) correctly notes that 360-degree evaluation models presume that employees can improve their performance, particularly in leadership venues, if they learn more about how their efforts affect others. Initially, 360-degree models were used to enhance employee development and to assist supervisors in improving their relationships with subordinates. This performance assessment method has been used in merit pay applications for local government (Fox and Klein 1996). However inclusive and innovative these models may be, these multi-appraiser models are not without their critics (Eichinger and Lombardo 2004). If done properly, the 360-degree models should be ongoing—with formal assessment at least twice per year—and employees, clients, and supervisors may not be willing to devote sufficient time to assessment (Ginsberg 1997).

Toegel and Conger (2003) propose that 360-degree assessment is better served with two articulations of such an instrument. One instrument should be designed to provide feedback to management to aid in employee development in the aggregate. The other instrument should be designed to measure and monitor performance outcomes.

In the future, greater emphasis will be placed upon collaborative processes to address performance management issues. For such systems to work as intended, it is strategically important to engage the supervisor and their superior in setting goals, *with* the employee being an active participant in goal development (Halachmi 1993). Active participation by employees in the performance appraisal process enhances perceptions of system effectiveness (Lovrich et al. 1980). Boyd and Gessner (2013) consider these collaborative models to be an ideal way to encourage organizational justice and empower employees. However, Roberts (2002, pp. 338–339) indicates that garnering credible employee participation requires a significant organizational commitment, and such approaches are hampered by environments characterized by distrust, favoritism, supervisor disinterest, and limited accountability to organizational leadership.

Performance Systems

In the following excerpt, Reinke considers the performance appraisal process as it is practiced in county government in the State of Georgia. In this particular study, she examines the technical characteristics of the appraisals and the preparation of supervisors to conduct such assessments in an overall quest to consider how important the perceived legitimacy of the process/instrument is to the overall appraisal system.

Consider the following questions as you review this excerpt.

1. How does Reinke operationalize the concept of legitimacy, and why does she argue that this is important in performance systems?
2. This study focused upon county government in a particular state. What factors, if any, might change in other parts of the United States? And at other levels of government?

Performance systems depict a holistic approach to improving performance and productivity in organizations. They are premised on the assumption that the employees in an organization, regardless of rank or decision-making level, can come to understand how they contribute to organizational goals, and that all activities within organizations can be analyzed to determine how they either contribute to or detract from the achievement of organizational ends. Performance appraisal of an individual, work group, or department would serve as separate components of a performance management system (Selden, Ingraham, and Jacobson 2001). The design of the job or the identification of specific knowledge, skills, or abilities associated with a particular position would be linked in a system approach to performance management. Assessment could not be considered without attention to all other central facets of HRM. In fact, performance systems are an integral part of strategic planning and should be viewed as a key feature of implementation efforts for organizations (Selden, Ingraham, and Jacobson 2001).

Gilbert (2007, p. 137) indicates that varying organizational factors, such as resource constraints and opportunities for performance management, converge on three distinct planes of decision making and action: *policy*, *strategic*, and *tactical* levels. His matrix echoes the logic of strategic planning: mission, goals and objectives, and action planning. At the *policy* level, we are concerned with maintaining an organization's fit to its environment, which, for both public and nonprofit organizations, means accommodating the interests of political actors, interest groups or stakeholders, and agency clientele (Gilbert 2007, p. 137). The challenge for managers is to mesh the culture of the organization with its mission, the expectations of stakeholders, and the development of the resources, technology, and workforce skills required to meet their respective organization's mission-defined challenges (Baird and Meshoulam 1988, p. 122). *Strategy* entails the specification of the necessary goals and objectives that give life to the mission; it requires the development of evaluative criteria to assess whether the goals and objectives are met (Gilbert 2007, p. 137). *Tactics* pertain to the specific actions to be taken to accomplish organizational goals and objectives (Gilbert 2007, p. 137). This is the area of organizational life that entails learning from experience on the part of 'street-level' personnel, and requires that the learning gained from active contact with clientele (internal and external) feeds back to the strategic and policy-making levels.

The public and nonprofit sectors may face somewhat different challenges as they attempt to assess performance for an organization, for workplace groups, and for individual employees. The often-ambiguous nature of public goals and the limitations of technology and resources that can be used for public action complicate and inhibit efforts to manage performance. Three central questions guide public organizations as they attempt to develop performance management systems: (1.) How do we define and assess performance? (2.) Who appraises whom? And (3.) for what purpose do we assess performance?

How Do We Define and Assess Performance?

Some government activities involve well-established processes with clearly defined outputs and beneficiaries. These activities can be measured, and improvements can be made to the processes

Excerpt 10.1 Trust in the Performance Appraisal Process

Performance appraisal assumes that employees and supervisors accept the process as legitimate. In this study, legitimacy is defined in terms of whether employees believe the process adequately evaluates individual performance and rewards good performance. If they do, the summative and developmental purposes of appraisal will be fulfilled. Employees will respond to information received in the appraisal process and alter their behavior to receive promised rewards (promotion, pay, etc.). Supervisors, on the other hand, will use the processes to identify employee needs for development and fitness for promotion or additional pay. If employees and supervisors do not accept the performance appraisal process as legitimate, then its purposes are thwarted regardless of the quality of the instrument or the processes supporting it (Dipboye & de Pontbriand, 1981; Hedge & Teachout, 2000; Landy, Barnes & Murphy, 1978; Lawler, 1967). . . .

[T]his study examines the role of leadership and trust in influencing acceptance of the appraisal process. [Specifically,] . . . this research examined the role of a particular leadership approach, servant leadership, and proposes that trust serves as a moderating variable between leadership and employee attitudes toward the appraisal process. . . .

The study population consisted of the 651 employees of a suburban county in Georgia. . . . [C]oncern existed over the adequacy of its performance appraisal system. Originally conceived when the county was much smaller, the existing system consisted of one standard form with which all employees were rated, listing 11 behaviors that were evaluated on a simple 1 to 5 scale, with an additional form for supervisory employees. Before embarking on change, the county wanted to know how employees felt about the existing system. This study was undertaken to examine those attitudes and determine the sources of dissatisfaction (if any). . . .

[T]rust emerged as the most important predictor of an attitude toward a performance appraisal process, in this instance, acceptance of the process. This supports the literature suggesting that no analysis of performance appraisal is complete that does not acknowledge its essentially interpersonal nature (Bowman, 1999) and its place as part of the ongoing relationship between the supervisor and employee.

Excerpt References

Bowman, J. S. (1999). Performance appraisal: Verisimilitude trumps veracity. *Public Personnel Management, 28*(4), 557–576.

Dipboye, R. L., & de Pontbriand, R. (1981). Correlates of employee reactions to performance appraisals and appraisal systems. *Journal of Applied Psychology, 66*(2), 248–251.

Hedge, J. W., & Teachout, M. S. (2000). Exploring the concept of acceptability as a criterion for evaluating performance measures. *Group and Organization Management, 25*(1), 22–55.

Landy, F. J., Barnes, J. L., & Murphy, K. R. (1978). Correlates of perceived fairness and accuracy of performance evaluation. *Journal of Applied Psychology, 63*(6), 751–754.

Lawler, E. E. (1967). The multitrait–multirater approach to measuring managerial job performance. *Journal of Applied Psychology, 51*(5, Pt. 1), 369–381.

Source: Reinke 2003.

involved in each system. For example, some local government functions are rather easily measured: park and recreation department program attendance, timely solid waste collection on fixed schedules, and water quality maintenance as documented in samples tested by scientifically qualified laboratories. State governments process insurance forms and pension checks, route child support payments, and authorize and either carry out or subcontract road construction projects. These activities lend themselves to systematic outcome measurement. Increasingly, we may even see these more or less routine activities provided by nongovernmental actors through contracting arrangements, precisely because they are more easily designed as delivery units and measured.

Unfortunately, in many other instances of public service delivery performance, levels cannot be readily measured in widely approved metrics. Characterizing the quality or effectiveness of many public programs is quite difficult, because the objectives used as yardsticks are often vague or overly simplistic. Identifying performance goals at an organizational level may not tidily devolve to an assessment of individual performance. Can we justly assess the performance of the public employees charged with implementing a particular program or developing a service when we are unable to assess organizational performance clearly?

For example, how do we assess the quality of education? If the quality of education is reflected in a student's preparation for a career, then it is easy to measure the number of graduates who successfully land jobs. However, this goal and this measure would not truly reflect the quality of the education effort because variables completely outside the control of the educator and the student play a role in the number of graduates who find work and the type of work they find. If we ask students (as clients) to assess the quality of their education, the criteria used for that assessment could differ widely: how quickly the class passes, how funny the instructor is, or how often they refer to course materials at work? Are any of these assessments more or less valid than the others? Do any of these assessment questions accurately reflect the quality of education? Even if we could clearly identify the indicators of performance, for individuals or organizations, then we are still faced with the appropriate mesh of performance appraisal technique and process (Olsen and Bennett 1975, 1976).

To Appraise or Be Appraised?

The constraints and opportunities posed by organizational structure, as well as the formal and informal distribution of power and authority, are important factors to consider in assessing performance. For example, using a group-based structure and rewarding group effort would work at cross-purposes with a performance appraisal system relying on the conventional, dyadic, supervisor–subordinate performance appraisal process. The assessment of group-based performance requires consideration of collective achievement by individuals in the group and judgments about their ability to contribute to the group effort. Group-based assessment requires due consideration of the ability of individual members to work with others to ensure that their knowledge, insights, and skills are shared within the work group. If we rely upon supervisors of the work group to assess performance, without considering the key perceptions held by a particular employee's peers, then we are receiving only a partial picture of performance. For project-based systems, a performance assessment frame linked to the project cycle may be more useful than assessing performance during set blocks of time. Conversely, if we opt for the TQM characterization as supervisors being the enablers of high performance, then we must incorporate employee evaluations of their supervisor in any group assessment process.

Can we hold public servants accountable in their performance assessment for the actions of individuals over whom they have no direct control? As may be rather common with the provision of public goods and services through nonprofit or private sector organizations, a public agency employee overseeing the program in question could be entirely dependent upon the activities of people outside the organization to implement a particular publicly supported program. Similarly, a work group within a public organization may include seasonal or temporary-contract employees, over whom the supervisor has only limited control. In these cases, their ability to manage the work of others over whom they may have no direct supervisory influence is crucial, yet extremely difficult to measure and assess uniformly. Failure to consider the structure of the organization and understand key agency processes at play leads to disappointing results with respect to performance improvement efforts.

For What Purpose Do We Assess Performance?

Decisions about what purposes are served in doing performance appraisal should comport with the organization's mission in general, and with the job-specific elements of work for which the employee or group of employees is held responsible. Performance appraisal can be delineated in terms of whether it is used to judge (or grade) employees, or used to develop their capacity to perform (Cummings and Schawab 1973, p. 5). Certainly, appraisal systems are founded on basic assumptions about people and their motivation, the links to performance that various benefits and incentives may have, and even whether employees can be largely trusted to do the job or must be controlled rather closely.

In other applications, employee assessment may be a means to punish detrimental behaviors or warn about the consequences of poor performance. Conversely, the same process can be used to reward favored activities or reinforce positive behaviors, such as the acquisition of competencies needed in the workplace. Many organizations link performance assessment with compensation and merit pay (Selden, Ingraham, and Jacobson 2001). Performance appraisal may also serve to help management identify employees for promotion, or select individuals for either reassignment when their skills are needed elsewhere in the organization or dismissal if performance is sub par. In these applications, appraisal serves as a means to judge the relative importance of individual employee contributions to the organization.

The performance outcomes managers may seek drive decisions about the subject of assessment (of groups or individuals). For example, if we want to know about employee–client relations, then we should probably use some assessment method that includes a survey of client opinions. If we would like to assess a work group or other collaborative effort within an organization, we would expect both peers and supervisors to appraise performance and work groups to assess other work groups.

The intent and focus of assessment will affect the performance management system adopted for an organization. It is important to note that production activities require different assessment approaches than service activities. Measurement may be entirely quantitative, or it may address performance appraisal through the use of qualitative indicators. Finally, the anticipated application of the performance information should be tied to the performance system.

Doing It Right: Effective Performance Appraisal and the Role of Leadership

Research indicates that managers and subordinates do not necessarily share the same perception of the performance appraisal (Reinke 2003; Longenecker, Gioia, and Sims 1978). In fact, Pulakos et al. (2012, p. 1) describe a clear disconnect between the ideal of performance management and its reality in organizations:

> When asked what purpose performance management *should* serve in organizations, employees, managers and HR professionals alike cite important outcomes such as improving performance

effectiveness and results, developing employees, and facilitating communication and information exchange between employees and managers. However, when a slightly different question is asked—what purpose *does* performance management serve—the responses are quite different. Most people say that in reality, performance management serves primarily only *administrative purposes*. These purposes include helping managers make pay and compensation decisions, providing documentation for the organization to defend itself in court, and enabling the organization to deal with poor performers.

Ultimately, for performance appraisal to be useful, employees and managers have to agree upon its purpose and believe that it is a legitimate and useful process (Maroney and Buckeley 1992; Reinke 2003). Increasing participation by employees in the appraisal process is positively associated with an enhanced perception of the effectiveness of the appraisal, the utility of the process, the legitimacy of the performance goals, and the relationship between employees and supervisors (Silverman and Wexley 1984).

Employees are clearly interested in an objective assessment of their performance (Lovrich et al. 1980), and, not surprisingly, favorable performance appraisals tend to enhance an employee's perception of the accuracy of performance appraisal (Stone and Stone 1984). However, the employee's perception about the accuracy of his or her own performance appraisal does not translate to a positive perception about the utility of the overall performance management system for the organization (Pearce and Porter 1986; Reinke 2003). Paarlberg and Lavigna (2010) propose that transformational leadership, coupled with hiring efforts to grow the ranks of employees with a strong public service motivation and better socializing of those new employees at the onset of their arrival, can set the context for a healthier performance system. Public service motivations alone are not sufficient, if the performance appraisal system is fundamentally incompatible (in terms of process, goals, or rewards) with such deeply intrinsic motivation. Organizations may not see dramatic productivity gains (Alonso and Lewis 2001; Oh and Lewis 2009).

No single template appraisal format is appropriate for all organizations. The most useful performance system is one in which the appraisal format establishes linkages to organizational goals (Greenburg 1986). Prescriptions for effective performance appraisal often focus upon developing instruments and procedures to support the traditional supervisor–employee models of assessment. However, summarizing the scholarship done on performance appraisal suggests that the following three general lessons can be applied:

1. The performance management system should be developed with specific intent rather than result from casual loading of faddish technical applications upon an existing system. For example, the evaluative role supervisors may play versus peers versus clients in evaluating the performance of a particular employee will change depending upon the intent of the assessment. If we want to discover how to improve customer service, then we have different expectations about who will appraise an employee's efforts than we might if we were using the performance management system solely to distribute internal rewards.

2. While the performance appraisal system should be job-related and used to develop and improve performance, it may be used additionally to address performance concerns at multiple levels— the organization, the work group or service unit, and for individual employees. To that end, if employees participate in establishing performance goals, their interests and concerns can be made an integral part of the performance system. A performance collaboration means that employee feedback cannot be limited to a response block in the 'Employee Comments' section of a template appraisal instrument.

3. Effective performance management must be linked to the manner in which positions/activities are identified and assigned—whether this is done through a traditional job analysis and classification model or reflects a work classification model. If performance assessment is not integrated into the manner in which work is structured—individual versus group, or perhaps task versus project—then the assessment instrument cannot discern relative levels of performance. For example, if all positions are carefully identified in terms of an individual employee holding a particular set of responsibilities relating to a clearly defined set of tasks, then assessment in terms of group-based effort in a project-driven environment would be most inappropriate.

Berman, West, and Wang (1999, pp. 15–16) join other public administration scholars in cautioning decision makers against quickly adding the latest fad or computer gadget to the performance management system, noting:

> As with all new productivity improvement efforts, in time the good is separated from the bad. As many human resource managers are trying new ways to increase their performance and provide accountability, new performance measures must be proposed, implemented and evaluated. Studies . . . should . . . examine whether these measures add value to the human resource function.

Summary

Performance assessment is a complex activity. Aside from the highly technical nature of identifying performance levels, we see enormous challenges in linking individual performance to organization-wide goals and productivity. Intuitively, a systemic approach to performance management is appealing, but much of the structure in organizations (established through analysis, classification, and compensation systems) must be integrated with performance management. In addition, it is difficult to dispense wholly with familiar practices such as supervisor–subordinate appraisal, which may suggest control and accountability, but often do not realistically reflect the changing work environment. As later chapters will demonstrate, performance assessment serves as a bridge between initial HR activities, such as job analysis, classification, recruitment, and selection, and subsequent concerns—namely, the development, training, and, if necessary, disciplining of employees.

A Manager's Vocabulary

- Performance appraisal
- Trait-based appraisal
- Achievement-based appraisal
- Competency-based appraisal
- Breadth of skill
- Depth of skill
- Graphic rating performance assessment instrument
- Ranking performance assessment instrument
- Forced choice performance assessment instrument
- Essay performance assessment instrument
- Objective/goal performance assessment instrument
- MBO
- BARS
- Critical incident

- Personal bias
- Halos and horns
- Constant error
- Recency
- Central tendency
- 360-degree evaluation
- Policy—performance matrix
- Strategy—performance matrix
- Tactics—performance matrix

Study Questions

1. How should performance be assessed for individuals?
2. How should performance be assessed for departments or work groups?
3. How should performance be assessed for the organization?
4. What performance assessment instrument might be appropriate for different jobs or organizations? How might the performance instrument differ for a position oriented toward routine duties versus a managerial position?

Exercise 10.1 Comparing Appraisal Instruments

Obtain three different performance appraisal forms from a public sector organization. If possible, obtain forms that reflect trait, achievement, competency-based, or some type of hybrid. Consider the following questions after you have examined the position appraisal forms:

1. What methods are used in the appraisal instrument (e.g., graphic rating, ranking, forced choice, BARS, essay, objective/goal, or critical incident)?
2. How well does each of the appraisal instruments capture performance?
3. Are the various levels of performance well articulated?
4. Which instrument would you prefer? Why?
5. Could these performance appraisal instruments be used easily for different jobs? What modifications might be necessary?
6. How well do the methods used for each appraisal instrument reflect the performance levels that we wish to assess in each position?

References

Alonso, Pablo, and Gregory B. Lewis. 2001. "Public Service Motivation and Job Performance: Evidence from the Federal Sector." *The American Review of Public Administration* 31 (4): 363–380.

Ayers, Rebecca S. 2013. "Building Goal Alignment in Federal Agencies' Performance Appraisal Programs." *Public Personnel Management* 42 (4): 495–520.

Baird, Lloyd, and Ilan Meshoulam. 1988. "Managing Two Fits of Strategic Human Resource Management." *Academy of Management Review* 13 (1): 116–128.

Berman, Evan M., Jonathan P. West, and XiaoHu Wang. 1999. "Using Performance Measurement in Human Resource Management." *Review of Public Personnel Administration* 29 (2): 5–17.

Bernardin, H. J., and Richard W. Beatty. 1986. *Performance Appraisal: Assessing Human Behavior at Work*. Boston, MA: Kent.

Biro, Meghan M. 2013. "7 Hottest Trends in HR Technology." *Forbes* (October 6). www.forbes.com/sites/meghanbiro/2013/10/06/7-hottest-trends-in-hr-technology/ (accessed January 15, 2015).

Boyd, Neil, and Brooke Gessner. 2013. "Human Resource Performance Metrics: Methods and Processes that Demonstrate You Care." *Cross Cultural Management* 20 (2): 251–273.

Brown, Michelle, and John Benson. 2003. "Rated to Exhaustion? Reactions to Performance Appraisal Processes." *Industrial Relations Journal* 34 (1): 67–81.

Crilly, Donal, and Pamela Sloan. 2012. "Enterprise Logic: Explaining Corporate Attention to Stakeholders from the 'Inside–Out'." *Strategic Management Journal* 33 (10): 1174–1193.

Cummings, Larry L., and Donald P. Schawab. 1973. *Performance in Organizations: Determinants and Appraisal.* Glenview, IL: Scott, Foresman.

Daley, Dennis M. 1992. *Performance Appraisal in the Public Sector.* Westport, CT: Quorum Books.

———. 2008. "The Burden of Dealing with Poor Performers: Wear and Tear on Supervisory Organizational Engagement." *Review of Public Personnel Administration* 28 (1): 44–59.

Dorfman, Peter W., Walter G. Stephan, and John Loveland. 1986. "Performance Appraisal Behaviors: Supervisor Perceptions and Subordinate Reactions." *Personnel Psychology* 39 (3): 579–597.

Eichinger, Robert W., and Michael M. Lombardo. 2004. "Patterns of Rater Accuracy in 360-Degree Feedback." *Human Resource Planning* 27 (4): 23–25.

Fox, James, and Charles Klein. 1996. "The 360-Degree Evaluation." *Public Management* 78 (11): 20–22.

Gilbert, Thomas F. 2007. *Human Competence—Engineering Worthy Performance.* Tribute ed. San Francisco. CA: Pfeiffer.

Ginsberg, Steven. 1997. "In a New Approach to Evaluations, Everyone's a Critic." *The Washington Post.* Sunday, July 27, H4.

Greenburg, Jerald. 1986. "Determinants of Perceived Fairness of Performance Evaluation." *Journal of Applied Psychology* 71 (2): 340–342.

Halachmi, Arie. 1993. "From Performance Appraisal to Performance Targeting." *Public Personnel Management* 22 (2): 323–344.

Hays, Steven W., and Richard C. Kearney. 2001. "Anticipated Changes in Human Resource Management: Views from the Field." *Public Administration Review* 61 (5): 585–597.

Heslin, Peter A., and Don VandeWalle. 2008. "Managers' Implicit Assumptions About Personnel." *Current Directions in Psychological Science* 17 (3): 219–223.

Islam, Gazi. 2013. "Recognizing Employees: Reification, Dignity and Promoting Care in Management." *Cross Cultural Management* 20 (2): 235–250.

Kalman, Frank. 2011. "Technology's Fix for the Performance Review." *Talent Management* (September 1). www.talentmgt.com/articles/print/technology-s-fix-for-the-performance-review/ (accessed January 15, 2015).

Longenecker, Clinton O., D. A. Gioia, and H. P. Sims. 1978. "Behind the Mask: The Politics of Employee Appraisal." *The Academy of Management Executives* 1 (3): 183–193.

Lovrich, Nicholas P., Jr., Paul L. Shaffer, Ronald H. Hopkins, and Donald A. Yale. 1980. "Do Public Servants Welcome or Fear Merit Evaluation of Their Performance?" *Public Administration Review* 40 (3): 214–222.

Maroney, Bernard P., and M. Ronald Buckeley. 1992. "Does Research in Performance Appraisal Influence the Practice of Performance Appraisal? Regretfully Not!" *Public Personnel Management* 21 (2): 185–196.

Murphy, Kevin R., and Jeanette N. Cleveland. 1991. *Performance Appraisal: An Organizational Perspective.* Boston, MA: Allyn & Bacon.

Oh, Seong Soo, and Gregory B. Lewis. 2009. "Can Performance Appraisal Systems Inspire Intrinsically Motivated Employees?" *Review of Public Personnel Administration* 29 (3): 158–167.

Olsen, L. O., and A. C. Bennett. 1975. "Performance Appraisal: Management Technique of Social Process? Part I—Management Technique." *Management Review* 64 (12): 18–23.

———. 1976. "Performance Appraisal: Management Technique or Social Process?" Part II—Social Process." *Management Review* 65 (1): 22–28.

Paarlberg, Laurie E., and Bob Lavigna. 2010. "Transformational Leadership and Public Service Motivation: Driving Individual and Organizational Performance." *Public Administration Review* 70 (5): 710–718.

Pearce, Joan L., and Lyman W. Porter. 1986. "Employee Responses to Formal Performance Appraisal Feedback." *Journal of Applied Psychology* 71 (2): 211–218.

Pulakos, Elaine D., Rose A. Mueller-Hanson, Ryan S. O'Leary, and Michael M. Meyrowitz. 2012. "Building a High-Performance Culture: A Fresh Look at Performance Management." SHRM Foundation. www.shrmfoundation.org (accessed January 11, 2015).

Quinones, Miguel J., Keven Ford, and Mark S. Teachout. 1995. "The Relationship Between Work Experience and Job Performance: A Conceptual and Meta-Analytic Review." *Personnel Psychology* 48 (4): 887–909.

Reinke, Saundra J. 2003. "Does the Form Really Matter? Leadership, Trust, and Acceptance of the Performance Appraisal Process." *Review of Public Personnel Administration* 23 (1): 23–37.

Roberts, Gary E. 2002. "Employee Performance Appraisal System Participation." *Public Personnel Management* 31 (3): 333–342.

Selden, Sally Coleman, Pat Ingraham, and Willow Jacobson. 2001. "Human Resource Practices in State Governments: Findings from a National Survey." *Public Administration Review* 61 (5): 598–607.

Shareef, Reginald. 1994. "Skill-Based Pay in the Public Sector." *Review of Public Personnel Administration* 14 (3): 60–74.

Silverman, Stanley B., and Kenneth N. Wexley. 1984. "Reactions of Employees to Performance Appraisal Interviewers as a Function of their Participation in Rating Scale Development." *Personnel Psychology* 37 (4): 703–710.

Stone, Eugene F., and Dianna L. Stone. 1984. "The Effects of Multiple Sources of Performance Feedback and Feedback Favorability on Self-perceived Task Competence and Perceived Feedback Accuracy." *Journal of Management* 10 (3): 371–378.

Tett, Robert P., Douglas N. Jackson, Mitchell Rothstein, and John R. Reddon. 1994. "Meta-Analysis of Personality–Job Performance Relations: A Reply to Ones, Mount, Barrick, and Hunter." *Personnel Psychology* 47 (1): 157–170.

Toegel, Ginka, and Jay A. Conger. 2003. "360-Degree Assessment: Time for Reinvention." *Academy of Management Learning & Education* 2 (3): 297–311.

Tornow, Walter W. 1993. "Introduction to Special Issue on 360-degree Feedback." *Human Resource Management* 32 (2–3): 211–219.

11 Human Resource Development

Learning Objectives

- Recognize the need for employee development.
- Understand the major strategies and phases of human resource development programs.
- Understand the implications for other functional areas, especially labor relations and performance management.

Human resource development (HRD) is the application of strategies and interventions designed to enhance the knowledge and skills of individuals to improve their capacity to contribute to their organizations, promote their careers, and improve their quality of life. The Academy of Human Resource Development defines HRD as a profession "that focuses on improving individual and organizational performance through learning" (Schmitz 1999).

The foundation of HRD is 'continual learning' achieved through a combination of individual learning strategies, formal training programs, or group/team learning approaches. The conventional strategy used for HRD has been the provision of formal training programs focusing on specific job skills for line employees and the development of supervisory and managerial skills among administrative personnel. Conventional training is still an important function of HRD, and classroom instruction remains the commonest HRD method of teaching. However, the sizable cost of training and the paucity of evidence documenting training benefits can lead to careful scrutiny of the HRD function. New methods of HRD are being introduced to enable individuals to have greater control over their own learning strategies, and to help organizations target their resources for specific learning objectives more effectively.

The Need for HRD

Members of the modern public workforce must possess much more knowledge and many more skills than the stereotypical bureaucrats of the past were expected to command. Public and nonprofit employees and their administrators must now be a resource to the citizenry and coworkers by being skilled in a wide range of competencies and being adaptable to rapidly changing workplace and societal demands. Public interest workers frequently facilitate discussions between disparate groups and make difficult decisions with scarce resources, while attempting to ensure equal access and maintain public accountability. All of this knowledge and these skills must be applied to community problems and issues efficiently and effectively, even though, in most situations, there is little prospect for significant pay incentives or available funds dedicated to keeping employees up to date on current information. Newly created knowledge and skill updates will be in great demand, but resources to obtain that knowledge and those skills will likely continue to be limited. Because of these predictable constraints, the need to find cost-effective ways of developing employees will be important to organizations seeking the best ways of serving the public.

In some ways, HRD is related to the field of organizational development: an important aspect of organizational development is developing methods for organizations to promote ongoing employee and organizational learning. According to Peter Senge (1990), a "culture of learning" is increasingly important in organizations, not only for individuals who want to increase their knowledge and skills, but also for the organizations themselves, as their members share insights, make use of institutional knowledge, and benefit from their diverse experiences. Organizations can learn through the process of collectively solving important management and operational problems, or through active participation in planning. Organizations can further develop their learning capacity through collaboration and cooperation with external organizations, such as universities, civic organizations, and other public agencies. By comparing operations and practices with those of similar jurisdictions, organizations can learn valuable lessons from the experiential knowledge gained by others who face similar challenges. By teaming up with university researchers, organizations can often learn about the lessons of public administration research conducted around the United States and in other countries.

HRD strategies focus on the development of the individual in the context of the needs of the organization. Although the focus of HRD is often on the individual or on small work groups, the objective of HRD practices overall is to facilitate the accomplishment of the mission of the organization. Training, mentoring, job rotations, apprenticeships, and other HRD strategies should be directed principally toward the improvement of the ability of individuals to help the organization provide public goods and services more effectively.

Public and nonprofit sector managers and HRD professionals need to develop and pursue multiple strategies to accommodate change. A comprehensive strategy of continuous employee development is more effective than isolated training sessions or periodic workshops. In addition, as a supplement to the overall employee development effort, a sort of 'just-in-time' employee development program is often deployed, in conjunction with ongoing development strategies, to provide learning opportunities in specific knowledge and skills as they are needed for time-sensitive requirements of the organizations.

One of the most important needs for employee development derives from the common practice of promoting individuals to supervisory positions who have had no prior supervisory training or experience. This is particularly true in the public sector where an employee is promoted to a supervisory position because he or she has performed well in an operational position. The practice of promoting from within is commendable generally, but the employee may be unable to function effectively as a supervisor without additional targeted training focused on supervisory tasks and responsibilities. Employee development initiatives such as mentoring, internships, and training can be useful ways of improving supervision for those who have not had the benefit of management education.

Another important reason for emphasizing employee development stems from the fact that a portion of the contemporary workforce may not have the requisite communication or analytical skills to be functional in the contemporary workplace. Exhibit 11.1 describes four types of literacy relevant to the adult workforce—prose, document, quantitative, and digital. The National Center for Educational Statistics (2003), in measuring prose, document, and quantitative literacy, notes no significant change in prose or document literacy between 1992 and 2003, but reports a slight increase in quantitative literacy. Anderson and Ricks (1993) found that some aspect of illiteracy, within the categories of prose, document, and quantitative, affects more than half (61 percent) of the local government workforce. Both job applicants and current employees may sometimes be deficient in language and

---

Exhibit 11.1 Adult Workforce Literacy Categories

- *Prose*: The knowledge and skills needed to perform prose tasks (i.e., to search, comprehend, and use continuous texts). Examples include editorials, news stories, brochures, and instructional materials.
- *Document*: The knowledge and skills needed to perform document tasks (i.e., to search, comprehend, and use noncontinuous texts in various formats). Examples include job applications, payroll forms, transportation schedules, maps, tables, and drug or food labels.
- *Quantitative*: The knowledge and skills required to perform quantitative tasks (i.e., to identify and perform computations, either alone or sequentially, using numbers embedded in printed materials). Examples include balancing a checkbook, figuring out a tip, completing an order form, or determining an amount.
- *Digital*: The knowledge and skills required to access and use software applications and hardware devices, to access the Internet, to understand digital content and applications, and to create such content. Digital literacy requires prose, document, and quantitative literacy, in addition to knowledge and skills with technology.

Source: Prose, document, and quantitative literacy definitions from National Center for Educational Statistics 2003. The definition of digital literacy is derived from the U.S. Department of Commerce 2011 and from Media Awareness Network 2010.

---

math skills. According to the Anderson and Ricks study (1993, p. 145), some local governments identified employees who were unable to write clear reports or read and understand instructions adequately. Murray and Pérez (2014, p. 85) describe use of communication technology (e.g., all forms of social media and the equipment used to access such) as another distinct form of literacy (characterized as digital literacy). The U.S. Department of Commerce (2011) indicates that 96 percent of employees use communication technologies during their work life, and 62 percent rely upon the Internet. Unfortunately, despite the frequency with which individuals interact with technology and the Internet, they still may lack the specific knowledge and derivative skills necessary to use such digital technology to solve problems or create usable knowledge for the workplace (Katz and Macklin 2007; Murray and Pérez 2014). Clearly, the cumulative impacts of these gaps in the multiple dimensions of literacy have implications for performance generally, but also for workplace safety and public service.

Public and Nonprofit Budgets and HRD

Despite the demonstrated need for employee development in public organizations, HRD is often largely neglected as a budget priority and is typically the first budget item to be reduced when organizations are required to trim their costs. The relatively low status of HRD in budgetary contests for resources is a problem for a number of reasons. Training and employee development are usually not viewed as the central function of most public agencies. The responsibility of public works departments, for example, is to provide clean and safe roads, water, and sewer systems. Health and welfare departments are focused on social services and public health. Training and other development programs can be viewed as taking employees away from these central functions and adversely affecting

training programs 1st to go.

the already overly stretched resources of the agency. HRD programs are considered desirable, but, unfortunately, they tend to be viewed as peripheral to the central purpose of most public agencies. When cost cutting becomes necessary, it is politically more palatable to cut training programs than to eliminate direct services and jobs in the labor-intensive environment of most public agencies.

Another reason for the low status accorded to HRD is the difficulty of seeing immediate benefits from such practices as training, job rotation, educational incentives, internships, and mentoring. Most people feel there is indeed some benefit to these practices from their own experience with them, but placing a dollar amount on the benefits is rather difficult. The benefits of learning are often intangible and may only manifest over a long period of time. Thus, the value is difficult to estimate, and its immediate effects may be indirect and difficult to see. This transferability problem leads many managers to doubt the efficacy of employee development programs. Frequently, the most easily perceived benefits of employee development are realized only after several years, whereas the up-front costs are immediate. The costs of development programs are generally more visible than the benefits, making the cost-to-benefit ratio of HRD programs difficult to determine. Public and nonprofit sector managers and their respective HRD professionals are under continuing pressure to find ways of more accurately measuring the benefits of employee development programs, and they are expected to be able to target training and development initiatives directly to meet the priority contemporary needs of line managers.

In a number of public agencies, however, training and development are viewed as essential to the operation of the organization. Police, fire, and emergency medical service agencies, for example, spend large amounts of time and money on established employee development programs. In these agencies, training is viewed as essential because of the liabilities to the organization if employees make mistakes in high-risk situations. They understand that they can deliver the best service possible (often in life-and-death situations) only when appropriate training on all expected stressful situations is provided. Other public sector functions such as finance, auditing, and information management are not as immediately concerned with life-and-death problems, but are nonetheless faced with public service situations that pose financial or data liabilities where poor performance can adversely affect public confidence in government.

Wise managers see the need to keep employees up to date on the information and skills needed to perform at their best. The first requirement of a successful employee development strategy is genuine commitment at the top of the organization. When top management is convinced of the benefits of HRD programs and is willing to commit the necessary resources, employees can use these programs to their full potential, and organizations can derive the full short-term and long-term benefits of investment in their employees.

HRD Strategies

The commonest forms of employee development are often not considered part of HRD. As Mosher (1982) argues in the Chapter 1 reading, in one sense the nation's largest HRD program is composed of its system of public schools and its community colleges, colleges, and universities. For the most part, these critical social institutions exist to prepare individuals for professions and vocations. Most organizations—public, nonprofit, and private alike—look primarily to the education system for new recruits. Except for knowledge and skills that are unique to each organization, students learn the fundamental skills and information needed to perform at an entry level in almost any profession. In addition to classroom instruction, colleges and universities often require or recommend service-learning, short-term internships, cooperative experiences, and apprenticeships of various types to help students make the transition from school to the workplace. The experiential learning approaches help students apply content from traditional instruction and acquire skills that can often be most effectively acquired only in on-the-job settings.

As Exhibit 11.2 illustrates, HRD strategies draw on a wide variety of methods designed to help employees learn for the purpose of keeping up with developments in their field, improving their overall capabilities, enhancing their workplace performance, and adapting to a rapidly changing environment. Training is the commonest method of structured, purpose-driven learning for the workplace. Many training techniques are instructor-oriented, meaning they are designed and delivered by an instructor who assumes much of the responsibility for imparting learning. Most HRD professionals believe that work-related learning will become increasingly important for all jobs in the future, given the rapid pace of technology-driven change in so many aspects of contemporary society. However, the learning taking place will be less formal, more individual-oriented, and structured within the parameters of the organization's mission. Individual learning strategies are intended to assist employees to become more responsible for their own learning and, thus, more inclined to search out the increasingly diverse types and channels of learning becoming available.

Organizations can facilitate learning by providing opportunities for employees to progress in their careers while accomplishing organizational objectives. As shown in Exhibit 11.3 and referenced in discussions earlier in this text on performance systems, a system-wide approach to HRM entails less mindless reliance on standard processes and more emphasis on extensive knowledge of those standard processes in order to apply them to new and emerging circumstances. Learning is an essential characteristic of successful organizations that are required to respond to change, and research on comparative organizational performance strongly suggests that successful organizations adapt to changing demands principally through the ability of their employees and administrators to learn from their own experience and that of others doing comparable work (Cosier and Dalton 1993, p. 38).

What about motivational speakers?

Technology and HRD

Many methods may be used to advance individual and organizational learning, and, as technology advances, more methods are added to this list virtually every day. The use of the Internet is a major resource for learning. Social media and a variety of image transmission technologies, such as Skype or FaceTime, give us new opportunities to work together regardless of physical location. Whatever the technique, the objective is to facilitate continuous learning to keep pace with the increasing demands placed on public employees and the formal organizations in which they work. Some of the most exciting developments in HRD are the emerging technologies developed for delivering timely information to employees. Technology has provided access to learning platforms in operation virtually anytime and anywhere. This is indeed important; however, it is also true that simply providing access does not equate to training, much less to effective learning or mastery of new concepts, as we will show further into this chapter.

Employee Training

targeted training

Training is the most common form of HRD intervention in organizations. Indeed, many employees travel great distances to conferences and workshops to receive training and technical updates in their respective professional and occupational fields. Despite the prevalence of training in the work environment, much of what is conducted under the name of 'training' is largely ineffective or unproductive. To be effective, training must be targeted to meet the needs of the organization and the employee, it must be designed appropriately, and it must be evaluated carefully to ensure its continued effectiveness, given the rapid pace of change requiring ongoing attention to new developments.

Exhibit 11.2 Individual Learning Strategies

- *Individual development plan*: This formal document outlines an individual's learning and development goals. An employee and supervisor jointly develop the training, education, and development activities to acquire position competencies.
- *Special projects and assignments*: These temporary duties are intended to broaden/ enhance an employee's knowledge or augment the skills on a team. These may include shadowing (an employee observes another) or a rotation (employee transfers to a different unit or duty area).
- *Coaching*: A supervisor or employee with specific expertise observes an individual at work and provides direct feedback and problem solving.
- *Mentoring*: Senior and junior employees are informally or formally partnered for the purpose of support, advice, and career guidance.
- *Job aids*: These reference materials offer instructions and step-by-step explanations for tasks. Examples include checklists, decision charts, policy/procedure manuals, FAQs, and work samples.
- *Manager as teacher*: Managers frame their role as that of teacher or facilitator and both demonstrate preferred skills and behaviors and serve as an on-the-job instructional resource.
- *Learning groups/teams*: Employees with shared interests or duties meet to exchange ideas, tips, and resources, and the ongoing peer support allows individuals to reinforce KSAs acquired in a problem-specific context.
- *Self-directed learning*: Many individuals have the initiative to seek out development activities to enhance their skills or to support their professional aspirations. These self-paced activities may include online videos, professional journals, or online courses.
- *Classroom learning*: Classrooms may be specific to the worksite or accessed through a college or university. Such training might include a variety of pedagogies, including role-playing, experiential activities, and simulations conducted with an instructor or facilitator in a face-to-face setting.
- *Distance learning*: This is similar to classroom learning, but without the benefit of face-to-face interaction with the instructor and/or other class members.
- *Online learning*: This approach may integrate a vast content and approach but shares an Internet-based delivery mode.
- *Informational interviews*: Employees seek targeted, specific information from key personnel.
- *Discussion forum*: Similar to the learning groups/team, a collection of individuals with shared interests or job responsibilities exchange information in a networked setting and can be either face to face or online. Listserves are a common option.

Source: Adapted from U.S. Office of Personnel Management 2005a.

Exhibit 11.3 Organizations and Learning

- *Personal mastery*: Employees engage in continual learning at all career levels to enhance earned credentials, acquire current skills, and hone competencies. Individual employee efforts become part of a career management system within the organization.
- *Team learning*: Deliverables are often a product of teams in the contemporary organization. Individuals must be able to learn in a collective setting and coordinate the multiplicity of skills and competencies to a team effort.
- *Mental models*: The organizational framework recognizes that change and innovation are the norm, and competitive workforces celebrate skill development and flexibility to better adapt to opportunities and challenges.
- *Shared vision*: Organizational leadership (and this includes all management levels and responsibilities) must share a view of the organization's mission.
- *Systems thinking*: This entails a holistic approach to organizational improvement that realizes a team-based framework across all vertical and horizontal levels of the organization and across all functional areas.

Source: Adapted from U.S. Office of Personnel Management 2005b and Senge 1990.

Public sector training entails instruction in a large number of topics, including training for job skills, client service, supervisory and interpersonal skills, team building, policy development and analysis, and organization culture. The variety of topics covered in training programs can be divided into types according to the designated recipient of the training: orientation for new employees, followed by development programs for rank-and-file employees, supervisors, managers, and executives (Van Wart 1993).

Orientation Training

Orientation training is designed to give *new employees* an understanding of the mission of the organization and the specific duties to be performed, to give maximum possible expression to organizational goals and objectives. The first training an employee should experience upon entering an organization is an orientation to the organization, to their job, and to their place in the organization. The importance of orientation is noted in Chapter 8 as part of the recruitment and selection cycle. In addition to the utility of having new employees understand their way around the organization, employee orientation benefits the organization and the employee in a number of important ways. Orientation helps reduce start-up costs by allowing the employee to perform immediately upon starting the job and cuts down on employee turnover because employees experience less stress through knowing what to expect on the job (Buford 1991, p. 200).

According to Beeler (1994, pp. 13–17), in orientation training, employees should:

- become acquainted with the purpose, mission, and services of the organization;
- learn about the key people and culture of the organization and the location of important physical facilities;

- become familiar with the compensation and benefit programs of the organization;
- understand all safety rules and regulations;
- learn about the structure and functions of their assigned department, who their supervisors and coworkers are, and what duties, responsibilities, and behaviors are expected of them on their specific job.

Employee Development Training

Training for employee development is typically focused on improving the performance of continuing employees in their particular job knowledge and skills. On-the-job training is frequently used to demonstrate job functions. Classroom sessions are used to convey general information. Supervisory development involves new and continuing frontline managers and develops skills such as delegation, effective use of techniques employed in the building and sustaining of employee motivation, interpersonal communications, and how to work with small groups to do problem solving and build teamwork. Supervisors are often taught by a 'tell–show–do' method, where supervisory practices are discussed and demonstrated, and the trainees then practice each of the skills. A debriefing session is often conducted after the practice of the skill in question, for trainers to answer any questions and clarify what are taken to be exemplary supervisory practices.

Management and Executive Training

Management and executive development is targeted at upper-level managers and focuses on the understanding of management theory, as well as involvement in discussions about how to perform important management duties, such as coaching, mentoring, and the building of administrative teams and problem-solving teams across intra- and interorganizational boundaries. Managers are responsible for oversight of personnel functions, and training is often directed toward deepening their understanding of contemporary HRM trends and best practices. Managers often receive training through methods such as role-playing, simulations, group analysis of case studies, active learning exercises, and the use of applied projects in which the dynamics of management theories are shown to be in play. Executive development includes broader conceptual and organizational issues, such as policy development and analysis, politics, strategic planning, negotiation, media relations and image management, intergovernmental networking, leadership studies, and organizational culture. Executive development programs are often done in small groups or are self-directed, limited only by the time constraints and costs involved. Public sector middle management and executive-level development programs have been developed in nearly every state.

Training Phases

Effective training for managers and employees is a much more complicated undertaking than simply sending someone to a conference or arranging for a motivational speaker. These actions can be useful steps to take, but they may not be what people really need to perform their job duties better. To be effective, training should address the actual needs of individuals and the organizations in which they are working, and should be designed to teach individuals in ways they are most able to internalize and then transfer the information and skills taught to their own work in their own organizations. Most scholars generally agree that training occurs in three broad phases: assessment, design and delivery, and evaluation (Fisher, Schoenfeldt, and Shaw 1996; Van Wart 1998, 2010).

Assessment

The first phase entails the systematic assessment of the need for training. There are many reasons training may be needed: some reasons relate to the benefit of the organization, others for the department or subunit within the organization, and others arise from what the individual needs to learn to do the job that has been assigned to them. Oftentimes, however, training is conducted without first determining which employees need the training in question. This haphazard approach to training can result in a great deal of wasted time for employees and a bad reputation for those providing the training.

Ideally, training should be designed to meet the needs of the organization and those who work there. Management fads are frequently the subject matter for training, but these topics can be counterproductive if the employees taking part in the sessions have greater training needs that are being neglected.

Organizations make assessments by determining, then analyzing the difference (or gap) between, what employees need to know and should be doing and what they already know and actually are doing. Training needs assessments typically investigate three particular organizational domains: organizational climate, job demands, and individual employees' capacity to perform and expand their range of activity.

Organizational climate assessments generally analyze the organization's mission, goals, and culture. They seek to determine if employees understand the stated mission and goals of the organization. Do they share the values of the organization and understand what is accepted as ethical behavior? An organizational assessment could also analyze the familiarity of employees with agency policies, such as personnel practices and equal employment guidelines. Stakeholder assessments of clients, citizens, and employees can show how these important groups view the organization and, in some cases, identify what the organization can do to serve their needs more appropriately. The organization may also want to assess its overall performance in relation to its own standards or the performance of similar types of organization, a practice known as benchmarking. Each of these organizational assessments can provide management and trainers with valuable information about the needs of the organization, information that can then be applied to the design of the training program and the structure of the evaluation phase.

Job demands assessments analyze the duties, responsibilities, skills, and knowledge that make up a job and determine which areas should be the subject of training. Some aspect of a job may involve learning how to make use of new technology or how to comply with new regulatory guidelines (e.g., workplace safety provisions), and these developments should be presented to employees who actually need the new information. In some cases, there may be a general problem of performance among those responsible for a specific task. Training may be needed to improve performance for all employees in a particular job classification. For example, if it is found that law enforcement officers are 'profiling' minority youth in traffic stops—i.e., disproportionately detaining minority drivers— a department-wide training program would be indicated.

Job demands assessment is probably the most common form of training assessment done. It can be used to identify job duties and responsibilities and the associated knowledge and skills needed to perform job tasks. Subject matter experts can be used to make certain that the essential duties and responsibilities are identified. The objective of the job demands assessment is to determine what type of training is needed to either help employees learn a new task or improve performance on existing work. Employees can be asked by survey or interview whether they see a need for additional training in any of their job duties and responsibilities. In addition, a performance audit can be conducted of work groups or individual employees to determine whether there are any common unacknowledged deficiencies in the knowledge or skill required to perform specific jobs that could be addressed in a targeted training intervention.

Individual assessments are done to help individuals improve their work performance. This assessment can help managers or trainers identify which individuals need to be trained and what type, and level, of training they need. In some cases, remedial skills training is required to bring employees up to their expected job level. Employees may also be trained in the jobs of coworkers, so that work team members are familiar with the jobs of other members, or they may learn to perform at the next job level in preparation for a promotion. Supervisors can provide valuable input as to which employees should receive training as identified from performance appraisals and employee development plans. Employees can also identify any legally mandated or professional training needs that require the attention of the organization, as well as pinpoint any self-identified deficiencies that they themselves are willing to address through training.

Design and Delivery

The second phase of training entails formulating the training design and planning its delivery. This phase involves conceptualizing a plan of how the training will take place, deciding what instructional methods will be used, as well as determining the time required, the specific teaching aids and materials needed, and any administrative considerations to be accommodated within the organization.

Once the training needs and participants are identified, a training program can be designed to meet the needs of both employees and their organization. The training intervention begins by identifying the training objectives and then designing the best approach to achieve these objectives.

Training Objectives

Training programs should be bounded by the mission of the organization and be directly related to problems existing in the organizations in question with respect to mission accomplishment. Therefore, the first step in training design is to establish the objectives of the training program as they are derived from the organizational mission. Administrative problems affecting mission accomplishment typically exist at three distinct levels—context, process, and behavior. Context problems arise when the organization's mission is insufficiently understood and employers are concentrating their efforts on inappropriate goals vis-à-vis that mission. Process problems arise when needed procedures for deciding action are either nonexistent or are being circumvented. Behavioral problems arise when organization members either cannot or will not do the mission-related things required of them in their work. For training to be effective, it needs to be directed appropriately to the context, process, or behavior problems clearly identified at the outset.

Training objectives should be measurable and have training evaluation in mind (Buford 1991, p. 201). Evaluation of training programs can be made by asking participants about the impact of training and measuring outcomes after participants have had time to practice the principles taught. Questions such as these are typically posed to training participants: What did they learn? How was their behavior at work affected? What actual improved performance results do they believe are attributable to the training intervention (Kirkpatrick 1983)? What skills or competencies were acquired in training? Were the skills or competencies subsequently demonstrated at the work site? What knowledge was acquired, and how might it be applied in the workplace? These questions may be assessed periodically as appropriate (e.g., immediately after the training and again, after a 3-month interval).

Training Design

Once training objectives are identified, the trainer can design the best instructional approach to achieve these objectives. In the development of the design, the trainer should consider the type of individual receiving the training, the type of task to be trained, the principles of learning that apply for optimum learning, cost controls, and the most appropriate methods to be used to achieve learning by the participants.

Adult learners have a significant body of knowledge gained through life experience. This knowledge can be a highly valuable resource for the instructor to help participants understand related learning objectives. For example, when the topic is how the hiring process should work in a personnel office, there is no substitute for the experience participants have had when they have applied for jobs to show the appropriate ways and inappropriate ways to structure and carry out a hire.

Adults are usually willing to take responsibility for their own learning. They can see the relationship of learning to their lives and understand the value of learning to their own well-being. Adult learners tend to be problem-centered, tend to take training to resolve a current problem or need, and want the training to be relevant to the workplace challenges they face. Consequently, it is important for training to be focused, rather than generic, and for the instructor to help participants apply the concepts learned in the training to their workplace circumstances. Finally, adults generally want to be actively involved in the learning process—they want to discuss how ideas apply to themselves and their own circumstances, and they want to practice the techniques or skills that are presented before trying them out in the work setting.

Our understanding of how people learn has changed from the traditional teacher-oriented model toward an appreciation of how participants perceive and process information. Learning is a process whereby individuals make sense of the world around them. Typically, learning is the result of perceiving a problem, clarifying the nature of the problem, and developing possible solutions (Dewey 1938). This process of problem solving through hypothesis testing is known as the 'scientific method'. Scientists use it to learn formally about their disciplines and to formulate generalizations and theories about their subject of study. However, this method is not exclusive to scientists—virtually all of us make use of this process informally as we seek to understand our world and solve our own problems. We encounter a problem, think of what the cause might be, and try out possible solutions. The knowledge gained from these problem-solving experiences is in time transformed into learning, as individuals think about their experiences and apply the principles formulated through experience to other related problems (Kolb 1984). Sims (1993, p. 249) explains that learning is "more than a stimulus-response process. Thinking and analysis occur during reflection and generalization, as well as in the testing of hypotheses."

To this end, scholars have identified seven fundamental training principles derived from the literature on learning theory that organizations can use to help training participants gain the most from their formal training experiences (Van Wart, Cayer, and Cook 1993):

- Foster participant goal setting.
- Increase the similarity of training to the work environment.
- Use underlying principles.
- Increase the organization of the material.
- Actively involve the learner.
- Give feedback.
- Use a variety of techniques and stimuli.

Participant goal setting also begins with an accurate needs assessment, as training participants should be able to make the connection between the training offered and their ability to perform better at their jobs. Training participants should also prepare to receive the training that is prepared for them (Noe 1986) by acquiring any prerequisite experience, skills, or knowledge required to understand the material presented.

Training transferability is enhanced when participants can relate what is being discussed in the training to their work situations and is made more realistic through the use of participative teaching methods (e.g., case studies, real work examples, role-playing, simulations, and site visits). Participants are better able to retain the training content when they have the opportunity to apply the training content to a workplace setting. Periodic review sessions will also support application and retention of training content. Learning theory suggests that, when participants understand underlying principles behind the specific application taught, they are able to apply these principles to new situations as they arise. One of the oldest methods of involving participants was effectively demonstrated by Socrates, who asked questions to help students come to desired conclusions themselves and to generate open discussion. Active engagement can also be accomplished through structured debates, and using both small breakout groups and large whole groups facilitates discussions. A concluding segment or debriefing session can result in useful discussion following a case study, a simulation, or self-assessment exercise. Trainees may also be given assignments for homework, case studies, or practice exercises. They can be assigned to go to a work setting to observe or practice the material discussed in the training session. Discussion of the results of these assignments can also enhance the active involvement of training participants.

Individuals are able to learn more efficiently when the instructor provides regular feedback to the participants regarding their progress and with respect to opportunities for exploring more deeply newfound ideas. Many people are motivated by achievement and need a specific goal to help them focus their learning. Periodic feedback helps training participants know if they are working in the right direction as is intended by the instructor. Feedback also helps trainees know if they are doing well at learning what they are supposed to learn, in the opinion of the instructor, and whether they are applying the principles in ways that were intended. Another valuable quality of feedback is that it provides an opportunity for participants to discuss the implications of the principles presented and explores ways these principles will apply to their own work situations.

Presenting information in a variety of ways helps participants understand the concepts under consideration more fully and makes the training more interesting and enjoyable. Almost half (47 percent) of training hours are still delivered by an instructor in a classroom setting, and for years the lecture was the near-exclusive method of presenting information (Training Industry Report 2014, p. 24). This method is clearly effective for some subjects, and a 'lecturette' may be useful in introducing topics. However, many people benefit from using more of their senses in the learning process— sight, sound, and tactile learning applications are quite useful. For example, in contemporary kindergartens, teachers use small blocks to demonstrate math concepts, or ask students to clap their way through syllables, or teach sign language while working on spelling. These applications are ways for learners to be more actively involved in learning, rather than just listening to a teacher. Participants can learn by remembering the touch, the sound, and the experience of performing a task. Not surprisingly, research indicates that 29.1 percent of training hours are delivered with blended learning techniques, and that using multiple approaches can be cost effective (Lothridge, Fox, and Fynan 2013; Training Industry Report 2014, p. 24).

In very practical terms, the organization of training materials has a major impact on the ability of participants to learn the desired skills and/or knowledge being taught. A clear, logical format helps trainees follow the presentation and apply the material to familiar situations. The training should have written objectives and an outline of how concepts or methods will be presented. Visual aids such as graphs, tables, pictures, and videos are also useful for promoting both understanding and retention. However, a word of caution is warranted regarding the use of training techniques and multimedia: it is easy to fall into the trap of substituting gimmicks for substance. A video, by itself, does not teach effectively: its relevance to the learning objective must be made clear to training participants. Exercises, simulations, overheads, computer displays, and other training techniques are very useful methods, but they are just tools.

The toolbox analogy is useful when training programs are being designed. There are many methods, each with particular appropriate applications. The right tool for the right job can result in a valuable learning experience for participants; the wrong tool can be clumsy and awkward, and training participants will be left wondering what the trainer was trying to accomplish. Effective training design and delivery require the appropriate training method being matched to the subject matter and learning objectives. Skillful application of methods is the means to learning, not the end. Training must be designed to help participants achieve learning objectives. Effective trainers use a variety of tools to tie together a conceptual theme or to illustrate a point that needs to be made. Training should not be unfocused in its learning objectives nor just offer entertainment. The limited time available for training in most organizations is far too valuable to be wasted in this manner.

Evaluation

The third and final phase is a systematic evaluation of the learning that took place as a result of the training. Evaluation begins with the learning objectives established when the training program was designed. The evaluation procedure should lead to a valid assessment of how well the training achieved specific learning objectives. As training is conducted with the objective of imparting information, learning a skill, or realizing some tangible result, the evaluation of training should determine whether these purposes were realized. Because of the limited organizational resources devoted to training and other HRD practices, managers must be able to see the return on investment—they need to document the benefits of training and observe measurable changes in performance. Training must be competency-driven, transformational, quantifiable, and technology-based to the maximum extent possible (Peak 1997).

Often, training involves some type of feedback instrument, such as an evaluation form that tells the trainer if participants enjoyed the training experience, or if they believed it useful in application to their jobs. This type of evaluation measures the reaction of participants to the training, and this is indeed useful information to some extent. Although helpful for some instructional purposes, participant end-of-session reactions do not really document whether the trainees participating actually learned anything of lasting value. A good evaluation would measure: (1.) participant reaction, as well as (2.) actual learning, (3.) whether behavior changed, and (4.) whether real positive results were realized in the workplace setting as a result of the training (Kirkpatrick 1983).

An effective evaluation would include all four elements of evaluation, if each is appropriate to the training's learning objectives. Reaction could be measured by evaluation surveys administered at the end of a training session or program. Learning can be measured by testing the participant for content knowledge immediately after the training and after a period of time has passed. Behavior is usually measured by observation by qualified evaluators, such as supervisors or others who know how a job should be performed. Performance results may be measured through observation or in quantitative terms, such as number of errors, complaints, cases completed, and other such measures of productivity.

Useful training evaluation requires an evaluation design that measures actual changes in learning, behavior, or results that are related to the training experience. The evaluation may also be used to determine if training participants were able to reach a specified level of performance or competence. The simplest method of evaluation is to measure knowledge, skill, behavior, or results after training is completed. This post-test-only design cannot measure change, because there was no measurement before training occurred, but it can be useful for measuring whether a standard of performance or level of knowledge has been achieved. For example, you may want to know if training resulted in all firefighters being able to identify critical equipment for use on the scene of an incident. Even in this case, it would be possible that the training had no effect on the learning of firefighters. They may have learned about this equipment on another job or in school. More definitive evaluations measure both a group that has received the training and one that has not received the training.

Pre-/Post-test

In this design, a group that will receive training can be measured before and again after training to see if a change took place because of training. Used frequently, this design requires sufficient planning to test the group before training. It has the drawback of assuming that any change was the result of training. Unfortunately, many factors could have influenced change during the time period between the pre-test and the post-test.

Control Group

A second design measures two groups, one that received the training and a control group that did not receive the training. The results from both groups are compared, and the difference should be the result of training. The problem with this method is more serious than the first, as no two groups are exactly alike, and many factors could account for differences between groups besides a training intervention.

It is possible to resolve the disadvantages of both designs by combining these two evaluation techniques. A pre-test/post-test is conducted on the group that receives training and on the control group that does not receive training. In this way, differences between groups are accounted for in the quasi-experimental design, and intervening factors are less likely to interfere in both groups. Whatever method is used to evaluate training, the important thing to remember is that you want to measure results that can be directly attributable to the training received.

Introduction to the Reading

A desire for value-added training merges with practical considerations in the following excerpt from a report from the U.S. Merit Systems Protection Board. This reading considers the importance of competencies and differentiates between categories of competencies in terms of what has been learned about the utility of training—that is, the degree of 'trainability' associated with a particular subject matter and the people designated to receive training in it. Consider the following questions:

1. How do the employees discussed in the report variously describe training needs?
2. How does this excerpt define a 'competency'?
3. How does the discussion of competencies and trainability relate to other functional activities in personnel such as job analysis or design? Recruitment and selection? Performance management?
4. What is 'trainability' and why might it be a useful concept as we evaluate the utility of training investments?

Excerpt 11.1 Competencies and Trainability

Competencies have three defining characteristics. First, they are not related just to a job but to superior performance on that job. . . . Second, competencies are closely related to general human abilities. . . . Finally, competency models do not consist only of relatively short lists of job-related abilities. These abilities are prioritized by the number and importance of the job tasks that each competency enables an employee to perform. This prioritization can be used for a number of practical human resource purposes, including deciding which competencies to assess for hiring or promotion and which to target for training. The relationship between competencies and general human abilities makes competencies a particularly useful language for examining the job-related abilities that employees may or may not develop through training. . . .

Knowledge . . . competencies include job knowledge, academic subjects, and knowledge of laws, policies, and regulations. Research indicates that this type of material is learnable by most people when it is presented in a well-designed way (Gagne et al. 2004) . . . knowledge competencies are *highly trainable*—they can be readily learned in training classes by almost all learners.

Language . . . competencies include reading, writing, learning other languages, editing, preparing lengthy documents, and preparing and giving speeches to large audiences. . . . Linguistic abilities often emerge as a separate type of ability or "intelligence" in factor analytic studies of human abilities . . . Language competencies are classified as *moderately trainable*— they can be learned, but how well they are learned is constrained by a person's natural talent for language.

Social . . . competencies help us get along with other people. They range from basic interpersonal skills and teamwork to more specialized abilities to negotiate, manage conflict, and foster diversity. They include the ability to work well with customers, those in authority, and "difficult people." . . . Social competencies are considered *moderately trainable*—improving them through training is constrained by each learner's individual level of talent.

Reasoning . . . competencies are based on logic and mathematics, and include such practical competencies as analysis, troubleshooting, and computer programming. [These] . . . competencies are considered *moderately trainable*—reasoning strategies can be taught, but the competencies also have a natural ability component.

Motivation . . . competencies capture employee willingness to perform work. They include personal characteristics such as resilience in the face of difficulty, integrity, and public-spiritedness. . . . [As these competencies are linked to personal characteristics,] motivation competencies are *less trainable*.

Mental Style . . . competencies include long-term mental habits such as flexibility, integrity or conscientiousness, creativity, ability to deal with complexity, rapid learning ability, stamina, and decisiveness [Coburn 2000; Wong et al. 2003; Cerinsek and Dolinsek 2009]. [Because these competencies are also linked to personal characteristics, these too] . . . are considered *less trainable*.

These six competency categories are directly related to competency trainability. Training that targets Knowledge competencies is more likely to be successful. On the other hand, it is very difficult to change Motivation and Mental Style competencies through training. Each person brings some level of natural ability to any attempt to improve Language, Social, or

Reasoning competencies. Within these limits, training can produce improvement in such moderately trainable competencies.

Excerpt References

Cerinsek, Gregor and Slavko Dolinsek. 2009. "Identifying employees' innovation competency in organizations," *International Journal of Innovation and Learning* 6(2): 164–177.

Coburn, William E. 2000. *The Reagan Way: Using Leadership Skills for Strategic Success.* Carlisle Barracks, PA: U.S. Army War College.

Gagne, Robert M., Walter W. Wager, Katharine Golas, and John M. Keller. 2004. *Principles of Instructional Design.* New York: Wadsworth.

Wong, Leonard Wong, Stephen Gerras, William Kidd, Robert Pricone, and Richard Swengros. 2003. *Strategic Leadership Competencies.* Strategic Studies Institute, U.S. Army War College, Carlisle Barracks, PA.

Source: Excerpt from pp. 10–16, U.S. Merit Systems Protection Board. 2011. "Making the Right Connections: Targeting The Best Competencies For Training." www.mspb.gov/studies/browsestudies.htm (accessed May 9, 2014).

HRD Practices in Government

Effective HRD practices are becoming increasingly important to the performance of public, private, and nonprofit organizations. This significance is reflected in the amount of money spent annually on employee training, management training, executive leadership development, and organizational development. Schmitz (1999) estimated that 1995 HRD expenditures across all sectors of the U.S. economy approached nearly $200 billion. The 2014 Training Industry Report represents U.S.-based corporations and educational institutions with 100 or more employees (but does *not* include state, local, or federal agencies or nonprofit organizations). Per this report, training expenditures had increased to $61.8 billion (Training Industry Report 2014, p. 17). Training hours annualized per employee are approximately 40.7 (p. 19), and most training is targeted at nonexempt employees. Estimates for expenditures solely within government are difficult to identify, and as such this is an excellent area for research. However, a great deal of training is contracted, and the OPM maintains a list of approved federal contractors and offers ongoing programming for state and local governments (U.S. Office of Personnel Management 2015a). In addition, federal agencies have detailed reporting requirements regarding certain required data elements, such as training purpose, delivery type, and various cost categorizations (e.g., per diem, travel, tuition, etc.; U.S. Office of Personnel Management 2008, pp. 6–7).

According to Wiley (1995) certification, accreditation, and licensure are ways to document the credentials of an individual or an organization. Certification and accreditation are both administered by professional associations, often nonprofit collectives of related discipline-specific professionals. Licensure usually rests at the individual level and is administered by a government or political jurisdiction. These processes serve to verify some level of knowledge or competency attainment and may serve a gate-keeping function to affirm to those without expertise in a particular field that citizens and clients are benefiting from the judgment and efforts of such an expert. Wiley (1995) argues that these verifications offer clear benefits to individuals, organizations, and professions in serving as proxies to verify knowledge, offer evidence regarding professional currency in a particular field, and codify a body of knowledge regarding a profession or occupation. Levit (1995) concurs with Drucker's (1980) observation that certification and the like encourage the public and elected officials to take the profession of public management seriously. Those who challenge the utility of certification ask about the relationship between certification and performance (e.g., just because someone can does not mean that they will). Levit (1995) expresses concern that certification may lock in the scope of knowledge and skills of a profession, limiting its ability to grow and develop. Wilhelm (1995) observes that many professions have not yet reached agreement on what the essential characteristics of the profession are, or even on what constitutes competency in the performance of job duties and responsibilities. Gazell and Pugh (1993) contend that the history of such efforts suggests that challenges in identifying a single organization to administer the certification are often significant obstacles precluding action. This results in a form of professional fragmentation, as multiple associations offer similar certifications, and people outside the field are at a loss to distinguish one from another.

A number of professions have historically awarded certification to those who have met the educational and practical requirements of the profession. Associations for public accountants, attorneys, and engineers certify that qualified individuals have met their requirements for official certification. A number of public sector professionals have developed certification programs (Black and Everand 1992). The International Institute for Municipal Clerks certifies local government clerks, and the Municipal Treasurers Association of the United States and Canada certifies city treasurers. Thirty-six states have developed certified public manager programs, consisting of 300 hours of formal management training for state managers, and thirty-two of those states maintain formal accreditation with the National Certified Public Manager Consortium (2015). Certification in the nonprofit realm continues to grow through efforts by organizations such as the Nonprofit Leadership Alliance (2015; formerly American Humanics) and the Association for Research on Nonprofit Organizations and Voluntary Action (2015).

The maturation of public and nonprofit administration is also reflected in the large number of graduate programs in public administration and the growing number of nonprofit degree programs in existence across the country. In addition, the accreditation efforts of the Network of Schools of Public Policy, Affairs and Administration (Hays and Duke 1996) serve to affirm a shared set of competencies for those earning certain graduate degrees or studying in a particular professional emphasis area.

Perennial Training Topics: Ethics and Diversity

Diversity Training

An increasing demand for employee development has been in part the result of the increased diversity of the U.S. workforce. As the demography of the workforce continues to broaden in its diversity, organizations must adjust personnel functions to accommodate newly recognized needs of both their current and future employees.

When discussing diversity, we include individuals from many different backgrounds who have different experiences, outward characteristics, and cultural heritages and can offer a unique range of perspectives for the benefit of the group or organization as a whole. These differences may include differences in language, culture, race, ethnicity, age, sex, religion, disability, nationality, region, or other distinctions. Everyone is included in a diverse workforce, and the needs of all individuals are viewed as deserving equal acknowledgment. The focus is less on differences than on the contribution of each perspective to the implementation of the goals of the agency and its service delivery to internal and external communities. In many ways, attending to the enhancement of diversity and the creative blending of diverse perspective is the hallmark of a learning organization.

Public and nonprofit organizations have decided that it is wise for them to encourage and appreciate diversity as they endeavor to serve the needs of their clientele and citizenry. As is the case during any time of transition, some employees accustomed to a relatively homogeneous workplace community may experience difficulty adjusting to or understanding the changes going on around them. In response to the needs of a diverse workforce and multicultural citizenry, public and nonprofit organizations around the country have implemented diversity training programs. According to the U.S. Office of Personnel Management (2015b), the goals of diversity training include:

- the legal and statutory requirements for EEO and AA that support diversity in the federal government and in private industry;
- understanding that diversity is the similarities, as well as the differences, among and between individuals at all levels of the organization, and in society at large; and
- understanding how diversity contributes to a richness in the organization by giving a variety of views, approaches, and actions to use in strategic planning, tactical planning, problem solving, and decision making.

State and local governments often draw upon federal online resources to support their training initiatives. There are a variety of resources on federal and many state government sites in support of diversity training, including full curriculum outlines. In practical terms, the U.S. Office of Personnel Management (2015b) recommends that agencies focus on the following:

- *Interpersonal skills*: Federal employees need to provide services to, work with, and manage persons and groups with similarities and differences.
- *Behavior*: Federal employees are expected to exhibit in all workplace contacts behavior that respects each individual, preserves human dignity, honors personal privacy, and values individual differences, as well as common characteristics.
- *The work environment*: Federal employees need to appreciate diversity and understand its demonstrated relationship to effectiveness and efficiencies in organizational performance.

Ethics Training

Federal, state, and local government employees are increasingly under public scrutiny. Even the appearance of unethical conduct can lead to negative media exposure and public criticism. For this reason, many public organizations require ethics training for all of their employees. Such training is appropriate for nonprofit organizations responsible for handling resources for their clientele or working to educate public decision makers about policy changes occasioned by changes in society. Training about the federal laws, state statutes, or local government ordinances governing a particular jurisdiction is known as 'rules-based' training, and training sessions on these topics are fairly common after any noteworthy new laws or ordinances come into effect. Ethics commissions exist in forty-two states, and, even in states without such commissions, oversight is codified and implemented, either through statute, an executive office such as the attorney general, or a committee in the house or senate of a given state (National Conference of State Legislatures 2014). Municipalities and county governments often use variations to model what is used in their respective states. In addition, some states extend the rule-specific training to a general ethics education that may include principles of ethical decision making (National Conference of State Legislatures 2015). According to Kerns and Moore (2003), many states offer online ethics training and either encourage or outright mandate state employees, as well as those who lobby state government, to participate and acquire a certificate of training completion.

To establish standards of ethical conduct, many professional organizations have established *codes of ethical conduct* (American Society for Public Administration 2013), and, in some cases, law has established a framework for ethical behavior. The Ethics in Government Act of 1978 represents an early attempt to establish a code of conduct for federal employees. The Act established the Office of Government Ethics (2015; OGE), the mission of which is to prevent and resolve conflicts of interest and promote high ethical standards for federal government employees. The OGE provides resources for executive agencies that offer ethics training for their employees, and it publishes an extensive quarterly training schedule featuring detailed classes available for federal employees. In addition to the most recent executive order dealing with ethics, Executive Order 13490 (2009), the OGE's training programs are designed around Executive Order 12674 (1989) and Executive Order 12731 (1990), which outline fourteen "principles of ethical conduct for government officers and employees" to "ensure that every citizen can have complete confidence in the integrity of the Federal government" (Executive Order 12674, April 12, 1989).

Summary

The HRM department in public and nonprofit organizations often performs the HRD function. In smaller jurisdictions or nonprofits, much of this domain may be left to individual supervisors. Some of the most important responsibilities of HRM are to see to it that the organization is staffed with employees possessing appropriate knowledge and skills to carry out the organization's mission, and to develop and advance employees to satisfy both their professional needs and the needs of the organization. Employees are usually hired with the fundamental professional knowledge and experience needed to perform their duties on the job, but they need to learn the unique requirements of a specific job and the special circumstances of the organization within which the job is carried out. Organizations seek to hire people who can adjust quickly to the particular responsibilities and culture of an organization and adapt well to the changes that occur in the work or profession as time goes on.

However, although staffing and training and employee development are essential elements of the personnel office's duties, HRD professionals are no longer simply 'the people who do training'. The HRD manager is increasingly likely to be serving as the key link between leadership, the employees, and an organization's mission and goals. HRD professionals facilitate learning in consultation with functional managers and leaders in the various HRD programs of contemporary organizations (Nadler and Nadler 1989). As such, they must stay current with changes occurring within and outside the organization, and they must help managers adjust to change by acquiring the knowledge and skills needed to perform in a dynamic social environment. HRD professionals must be learning specialists skilled in the use of instructional technologies, knowledgeable regarding the application of adult learning principles, and consultants to management on workplace learning needs and the development of effective strategies to address those needs.

A Manager's Vocabulary

- Human resource development
- Mentoring
- Training phases
- Training principles

- Trainability
- Certification
- Licensure
- Accreditation

Study Questions

1. What are the greatest needs for training in the public agency or nonprofit organization where you work or with which you are most familiar?
2. Is it necessary for other areas of government to budget as much for training and development as public safety departments do? Why, or why not?
3. What actions could federal, state, and local government do to help high-school students prepare for meaningful work in the public service or nonprofit arena?
4. Which individual learning strategies and organizational learning strategies are the most effective or least effective in your own experience?
5. What phase of training is generally most neglected? How does this largely neglected activity affect the effectiveness of training programs?

Exercise 11.1 Needs Assessment

You have been asked by the director of your MPA graduate program to recommend changes to the program in place for teaching public administration for MPA students. She has requested that you provide her with the topics you believe should be included in the newly fashioned program, categorized by major course headings. Develop a plan for assessing the educational needs of a modern public administration curriculum, prepare a survey of an important group of persons who are knowledgeable about the current needs of public administration professionals, and survey at least ten people using your instrument. Analyze the data and make recommendations to the program director.

References

American Society for Public Administration. 2013. "ASPA Code of Ethics." www.aspanet.org/public/ASPA/About_ASPA/Code_of_Ethics/ASPA/Resources/Code_of_Ethics/Code_of_Ethics1.aspx?hkey=222cd7a5-3997-425a-8a12-5284f81046a8 (accessed June 27, 2015).

Anderson, Claire J., and Betty Roper Ricks. 1993. "Illiteracy—The Neglected Enemy in Public Service." *Public Personnel Management* 22 (1): 137–152.

Association for Research on Nonprofit Organizations and Voluntary Action. 2015. "About ARNOVA." www.arnova.org (accessed January 21, 2015).

Beeler, Cheryl. 1994. "Roll Out the Welcome Wagon." *Public Management* 76 (8): 13–17.

Black, Homer S., and Kenneth E. Everand. 1992. "The Academy of Administrative Management: Path to the Professional Management Certification." *Management World* 20 (1): 6–7.

Buford, James A., Jr. 1991. *Personnel Management and Human Resources in Local Government: Concepts and Applications for Students and Practitioners.* Auburn, AL: Center for Government Services.

Cosier, Richard A., and Dan R. Dalton. 1993. "Management Training and Development in a Nonprofit Organization." *Public Personnel Management* 22 (1): 37–42.

Dewey, John. 1938. *Democracy and Education.* New York: MacMillan.

Drucker, Peter. 1980. "The Deadly Sins of Public Administration." *Public Administration Review* 40 (2): 103–106.

Executive Order No. 12674, 54 Fed. Reg. 15159, April 12, 1989.

Executive Order No. 12731, 55 Fed. Reg. 42547, October 17, 1990.

Executive Order No. 13490, 74 Fed. Reg. 4893, January 21, 2009.

Fisher, Cynthia D., Lyle F. Schoenfeldt, and James B. Shaw. 1996. *Human Resource Management*, 3rd ed. Boston, MA: Houghton Mifflin.

Gazell, James, and Darrell Pugh. 1993. "The Future of Professionalization and Professionalism in Public Administration: Advancements, Barriers, and Prospects." *International Journal of Public Administration* 16 (12): 1933–1964.

Hays, Steven W., and Bruce Duke. 1996. "Professional Certification in Public Management: A Status Report and Proposal." *Public Administration Review* 56 (5): 425–432.

Katz, Irwin R., and Alexius Smith Macklin. 2007. "Information and Communication Technology (ICT) Literacy: Integration and Assessment in Higher Education." *Systemics, Cybernetics and Informatics* 5 (4): 50–55.

Kerns, Peggy, and Nicole Casal Moore. 2003. "Ethics Training." www.ncsl.org/research/ethics/legisbrief-ethics-training.aspx (accessed January 21, 2015).

Kirkpatrick, Donald L. 1983. "Four Steps to Measuring Training Effectiveness." *Personnel Administrator* 28 (11): 19–25.

Kolb, David A. 1984. *Experiential Learning: Experience as a Source of Learning and Development*. Englewood Cliffs, NJ: Prentice-Hall.

Levit, Robert A. 1995. "Response to Reexamining Professional Certification in Human Resource Management by Carolyn Wiley." *Human Resource Management* 34 (2): 291–294.

Lothridge, Kevin, Jamie Fox, and Eileen Fynan. 2013. "Blended Learning: Efficient, Timely and Cost Effective." *Australian Journal of Forensic Sciences* 45 (4): 407–416.

Media Awareness Network. 2010. "Digital Literacy in Canada: From Inclusion to Transformation." www.ic.gc.ca/eic/site/028.nsf/eng/00454.html (accessed January 19, 2015).

Mosher, Frederick C. 1982. *Democracy and the Public Service*. New York: Oxford University Press.

Murray, Meg Coffin, and Jorge Pérez. 2014. "Unraveling the Digital Literacy Paradox: How Higher Education Fails at the Fourth Literacy." *Issues in Informing Science and Information Technology* 11: 85–100.

Nadler, Leonard, and Zeace Nadler. 1989. *Developing Human Resources*, 3rd ed. San Francisco, CA: Jossey-Bass.

National Center for Educational Statistics. 2003. "National Assessment of Adult Literacy." www.nces.ed.gov/naal (accessed January 19, 2015).

National Certified Public Manager Consortium. 2015. "Members." cpmconsortium.org (accessed January 21, 2015).

National Conference of State Legislatures. 2014. "Ethics Oversight." www.ncsl.org/research/ethics/state-ethics-commissions.aspx (accessed January 21, 2015).

———. 2015. "Ethics Training Resources." www.ncsl.org/research/ethics/ethics-training-resources.aspx (accessed January 21, 2015).

Noe, Raymond A. 1986. "Trainees' Attributes and Attitudes: Neglected Influences on Training Effectiveness." *Academy of Management Review* 11 (4): 736–749.

Nonprofit Leadership Alliance. 2015. "Certified Nonprofit Professionals." http://nonprofitleadershipalliance.org (accessed January 21, 2015).

Peak, Martha H. 1997. "Training: No Longer for the Fainthearted." *Management Review* 86 (2): 23–27.

Schmitz, J. 1999. "Information about the Human Resource Development Profession." Academy of Human Resource Development. www.ahrd.org/profession.htm (accessed February 11, 1999).

Senge, Peter. 1990. *The Fifth Discipline: The Art and Practice of the Learning Organization*. New York: Doubleday/Currency.

Sims, Ronald. 1993. "The Enhancement of Learning in Public Sector Training Programs." *Public Personnel Management* 22 (2): 243–255.

Training Industry Report. 2014. *Training*. November/December. www.trainingmag.com/trgmag-article/2014-training-industry-report (accessed January 19, 2015).

U.S. Department of Commerce. 2011. "Fact Sheet: Digital Literacy." www.commerce.gov (accessed January 19, 2015).

U.S. Office of Government Ethics. 2015. "Mission and Responsibilities." www.oge.gov (accessed January 21, 2015).

U.S. Office of Personnel Management. 2005a. "Learning Strategies for Creating a Continuous Learning Environment." pp. 1–11. http://opm.gov/hcaaf_resourcecenter_assets/lead_tool4.pdf (accessed January 19, 2015).

——. 2005b. "Fostering a Learning Organization." pp. 1–4. http://opm.gov/hcaaf_resourcecenter_assets/lead_tool8.pdf (accessed January 19, 2015).

——. 2008. "Guide for Collection and Management of Training Information." pp. i—35. http://opm.gov/hrd/lead/pubs/guide_for_collect_mgmt_of_training_info.pdf (accessed January 19, 2015).

——. 2015a. "Resources for Procuring the 'Right' Learning Management System." pp. 1–6. http://opm.gov/hrd/lead/pubs/resourcesforprocuringanlms2.pdf (accessed January 19, 2015).

——. 2015b. "Conducting Diversity Training." www.opm.gov/policy-data-oversight/training-and-development/reporting-training-data/#url=Conducting-Diversity-Training (retrieved January 21, 2015).

Van Wart, Montgomery. 1993. "Providing a Base for Executive Development at the State Level." *Public Personnel Management* 22 (2): 269–282.

——. 1998. "Organizational Investment in Employee Development." In *Handbook of Human Resource Management in Government*. Ed. Stephen E. Condrey, 276–297. San Francisco, CA: Jossey Bass.

——. 2010. "Increasing Organizational Investment in Employee Development." In *Handbook of Human Resource Management in Government*, 3rd ed., Ed. Stephen E. Condrey, 299–322. San Francisco, CA: Jossey Bass.

Van Wart, Montgomery, N. Joseph Cayer, and S. Cook. 1993. *Handbook of Training and Development for the Public Sector*. San Francisco, CA: Jossey-Bass.

Wiley, Carolyn. 1995. "Reexamining Professional Certification in Human Resource Management." *Human Resource Management* 34 (2): 269–290.

Wilhelm, Warren R. 1995. "Response to Reexamining Professional Certification in Human Resource Management by Carolyn Wiley." *Human Resource Management* 34 (2): 295–297.

12 Discipline and Dismissal

Learning Objectives

- Be able to differentiate development from discipline.
- Understand rights, responsibilities, and due process in discipline and dismissal.
- Be able to differentiate misbehavior from performance issues.
- Understand workplace aggression.
- Understand the implications of privacy and public safety in regard to employee discipline.

Two of the most important and challenging functions of management are the exercise of consistent and fair discipline and the infrequent dismissal of incompetent or unethical employees. Discussions about public personnel frequently raise the specter of public agency managers so bound by red tape and due process requirements that they are incapable of disciplining recalcitrant and ineffective employees who earn generous wages, but offer little in return. This commonplace conception of public sector management is not only an egregious exaggeration, but also constitutes a disservice to the vast majority of public sector employees and supervisory personnel at all levels of government. According to Daley (2008, p. 45):

> "With civil service rules you just can't fire anyone" is a legendary complaint. However, the reality is quite different virtually everywhere in public service. Poor performers are regularly dealt with through performance improvement plans, probationary conditions, transfers, and ultimately termination if corrected workplace behavior or performance do not improve. Although terminations make up a relatively small proportion of turnover figures, this is as it should be in personnel selection and training systems working as they should. However, poor performers are to be found in even the most effective selection and employee development systems, and they can cost the organization dearly in terms of lost productivity. The direct loss in productivity is compounded in terms of the bad example set for other employees and the inefficiency that is introduced into workplace team efforts.

In a study of federal managers, Daley (2008) acknowledges that maintaining employee discipline can be both frustrating and somewhat dissatisfying for supervisors, who benefit from clear, measurable goal setting and senior management's support for, and acknowledgment of, the importance of responsive disciplinary practices and access to resources required to handle this function.

Clear definitions grant us a useful springboard for this discussion. Discipline can mean a positive or negative action imposed by another, as in the "instruction designed to train to proper conduct or action" or "the punishment inflicted by way of correction" (*Random House Dictionary* 1980,

p. 249). Alternatively, discipline can imply autonomous change in the sense of personal self-control and sense of purpose, as occurs in "the training effect of experience" (*Random House Dictionary* 1980, p. 249). The difference between these two distinct conceptions of discipline draws from the locus of control. Who is it that opts for or imposes the change/correction?

Dismissal simply means "to discharge" (*Random House Dictionary* 1980, p. 252), but euphemisms we use to discuss these concepts generally reflect the discomfort and concerns all managers (public, private, and nonprofit alike) share about the notion of disciplinary action generally and employee dismissal in particular. When employee actions are not consistent with the goals of the organization, either the goals or the actions of the employees must change. As we learned in Chapter 5, to remain effective, organizations must evaluate goals constantly through strategic planning efforts to ensure that operational goals appropriately address the mission of the organization. If such organizational goals are appropriate reflections of the organizational mission, then performance concerns or workplace disputes may necessitate behavior change on the part of employees or a restructured workforce. This line of reasoning seems quite logical and sequential in the abstract. Disciplinary action and—at the extreme—discharge, however, are very nearly always complicated and emotionally charged areas of personnel management. This is the case because we need to concern ourselves with the tension between consideration for the fair and just treatment of an individual employee and concerns about the achievement of organizational objectives.

This tension is heightened in public sector organizations for several reasons. First, public sector employees are citizens who hold employment rights and protections—by statute and under the U.S. Constitution—to which neither nonprofit nor for-profit employees can lay claim in their dealings with their employers. Second, public employees are concerned with delivering often-essential public goods and services for citizens and their communities. An inability to perform in this context may be harmful to others beyond a simple decline in service or production in a for-profit organization. However, nonprofit and for-profit organizations that deliver public goods through contract and grant arrangements share this concern. Finally, in the broader context of environmental conditions for public agencies, public sector employees are held strictly accountable for their actions as agents of the people. Public employees should be productive and professional; they are subject to public scrutiny in all of their public actions. For example, public sector employees work in public organizations that are often mandated to 'do more with less', while staying current with technological change; the term "unfunded mandates" is a frequent refrain heard in public agencies subject to legislative bodies and political executives that raise the bar of public expectations without providing the resources required for meeting those expectations. Not surprisingly, under these all too common circumstances, tensions can erupt into conflict between individuals and among groups within organizations and between the supervisory staff of organizations and their employees.

Performance Management or Discipline?

Managing employees is generally a complex activity, even in the stablest of times. The manner in which the workplace accommodates social change during periods of changing values and technology is of particular interest given our era of cultural transformation. In addition to the challenge of managing performance when work and workplace technology are in flux, we must also consider an increasingly broad range of human behavior in organizations. Changing social norms lead to differences in how people believe they should or can act toward others in the workplace, and how they should be treated in that same environment. What we may define as inappropriate behavior today may have been condoned with a wink or a shrug only a decade or so ago. Violence and other forms of dysfunction in private lives often spill into the workplace. Harassment of others because of difference in gender, sexuality, ethnicity, age, or ability is not a relic of the pre-civil-rights-era past, but rather a far too common contemporary occurrence. Managers must not permit harassment, violence, and other such behaviors in the workplace that demean others and detract from the delivery of public services to go unaddressed.

At a fundamental level, supervisory staff in organizations must be able to distinguish between low performance due to factors potentially addressed through training and employee development as opposed to factors arising from an employee's unwillingness or underlying incapacity to respond to the demands of a given position. In other situations, the employee's performance per se may be acceptable in a technical sense, but his/her behavior does not meet the organization's workplace standard reflecting the duly established and periodically renewed goals and objectives of the organization.

When an employee's performance is insufficient, or when an employee's behavior threatens individual and/or organizational effort, organizations are duty bound to address these problems. Aufrecht (1996) argues that organizations must consider the costs to the organization when employees are not disciplined for failure to meet organizational standards or to observe organizational rules. Inappropriate, inconsistent, and inadequate discipline to address problems with employee behavior and performance has serious long-term implications for public sector organizations in relation to citizen perceptions of government performance, employee motivation and morale, and degraded organizational capacity.

"The cumulative effect on society of poor public sector discipline practice is to increase public cynicism about government" (Aufrecht 1996, p. 172). Much of the lore surrounding government incompetence derives from horror stories about how incompetent public employees have absolute protection from termination. The perception that public sector management is greatly impeded because of civil service protections, union advocacy, and employment rights is an impetus for those who advocate for government downsizing.

Discipline

Discipline implies corrective action through education or punitive actions intended to modify employee behavior or performance so that the employee's actions are compatible with organizational goals, norms, and performance expectations. The punitive *adverse actions* that can take place are purposeful decisions made by an organization that disadvantage an employee in some way; in the public service, such decisions must be for *just cause*, that is they must be based upon specific and job-related factors (Hays 1995). Adverse action, taken in response to behavioral problems, requires that an employee must have a clear understanding of what constitutes appropriate behavior in a particular situation. Additionally, adverse action, taken in response to unacceptable performance, implies that supervisors have assessed and documented inadequate performance prior to initiating any adverse action. Discipline, like performance appraisal or job analysis, should not be based on personal factors, but rather a response to an action, performance, or job requirement, and should be consistent for all employees in like situations in terms of penalty and progression (Hays 1995, pp. 152–154).

Disciplinary action in contemporary public sector work settings requires that we consider the scope of responsibilities as well as the authority structure within the organization. For example, supervisors should consider the employee's role and how his or her conduct is assessed compared with similar behaviors by nonpublic employees. There may be different standards in place to assess public versus nonpublic employees. In addition, when an employee's responsibilities are contingent

---

Exhibit 12.1 Just Cause

Before organizations act against an employee for poor performance, they should:

1. inform the employee of the critical job elements in which he or she is deficient;
2. inform the employee what is required under those critical elements;
3. inform the employee that failure to fulfill the elements may lead to demotion or removal;
4. provide the employee an opportunity to improve his or her performance; and
5. assist the employee in improving his or her performance.

Source: U.S. Merit Systems Protection Board 2003.

---

upon the efforts of a work group, disciplinary action may be handled differently than when an employee is more autonomous. It is also important to consider whether the employee exercises authority over others within the organization or has significant decision-making authority over constituents outside the organization.

Aufrecht argues that discipline is a means to ensure that employee effort is coordinated and contributes to movement toward the attainment of the organization's mission (1996, p. 178). In theory, the policies, procedures, and rules of behavior that an organization establishes should facilitate this effort at coordination on the part of supervisory personnel. If an employee does not comply with established policies or codes of conduct (e.g., professional attire, no use of profanity, etc.), Aufrecht argues that a supervisor can then respond in two general ways: modifying employee behavior through the threat of use of adverse actions or removing the employee from the position (p. 178). In particular, Aufrecht (1996, pp. 185–186) notes, "there is no formula available for determining the proper corrective action in an organizational discipline case. There are too many competing values and variables. Human beings ultimately must make judgments."

The following sections address these supervisory judgments in greater detail and summarize prevailing thought about proper organizational guidelines for maintaining discipline and, when necessary, moving toward discharge. Because employment law is a highly developed legal practice specialty in American society, much of what we use as a set of practical guidelines for adverse action derives from court cases and interpretations of administrative law judges' rulings in cases of contested discharge ('wrongful termination'). Managers and supervisors should consult with organizational employment law specialists in this regard for the most recent and germane interpretation.

Disciplinary Action

Disciplinary action varies along three fundamental dimensions: (1.) according to the degree of formality employed, (2.) according to the punitive versus corrective intent held by the organization and the intent of the employee, and (3.) according to the locus of control in terms of centralization or decentralization of disciplinary policy. Carter and Harrington (1991, pp. 201–207, 545) offer an interesting logic of how formality and informality in administrative action are associated with response. We develop this logic in Exhibit 12.2. Proportionality dictates that disciplinary action should be commensurate with the severity of the consequences of the behavior or the magnitude of the performance gap.

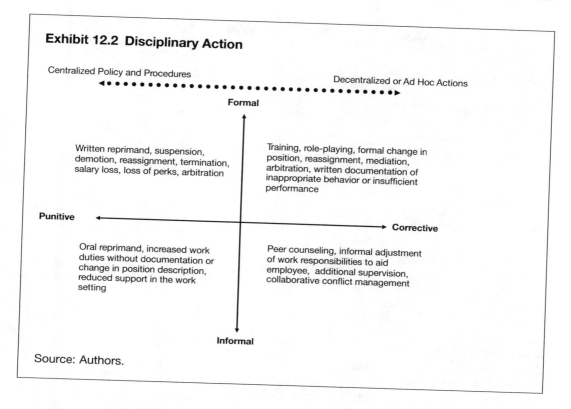

Exhibit 12.2 Disciplinary Action

Centralized Policy and Procedures ←•••••••••••••••••••••••••••••••••→ Decentralized or Ad Hoc Actions

Formal

Written reprimand, suspension, demotion, reassignment, termination, salary loss, loss of perks, arbitration

Training, role-playing, formal change in position, reassignment, mediation, arbitration, written documentation of inappropriate behavior or insufficient performance

Punitive ←——————————————→ **Corrective**

Oral reprimand, increased work duties without documentation or change in position description, reduced support in the work setting

Peer counseling, informal adjustment of work responsibilities to aid employee, additional supervision, collaborative conflict management

Informal

Source: Authors.

Formality

Disciplinary responses vary according to the degree to which discipline is recorded, documented, and codified within the organizational memory. Highly informal discipline is likely to be unwritten and is generally intended to be corrective without presumption of a pattern of inappropriate behavior or performance on the part of the employee. Formality in disciplinary method increases with a written record of the action taken by the employee and the specific organizational response to that action. In addition to the record, formality will increase with the number of procedures in place orchestrating the process and the potential outcomes for disciplinary action.

Intent

Consideration of intent requires two perspectives: the employee's view and that held by the organization. Disciplinary efforts differ according to whether we attempt to enhance an employee's performance (e.g., offer training or adapt a work structure), or to remove some privilege as an incentive to change behavior (suspend, loss of a benefit). From an employee's perspective, we may also need to consider their intention. Stone (1997) suggests that, in U.S. society, we are preoccupied with causality. If something is a problem, then we must root out the cause. If we find the cause, we eliminate it and, in doing so, we eliminate the problem.

To this end, Stone characterizes dimensions of intentionality (1997, pp. 188–195). Did we intend our actions, and did we know what the outcome might be? In terms of public sector workplace discipline, we need to consider whether an employee intends a behavior or performance level and whether they understand the negative ramifications of their action or behavior. If there is no intent and no understanding of the ramifications, then efforts to enhance the employee's understanding or skills through training or perhaps a restructuring of a position or work schedule are appropriate corrective actions.

If the employee demonstrates intent and a lack of concern about the outcomes, then punitive rather than corrective actions may be necessary. The problem in carrying out this line of thinking lies in demonstrating intent and documenting understanding; such demonstration and documentation are time-consuming and difficult undertakings for most supervisors and managers.

Locus of Control

Ideally, the difficulty in assessing intent and managing performance means that consistency and objectivity are critical components of maintaining discipline. Because individuals are unique, and situations of misconduct vary widely, developing a policy for discipline is difficult, and there are often more exceptions to the rule than cases fitting an established policy. Supervisors may need to exercise greater discretion and informality in managing performance or responding to employee behaviors than a formal policy may allow. Should control rest with the supervisor, as in a decentralized system? Or, conversely, should control be consolidated in a centralized system through standardized procedures and 'one-size-fits-all' responses to discipline? The flexibility of decentralized disciplinary systems comes at the high price of inconsistency in the treatment of similar cases—a fruitful area for contesting an adverse action in a grievance or filing a wrongful discharge suit.

Ethical Considerations

One ethical consideration centers on measuring performance in group work settings. Sewell considers peer surveillance in team-based employment settings (1998), suggesting two forms of surveillance— vertical surveillance (e.g., electronic monitoring) and horizontal surveillance (e.g., peer monitoring)— to maintain control and enforce disciplinary norms in group-based work settings (p. 414). Group-based work arrangements may offer a useful means of maintaining discipline in organizations, as the team members impose informal discipline to ensure compliance with team/organizational goals (Barker 1993). However, reliance upon informal means to manage disciplinary issues may offer the potential for abuse of authority and violation of employee rights. Certainly, informal norms have served to both encourage and discourage a variety of workplace behaviors that are now inappropriate and sanctioned by law, including sexual harassment and retaliatory action against whistleblowers.

Another ethical consideration is trust. Trust is an important dimension of disciplinary action. Employees must trust that supervisors will not arbitrarily charge subordinates with wrongdoing. Carnevale (1995) argues that high-trust actions include forming coalitions, keeping promises, and being civil, whereas low-trust actions include deceit, harboring grudges, and insincerity. Charges of inappropriate behavior, and any resulting sanctions, require sufficient evidence and documentation. Employees must believe that they will have the opportunity to challenge accusations. Punishment or correction applied without due process is unethical, might result in civil penalties, and will likely harm workplace morale and motivation. Unfortunately, management must sometimes codify commonsense to ensure uniform and consistent approaches to managing employees in the workplace (Carnevale 1995, p. 145):

> Trust is influenced by the interaction of power, politics, and conflict in organizations . . . the mere presence of these factors is not unusual or predictive of low trust . . . what counts is what

kinds of power, politics, and conflict organizations experience and how they choose to deal with these challenges. If they are managed in moral and ethical ways, these issues present as much opportunity as threat.

Modifying Employee Behavior: Progressive Discipline

In progressive discipline systems, supervisors combine various corrective and punitive actions and vary the remedy for misconduct in accord with an assessment of intent, the frequency of violations, and the magnitude of the problem being addressed (Hays 1995, p. 154). In theory, most behavior problems arise from situations where corrective employee assistance is the appropriate response. However, if a behavior or performance problem continues or increases in severity over time, then the scope of the correction or punishment will escalate in response. Developmental discipline corrects inappropriate behavior by taking a rehabilitative outlook on problematic performance and/or conduct situations and precludes the use of punishment for past actions by employees—be it misconduct or insufficient performance—until it is clear that the employee is unwilling or unable to benefit from the rehabilitative effort (Hays 1995, p. 156).

In most cases, the first step in the progressive discipline model is to talk to the employee about the problem in some depth, in an informal, private setting (Smith 1998, p. 18). A useful approach to progressive discipline is to begin as a problem solver. At this point, the supervisor can discuss the expectations for performance or behavior. She or he may discover that training deficiencies are contributing to insufficient performance, or perhaps that personal issues are prompting inappropriate behaviors at work.

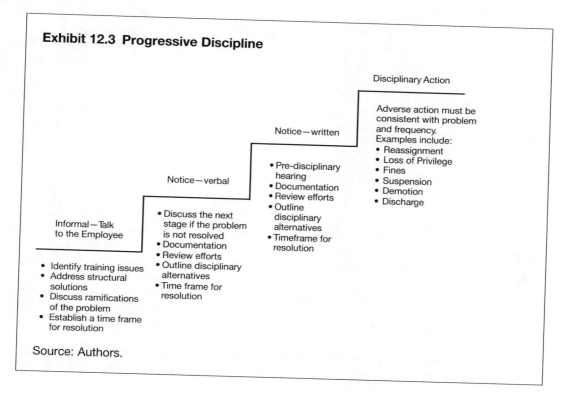

Exhibit 12.3 Progressive Discipline

Disciplinary Action

Notice—written

Adverse action must be consistent with problem and frequency.
Examples include:
• Reassignment
• Loss of Privilege
• Fines
• Suspension
• Demotion
• Discharge

Notice—verbal

• Pre-disciplinary hearing
• Documentation
• Review efforts
• Outline disciplinary alternatives
• Timeframe for resolution

Informal—Talk to the Employee

• Discuss the next stage if the problem is not resolved
• Documentation
• Review efforts
• Outline disciplinary alternatives
• Time frame for resolution

• Identify training issues
• Address structural solutions
• Discuss ramifications of the problem
• Establish a time frame for resolution

Source: Authors.

As discussed in Chapter 10, various factors can contribute to employee performance. Personal role demands, such as child- or eldercare, often affect employee performance and workplace behavior. If an employee is experiencing violence or harassment in the workplace, or has insufficient training or experience to perform when the demands of a position have changed, then a supervisor could employ a number of strategies to address any resultant performance problems. Strategies include counseling referrals, disciplinary action for harassing employees, or targeted training.

If performance issues continue, the supervisor must then discuss the problem with the employee again, notifying them that the next stage will be a written notice about unacceptable behavior or performance. Written guidelines for remedying the performance issue should be provided to the employee and included in his/her personnel file (Smith 1998, p. 18). Documentation is critical at this stage. Before any adverse action occurs, the employee should have the opportunity to respond in a pre-disciplinary hearing (Smith 1998, p. 18). Necessary disciplinary action that may ensue after due process hearings could include suspension with or without compensation, fines or pay reductions, or removal from the position or work setting through demotion, reassignment to another position away from the work unit where problems persisted, or discharge from the organization.

Demotions and Reassignment

When counseling, development, or less-dramatic sanctions are not effective in addressing inappropriate behavior or deficient performance, supervisors may employ additional remedies. If due process guidelines have been met, then demotion might be an appropriate response when the employee is unable to perform in the position owing to some gap in skill or competency that cannot be remedied either through training or via mentorship. When performance levels do not improve in response to training, or when the employee is unwilling to participate in such training, then a reduction in grade/ class/position may be the best action for both the employee and the employing organization.

Reassignment may be a useful action if the problem lies with the work setting, the demands of a particular position, or the presence of interpersonal disputes. If, for example, the employee is late to work because of their personal obligations coupled with the location of the work site, creative performance solutions could entail a transfer to a site better situated for the employee (if this is feasible) or even flexible scheduling or telecommuting. Transfers are not necessarily punitive, but may reflect an appropriate accommodation to retain an employee struggling in one setting but contributing effectively in another.

Discharge

Sometimes, the most viable option is to discharge the employee. Discharge in the public sector requires just cause. However, even with cause well established, managers may be unwilling to discharge employees. Klaas and Dell'omo (1997) explain that managers may be unwilling to pursue the necessary actions to discharge an employee when they believe that the effort to do so would be great owing to restrictive disciplinary procedures or when just cause was not established unequivocally in a legal sense. This scenario may be especially likely when past supervisors neglected to manage the performance of employees and systematically overlooked transgressions. In addition, a supervisor may be unwilling to pursue discharge without clearly established cause if the employee is likely to grieve and will have the benefit of legal counsel (Klaas and Dell'omo 1997, p. 934). Furthermore, Springer (1996, p. 16) cautions:

> While an employer's best defense against a wrongful discharge claim often is established through careful employee selection and consistent disciplinary procedures, the manner in which the

employee is terminated also is important in protecting against liability. The best methods of minimizing claims associated with termination coincide with those methods dictated by good business judgment and common sense.

Rights, Responsibilities, and Due Process

[handwritten: Cleveland V Board of Ed.]

Chapter 3 examined how the courts have come to treat the rights of public sector employees. Although public employees were originally viewed as exempt from employment rights by virtue of the doctrines of privilege and sovereignty, the contemporary interpretation is that public employees are entitled to strong protection against arbitrary or capricious actions by supervisors by virtue of the constitutional protections available to all citizens against government action that affects them adversely. Among the most important of these protections with respect to public employment are due process rights, which constrain government from taking a citizen's property without due process of law. Public sector employees generally hold a bona fide property right in their jobs once they have passed their period of probationary service. Consequently, any adverse action taken by government against an employee requires careful consideration and awareness of due process rights, should such actions be contested by the employee. Although legal interpretation does not usually hold that private and nonprofit sector employees enjoy a property right in their employment, due process procedures are nonetheless recommended in the case of adverse action. Bohlander (1989, p. 339) notes that the right to challenge an adverse action is a generally accepted foundation of workplace democracy, regardless of sector of employment. In general, the appeal or grievance process should be commensurate in formality to the consequence facing the employee (*Board of Regents v. Roth* 1972).

[handwritten margin note: public citizens and property rights]

Procedures for appealing a discharge will vary somewhat across jurisdictions and across agencies, but most public organizations and government jurisdictions have formal, written guidelines (Daley 1993, p. 158). In a unionized setting, the procedures are established through contract language for specific groups of employees. Usually, these procedures include notifying the appropriate supervisor of a challenge filed by an employee. Next, the union representatives and/or liaisons in the personnel office would receive an oral notice. Written notices of challenge are necessary steps in most processes, and the same individuals will be likely to receive these. The process continues until resolution is reached. A final arbitration hearing is a common endpoint.

Some organizations have established independent mechanisms to manage disputes, or ombud offices as places for employees to take issues for a neutral hearing and informal resolution of issues. These activities vary according to the level of formality and the specific steps involved. Usually, organizational policies identify the contact chain and specify the oral/written nature of the challenge. In addition, policies usually outline appropriate forms of documentation and identify the expectations of due process.

Although most union contracts specify grievance procedures, many organizations establish independent grievance systems. Independent grievance systems established collaboratively by employees and management offer important advantages to public sector organizations. First, it is possible to streamline independent systems to manage disputes to offer "timely workplace justice" (Bohlander 1989, p. 339). Second, Bohlander continues (p. 340) to note that employee disputes may not be bound by contract language in an independent system, but it could reflect an open forum for concerns. Certainly, independent grievance systems could improve conflict management practices by reducing the adversarial nature of the process. Finally, independent grievance systems can be a means to enhance individual performance by identifying problems in policy and practice that impede an employee's ability to do their work.

The term at-will employment is drawn from a court decision in which it was held that an employer does not have to provide cause to discharge an employee in some circumstances (*Payne v. Western and Atlantic RA Company* 1884). Employment-at-will can be used to prevent employees from asserting a property right (Hays 1995, p. 151). There are, however, some limitations to employer action, despite the strength of the at-will employment doctrine.

Civil rights legislation intercedes in the employment relationship to protect certain groups of people who have "suspect classification" status under the law by virtue of their vulnerability or having suffered a pattern of *de jure* discrimination historically (e.g., minors, the mentally ill, minorities, women, persons over forty). Formal collective bargaining contracts can serve to constrain and proscribe employer action against an employee through procedural agreements regarding disciplinary procedures, grievance and appeal structures, and scope-of-work agreements. The at-will employment doctrine has limited application and is expressly limited when the employer action violates the public interest (e.g., involves retribution for whistleblowing; *Palmateer v. International Harvester* 1981). The doctrine is also limited when there is a presumption of a contract between the employer and employee (*Touissant v. Blue Cross and Blue Shield of Michigan* 1980), or when the employer acts with malicious intent (*Monge v. Beebe Rubber Company* 1974), or denies an employee compensation or benefit due (*Fortune v. National Cash Register Co.* 1977). Although at-will employment is usually associated with the private sector and with political appointees in the public service, states such as Georgia, Wisconsin, and Florida are using variants more broadly than just for political appointees. In Georgia, new employees are hired as unclassified personnel and considered at-will by the Georgia State Personnel Board. This designation means that they do not have the same formal protections held by other state employees in Georgia.

The ADA offers additional legal protections to ensure that employees, public or private, receive sufficient opportunity to perform. However, ADA protections do not extend to disciplinary actions in the case of violence-free workplace policies when a previously protected employee threatens another (*Palmer v. Circuit Court of Cook County Illinois* 1997).

In addition, various whistleblower regulations (see Chapter 4) protect employees from adverse action in retaliation for reports of wrongdoing. At the federal level, the Civil Service Reform Act of 1978—and as expanded in the Whistleblower Protection Act of 1989—established the parameters for such protection. According to a study conducted by the U.S. Merit Systems Protection Board, federal employees appear to be willing to report illegal/wasteful activities such as waste due to poor management, practices that expose employees or constituents to danger, or overt bribery and theft (U.S. Merit Systems Protection Board 2010). Unfortunately, more than one-third of the employees who had made such reports have experienced retaliatory acts, ranging from informal harassment or denial of some organizational benefit to demotion, reassignment, or even suspension.

Disciplinary Investigations

Procedural due process is an important underlying principle in disciplinary investigations. Employers must have sufficient evidence prior to taking adverse action. That evidence should demonstrate the magnitude of the problem, thereby guiding the most appropriate approach to discipline. Disciplinary investigations are not bound by the probable cause standard used in criminal proceedings in the judicial system. Courts recognize that employers enjoy a right to maintain supervision over their employees. However, employers do need to prevent bias in the investigations they carry out (they should not single out individuals who require closer supervision than other employees do), and they need to acquire evidence systematically as documentation for any disciplinary action. It is not always necessary to 'catch employees red-handed', but employers must recognize the fact that organizations must establish and make use of appropriate procedures to prevent wrongdoing and must have clear policies that identify appropriate versus inappropriate behavior.

Managing Discipline and Dismissal

Consistency and civility are vital components of effective discipline and important to mitigate the fallout of dismissals for the terminated employee as well as his or her former colleagues. Disrespect, whether shown by an employee to a supervisor or client or demonstrated by a supervisor toward his or her subordinate, is never acceptable. A positive, respectful approach to communicating with others during a dispute of any type can diffuse emotional and threatening situations. Clearly, calmly, and respectfully stating a view can contribute to a positive hearing by another person. Allowing another person to retain dignity during a trying situation is important.

Managers utilize different approaches to dealing with disciplinary actions, depending upon the employee's length of service or the supervisor's perception about the amount of time and effort that the disciplinary action would entail (Rollinson et al. 1996). However, Bennett (1998) found that uniformity in the magnitude of adverse disciplinary actions and consistency in their application are important, because "unfair allocations not only result in dissatisfaction and anger with the perceived unfair procedure but also aggressive behaviors" (p. 259).

The organizational and interpersonal justice scholarship offers interesting guidance to managers seeking to reduce the residual frustration that may accompany conflicts between employees or issues between supervisors and subordinates. The overview of alternative conflict management styles from Chapter 5 also offers a useful application in considering workplace conflicts between groups and individuals. Nesbit, Nabatchi, and Bingham (2012) found that greater collaborative processes during mediation benefitted parties to disputes by resulting in a more satisfactory settlement. In fact, alternative dispute resolution processes featuring more collaborative approaches associate, in aggregate, with positive performance and beneficial workplace climate effects (Poitras and LeTareau 2008).

As a complement to process, supervisory approaches to discipline matter as well. In a study considering differences between female and male supervisors and perceptions of fairness held by employees who were subject to disciplinary action, Cole (2004, p. 274) found that certain supervisory communication styles constitute a more effective means to attain positive outcomes and facilitate ongoing work relationships:

> Numerous behaviours associated with verbal and nonverbal communication, leadership style and interactional justice . . . are positively correlated with disciplinary fairness ratings. Specifically, the ten behaviours identified were: a positive demeanour, neutrality, transformational leadership, referent power, conversational maintenance, fact finding, tentativeness, interactional justice, giving explanations and active listening.

Introduction to the Reading

The following reading offers an overview of alternatives to traditional approaches to correcting the behavior and performance of employees. The MSPB conducts regular research regarding processes under its statutory scope of responsibility. The following excerpt is from the executive summary of a study conducted with more than twenty administrative units in the federal government. In addition to a survey, the MSPB researchers interviewed management and labor organizations involved on a regular basis in disciplinary efforts at the federal level. As you read the excerpt, consider the following questions:

1. How does traditional discipline differ from alternatives?
2. How well has the U.S. federal government done in adopting effective alternative discipline processes?
3. What policies regarding alternative discipline procedures has your agency or organization adopted (or an agency located in your area)?

Excerpt 12.1 Alternative Discipline as a Creative Solution

While alternative discipline is not easily defined because it can take many forms, a simplified explanation is that alternative discipline is an effort, undertaken by an employer, to address employee misconduct using a method other than traditional discipline. Traditional discipline is most often a reprimand (sometimes called an admonishment), suspension, change to lower grade, or removal based upon the employee having engaged in conduct that damaged the efficiency of the service. Alternative discipline is management taking a different course of action to address the misconduct. . . .

The major findings from our study of alternative discipline [include these points]. The level of guidance on alternative discipline that agencies provide to their workforce varied greatly by agency, but in most agencies there was little or no guidance. Only 7 of our 46 responding organizations told us their agency has a formal agency-wide policy. However, 80 percent of those organizations *without* such a policy are permitted by the agency to use alternative discipline on an ad hoc basis. Training was also missing in most agencies. Of the 37 organizations permitted to use alternative discipline, only 2 organizations reported that their agency provides specific training on alternative discipline to personnelists, supervisors or employees. Only a few organizations indicated they keep track of alternative discipline as a program. Seven of the 37 organizations that use alternative discipline reported that they track its use, while only 3 keep track of how often the alternative discipline successfully modifies the conduct. A few agencies use alternative methods automatically, with little or no assessment of the employee or possible nuances of the particular situation. However, the overwhelming majority of agencies encourage managers to assess the situation on a case by case basis to determine what approach is most likely to resolve the situation. Some agencies limit the use of alternative discipline to low-level offenses or early offenses, while others use it primarily as a final effort before removal. Almost all responding organizations indicated that when alternative discipline occurs, it is the result of an agreement between the agency and the individual employee as opposed to being unilaterally imposed by the agency without consulting the employee. When alternative discipline is addressed in a collective bargaining agreement, it tends to be an option for management rather than a requirement. (The U.S. Postal Service is a notable exception.) The following is not a "new" finding, but this report reiterates that: Alternative discipline agreements are contracts. Thus, how they are formed, executed, enforced, and potentially breached will be evaluated by legal standards if a party seeks MSPB or judicial enforcement.

Recommendations

1. Managers and human resources personnel should consult with legal counsel when implementing an alternative discipline agreement that requires the employee's consent. It is extremely important for agreements to meet certain legal requirements to form a valid agreement. We strongly recommend that a legal advisor review such agreements.
2. Agencies should develop policies, or at least provide guidance, on the use of alternative discipline in order to ensure that human resources staff can properly advise managers on the issues to consider when determining if alternative discipline is appropriate and, if so, what approaches should be considered.

3. Managers should be trained, before the problem arises, on the existence of alternative discipline and the basic principles behind it. Knowing that alternative discipline is available may help managers to effectuate an early intervention before the poor conduct worsens. Agencies have a responsibility to ensure their supervisors develop the necessary skills and have the required knowledge of Federal rules in order to address conduct issues. We recommend that training in this area include information about when and how to use alternative discipline.

4. Agencies should, in general, avoid inflexible rules on the use of alternative discipline: Not every situation is appropriate for alternative discipline, and it should not be used if management has reason to believe traditional discipline is likely to be more effective. However, where management has reason to believe alternative discipline will be more likely to effect the necessary change, we recommend that management be given the opportunity to try an alternative approach.

Source: Excerpt drawn from pp. i–iv of U.S. Merit Systems Protection Board 2008.

[handwritten margin note: Workplace and aggression article]

Workplace Aggression

A broader construct of workplace aggression, according to Baron and Neuman (1996), includes interpersonal aggression, as well as aggression by an individual or group targeted at the organization or organizational mission such as the "guerilla governance" or "clandestine dissent" articulated by O'Leary (2006). Like the guerilla governance described by O'Leary, interpersonal workplace aggression may be rationalized by the aggressor as necessary to achieve some greater purpose, but ultimately may cause undue harm and may incorporate action/intent outside formal organizational goals and processes. Some forms of workplace aggression have legal ramifications, (e.g., repeated hostility due to the target's race, color, religion, national origin, sex, disability, or age). As discussed in Chapter 3, these instances are actionable through the U.S. Civil Rights Acts, the U.S. Age Discrimination in Employment Acts, the U.S. Rehabilitation Act, and U.S. Americans with Disabilities Act. When not linked to status categories protected by statute, individuals harmed by aggressive actions from coworkers, subordinates, or supervisors have limited legal options. In fact, these aggressive behaviors may be condoned by either the organization or workgroup (Brodsky 1976).

Hornstein (1976) has argued that aggression is a function of definition and attribution in that 'we' are "individuals with common concerns, hopes, loves and fears . . . people who share belief in cherished symbols and have an identify and a life much like one another" (p. 136). Conversely, 'they' are outsiders and, thus labeled, are readily dehumanized, easily differentiated, and subject to a range of cruel and egregious behavior orchestrated or tolerated by 'we'.

While we lament the decline of civility in public settings, the harms are not as simple as wounded feelings in the workplace (Mahtesian 1997). It probably is not necessary to offer a list of incidents of workplace violence to illustrate that there is a problem. Unfortunately, each of us can list events in schools, in public organizations, and in private organizations in which people have been subject to indignity, injuries, and even death. It is not endemic to any single government level or agency, nor is it necessarily a problem of urbanization. Violence in the workplace may directly affect large numbers of people, or it can arise from an incident between two employees. In some situations,

---

Exhibit 12.4 Responses to Problematic Workplace Behaviors

Behavior	Response
Anger (excludes anger expressed in ways that you feel are dangerous or may be violent)	1. Assume anger comes from fear or an attempt to get your attention 2. Avoid defensive responses 3. Use emotional defusing listening techniques: • Reframe angry comments into work-related issues • Refer the individual to counseling • Use mapping technique to identify possible fears and respond at the fear/need level
Personal self-interest	1. Reframe as larger work issues
Interrupts when you are giving feedback	1. Listen, then return to your planned discussion rather than be drawn off-topic
Argumentativeness	1. Ask for ideas and help in solving the problem instead of critique 2. Assign the individual tasks requiring analytical ability 3. Use the "Yes . . . and" technique
Negativity or sarcasm	1. Ignore the negative comments and go on 2. Reframe the comments 3. Refer to department statements of common value or respectful workplace 4. Coach the individual on how to restate the comment more productively

Source: From McCorkle and Witt 2014, p. 109, Table 7.1.

---

domestic violence can spill over into the workplace through diminished performance or behavioral problems, or in incidents of physical or emotional abuse played out at work. Many organizations are putting into place explicit policies and procedures for a violence-free workplace and providing corrective alternatives such as training and constructive conflict management mechanisms to manage employee disputes in situations where the risk of escalation is present.

Public, private, and nonprofit sector organizations now find that, in addition to managing traditional workplace interactions among employees, they have to develop structural and procedural remedies to protect their employees and constituents from incivilities. Managing workplace aggression entails some of the same protocols as dealing with any other type of eschewed behavior in the organization—namely, instituting a combination of policies and procedures, organizational culture changes, and professional conduct code development, advocating for relevant external statutes, and summarizing case law updates as courts adjudicate disputes. In addition, supervisors can integrate standards related to a collegial work environment into the performance processes. Recruiters and those hiring can communicate expectations during recruitment and selection. Arguably, a civil and mutually supportive work environment would be a plus in recruiting and certainly is especially important to employees seeking work–life balance.

Exhibit 12.5 Institutional Betrayal and Sexual Harassment

Recently, high-profile cases in universities and the military have demonstrated that sexual harassment is a problem in these venerable institutions. Regardless of gender or age, people in a variety of work contexts have experienced such harassment from individuals in a position of power or trust. Research generally indicates that work settings with a large number of male workers and traditionally male occupations mesh with negative attitudes toward women, and the employees in those settings are more likely to tolerate sexual harassment of women (Vogt et al. 2007). However, men report sexual harassment as well in the military, and race appears to play a role, as Settles, Buchanan, and Colar (2012) report this occurrence was more likely for African American than Anglo men, though military rank was a factor. Discussions of sexual harassment and an appropriate organizational response to disciplining are sometimes misdirected, with comments about the proportion of women in the workplace. In a class discussion several years back, a male student reported his stunned epiphany after reading the excellent Fitzgerald, Swan, and Fischer (1995, p. 132) article in which those authors observed that:

> unlike cases of racial and religious harassment, where offensive behavior is assumed to be unwelcome, [courts place] welcomeness at the heart of the sexual harassment inquiry and burden . . . the victim with proving she neither invited nor welcomed the conduct of which she is complaining.

"Why," this student asked, "would we *presume* someone is interested . . . especially at work? Why should you have to do anything but say, 'no, thanks'." Why, indeed? Certainly, the notion that these incidents occur in public service organizations is somehow even more egregious. Smith and Freyd (2014) reference "institutional betrayal" as a phenomenon that occurs when respected institutions deal with predatory or malicious behavior within the organization by disenfranchising the victim. Certain characteristics seem to be shared among those organizations viewed as 'betraying' individuals who report trauma (2014, p. 580):

- "clearly defined group identities with inflexible requirements for membership";
- "institutions or their leaders enjoy an elevated role within the community or society";
- "performance or reputation is valued over, or divorced from, the well-being of members."

Vogt et al. (2007) found that sexual harassment training appeared to associate with positive attitudes toward women, but training alone is insufficient. Firestone and Harris (2003) recommend sexual harassment prevention in the military requires explicit public statements damning harassing behavior coupled with channels to report harassment outside the chain of command that protect the target from retaliation. The best organizational response to harassment of this nature is similar to what should occur with hostile or uncivil workplace misbehavior of any kind—clarity and consistency:

- clear policies outlining the standards for professional behavior;
- clear reporting channels and institutional support of the right for a target to challenge inappropriate behavior;
- consistent training and organization-wide statements against harassment;
- consistent application of disciplinary penalties and remedies.

Source: Drafted by authors; references are included in the reference section of this chapter.

Emerging Concerns and Considerations

Work Arrangements

One area in which changing work arrangements may affect the management and discipline of employees is telecommuting and flexible scheduling. Expectations about employee performance and behavior in the workplace change with the status of the employee in the organization and the nature or scope of responsibilities. The adoption of flexible work arrangements such as telecommuting and flexible scheduling will mean that different expectations will emerge about how employees will communicate with their supervisors and with one and other. Changing to work done and evaluated on the basis of groups also results in shifts in reporting and monitoring relationships observed in performance management systems.

Another emerging concern related to work arrangements pertains to employees with probationary status. According to the MSPB (2006), *Van Wersch v. Department of Health & Human Services* (1999) and *McCormick v. Department of the Air Force* (2002) challenge the traditional assumption that supervisors had greater dismissal latitude during probationary periods. A probationary period has often been treated as a continuation of the overall assessment process of selection and included the presumption that the probationary employee had quite limited procedural and appeal rights compared with regular employees. Managers could then dismiss the probationer who was not performing to standard without the same due process considerations. Instead, *Van Wersch* (1999) and *McCormick* (2002) may extend in good part the process recommendations noted in Exhibit 13.2 to probationary employees. The best response to discipline and dismissal is to default to the well-established due process protocols, regardless of the probationary status of the employee.

Technology

Technology has influenced discipline as much as it has increased the speed of activity in the workplace. Policies are critical as a foundation for performance and behavior in the organization. Supervisors should *not* presume that the parameters for basic courtesy and responsible use of technology are obvious and widely accepted practices. Clearly, the access to and/or transmission of threatening or obscene material are issues requiring sanction. In a public sector organization, Hatch Act provisions regarding the separation of partisan political work from public service work may place political content under scrutiny.

The seduction of electronic communication has tempted some employees to believe that their workplace communications are entirely private. However, as you discovered in Chapter 4, there are few privacy protections in place for public sector employees. With properly framed policies on email, the use of computer equipment, and communication norms, employees can be held accountable for the types of material that they access through the Internet (*Urofsy et al., v. Gilmore* 1999) and for Internet-based communication (*Fraser v. Nationwide Mutual Insurance Co.* 2003).

Employers may monitor employee behaviors with increasingly sophisticated technologies (Bogard 1996; Lyon 1993). Some analysts raise strong concerns about the erosion of all forms of privacy generally in a technology-driven society in the workplace (Lane 2003). However, other management scholars suggest that a balance between privacy and an employer's legitimate need to monitor workplace activities can be achieved (Stanton and Stam 2006). Surveillance cameras, recording equipment, and software to monitor Internet usage and electronic mail may mean that most of these actions are recorded in some archival record for later retrieval. Thus, an employee's stellar performance in working with citizens will be recorded for his or her supervisor to use in the next performance appraisal. However, it may also mean that an employee's habit of borrowing office supplies or another worker's propensity to play video games at her desk will be on permanent record. Technology has also expanded the scope of investigation of employee wrongdoing in more serious matters (Ferraro 2012).

Technology may also help manage incidents of workplace violence. Electronic surveillance equipment can be used to monitor performance levels and employee behavior that could be considered to be threatening to others. Other forms of technology include metal detectors or security badges to control entry into the workplace, cameras, cell phones, and tablets for field-based personnel, so that continuous contact with supervisors can be maintained despite the distance from an office setting. These may be used to record behavioral or performance concerns and serve as documentation during disciplinary actions.

Diversity

In the Winter Commission report on state and local public service (National Commission on the State and Local Public Service 1993), academics and practitioners alike noted a clear disparity between the demographic composition of people in public service and that of the general citizenry. The Commission called for "aggressive recruitment" of underrepresented groups, an undertaking that will necessarily serve to deepen further the diversity of values present in the public work force (p. 31). Diversity demands that managers understand effective methods of handling conflict between employees who possess differing values. A diverse work environment does not magically translate to enhanced productivity. Individuals vary in terms of their skills levels in responding to misunderstood or unexpected behaviors. Triandis (1995, p. 31) explained the subconscious factors at play in the workplace when individuals find themselves faced with unexpected differences or situations:

> Similarity leads to feeling good . . . and to interpersonal attraction . . . the greater the perceived similarity and the opportunity for contact, the more rewards are experienced, which results in more interaction as well as in more positive intergroup attitudes . . . positive intergroup attitudes can be eliminated or seriously reduced if there is much intergroup anxiety . . . cultural distance increases intergroup anxiety . . . any factor that increases uncertainty about how to behave in social situations, or in the individual's sense of control over the outcomes of the social interaction, increases anxiety.

Contemporary public sector managers clearly need skills for managing various forms of routine conflict, and these skills are especially germane in light of the demographically diverse workforce of this century. Managers who choose to address disputes between employees or between an employee and an important organizational norm can manage conflict by emphasizing shared goals, celebrating difference, developing cross-cultural training, and emphasizing effort as well as ability in performance (Triandis 1995). If the overall goal is to achieve the organizational mission that, in the public sector, requires action for the public interest, then common ground should be possible to discover, and its discovery should lead to productive public sector actions.

Although organizations could continue to pursue the zero-sum politics of yore, doing so will hamper achievement of the public interest—a mission held by public and nonprofit organizations alike. Ruthless competition, whether between individuals, or between and within groups, for position, resources, and dominance must acquiesce to collaborative arrangements in which all gain in pursuit of a common vision. The collaborative approach is a better tool, because the rule of the high-performing organization is precisely that the sum is greater than its parts (Triandis 1995, p. 130).

Summary

Throughout this chapter, several principal themes have emerged. Supervisors should treat employees with dignity and compassion, and in a consistent and predictable manner. Managing disciplinary action is as necessary as facilitating the training and development of employees, assessing performance, or dealing with any other functional area within personnel administration. Necessary disciplinary actions taken by managers and supervisors should focus on achieving organizational goals, rather than resorting to adverse actions born of malice, frustration, or vindictiveness.

The differences that will arise in the contemporary environment facing public and nonprofit organizations and the disputes these differences might occasion do not necessarily reflect efforts to supersede organizational goals or a supervisor's direction. Conflict in the workplace may be a result of personal factors, cultural differences, unclear standards, or some aspects of work structure. Clear workplace standards that outline appropriate and inappropriate behavior are important to protect the interests of employees and employers alike. To this end, the following chapter on policy and procedures offers some guidance to professional judgment. Managers cannot avoid the need for discipline upon occasion so that organizations meet the public interest, but such discipline need not be a harsh, ethically depleted endeavor.

A Manager's Vocabulary

- Discipline
- Dismissal/discharge
- Due process
- Just cause
- Adverse action
- Progressive discipline

Study Questions

1. What is discipline?
2. Why is due process important?
3. How should disciplinary problems be handled? Why?
4. What is the role of power in discipline? And in dismissal?
5. What are some of the implications of 'at-will' employment for public sector employees?
6. How might changing work arrangements such as the use of temporary versus permanent employees affect employment protections?
7. What is progressive discipline?

Exercise 12.1 Discipline Hypotheticals

What would you do in the following situations?

1. An employee who began working 6 months ago requests a transfer, complaining about coworkers who tell jokes while the team is working on a job. The employee describes feeling routinely embarrassed at the content of the jokes that often are negative or mock individuals and general groups. The jokes are not explicitly sexual and do not overtly reference individuals who are protected through Title VII. The employee is too embarrassed to raise concerns with the coworkers.

2. An employee reports that a coworker is hindering his/her ability to get the job done by not delivering messages, 'losing' interoffice mail, not inviting the person to important meetings, or removing items from the work area that are necessary to do the job.

3. An employee reports his/her boss yells, labels the employee as 'too stupid to work here', and makes faces (e.g., eye rolling or smirking) whenever the employee speaks.

4. One of the employees recently became pregnant. The topic of conversation in the close work environment now includes intimate details regarding the pregnancy, childbirth, or breastfeeding. Another employee expressed his discomfort at the topic, but his coworkers have continued these discussions.

References

Aufrecht, Steven E. 1996. "Toward a Model for Determining Appropriate Corrective Action in Public Employee Discipline." *Journal of Collective Negotiations in the Public Sector* 25 (3): 171–198.

Barker, James R. 1993. "Tightening the Iron Cage: Concertive Control in Self-Managing Teams." *Administrative Science Quarterly* 38 (3): 408–437.

Baron, Robert A., and Joel H. Neuman. 1996. "Workplace Violence and Workplace Aggression: Evidence on Their Relative Frequency and Potential Causes." *Aggressive Behavior* 22(3): 161–173.

Bennett, Rebecca J. 1998. "Taking the Sting Out of the Whip: Reactions to Consistent Punishment for Unethical Behavior." *Journal of Experimental Psychology* 4 (3): 248–262.

Board of Regents v. Roth, 408 U.S. 564 (1972).

Bogard, William. 1996. *The Simulation of Surveillance: Hypercontrol in Telematic Societies*. Cambridge, UK: Cambridge University Press.

Bohlander, George W. 1989. "Public Sector Independent Grievance Systems: Methods and Procedures." *Public Personnel Management* 18 (3): 339–354.

Brodsky, Carroll M. 1976. *The Harassed Worker*. Lexington, MA: Lexington Books.

Carnevale, David G. 1995. *Trustworthy Government: Leadership and Management Strategies for Building Trust and High Performance*. San Francisco, CA: Jossey-Bass.

Carter, Lief H., and Christine B. Harrington. 1991. *Administrative Law and Politics*, 2nd ed. New York: HarperCollins.

Civil Service Reform Act of 1978, Pub L. 95–454, 92 Stat 1111.

Cole, Nina D. 2004. "Gender Differences in Perceived Disciplinary Fairness." *Gender, Work and Organization* 11 (3): 254–279.

Daley, Dennis M. 1993. "Formal Disciplinary Procedures and Conflict Resolution Remedies: Availability and the Effects of Size and City Manager Among North Carolina Municipalities." *Public Personnel Management* 22 (1): 153–166.

———. 2008. "The Burden of Dealing with Poor Performers." *Review of Public Personnel Administration* 28 (1): 44–59.

Ferraro, Eugene. 2012. *Investigations in the Workplace*. Boca Raton, FL: CRC Press.

Firestone, Juanita M., and Richard J. Harris. 2003. "Perceptions of Effectiveness of Responses to Sexual Harassment in the U.S. Military, 1988 and 1995." *Gender, Work and Organization* 10 (1): 42–64.

Fitzgerald, Louise F., Suzanne Swan, and Karla Fischer. 1995. "Why Didn't She Just Report Him? The Psychological and Legal Implications of Women's Responses to Sexual Harassment." *Journal of Social Issues* 51 (1): 117–138.

Fortune v. National Cash Register Co., 373 Mass. 96, 36 N.E. 2d 1251 (1977).

Fraser v. Nationwide Mutual Insurance Co., 2003 U.S. App., 3rd Cir. (2003).

Hays, Steven W. 1995. "Employee Discipline and Removal: Coping with Job Security." In *Public Personnel Administration: Problems and Prospects*, 3rd ed., Eds. Steven W. Hays and Richard C. Kearney, 145–161. Englewood Cliffs, NJ: Prentice-Hall.

Hornstein, Harvey A. 1976. *Cruelty and Kindness.* Englewood Cliffs, NJ: Prentice-Hall.

Klaas, Brian S., and Gregory G. Dell'omo. 1997. "Managerial Use of Dismissal: Organizational-Level Determinants." *Personnel Psychology* 50 (4): 927–954.

Lane, Frederick S. 2003. *The Naked Employee: How Technology is Compromising Workplace Privacy*. New York: AMACOM.

Lyon, David. 1993. "An Electronic Panopticon? A Sociological Critique of Surveillance Theory." *Sociological Review* 41 (4): 653–678.

McCorkle, Suzanne, and Stephanie L. Witt. 2014. *People Skills for Public Managers*. Armonk, NY: M. E. Sharpe.

McCormick v. Department of the Air Force, 307 F.3d 1339 (Fed. Cir. 2002), pet. for reh'g en banc denied, 329 F.3d 1354 (Fed. Cir. 2003).

Mahtesian, Charles. 1997. "The Politics of Ugliness." *Governing* 10 (9): 18–22.

Monge v. Beebe Rubber Company, 114 N.H. 130, 316, A.2d 549 (1974).

National Commission on the State and Local Public Service. 1993. "Winter Commission." *Hard Truths/Tough Choices: An Agenda for State and Local Reform*. Albany, NY: Nelson Rockefeller Institute of Government.

Nesbit, Rebecca, Tina Nabatchi, and Lisa Blomgren Bingham. 2012. "Employees, Supervisors, and Workplace Mediation: Experiences of Justice and Settlement." *Review of Public Personnel Administration* 32 (3): 260–287.

O'Leary, Rosemary. 2006. *The Ethics of Dissent: Managing Guerilla Government*. Washington, DC: CQ Press.

Palmateer v. International Harvester, 85 Ill. 2d 124, 421 N.E. 2d 876 (1981).

Palmer v. Circuit Court of Cook County Illinois, 117 F.3d 351, 7th Cir (1997).

Payne v. Western and Atlantic RA Company, 82 Tenn. 597 (1884).

Poitras, Jean, and Aurélia LeTareau. 2008. "Dispute Resolution Patterns and Organizational Dispute States." *International Journal of Conflict Management* 19 (1): 72–87.

Random House Dictionary. 1980. New York: Random House.

Rollinson, Derek, Caroline Hook, Margaret Foot, and Janet Handley. 1996. "Supervisor and Manager Styles in Handling Discipline and Grievance: Approaches to Handling Discipline and Grievance." *Personnel Review* 25 (4): 38–55.

Settles, Isis H., NiCole T. Buchanan, and Brian K. Colar. 2012. "The Impact of Race and Rank on the Sexual Harassment of Black and White Men in the U.S. Military." *Psychology of Men & Masculinity* 13 (3): 256–263.

Sewell, Graham. 1998. "The Discipline of Teams: The Control of Team-Based Industrial Work Through Electronic and Peer Surveillance." *Administrative Science Quarterly* 43 (2): 397–420.

Smith, Carly Parnitzke, and Jennifer J. Freyd. 2014. "Institutional Betrayal." *American Psychologist* 69 (6): 575–587.

Smith, Maureen. 1998. "Progressive Discipline in the Workplace." *IMPA News* 64 (11): 18.

Springer, Bettye. 1996. "Terminating Problem Employees." *Public Management* 78 (4): 16–17.

Stanton, Jeffrey M., and Kathryn R. Stam. 2006. *The Visible Employee: Using Workplace Monitoring and Surveillance to Protect Information Assets without Compromising Employee Privacy or Trust*. Medford, NJ: Information Today.

Stone, Deborah. 1997. *Policy Paradox: The Art of Political Decision Making*. New York: W. W. Norton.

Touissant v. Blue Cross and Blue Shield of Michigan, 408 Mich. 579, 292 N.W.2d 880 (1980).

Triandis, Harry C. 1995. "A Theoretical Framework for the Study of Diversity." In *Diversity in Organizations*, Eds. Martin M. Chemers, Stuart Oskamp, and Mark A. Costanzo, 11–36. Thousand Oaks, CA: Sage.

Urofsy et al., v. Gilmore, 167 F.3d 191, 4th Cir. (1999).

U.S. Merit Systems Protection Board. 2003. "Firing Poor Performers: Part III." *Issues of Merit* (July): 5. www.mspb.gov/studies/newsletters.htm (accessed April 1, 2014).

———. 2006. "Navigating the Probationary Period after Van Wersch and McCormick." www.mspb.gov/studies/browsestudies.htm (accessed April 22, 2014).

———. 2008. "Alternative Discipline: Creative Solutions for Agencies to Effectively Address Employee Misconduct." www.mspb.gov/studies/browsestudies.htm (accessed April 22, 2014).

———. 2010. "Whistleblower Protections for Federal Employees: A Report to the President and the Congress of the United States." (September), pp. 51–52.

Van Wersch v. Department of Health & Human Services, 197 F.3d 1144 (Fed. Cir. 1999).

Vogt, Dawne, Tamara A. Bruce, Amy E. Street, and Jane Stafford. 2007. "Attitudes Toward Women and Tolerance for Sexual Harassment Among Reservists." *Violence Against Women* 13 (9): 879–900.

Whistleblower Protection Act of 1989, Pub. L. 101–12, 103 Stat. 1465.

13 Efficiency, Effectiveness, and Risk Management

Learning Objectives

- Understand the importance of policies and procedures in organizations.
- Consider practical approaches to policy development.

References abound throughout this book to the importance of policies and procedures in HRM. Unfortunately, although scholars commonly refer to the critical role of policies and procedures, textbooks in HRM or public administration do not usually consider in any detail the practical concerns facing managers who must draft such workplace policy documents. For example, if disciplinary action is being contemplated, it is vital that there is a clearly articulated policy that differentiates between appropriate and inappropriate workplace behavior. What should be included in such a policy? How should the content of such policies be derived? How should disciplinary action documents be worded? What are the ramifications of having no policy at all in place when the need for disciplinary action arises?

Often, employees and managers do not realize that nearly any written document used to guide employee management processes becomes a de facto addition to the work unit's policy and procedures 'manual'. Thus, if an admissions committee at a university, for example, wishes to develop a rubric for use in evaluating applicants, then that document becomes, in effect, part of that department's policies and procedures. If this is the case, then the department assumes liability if that rubric is not applied uniformly and consistently. If one person either chose not to use the rubric or applied the constructs therein differently than others, then this might open the door for challenge by a student who was not admitted to a particular degree program.

Policies in the context of HRM suggest general guidelines or principles that reflect prudent and practical considerations in the achievement of the organization's mission. A procedure is generally considered to be the step-by-step, detailed account of the best method to accomplish a desired goal. A policy may represent a general overview or framework for the accomplishment of particular goals in terms of specific modes of operation, such as setting out in policy statements general expectations about the manner in which recruiting and selection activities will be conducted (e.g., broadly framed distribution of notices of vacancy, open process of candidate meetings, systematic contact with all references, etc.). A procedure could entail the specific tasks and recommendations for the manner of their completion, as in the case of specific steps a manager must take to announce a position opening and initiate a job search, and the minimum and maximum number of candidates to be considered within a given period of time.

Unfortunately, it is all too commonplace to have policies in effect that were written to control behavior in reaction to *past problems* rather than reflecting the more proactive orientation of facilitating high levels of performance. Policies are often considered to be a means of preempting problems or offering general, tried-and-true approaches to handling repeatedly initiated activities in the organization. In this way, policies and procedures constitute an important form of risk management in any organization.

Risk management refers to the efforts of organizations to manage their exposure to potential loss or hazard, including exposure to lawsuits by persons alleging unfair treatment. Risk managers deal with problems that organizations confront with parties external to the organization (e.g., managing the effects of a policy decision adversely affecting community members). In many cases, risk management has also been the responsibility that a public organization has to provide protection for a community in the case of a natural disaster. Risk managers also address some problems arising from internal organizational operations, such as production processes, service provision, or management programs wherein employees are owed due consideration for workplace safety provisions. Of course, these several types of problem can have implications for others outside the organization, but for our purposes let us focus upon the HR arena.

Zeckhauser and Viscusi (1996) discuss the role that government should play in managing risk and ask how government might determine how much of a focus should be placed on managing anticipated, but not yet realized, risk. They caution that, "government policy should not mirror citizens' irrationalities but, rather, should promote the decisions people would make if they understood risks correctly and made sound decisions based on this understanding" (p. 142).

Why Do We Need Rules?

Max Weber offers a quite contemporary-sounding depiction of the importance of written policies and procedures in public administration. As he points out, uniform policies in most cases are established to be able to address legal issues should they arise, and are nearly always developed from the perspective of managers, to establish and maintain uniform practice within the organization by employees.

> The management of the office follows general rules, which are more or less stable, more or less exhaustive, and which can be learned. Knowledge of these rules represents a special technical learning which the official[s] in a bureaucracy possess. It involves jurisprudence and entails the system of administrative and business management practices that give life to the mission and goals of an organization. The reduction of modern office management to a complex web of operational rules is deeply embedded in its very nature.
>
> (Weber 1996, p. 81)

Generally, policy/procedure manuals are used to communicate expectations about performance and conduct in the workplace, and they may describe as well employee benefits and any protections they may enjoy at the expense of the organization (DiNome, Yaklin, and Rosenbloom 1999, p. 93). In the contemporary setting, policy manuals often provide a means to codify the organization's vision, mission, and goals as developed through the strategic planning process. This document may or may not be considered an employee handbook, depending upon the circumstance, but quite often employee handbooks are used to communicate the policies and procedures of the organization and to more fully explain the terms of employment (Bithell 1999, p. 3d). Formal policies and procedures and related employment guidelines that are published in organizational employee handbooks are often used as a reference in judicial and quasi-judicial proceedings, to resolve personnel disputes which arise between employees and their public agency or nonprofit organization employers.

Language

Because legal and administrative proceedings may come to rely upon employee handbooks and an organization's policies and procedures to address personnel grievances and disputes, the precise language used in the manual is clearly very important. Experienced HR managers commonly recommend that certain specific policy statements and topics be included in such employment documents to protect the interests of the organization and its supervisory and administrative cadre.

For example, recall our discussion about at-will employment in earlier chapters. The written and oral statements made in an organization can suggest contractual intent in some states (Bithell 1999; DiNome, Yaklin, and Rosenbloom 1999). If appropriate disclaimers are not included in the employee handbook, or in the organization's policies and within its procedures, then the substance of the handbook could lead to an implied contract. In this case, and if state law provides remedy, employees may be able to sue the employer for breach of contract if enumerated policies are not implemented in practice or, alternatively, if policies change substantively without sufficient notice to employees (Bithell 1999, p. 3d; DiNome, Yaklin, and Rosenbloom 1999, p. 94).

Recommended Statements and Topics

The potential for implied contract in the case of at-will employees, together with the potential for additional employment guarantees for others protected by civil service tenure, demands that government employee handbooks include pertinent disclaimer statements and a written form upon which the employees can acknowledge receipt and indicate comprehension of the handbook. In addition, DiNome and associates (1999, pp. 94–121) suggest including sections such as the following: political patronage, EEO, sexual harassment and discrimination, the FMLA, workplace violence, whistleblower protection, and grievance procedures. Policies on civility in discourse and interpersonal relations and social media use during both work and private time are also increasingly commonly found sections.

Policies: Means to Control or Facilitate?

The competing purposes of policies and procedures echo a tension that we have seen in a variety of topics in this text. For example, consider the implications of policies and procedures in terms of a performance system (Chapter 11). Do we look to policies as a means to control behavior, so that we can achieve organizational goals, or should policies serve to establish broad parameters within which managers may exercise some degree of discretion? Entrepreneurial public management is considered to be a risk-taking enterprise wherein management decisions are streamlined to permit timely initiatives, authority is decentralized to encourage organizational learning, and accountability to customer/citizen satisfaction dominates the framing of administrative actions (Moon 1999). "Innovative public managers are entrepreneurial. They take risks . . . with an opportunistic bias toward action and a conscious underestimation of bureaucratic and political obstacles their innovations face" (Sanger and Levin 1992, p. 88). In the contemporary setting of government reform, there is indeed a tension between risk management (minimized exposure) and risk-taking (maximized innovation) to promote the public interest.

Policies may enhance productivity by limiting those behaviors that had previously impeded performance. For example, Katz reports that a zero tolerance policy on violence in a school district had measurable benefits for productivity. Before the application of the zero tolerance policy, the Calcasieu Public School system in Lake Charles, Louisiana lost more than 240 teacher workdays in antiviolence-related activity; since the policy was adopted, only 6 hours of teacher time have been lost from the classroom (Katz 1999).

Policies also may serve to facilitate performance by clearly defining latitude and discretion, as in the case of the TQM model. Zeckhauser and Viscusi (1996) advocate policies that offer critical parameters, but that, at the same time, provide the latitude necessary for the exercise of considerable discretion in policy implementation. Policies may serve to guide people to manage the foreseeable disputes that will occur in interactions among people. The 'rules of engagement' to be followed during situations of workplace conflict can be established through policies such as those specified in grievance policies (Chapter 13).

Policies are also used as a means to communicate about the distribution of resources and sanctions within an organization. Employees can read the manual to learn about how to request training opportunities or inquire about benefits that might accrue from certain performance levels, or to determine the benefits accruing to longevity with the organization. Policies can detail the sanctions that may be imposed for certain behaviors, and can identify the types of behavior that will either be rewarded or sanctioned. Policies may articulate what is meant by sick leave versus other forms of excused absence (e.g., compensated jury duty, personal days off, or bereavement leave). Employees can discover what is meant by a standard workweek proper attire, or what the expected times may be for arrival and departure from work. Expectations about licensure, certifications, or accreditation may be detailed, with pertinent timelines and provisions for exemptions and waivers.

Most public sector organizations or their political jurisdictions develop their own broad policies and workplace guidelines, or they receive some portion of these policies through federal or state statutes. The topics covered in policy will vary considerably by jurisdiction; most sets of policies include general provisions that reflect the chapter titles used in this book. Additional provisions reflect the expectations and historical experiences of specific jurisdictions and public agencies. Individual agencies and governmental departments may have some latitude in developing their own policies and procedures, though in most cases some guidance will be provided through a central HR office for a state, county, or municipality. At the federal level, the Office of Personnel Management has the responsibility for most federal departments and bureaus. Exhibit 13.1 offers some suggestions about useful policies to address in the workplace.

New Policies for an Evolving Workplace

Throughout this book, we have discussed the ways in which the work environment is changing and the new demands these changes hold for both HR specialists and line managers and supervisors. Some evolving policy areas that are particularly critical for public agency and nonprofit organization managers are detailed below.

Diversity

An organization may have formal policies in place to laud the benefits of diversity. As diversity in the workforce is an important means of socializing members of an organization to consider alternatives to stereotypical gender-, racial-, and ethnic-associated roles and behaviors, a coherent set of policies requires that a wide range of policies should be reviewed to be certain that they are consistent with an overarching organizational objective of diversity promotion. For example, if an organization has policies in place that might reflect stereotypes held about the relative skills, strengths, capacities, or aptitudes of women versus men in staffing scenarios, then this results in a dilemma. Policies that exclude people from work because of gender are discriminatory, unless the agency can establish a BFOQ (Thompson and Worthington 1993, p. 18).

Exhibit 13.1 Sample Policy Manual Topics

Staffing

- Job announcements
- Hiring and selection procedures
- Nepotism policy
- Minimum age of employees
- Reemployment and reinstatement policy
- Reference checks
- Driving policy
- Employment processing
- Classification policy
- Volunteer or Intern policy

Salary and Benefits

- Salary warrants
- Health insurance benefits
- Retirement benefits
- Deductions—withholding tax, retirement, insurance, bonds, deferred compensation
- Salary adjustments—regular increases, longevity pay, merit increases, promotion, demotion, salary decreases
- Garnishment—IRS, child support

Attendance and Leave

- Work hours
- Overtime (FLSA, exempt and nonexempt)
- Holidays
- Leave—annual/vacation, sick, compensatory, emergency, extended sick leave, sick leave pool, military, volunteer fireman's, seeing-eye dog training, jury duty, judicial witness, educational, short/extended leave without pay

Employee Relations

- Performance evaluations
- Employee recognition program
- Employee assistance program
- Safety policy
- Smoking policy
- Temporary reassignment or removal from workplace
- Suspension with pay for investigative purposes
- Reprimands—verbal, written
- Probation
- Disciplinary suspension

- Salary decrease/demotions
- Participation in employee organizations and associations
- Drug-free workplace policy

Ethics

- Ethics policy
- Political activities
- Outside or dual employment with the state
- Prohibited activities
- Conflict of interest and standards of conduct
- Civility and respectful conduct

General Management

- Conferences
- Travel and reimbursement
- Workers' compensation
- Emergency evacuation procedures
- Personnel files (access and confidentiality)
- Agency rules, work rules, ability to perform duties, quality/quantity of work, management directed transfers, reassignments, reorganizations, facilities use, witness fees

Complaints and Grievances

- Complaint policy
- Grievance policy

Equal Employment and Affirmative Action

- EEO employer
- Prohibition against discrimination on basis of age, sex, race, color, religion, national origin, or disability
- Disabled/reasonable accommodation
- Sexual harassment
- EEO complaint procedures
- AA
- Work force diversity

Job Separations

- Resignations/transfers
- Retirement
- RIF
- Death
- Dismissals

Technology

- Personal technology use during work hours
- Social media
- Personal use of organization equipment

Source: The authors identified a number of policies based upon their collective experiences. Additionally, part of the formatting, as well as certain recommended policy topics, was drawn from the Texas State Office of Risk Management 2015.

Diversity policy that is included in employee handbooks can serve as a critical mechanism to communicate expectations about tolerance of, and appreciation for, difference in the workplace. Clear policy in this regard is related to other policies, such as workplace violence, sexual harassment, privacy, and disciplinary action. Policies in these areas should offer consistent standards of behavior and provide explicit guidelines for the reporting of wrongful conduct. At the same time, policies must advise employees of the rights of due process in force for those who are accused of engaging in unacceptable behaviors.

Workplace Aggression

As we discussed in Chapter 12, workplace aggression encapsulates efforts by individuals to harm others with whom they work, or have worked, or to harm the organization in which they are presently, or were previously, employed (Baron and Neuman 1996; Neuman and Baron 1998). Although there are laws and policies against sexual harassment, and although the courts have sought to clarify interpretation of these statutes and agency rules, it still appears that a great deal more guidance in this area may be necessary in the contemporary workplace.

Sexual harassment has been defined by a series of court decisions. Currently, employers are liable for a hostile environment that results in some detriment to an employee's work (*Burlington Industries Inc. v. Ellerth* 1998; *Faragher v. City of Boca Raton* 1998; *Harris v. Forklift Systems Inc.* 1993; *Meritor Savings Bank v. Vinson* 1986). Given this line of litigation and the standards set by U.S. courts, organizations benefit greatly from having a clear policy response. Because malicious and debilitating treatment of others may not be limited solely to sexual behavior, agency policies can address potential problems, even though current court interpretation specific to nonsexual harassment is either lacking, somewhat unclear, or inconsistent (Yamada 2000).

Incidents of mass violence in public schools and in work settings continue to shock society and have prompted violence-free policies in public and private organizations. State and local governments have responded to these issues with policies to guide departments. The State of New York's Public Employee Safety and Health department (2015, paragraph 4) prescribes that municipalities and state agencies do the following:

1. **Develop and post a written policy statement** about the employer's workplace violence prevention program goals and objectives.
2. **Conduct a risk evaluation** by examining the workplace for potential hazards related to workplace violence.

3. **Develop a workplace violence prevention program** (preferably in writing, although that is only required for employers with 20 or more full-time permanent employees) that explains how the policy is actually going to be implemented. The program will include details about the risks that were identified in the evaluation and describe how the employer will address those risks. It will also include a system to report any incidents of workplace violence, among other things.

4. **Provide training and information for employees** around the workplace violence prevention program including any risk factors identified and what employees can do to protect themselves.

5. **Document workplace violence incidents** and maintain those records.

Safety

Beyond policies to respond to outright forms of aggression, public agencies must abide by state and federal statutes affording protections to employees and specifying appropriate workplace safety measures. In addition, the agency may be faced with the dilemma of how paternalistic they can or should be in the assignment of safety-related policies. Consider, for example, the case of employees who work with chemicals that have been associated with fetus abnormality and death, while recalling that the only exemption for sex discrimination is for a BFOQ. Although agencies cannot exclude people from certain work or work areas because of gender, they may still face liability if a fetus is harmed (Thompson and Worthington 1993). This may then be an example of a situation where establishing a safety-related policy and an organization's need to manage risk might be quite challenging to negotiate.

Note also that the issue of volunteer management has implications here. We tend to consider staffing to be limited to paid personnel; however, in both public and nonprofit organizations, it is quite common to find volunteers who handle a variety of responsibilities in the workplace. The Nonprofit Risk Management Center is a nonprofit organization that provides resources to nonprofit organizations for addressing all manner of risks that these organizations might face. The Center's recommendations specifically reference volunteers as well as paid employees in workplace safety policy recommendations (2015, paragraph 1).

> It is up to the management of a nonprofit to vigilantly protect staff safety. Implementing a safety policy for your organization should be a top priority. Staff—paid employees and unpaid volunteers—should be encouraged to report any unsafe conditions right away and should be trained how to react in an emergency involving potential violence at the workplace.

Privacy

Supervisors must balance a valid concern about monitoring employee behavior in the workplace with due respect for their privacy. Intrusions upon an employee's privacy could lead to problems with morale and, under some circumstances, even provoke legal challenge (Kilker 1999). As noted in Chapter 4, employers have substantial latitude in terms of the workplace. For example, desks and lockers can be inspected under certain circumstances, but the scope of this inspection could be subject to an impartial party investigation as to whether employees could enjoy a 'reasonable expectation of privacy' in any particular formal complaint. The policy language becomes important here in contributing to what the scope of that reasonable expectation might be in an agency or nonprofit organization. Certainly, the policy language used can provide notice to employees about what materials may be subject to review by supervisors. However, this issue is under frequent review by the courts, and growing sophistication in technology means that application of Fourth Amendment protection will continue to evolve.

Personal Relationships

That employees develop friendships in the workplace should not be surprising, given the amount of time we spend at work and the logic that people who have something in common, even if it is their office, may tend to develop friendships. Generally, platonic friendships that tend to occur in the workplace are treated as a positive outgrowth of work, although there are generally some cautions against demonstrating favoritism. However, relationships that extend beyond friendship tend to cause quite a stir. Sexual harassment policy addresses behavior that is unwelcome and creates a hostile environment, but how should organizations respond when the relationship is, at least initially, welcomed by both parties?

Workplace disruption may occur, not because of problems between the involved parties, but because of concerns held by other employees. Perceptions of favoritism, eroded privacy, or the social implications when one party is married to another person can create discomfort and discord in the workplace. Recent accounts of adultery and fraternization in the military certainly have heightened the profile of these relationships in the public sector, but their occurrence in any organization is not a novelty. Meyer (1998, p. 57) notes that, "although firms probably can't and shouldn't try to stop love in the workplace, they should take steps to protect themselves and ensure that the work environment is healthy, professional and productive."

Location and Structure of Work

As employees consider alternative work arrangements, such as formal telecommuting and flex-design, it may be necessary to revise existing policies that reflect a more traditional pattern of office work, with fixed hours and place of work. Time frames will differ, as will expectations about arrival and departure times and forms of effort reporting to supervisory staff. Policy artifacts such as language about an 8:00 A.M. start time could be subject to equity challenges.

Technology

As technology has increased the speed of activity in the workplace, so too has it influenced discipline. Often, organizations address the use of technology primarily within policies on communications or information systems. These may include applications ranging from telephones and voicemail to personal computers and tablets linked to the organization's server/Internet protocols, as well as the use of personal devices. Policies should acknowledge the organization's right/intention to monitor technology and articulate when and how employees can use both the agency's equipment and their personal devices. Supervisors should not presume that the parameters for basic courtesy and responsible use of technology are obvious and accepted practices.

Jacobson and Tufts (2013) report on a content analysis of state policies on social media use. They expressed particular concern about how well such policies explain the parameters on employee use of social media and what the implications might be for protections of employee speech (p. 102):

> When covered at all, First Amendment rights are addressed in an indirect manner and lack a clear indication of what constitutes protected speech. Many of the policies reference the blurring

of professional and personal roles, but the discussion lacks little direction in terms of what that means for actions outside of warning the employees to be aware of this issue.

As Chapter 3 noted, employees do have some protections with regard to speech. However, case law suggests this is a function of whether or not their actions/speech occur in the conduct of their job responsibilities. In general terms, accessing or transmitting threatening or obscene material is clearly problematic. However, in a public sector organization, Hatch Act provisions may place political content under scrutiny as well. Generally, it is wise to identify the uses to be made of computers and related equipment and software, and those uses should be related directly to the organization's mission. Other policies such as intellectual property, privacy, or sexual harassment still apply in conjunction with technology policy, especially in relationship to Internet access and use.

Introduction to the Reading

The excerpt for this chapter was developed by Kevin Richert, an experienced journalist, who was charged with making recommendations about technology policy for the contemporary workplace while enrolled in an MPA class in 2014. Confusion over social media policy is understandable, as social media evolve daily. However, as we discussed in previous chapters in this book, public and nonprofit organizations must respond to emerging technologies with policies that are both clear and consistent with existing organizational policies and federal and state statutes. Note that Mr. Richert considers the importance of performance metrics for an organization as part of a policy on social media use. As you read the following, consider a single question: What would be a good social media policy in your organization?

Policy Development in Practice

The employee handbook/general workplace policies and procedures can be used both to establish uniform procedures to enhance productivity and to communicate the scope of employee rights and responsibilities. Rudolph (1998) addressed the importance of managing risk for elected and appointed public officials in response to decisions that could give rise to civil rights, privacy, or access challenges. Exhibit 13.2 offers a basic checklist that he developed as a guideline for public officials, but this applies well to all public and nonprofit organizations.

All employees should have copies of, or at least access to, department and agency policies. In addition, they should be asked to sign statements indicating that they understand the policies and are willing to abide by them. Expectations of employees should be documented, and this extends to retaining minutes of meetings wherein expectations were communicated, even if such meetings are not open to the public. Although it may be difficult for small jurisdictions to do so, it would probably be prudent for any policies or procedures to be reviewed by legal counsel to ensure that legal expectations for due process and statutory guidelines established in different states are properly observed. Many state and national associations of cities, counties, school boards, or other local government interest groups offer *model policies and policy manuals* that have been vetted by counsel to assist small jurisdictions.

The general approach to developing policies should probably consider basic standards of courtesy and commonsense, though commonsense and constitutional interpretation on occasion may not go hand in hand (DiNome, Yaklin, and Rosenbloom 1999). Just as we need to have a legitimate rationale in the workplace for considering personal characteristics such as age or race in assessing the ability

Excerpt 13.1 Developing a Social Media Policy

Drafting the social media policy. Assuming that an agency is just trying to improve its existing social media practices—and not cleaning up after a trainwreck—I would draft the policy by working with staffers who have already worked on projects on the agency's behalf. I'd want to build on what has been done, to avoid making the same mistakes twice, and to seek buy-in from the people already on the front lines. I would convene a focus group, including social media thought leaders from the community, constituents who use existing agency platforms, and agency management.

Rolling out the policy. Training would be crucial, and needed at three levels.

- Training geared to social media newcomers—to the skeptics, but also the curious. Ideally, you'd like some of these staffers to jump on in time.
- Advanced training for social media-savvy staffers—for site administrators and the agency's frontline social media "voices."
- Management-level training. This would prepare managers for the times when they have to participate on social media platforms (such as an emergency). This training should make managers more comfortable with this new direction, solidifying buy-in from the top.

Measuring success. Fortunately, social media doesn't lack for metrics. By quantifying Facebook friends and "shares" and Twitter followers, retweets and "favorites," an agency can track its progress, weekly, monthly or over the course of a year. It would be realistic to expect steady and incremental growth, with occasional spikes at times of peak public interest. I would reconvene a focus group at the one-year mark—bringing back some of the people who were involved with the drafting process, as well as some new participants.

Excerpt References

This report incorporates ideas from social media policies developed by Austin, TX (2014); Boston, MA (2014); Fairfax County, VA (2014); Houston, TX (2014); the State of Idaho (2014); New York City (2014); Orange County, CA (2014); San Jose, CA (2014); and City of Seattle, WA (2014).

Source: Personal communication from Kevin Richert, 2014.

of an employee to perform, so must we have a legitimate rationale for references to gender, age, or race in workplace policies and procedures.

An important consideration in developing a policy is to consider how the policy itself will be established. Will employees have the opportunity to participate in its development, or will they simply receive some dictate? Ideally, employees can be involved in the periodic updating of policies and procedures; the employee involvement process can serve as an instructive policy review to affirm the logic and utility of the policies in application. Throughout the course of this book, we have emphasized the importance of systematic documentation. The policy and procedure manual can offer guidelines for gathering documentation about actions related to employment, including simple procedures on retention, collection, and scope.

Exhibit 13.2 Checklist for Risk Management and Employee Relations

- Are policies and procedures guiding personnel actions and workplace behaviors codified in writing?
- Are accurate and complete minutes of all meetings, both open and closed sessions, being properly recorded and maintained?
- Have all ordinances and administrative policies been reviewed by legal counsel in advance of implementation?
- Are the duties expected of individual employees codified in position descriptions and performance appraisals?
- Are the duties expected of employees legitimately related to the scope of the agency's responsibility?
- Have the policies and procedures been developed in accordance with state and local due process requirements?

Source: Adapted from Rudolph 1998, p. 166.

Ethical Considerations in Policy Development and Application

The ethics of policy development begin with what the intended outcomes of the policy are and discussions about who develops the policy and to whom it is intended to apply. A pressing concern in the development of policies and procedures rests with the intention of the document. If we look to policies and procedures to manage risk and anticipate that risk management must be a means to control behavior, then this suggests a particular approach to be taken in developing policies and procedures. If we instead consider that policies are a means to manage risk in order to provide employees with the latitude to perform and to self-manage their behavior and activities, then we are considering a very different outcome.

Hersey and Blanchard (1988, pp. 51–83) suggest that a manager guided by a control-oriented approach views employees as passive and dependent. In contrast, managers who perceive the importance of self-direction for employees might focus upon the importance of affiliation in the work setting, of creativity in performing even routine functions, and of promoting employee participation and decision making. The control approach contributes to a decidedly pessimistic and condemnatory public view of the public organization and its employees, encouraging organizational members to adopt a mentality perpetuating this negative view (Goodsell 1985, pp. 9–11; Hummel 1987, pp. 29–37; Lipsky 1980, pp. 479–483). Public organizations may seriously compromise their contribution to effective governance with practices that overly emphasize control over performance. These controlling practices are often enshrined in organizational policies.

Bozeman (2000) conceptualized ineffective organizational rules or policies as "red tape" in his now-classic treatment of excessive and counterproductive rules and policy prescriptions. More recently, scholars have introduced the concept of 'green tape', or rules that add utility in an organization. DeHart-Davis (2009, p. 362) extends Bozeman's analysis by differentiating between good and bad rules, noting that, "green tape is delineated by five attributes: (1) written requirements, (2) with valid means–ends relationships, which (3) employ optimal control, (4) are consistently applied, and have (5) purposes understood by stakeholders."

In this book, we have generally argued for great similarity between public and nonprofit organizations with regard to the logic of HRM. However, Feeney and Rainey (2010) argue that, in the area of 'red tape' and perception, there may be significant differences between managers in the public sector and those in the nonprofit realm. They note that, "respondents who work in the nonprofit sector report significantly lower levels of organizational red tape compared to public sector workers" (p. 814) and suggest that potential employees will make choices about whether or not to join an organization (or select between the public or nonprofit sectors) based upon their perception of whether or not an organization is bound by 'red tape'—a preponderance of ineffective, cumbersome rules. Thus, Feeney and Rainey (2010, p. 819) argue:

> significant variation in red tape perceptions related to reporting that the current job was chosen due to a motivation for career advancement (negative) and security (positive). This finding makes sense, if we think of red tape and personnel constraints as providing job security and also possibly rewarding job tenure. Those individuals seeking career advancement will seek positions in organizations with less red tape and personnel constraints. Similarly, it makes sense that people seeking job security will choose positions in organizations with more personnel rules and regulations protecting jobs.

Summary

HR policies and procedures in an organization are driven to a great extent by the functional activities that need to occur to ensure proper staffing. For example, in Chapter 7, we reviewed the importance of legal and managerial considerations in recruiting and selecting employees in public sector organizations. Clear guidelines must be established to offer decision makers the ability to identify and assess candidates in appropriate and uniform ways. Should managers have policies in addition to those legally required for AA? If so, what should these policies include? In Chapter 6, the logic of the analysis and classification system underscores policies and procedures that will be in place to identify the steps to be taken in developing new positions, evaluating current jobs, and establishing a framework for their evaluation and classification. Should we establish guidelines about when and how a manager might ask that a position be analyzed or evaluated? Do we need to specify the format for position descriptions, or simply leave this up to each manager? The discussion presented in Chapters 8 and 9 is explicit that guidelines are necessary to ensure equitable and appropriate compensation and benefit packaging. What types of concern might we want to address in policies? How would we handle issues relevant to when someone does and does not qualify for a benefit? How do we define benefits and the qualifications of recipients? Can someone use sick leave to care for an elderly parent? Policies are an important means to address these questions, to engage employees in discussions about their workplace, and to ensure that employees have the opportunity to understand their rights and responsibilities in the workplace.

A Manager's Vocabulary

- Policy
- Procedures
- Risk management
- Implied contract
- Reasonable expectations of privacy
- Red tape versus green tape

Study Questions

1. How can managers balance employee self-direction with legitimate needs for accountability and control?
2. How should an organization go about developing a policy and procedure manual or employee handbook?
3. Why are policies and procedures important?
4. How can managers address problems with implied contract in a policy manual?
5. What types of policy are important in your workplace?
6. What types of policy might be necessary in a regulatory agency versus one that distributes social benefits to others?
7. How important is the location or the mission of the organization to the content of the policy and procedure manual?

Exercise 13.1 Comparing Policies

Each student should come to class with a copy of a policy from a public organization. For ease of comparison, the students may wish to look for policies relevant to a particular topic, such as leave or privacy. Students should break into small groups to compare the policy in terms of the following:

- What substantive provisions are identified?
- How is specific content of the different policies similar in intent?
- How does the intent of the several policies differ?
- What assumptions about the role of the worker are communicated in each of the policies?
- What is missing in the policy statements that ought to be there?

References

Baron, Robert A., and Joel H. Neuman. 1996. "Workplace Violence and Workplace Aggression: Evidence on their Relative Frequency and Potential Causes." *Aggressive Behavior* 22 (3): 161–173.

Bithell, Walter. 1999. "Employee Handbook Can Open Communication." *The Idaho Statesman*, August 1, p. 3d.

Bozeman, Barry. 2000. *Bureaucracy and Red Tape*. Upper Saddle River, NJ: Prentice Hall.

Burlington Industries Inc. v. Ellerth, 524 U.S. 742 (1998).

City of Austin, Texas. 2014. "Communications." www.austintexas.gov/sites/default/files/files/Communications/social-media-policy.pdf (accessed by Kevin Richert, July 22, 2014).

City of Boston, Massachusetts. 2014. "Social Media Terms of Use for Visitors." www.cityofboston.gov/copyright/socialmedia.asp (accessed by Kevin Richert, July 22, 2014).

City of Houston, Texas. 2014. "Executive Orders." www.houstontx.gov/execorders/1-18.pdf (accessed by Kevin Richert, July 22, 2014).

City of San Jose, California. 2014. www.sanjoseca.gov/index.aspx (accessed by Kevin Richert, July 22, 2014).

City of Seattle, Washington. 2014. "Legislation, Policies & Standards." www.seattle.gov/pan/socialmediapolicy.htm (accessed by Kevin Richert, July 22, 2014).

DeHart-Davis, Leisha 2009. "Green Tape: A Theory of Effective Organizational Rules." *Journal of Public Administration Research and Theory* 19 (2): 361–384.

DiNome, John A., Saundra M. Yaklin, and David H. Rosenbloom. 1999. "Employee Rights: Avoiding Legal Liability." In *Human Resource Management in Local Government: An Essential Guide*, Ed. Siegrun Fox Freyss, 93–121. Washington, DC: International City/County Management Association.

Fairfax County, Virginia. 2014. "Office of Public Affairs." www.fairfaxcounty.gov/opa/fairfax-county-social-media-policy.pdf (accessed by Kevin Richert, July 22, 2014).

Faragher v. City of Boca Raton, 524 U.S. 775 (1998).

Feeney, Mary K., and Hal G. Rainey. 2010. "Personnel Flexibility and Red Tape in Public and Nonprofit Organizations: Distinctions Due to Institutional and Political Accountability." *Journal of Public Administration Research and Theory* 20 (4): 801–826.

Goodsell, Charles T. 1985. *The Case for Bureaucracy*. Chatham, NJ: Chatham House.

Harris v. Forklift Systems Inc., 510 U.S. 17 (1993).

Hersey, Paul, and Kenneth Blanchard. 1988. *Management of Organizational Behavior: Utilizing Human Resources*, 5th ed. Englewood Cliffs, NJ: Prentice Hall.

Hummel, Ralph P. 1987. *The Bureaucratic Experience*, 3rd ed. New York: St. Martin's Press.

Jacobson, Willow S., and Shannon Howle Tufts. 2013. "To Post or Not to Post: Employee Rights and Social Media." *Review of Public Personnel Administration* 33(1): 84–107.

Katz, David M. 1999. "School Violence Spurs Copycats, Prevention." *National Underwriting/Property & Casualty Risk & Benefits* 103 (24): 8–9.

Kilker, Patrick F. 1999. "Employee Privacy." *IPMA News* 65 (5; May): 21.

Lipsky, Michael. 1980. *Street-Level Bureaucracy*. Newbury Park, CA: Sage.

Meritor Savings Bank v. Vinson, 477 U.S. 57 (1986).

Meyer, Harvey R. 1998. "When Cupid Aims at the Workplace." *Nation's Business* 86 (7): 57–59.

Moon, Myuing Jae. 1999. "The Pursuit of Managerial Entrepreneurship: Does Organization Matter." *Public Administration Review* 59 (1): 31–44.

Neuman, Joel H., and Robert A. Baron. 1998. "Workplace Violence and Workplace Aggression: Evidence Concerning Specific Forms, Potential Causes, and Preferred Targets." *Journal of Management* 24 (3): 391–419.

New York City, New York. 2014. "Social Media Customer Use Policy." www1.nyc.gov/home/social-media-privacy-policy.page (accessed by Kevin Richert, July 22, 2014).

Nonprofit Risk Management Center. 2015. "Workplace Safety Policy Statement." www.nonprofitrisk.org/tools/workplace-safety/nonprofit/c1/policy.htm (accessed January 22, 2015).

Orange County, California. 2014. ocgov.com/civicax/filebank/blobdload.aspx (accessed by Kevin Richert, July 22, 2014).

Public Employee Safety and Health. 2015. "Workplace Violence Prevention Information." New York Department of Labor. www.labor.ny.gov/workerprotection/safetyhealth/workplaceviolence.shtm (accessed January 22, 2015).

Rudolph, Richard. 1998. "Public Officials Liability." *CPCU Journal* 51 (3): 164–170.

Sanger, Mary B., and Martin A. Levin. 1992. "Using Old Stuff in New Ways: Innovation as a Case of Evolutionary Tinkering." *Journal of Policy Analysis and Management* 11 (1): 88–115.

State of Idaho. 2014. "Idaho Technology Authority." ita.idaho.gov/psg/g330.pdf (accessed by Kevin Richert, July 22, 2014).

Texas State Office of Risk Management. 2015. "Chapter 2 Personnel Policies and Procedures." www.sorm.state.tx.us/rmtsa-guidelines-2/rmtsa-introduction/rmtsa-volume-four-table-of-contents/rmtsa-vol-iv-section-two-chapter-two (accessed January 22, 2015).

Thompson, James H., and James S. Worthington. 1993. "Risk Management: Identifying a Company's Vulnerability." *National Public Accountant* 38 (12): 18–22.

Weber, Max. 1996. "Bureaucracy." In *Classics of Organization Theory*, 4th ed., Eds. Jay M. Shafritz and J. Steven Ott, 80–85. Orlando, FL: Harcourt Brace.

Yamada, David. 2000. "The Phenomenon of 'Workplace Bullying' and the Need for Status-Blind Hostile Work Environment Protection." *The Georgetown Law Journal* 88: 475–536.

Zeckhauser, Richard J., and W. Kip Viscusi. 1996. "The Risk Management Dilemma." *Annals of the American Academy of Political & Social Science* 545: 121–144.

14 The Competent Manager

Learning Objectives

* Explore the demands made of managers in public and nonprofit organizations.
* Introduce the significance of leadership competencies as a way to improve citizen perception and trust in public and nonprofit sector managers.

In the preceding chapters, we have described the wide range of KSAs required of the public HR manager or the line manager concerned with HR issues. In addition to the themes of diversity, technology, and ethics, the related notions of competence and competencies have appeared throughout. In this final chapter, we consider the importance of HR for effective public service and the critical conduit leadership plays in translating the collection of KSAs arrayed in an organization's workforce into achievement of a public or nonprofit organization's vision and mission. Not surprisingly, Mesch (2010, p. s173) observe that:

> Of all the factors that contribute to organizational performance, the human element is the most fundamental. Managers across the public, private, and nonprofit sectors are increasingly recognizing that employees are their organization's most important assets and that the most significant source of competitive advantage comes from having the best systems in place for attracting, motivating, and managing their organization's human resources.

Whether positioned as a line manager or as a specialist in a centralized unit, the competent manager will be knowledgeable about the roles that an HR specialist must perform and the KSAs needed to be an effective manager in the modern environment. Personnel responsibilities are no longer limited to a centralized HR department, wherein staff conduct salary surveys and job audits. To contribute effectively to organizational goals, whether as a direct manager or a specialist performing HR functions, competent managers must understand a wide variety of tasks, ranging from expansive strategic thinking to the details of employee job descriptions.

Managers are asked to facilitate desired change within the organization. Such leadership requires an understanding of group dynamics and organizational skills, including consensus building, negotiating, and marketing. These organizational leaders may be located with HR, but they are just as likely to be distributed throughout the organization in direct service delivery, middle management, or at the senior executive levels. An organization is strengthened when all managers are well versed in the nuances of HRM.

Introduction to the Reading

For the most part, our purpose in this text has been to describe the objectives and processes in HRM relevant to a changing organizational environment and a very different world. These changes require new characteristics and competencies for HR professionals as they fulfill new roles. In the following reading, Houston and Harding (2013/2014) consider the concepts of competence and trust from the perspective of citizens. Administrators who act in the public service are in both public and nonprofit sector organizations.

The authors describe what might influence the perspective held by the citizenry (including demographic characteristics and partisanship) and what might be done to improve relations between citizens and those charged with acting in the public interest. As you read the following selection, consider that Houston and Harding describe alternative visions of public service—'new public management' (reforms based on performance benchmarking and efficiency incentives) or 'democratic administration' (public service through governance that is responsive and collaborative). What do their findings about perceptions of trust and competence tell managers in the public and nonprofit sectors about professional development and HRM practices?

New Roles and Competencies for Managers

A competency is defined as "a cluster of related knowledge, attitudes and skills that affects a major part of one's job" (Parry 1998, p. 59). Competencies are often derived by identifying high performing individuals doing similar work and finding the characteristics that distinguish them from others (Zemke and Zemke 1999). As Houston and Harding note (2013/2014, p. 53), "perceptions of competence correlate with whether government is doing what citizens want, while perceptions of trustworthiness are influenced by experiences with bureaucrats." As such, both competence and trustworthiness are social constructs derived from individual preferences (e.g., competence as a function of partisanship) and individual experiences (trustworthiness as a function of positive/productive experiences with a bureaucrat). When we discuss organizations performing in the public interest, we seek a blend of competence and trustworthiness in that, although we may not always agree with 'what' is being done, we believe professionals are acting responsively and responsibly.

Certainly, contemporary managers must be knowledgeable about the deliverables of their work unit and knowledgeable enough about HR functions to work with specialists to ensure that they can acquire and retain the best staff for their unit. HR specialists must be well versed in recruitment and selection, compensation and benefits, training, and development and performance management, as these techniques are necessary to accomplish the basic purpose of HRM. However, HR specialists must adapt to new roles in working with managers to provide the organization with basic HR services. These practical deliverables include finding qualified candidates to fill positions within the organization, developing and maintaining an equitable compensation and benefit system, providing programs to teach employees at all levels their legal and functional responsibilities, and working with other leaders to determine how the organization will operate (policies and procedures).

In the traditional approach to HRM, neither HR specialists nor managers with HR responsibilities (whether primary or secondary) considered themselves to be organizational leaders. HR was a support function, and the personnel office provided the gateway into the organization by screening applicants and developing qualified lists of candidates. It developed and maintained classification and compensation systems and sometimes provided training programs for employees. If personnel offices ventured into consulting with agency managers (welcome or not), it was to give legal advice, usually in cases of employee discipline or termination. Leadership was left to elected and appointed officials with responsibility for organizational mission and performance.

Excerpt 14.1 Public Trust in Government Administrators

It is worth noting that being a public employee does not affect one's level of trust. Perhaps this is because those working in government see exemplary public servants but also see waste and lack of commitment of other workers. Additionally, social capital theory is weakened as an explanation for these particularized trusting attitudes. It is possible that while civic engagement promotes social capital, it may not enhance confidence or trust in governmental officials. Alternatively, it may be that the measure used for civic engagement is too crude to uncover the effect on these trusting attitudes. Perhaps it is involvement in organizations that work directly with government agencies to promote civic ideals to develop social capital that translates to enhanced trust in administrators. . . .

[D]espite the rich theoretical literature that argues for a focus on democratic values and citizen involvement in public policy decisions, managerialism and a market orientation dominate reform efforts (e.g., New Public Management). The potential of these reforms to enhance trust in public services is limited, however, because they speak only to competence. Additional strategies that have the potential to improve the affective basis of trust are needed. . . .

First, a professional ethic for public administration must promote the duty of public service. As Svara writes: "If administrators are to serve the public, it must be clear that they are putting the public interest over self-interest" (2007, 28). Toward this end, Cooper (1991) states that administrators have an ethical responsibility to encourage citizen participation in the planning and provision of public services. Using citizenship theory as a basis for public administration ethics, Cooper (2004) presents an image of the administrator as a "professional citizen" that entails responsiveness to citizens and encouraging public engagement. As such, administration in a democratic process requires a demonstrated commitment to serve and a responsibility to share information with the public, ensure transparency, and support citizen participation (Svara 2007). Second, there is a need for enhanced professional training in the collaborative processes of governance. Specific topics may address how to effectively involve citizens in service planning and delivery, cultural awareness, conflict resolution, and listening skills. Third, information technology provides an opportunity to increase transparency and citizen participation. E-government has been offered as one tool for increasing interactions between citizens and government administrators with the intent of enhancing public service trustworthiness. Indeed, use of e-government is correlated with more positive assessments of services (or satisfaction) and trust in government (Welch, Hinnant, and Moon 2004). However, agency Web sites are largely used to provide information and to deliver services to "customers," not to meaningfully interact with citizens (Musso, Weare, and Hale 2000; Steyaert 2000). To the extent that e-government engenders trust in public agencies, it does so largely by enhancing perceptions of service delivery efficiency and effectiveness, not by increasing the types of interactions that engender a sense that bureaucrats are caring, responsive, and therefore trustworthy. As a consequence, Bovens and Zouridis (2002) worry that e-government actually decreases citizen interaction with agencies and increases the level of bureaucratic routinization, transforming street-level bureaucracy into screen-level bureaucracy. To take full advantage of electronic technology, agencies must develop the capacity for these tools to increase the quality of interactions with citizens and enhance responsiveness.

Excerpt References

Bovens, Mark, and Stavros Zouridis. 2002. "From Street-Level to System-Level Bureaucracies: How Information and Communication Technology Is Transforming Administration Discretion and Constitutional Control." *Public Administration Review* 62, no. 2:174–184.

Cooper, Terry L. 1991. *An Ethic of Citizenship for Public Administration*. Englewood Cliffs, NJ: Prentice Hall.

———. 2004. "Big Questions in Administrative Ethics: A Need for Focused, Collaborative Effort." *Public Administration Review* 64, no. 4:395–407.

Musso, Juliet, Christopher Weare, and Matt Hale. 2000. "Designing Web Technologies for Local Government Reform: Good Management or Good Democracy?" *Political Communication* 17, no. 1:1–19.

Steyaert, Jo. 2000. "Local Government Online and the Role of the President: Government Shop Versus the Electronic Community." *Social Science Computer Review* 18, no. 1:3–16.

Svara, James. 2007. *The Ethics Primer for Public Administrators in Government and Nonprofit Organizations*. Boston, MA: Jones & Bartlett.

Welch, Eric W., Charles C. Hinnant, and M. Jae Moon. 2004. "Linking Citizen Satisfaction with E-Government and Trust in Government." *Journal of Public Administration Research and Theory* 15, no. 3:371–391.

Source: Excerpt from pp. 64–68 of Houston and Harding 2013/2014.

New roles and expectations derived from the competency model of HRM require HR professionals to rewrite their old job descriptions. The traditional list of KSAs for an HR professional focused on technical abilities and knowledge of employment laws. These competencies were regulatory in focus. However, these are but a small portion of the knowledge and abilities required of the modern HR professional. Burke (1997) argued that, beyond the standard functional knowledge about personnel, successful HR professionals need expertise in nine areas: performance improvement, consequences of restructuring, management of organizational change, understanding of the impact of globalization, working in groups and teams, action learning, relationship building and interpersonal skills, work–life balance, organizational power shifts derived from technology, employee empowerment, and globalization.

Burke (1997) wrote about HR in general terms with a primary emphasis on the private, for-profit sector; his reference to globalization is, for example, most relevant to overseas operations in manufacturing firms. However, his recommendation can be distilled into four broad categories for our discussion in this final chapter: people, structure, tools, and applications.

People

Broadnax (2010, p. s178) argues that diversity in organizations:

> has improved their capacity to deliver higher-quality goods and services for the diverse populations they serve. However, embedded in the successes we have experienced thus far is the need to further define and refine where we wish to go with an evolving notion of what diversity in public organizations may mean in the not too distant future.

Given the opportunities presented by diversity, it is important to make careful use of KSA assessments and the resulting integrated model of needed organizational competencies in the development of a succession plan for organizations. The aging of the workforce represents both a crisis and an opportunity. Who will be prepared to succeed current managers who are expected to retire in the next decade? The 'crisis' can be avoided with a realistic succession plan derived from an analysis of the competencies needed to fill open upper-level managerial positions (U.S. Office of Personnel Management 1995, pp. 2–3).

As discussed throughout this book, demographic shifts will continue to change the composition of the workforce, just as those same shifts influence public policy preferences and the types of programming provided by the nonprofit sector. For example, Wolfe and Amirkhanyan (2010, p. s12) observe that, "changes in the age structure of the U.S. population will create serious fiscal pressures at the federal level . . . these demographic trends also will have a direct impact on the way state and local governments operate." In particular, population shifts are likely "to affect demands for both public and private assistance" (p. s16). Undoubtedly, we will continue to see collaborative service delivery arrangements between public organizations, especially at the state and local level, and nonprofit organizations. Wolfe and Amirkhanyan (2010) speculate that these arrangements will mean that nonprofit organizations must recruit employees with flexibility and an innovative attitude to succeed in these collaborative arrangements.

Leadership in today's environment includes developing an organizational culture for a learning organization (Harrison 1998) and building intellectual capital within the organization (Miller 1999). A learning organization is composed of individuals who capitalize on their successes and mistakes and seek to learn from those organizations that are successfully addressing the needs of the specific customer or general public. Leaders in these organizations know how to learn and teach this principle of learning in the organization by example and their organizational priorities (Briscoe and Hall 1999). The leader must be viewed as credible, and the people need to be cognizant of the leader's values and direction for the culture to be significantly affected (Edgeman and Dahlgaard 1998). High-performance agencies build the capacity to learn and the intellectual capital within their organizations to achieve higher levels of performance (Athey and Orth 1999). The competencies needed to build intellectual capital include expanding intelligence throughout the organization, encouraging innovation, and exercising integrity (Miller 1999).

Bennis (1999) argued that leaders in today's knowledge-intensive world must release the brainpower of their people and energize the know-how and creativity of their workforce. Leadership, accordingly "is the main instrument for leveraging intellectual capital" (Bennis 1999, p. 4). Thus, he explains that leaders who can build the intellectual capital of their organizations share five competencies (pp. 4–5):

> **Possess Passion and Purpose**. Leaders possess a strong determination to achieve a goal.
> **Generate and Sustain Trust**. Exemplary leaders demonstrate competence, constancy, caring, candor, and congruity.
> **Exhibit Hope and Optimism**. All successful leaders believe they can achieve what they set out to do.
> **Manifest a Bias for Action**. Convert purpose and vision into action, "a dream with a deadline."
> **Learn and Grow**. Create an environment for learning, thinking, and talking with new people from within and outside the organization.

Through leadership and the diversity of employees, organizations can position themselves to respond to the structural changes in their environments. Whether the environmental change comes from the political and legal realm or is a function of shifts within the organization, HRM can contribute to the organizational mission.

Structure

The trends described in the book will influence the ways that government implements the public interest. One of the rationales in developing a text that considered HR from a state and local perspective as much as possible is that we anticipate that state and local governments will play an increasingly important role in delivering services in our federal system. This supports Warner's projection (2010, p. s145) that:

> The twenty-first century must focus on rebuilding the capacity of local governments to finance critical infrastructure, attract and retain a skilled labor force, and engage citizen in designing innovative solutions to address public problems. Innovations in public service delivery will move beyond public private partnerships to models that more effectively balance accountability, equity, and efficiency concerns.

In addition, we continue to see adaptations of the tradition civil service models at the state and local levels of government. Since the passage of civil service reform statutes such as the Pendleton Act in 1883, personnel systems have striven for impartiality and objectivity with the "prime directive" to uphold merit principles. Decisions that had been made on the basis of political affiliation or social advantage, as in the patronage system, were no longer acceptable. In the merit system, job applicants and employees should be treated equally and equitably, with exclusive consideration of an individual's qualifications for job actions such as hiring or promotion. Over time, some personnel offices took this role of protector of the merit system to the extreme of ignoring organizational goals and department needs. A strict, cold, numeric rating could be applied to the number of candidates who could qualify for an interview list or to the list of those who should receive a performance (or merit) raise. Personnel rules were viewed as hard and inflexible, and managers began to seek ways around the system (Jorgensen, Fairless, and Patton 1996). It was, as Wallace Sayre (1948) described, "a triumph of technique over purpose."

Although rationalized as a way to ensure efficiency, these circumventions of the rules of the merit system are likely to lead to trouble. The legal environment within which HR must function for public organizations in particular can be highly complex. As Rosenbloom observes (2010, p. s176), "Today, one cannot practice public sector HRM without reference to judicial decisions." The sheer volume of case law affecting HR can be quite intimidating, and managers are correct to exercise some caution and draw upon the expertise of HR specialists to be certain that due process provisions are respected, whether or not a particular jurisdiction has a civil service system or must deal with unions and contracts.

Furthermore, organizations are moving increasingly toward using teams to accomplish their missions. As organization structures change to implement deliverables through team-based working groups, managers, and HR specialists, must collaborate to ensure that everyone learns the competencies necessary to make teams productive. These competencies include generating and refining ideas, organizing and integrating work, sustaining group esprit, and managing the boundaries of group responsibilities (Farren 1999).

Because of structural shifts in the level of government providing or facilitating services, the manner in which the services are provided, and the legal environment in which this must occur, HR managers and professionals have become accustomed to acting as an HR expert. In this capacity, they have generally provided technical expertise across the spectrum of HR functional practices and cautioned against potential infringement of personnel rules and employment laws. Because of the changing structural context, HR professionals must change their focus from being the regulator or watchdog of restrictive personnel policies to providing a wide range of services to their clientele within an organization.

The HR function serves many clients, beginning with the employee who receives needed information on conditions of employment and employee development services. Managers and supervisors are also clients who need consulting services on the full range of HR processes, from hiring to performance management. The organization itself is a client that requires HR services in planning for its needs for HR and organizing itself to create an environment for the maximum productivity of its employees. Ultimately, the citizen, as advocate and beneficiary of the democratic values of fairness and equality and the administrative values of efficiency and effectiveness, is a client of HR in public and nonprofit organizations.

Conceptualizing HR action as collaborative rather than regulatory emphasizes Houston and Harding's notions of trust and competence within the organization, as opposed to the more limited citizen–bureaucrat dynamic of the traditional HR approach. Sometimes, it is useful to remind ourselves that employees of public or nonprofit organizations are also part of the citizenry writ large, and managers, too, are simply one of many categories of employees of an organization.

Tools

In practice, individuals can use both 'ethics' and 'technology' to do their jobs more effectively and efficiently. The ethical leadership of managers can promote ethical behavior within the organization by modeling appropriate behavior, setting and articulating standards, and establishing a learning culture where employees can improve their application of ethical tools (Hassan, Wright, and Yukl 2014). Ethical leadership has a decided effect upon the health of an organization, reducing absenteeism and enhancing a climate wherein employees can identify and discuss ethical breaches (2014, p. 333). Hassan and colleagues argue that ethical leadership is so important for organizations that it should be a central component of employee development training for managers (2014, p. 341).

Using technology well means balancing the efficiency and effectiveness of the tools that technology provides without forgetting the importance of the human beings who are involved either as providers or recipients of public services. As Getha-Taylor (2010, p. s170) cautions:

> The first challenge to consider is the need to *balance virtual and personal connections*. The current explosive growth of membership in social and professional networking sites (Facebook, for example, counts more than 400 million active users) offers promise in its potential for expanded networks and improved collaboration.

However, simply because one can use asynchronous communication does not mean it is the best way to interact with colleagues in an organization or to reach citizens outside the organization. As we have discussed, there are a variety of legal issues involving employee speech through social media, and case law on this topic continues to emerge. Employees, like organizations, should have the means in place to review how their 'profile' is communicated to external audiences and constituencies. An employee who wishes to be viewed as a competent professional should ascertain that his/her personal profile in the virtual realm is compatible with that view.

Furthermore, the reality of uneven digital literacy and a 'digital divide' between those who have and can access technology and those who cannot should remind organizations of the importance of using multiple communication methods to reach stakeholders who lack Internet access. What are the implications when either individuals or organizations do not participate in networking sites? If, for example, an employee does not have a Facebook account or does not regularly check such a social media site, are they excluded from communications that might be provided within an organization about training opportunities, open positions, or other resources? For other employees, this may be the best method of communicating quickly.

Applications

Finally, in application, as described by Burke (1997), people use tools in the context of the structures of governance to forward the public interest. These applications include the means and ends of public service. Although the values of equity and equality remain paramount as the basis of merit principles, other values must also receive consideration when HR decisions are made. The accomplishment of organizational work goals is the reason for public and nonprofit agencies to exist. Therefore, managers, in partnership with HR specialists, should keep the values of effectiveness and efficiency in the operation of the agency as a top priority. Thus, managers with HR responsibilities, and the HR specialists with whom they work, are encouraged to (1.) assess and balance competing values and priorities; (2.) understand the public service environment; (3.) mentor, coach, and counsel with employees and agencies; (4.) provide citizen service; (5.) apply best practices; and (6.) promote work–life issues, including diversity in the workplace.

Understanding the core competencies needed to implement the mission of the organization helps managers and employees maintain a focus on their critical needs (Scarbrough 1998). As the work environment changes and organizations change over time, it is helpful to reassess what is being done to achieve the mission and stated focus of the organization. Some organizations may be in need of altering their direction, whereas others require reevaluation and renewal (Meschi 1999). Many public and private organizations are finding they need to form strategic alliances with others in order to accomplish their mission (Rule 1998).

Public and nonprofit organizations depend upon managers to provide needed knowledge and skills as organizations change direction and focus. Public service organizations seem to be in a constant state of reorganization, as policy priorities change or as new leaders enter office. Skilled managers are experts in organizational dynamics and serve as a resource to advise the administration on restructuring and change through their knowledge of organizational development principles and an understanding of the people and tools available to work within the structural parameters of the organization.

Summary

Contemporary public service organizations need leadership and the resources of a dynamic HR function to deal with transition and ongoing change. This type of leadership is not bound by formal authority patterns in a rigid hierarchy. Thus, managers in public and nonprofit organizations require a number of leadership KSAs to perform in new organizational roles. These professionals must be innovative and creative in finding new ways to accomplish organizational goals, while promoting adherence to laws, policies, and ethical practice in the realm of HRM. These professionals should work with others by consulting, counseling, influencing, negotiating, and collaborating. These professionals must promote integrity and trust.

Public service organizations must tap into their HR as they adopt a more strategic approach to serving the public interest. HR professionals must be integrated into the administrative team, as managers with HR expertise will be facilitators of organizational change, working with several agencies or departments to achieve broad goals and agency mission. Langbert (1999, p. 77) suggests that knowledge of the technical components of HR is, in some ways, secondary to management KSAs that include interpersonal skills, problem solving, and the ability to integrate HR with the broader public service mission. HR specialists, and the managers with whom they work, will be required to contribute to the organization with more than their traditional HR expertise: the new roles are strategic.

The knowledge and skills of HRM are neither static, nor sequential; the competencies of managers involved with HR are interconnected and complex. Some HR functions, such as strategic HRM and performance management, cut across all aspects of HRM. Other functions, such as compensation, depend on factors developed outside the organization, including the external labor market, classification systems, and labor contracts. The environment of the public workplace is continuously changing as the legislative branches write new laws and the courts interpret these against the Constitution. The environment is dynamic and unpredictable, and the added public and political aspects of public service HRM make the profession a difficult challenge. Personnel decisions can show up the next morning on the front page of the local newspaper. Public involvement in the budgeting process and in policy hearings have a direct impact on decisions made by public officials on matters such as salaries, benefits, labor contracts, employment requirements, and performance management. Counterbalancing the difficulty of operating in the public environment is the substantial satisfaction of accomplishing the objectives associated with the public interest through employees dedicated to public service.

A Manager's Vocabulary

- Leadership competencies
- Functional competencies
- Emerging HR roles
- Change agent
- Competency model

Study Questions

1. How have the roles performed by HR changed in recent years?
2. What new knowledge, skills, and abilities are required of managers who have HR responsibilities?
3. What values are important for HR professionals to consider when performing their various roles in public or nonprofit organizations?
4. Why should HR be a major consideration in the strategic direction of public and nonprofit organizations?
5. How might progressive organizations characterize a competent manager?
6. What core competencies are shared between HR professionals, managers, and other organizational leaders?

Exercises

Exercise 14.1 Core Competencies for Leadership Succession

Consider an organization with which you are familiar. Develop a list of core competencies that could be used in planning for leadership succession in this organization, and answer the following:

Who will be leaving the organization? What competencies will be lost? What additional competencies are needed for this organization? Who should be recruited? What should be tested for in the selection process? What topics should be provided in training programs? What other programs could be implemented to prepare the next generation of leaders?

Exercise 14.2 *Competencies Now versus Competencies Tomorrow*

Using your current job, a past job, or a job you would someday like to have, list the core competencies, leadership competencies, and functional competencies that have become obsolete in this job and the ones you anticipate will be needed to perform this job in the future.

References

Athey, Timothy R., and Michael S. Orth. 1999. "Emerging Competency Methods for the Future." *Human Resource Management* 38 (3): 220–222.

Bennis, Warren. 1999. "Five Competencies of New Leaders." *Executive Excellence* 16 (7): 4–5.

Briscoe, Jon P., and Douglas T. Hall. 1999. "Grooming and Picking Leaders Using Competency Frameworks: Do They Work? An Alternative Approach and New Guidelines for Practice." *Organizational Dynamics* 28 (2): 46–49.

Broadnax, Walter D. 2010. "Diversity in Public Organizations: A Work in Progress." *Public Administration Review* 70 (supplement): s177–s179.

Burke, W. Warner. 1997. "What Human Resource Practitioners Need to Know for the Twenty-First Century." *Human Resource Management* 36 (1): 71–79.

Edgeman, Rick L., and Jens J. Dahlgaard. 1998. "A Paradigm for Leadership Excellence." *Total Quality Management* 9 (4/5): 76–79.

Farren, Caela. 1999. "Smart Teams." *Executive Excellence* 16 (7): 14–15.

Getha-Taylor, Heather. 2010. "Human Relations 2.0." *Public Administration Review* 70 (supplement): s170–s172.

Harrison, Roy. 1998. "Intellectual Assets." *People Management* 4 (7): 33.

Hassan, Shahidul, Bradley E. Wright, and Gary Yukl. 2014. "Does Ethical Leadership Matter in Government? Effects on Organizational Commitment, Absenteeism, and Willingness to Report Ethical Problems." *Public Administration Review* 74 (3): 333–343.

Houston, David J., and Lauren Howard Harding. 2013/2014. "Public Trust in Government Administrators." *Public Integrity* 16 (1): 53–75.

Jorgensen, Lorna, Kelli Fairless, and W. David Patton. 1996. "Underground Merit Systems and the Balance Between Service and Compliance." *Review of Public Personnel Administration* 16 (2): 5–20.

Langbert, Mitchell. 1999. "Professors, Managers, and Human Resource Education." *Human Resource Management* 39 (1): 65–78.

Mesch, Debra J. 2010. "Management of Human Resources in 2020. The Outlook for Nonprofit Organizations." *Public Administration Review* 70 (supplement): s173–s174.

Meschi, Pierre-Xavier. 1999. "Competence Building and Corporate Renewal." *Business Strategy Review* 10 (2): 48–49.

Miller, William. 1999. "Building the Ultimate Resource." *Management Review* 88 (1): 42–46.

Parry, Scott B. 1998. "Just What Is a Competency? (And Why Should You Care?)." *Training* 35 (6): 58–64.

Rosenbloom, David H. 2010. "Public Sector Human Resource Management in 2020." *Public Administration Review* 70 (supplement): s175–s176.

Rule, Eric. 1998. "Competencies of High-Performing Strategic Alliances." *Strategy & Leadership* 26 (4): 36–37.

Sayre, Wallace S. 1948. "The Triumph of Techniques Over Purposes." *Public Administration Review* 8 (2): 134–137.

Scarbrough, Harry. 1998. "Path(ological) Dependency? Core Competencies from an Organizational Perspective." *British Journal of Management* 9 (3): 219–232.

U.S. Office of Personnel Management. 1995. *Executive Succession Planning Tool Kit*. Washington, DC: U.S. Government Printing Office.

Warner, Mildred E. 2010. "The Future of Local Government: Twenty-First-Century Challenges." *Public Administration Review* 70 (supplement): s145–s147.

Wolfe, Douglas A, and Anna A. Amirkhanyan. 2010. "Demographic Change and Its Public Sector Consequences." *Public Administration Review* 70 (supplement): s12–s23.

Zemke, Ron, and Susan Zemke. 1999. "Putting Competencies to Work." *Training* 36 (1): 70–75.

Index